God and Metaphysics

STUDIES IN ANALYTIC PHILOSOPHY
Quentin Smith, *Series Editor*

God and Metaphysics

Richard M. Gale

Prometheus Books
59 John Glenn Drive
Amherst, New York 14228-2119

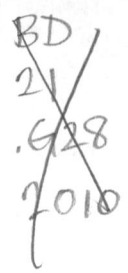

Published 2010 by Prometheus Books

God and Metaphysics. Copyright © 2010 by Richard M. Gale. All rights reserved. No part of this publication may be reproduced, stored in a retrieval system, or transmitted in any form or by any means, digital, electronic, mechanical, photocopying, recording, or otherwise, or conveyed via the Internet or a Web site without prior written permission of the publisher, except in the case of brief quotations embodied in critical articles and reviews.

Inquiries should be addressed to
Prometheus Books
59 John Glenn Drive
Amherst, New York 14228–2119
VOICE: 716–691–0133
FAX: 716–691–0137
WWW.PROMETHEUSBOOKS.COM

13 12 11 10 09   5 4 3 2 1

Library of Congress Cataloging-in-Publication Data

Gale, Richard M., 1932–.
　God and metaphysics / by Richard M. Gale.
　　　p. cm. — (Studies in analytic philosophy)
　ISBN 978–1–59102–269–5 (cloth : alk. paper)
　1. Philosophy. 2. Religion. I. Title.
BD21 .G28 2009
110—dc22

2009006024

Printed in the United States of America on acid-free paper

This book is dedicated to

Adolf Grünbaum

Dear friend and cherished mentor

This collection of seminal articles by Richard M. Gale represents the areas of philosophy to which he has made significant contributions—God, time, non-being, and pragmatism. His 1968 book, *The Language of Time*, along with his 1957 anthology, *The Philosophy of Time*, were instrumental in helping to stimulate philosophers to take seriously the opposition between the *A*- and *B*-theories of time. Articles that were important steps along the way to these publications are included, along with more recent work that he has done in this area.

Of special interest is his new cosmological argument (coauthored with Alexander Pruss) that is attracting considerable critical attention in professional journals. Other essays present Gale's searching criticisms of the numerous attempts to show that mystical experiences are cognitive and the free will defense of God in the face of the moral evil.

Gale's 1976 *Problems of Negation and Nonbeing*, the bulk of which is included in this volume, is the only book-length treatment of a nest of perplexing problems concerning the very distinction between positive and negative propositions, whether the latter are reducible to the former, and the status of nonoccurrent events, as well as a total nothingness.

Philosophers working on these topics will profit from reading Gale's works, which are models of clarity, leavened with humor.

CONTENTS

Autobiography 11

GOD

1. On the Cognitivity of Mystical Experiences 33

2. The Problem of Evil 55

3. God Eternal and Paul Helm 101

4. A New Cosmological Argument,
   coauthored with Alexander Pruss 123

5. A Response to Oppy and to Davey and Clifton, coauthored with Alexander Pruss … 143

6. The Ecumenicalism of William James … 157

TIME

7. Is It Now Now? … 179

8. McTaggart's Analysis of Time … 189

9. The Egocentric Particular and Token-Reflexive Analyses of Tense … 207

10. The Impossibility of Backward Causation … 225

11. An Identity Theory of the *A*- and *B*-Series, coauthored with Michelle C. M. Beer … 259

12. Disanalogies between Space and Time … 271

NONBEING

13. Negative Statements … 297

14. On What There Isn't … 323

15. Nonbeing and the Receptacle … 355

16. Could Logical Space Be Empty? … 385

AUTOBIOGRAPHY

I was born on July 13, 1932 in New York City of parents whose parents had immigrated from Poland/Russia in the latter part of the nineteenth century. My upbringing on the Upper West Side of Manhattan was uneventful. I attended public schools and was a very average student. My two-years-older sister, Zelda, was a brilliant student, and every teacher I had made a point to tell me about it, which queered school and intellectual things for me. This anti-intellectualism lasted throughout my life. Even today, I very rarely read anything that I don't have to read for something I am working on in philosophy. School was boring and triggered a deep sense that everything I was being taught wasn't true. For example, when I read in our geography text that Honduras raised and exported bananas a voice within me said "Bull shit!" I remember very little about my childhood, except for a pervasive feeling of detachment, a sense that I was a visiting cultural anthropologist from Arcturus 10 observing the strange rituals, practices, and customs of terran beings. This detachment from the commonplace was coupled with a sense of its unreality, if not in its existential sense at least in its evaluative sense. Thus, from my earliest years I had, without knowing it, the detached stance of the philosopher, the spectator of all time and eternity, bent on trying to understand a world that was not worth taking seriously. An outward observer never would have guessed that I was so out of it, since I dutifully went through all the outward behavior of a member of the tribe. I recited the Pledge of Allegiance, sang the national anthem, attended Sunday school at the Park Avenue Synagogue (which wasn't on Park Avenue!) where I subsequently was bar mitzvahed under Rabbi Milton Steinberg, a very great man.

The only thing I really enjoyed, except for my interactions with Rabbi Steinberg, was athletics. I was a member of varsity teams throughout my schooling, including college. I was a great player in practice but stank in the games because I did not know how to relax. Even today a small whiff of Ben Gay triggers in me a Proustian-type affective memory of how I felt when I missed a lay-up at a crucial point in the game or struck out with the bases loaded. What I like so much about philosophy is that it is not important how you can perform on the spur of the moment but what you can produce after you have had ample opportunities to rethink and rework issues. It is fortunate that I did not become a brain surgeon.

Another interest that sustained me during my precollege years was music, especially jazz. I grew up around jazz. My father, Moe Gale, was probably the most prominent person in black music, being the owner of the Savoy Ballroom and the personal manager of Chick Webb, Ella Fitzgerald, Cab Calloway, and the Ink Spots. He also had music publishing firms, both ASCAP and BMI, plus an agency, the Gale Agency, that booked many of the leading black jazz musicians, such as Dizzy Gillespie, Charley Parker, Lester Young, Art Tatum, Errol Garner, and Sarah Vaughn—all of whom I knew when a teenager. I studied a modified version of the Schillinger System of Musical Composition and Arranging with Edgar Sampson, who was the baritone saxophonist and arranger in the Chick Webb band and the composer of "Stompin at the Savoy" and "Don't Be that Way." I put together a six-piece combo in high school in which I played piano and did arrangements. After almost every gig we had to change our name so we could get another job. First we were "Richard Gale and His Manhattan Serenaders," then "Richard Gale and His Rhumba Orchestra," and finally "Richard Gale and His Society Orchestra." Our typical gig was a bar mitzvah in Brooklyn. No pay but all we could eat. We were a very oral bunch of guys.

Our ambition was to get a summer job at a resort in the Borscht Circuit in the Catskill Mountains, where they use sour cream for suntan lotion. I didn't want to use my father's pull to get the job, so I went on my own to a mountain booking agent named Jimmy Marks. He auditioned the band and told us that he could get us a summer-long job at a nonunion resort on Swan Lake, where all we had to do was play every evening in their night club, cut a show on Saturday night (you know, play "Chinatown, My Chinatown" behind the Chinese acrobats) and get into a volleyball game with the guests when they were short some players. I should have been suspicious of Jimmy because he always wore sunglasses, even in the middle of the winter. Periodically, I called him to find out when we would have our promised audition with the hotel owner and always got the same evasive reply, "Richard, I'm sweating it out." I managed to keep the band together for several months on the strength of his "sweating it out" assurances in spite of the extreme scepticism of some band members. I remember the trumpet player, Sid Davis, telling me that his father, although he never met me, was convinced that I was a phony and predicted that young Sid would be working in his refrigerator plant over the summer. Finally, it got to be a few days before the opening of the season on the Memorial Day Weekend, and when I called I got the answer that the hotel had just burned down but, in spite of this, I shouldn't lose heart since he was still sweating it out. The hardest thing I ever did was to inform the band members that there was no job. Many years later, when I was in the music publishing business, I heard a delightful Jimmy Marks story that put my agonizing experience in perspective. Jimmy had booked Larry Parks (the actor who played Al Jolson in the movie) into the Steel Pier in Atlantic City. Larry left his sweatshirt back stage and one of the chorus girls, knowing that Jimmy Marks was his agent, sent the sweat shirt to Jimmy Marks with a note on which was written "Larry Parks." It broke up Jimmy, because he took it as a gag gift from Larry, no doubt because he had been telling Larry that he was sweating it out.

I didn't much want to go to college but did so at my parent's urging. Since I loved music and was planning on going into the music business with my father, I thought it would be helpful and fun to get a Bachelor of Music degree, with a major in composition. I went to Ohio Wesleyan, which proved to be a very good choice but not for the reason that initially attracted me to the school. I had everything that it took to be a great composer except for talent. I wrote twelve-tone musical compositions, because I thought people wouldn't be too critical of them since they wouldn't expect to understand them. When one of my compositions was performed, the best that my fraternity brothers could say to me was, "Very interesting," which meant that they hated it.

Because most of my courses were in music and I was enrolled in the Air Force ROTC, I had almost no time for courses in other areas. But by a most fortunate accident I took Introduction to Philosophy in the spring term of my freshman year, having no idea of what philosophy is. My experience in this class, given by William F. Quillian, Jr., completely transformed my life. I finally found that which I was hungering for, though I did not know what it was. For the first time in my life I did something just for its own sake. It was a completely natural act and suddenly I became an outstanding student, at least in philosophy classes, though I continued to barely manage to get Bs in my other courses. In my junior year, two of my term papers received awards. I was slowly stepping out of my sister's shadow and beginning to believe in myself. I was most fortunate to have had an excellent teacher and mentor, Lloyd Easton, an Edgar Brightman student who specialized in American Hegelianism. He is the best teacher I ever had, and I owe him a great debt. Another seminal experience was hearing a guest lecture on John Dewey by George Raymond Geiger of Antioch College. His brilliance and humor blew me away, and I decided to follow his example and specialize in Dewey. This led to my writing a senior honors thesis on *The Aesthetic Theories of Kant and Dewey* under the direction of Easton and a visiting emeritus professor from the University of Minnesota, George Perrigio Conger (the author of *A Theory of Epitomizations*), a most delightful and fascinating man. It was the work of a mad dog Deweyite that made Kant look like he should have had his tenure revoked.

Immediately upon graduation in June of 1954 I went on active duty for two years in the United States Air Force as an intelligence officer with the 3rd Air Rescue Group in Nagoya, Japan. I was fortunate to have missed the Korean War by some nine months but still qualify for the GI benefits accorded to veterans of that war, which paid for all my expenses during the four years it took me to earn my PhD. I loved my time in the Air Force, maybe because I knew it was for only two years, after which I would have a wonderful life in the music business. When I wasn't in town doing wild things, I was reading philosophy back at the base.

The day after my hitch was up I began working for my father's BMI music publishing firms as a song plugger in June of 1956. My job was to romance disc jockeys so that I could get them to play our songs after they got recorded. Every couple of weeks I traveled to ten or so of the leading record cities, where in addition to spreading around some good cheer and fellowship I spread around a good deal of payola among disc jockeys and jukebox people. In order to make a dollar in the music business you had to be willing to give away half of it. We had many hits while I was with the firm, most notably "Don't Be Cruel" and "All Shook Up," both big hits for Elvis Presley whom we made a cowriter along with Otis Blackwell and with whose publishing firm we split the copyright. I remember my father saying to me that he would rather make 50 percent of a million dollars than a 100 percent of nothing. We also got our Blackwell song "There's No Time Like the Present" into Presley's first album. Little did I then realize how prophetic this title would be for my subsequent career in philosophy as a defender of the A-Theory of time.

To my amazement, I hated the business. I agonized over my many selves—the thought that each moment of actualization denied an infinite number of possibilities. I wasn't offended by the payola and the wheeling and dealing. To me it was just a part of the game, like stealing second base when you play the game of baseball. What turned me off was the thought that my success depended almost completely on my being able to manipulate people so that I could get them to do me favors. And to achieve this you had to hang out and be one of the boys: know what to laugh at, what to cry at. Again, I had the ability to fake it and appear from the outside to be well adjusted to my external circumstances. What really scared me was the thought that I was turning into the sort of person who is successful in this business. With every lie and hype-job I was slowly turning into Pinocchio, but minus any Jiminy Cricket for a conscience.

Fortunately, I continued to keep my interest in philosophy alive by taking a two-semester night course at NYU on existentialism. The instructor was William Barrett, the author of *Irrational Man*. Reading Kierkegaard's *Fear and Trembling* during the fall term was the most important event in my life. It proved to be the moral goose I needed to give me the strength and courage to leave the music business, to the great consternation of my parents, and do what I really loved, without any assurance that I would succeed. Barrett was brilliant at giving a secularized version of Kierkegaard, in particular his knight of infinite faith who can achieve authenticity only through making a very difficult decision that appears absurd to the rest of the world. The music business was my Regina! After months of agonizing I left the business and began graduate studies at NYU in the fall term of 1957.

Graduate school was paradise for me. Every day I had to pinch myself to believe that one could really make a living doing philosophy, and this feeling has never left me. No more agony-of-actualization angst for me, for I was now living in a way that was authentic for me. I broke very fast from the starting blocks, publishing several of my term papers in good refereed professional journals. These included "Russell's Drill Sergeant, Bricklayer and Dewey's Logic," *Journal of Philosophy*, 1959; "Natural Law and Human Rights," *Philosophy and Phenomenological Research*, 1960; "Mysticism and Philosophy," *Journal of Philosophy*, 1960; "Endorsing Predictions," *Philosophical Review*, 1961; "Professor Ducasse on Determinism," *Philosophy and Phenomenological Research*, 1961; "Tensed Statements," *Philosophical Quarterly*, 1962; "Can a Prediction 'Become True'?," *Philosophical Studies*, 1962; "Dewey and the Problem of the Alleged Futurity of Yesterday," *Philosophy and Phe-*

nomenological Research, 1962. For the most part, these articles are proof of the danger of rushing into premature publication. I remember Walter Stace, for whose course I wrote "Mysticism and Philosophy," saying just this to me when I asked him if I should publish it. My courage exceeded my ability.

I had a big advantage over my fellow students because I had a significant contrast in my life that enabled me to appreciate the life of the philosopher in a way that they, being fresh out of college, could not. Whenever I needed to psych myself up, all I had to do was to turn the radio on to an obnoxious payola disc jockey (Alan Freed, as a rule) and ask myself whether I wanted to contact him tonight. I was immediately back to work with full intensity. What I liked so much about the life of the philosopher is that your success depended upon what you could turn out, not on how *well liked* your were, as Willie Loman put it.

I had chosen NYU mainly because I still was an ardent Deweyite and wanted to study with Sidney Hook, the high priest of pragmatism. But while I did continue to pursue Dewey during my first year, terminating in a master's thesis on "Dewey and the Paradox of the Alleged Futurity of Yesterday," my interests took a decisive turn to ordinary language philosophy. Antony Flew was a visiting professor in the fall term of 1957 and I took his class on topics in ordinary language philosophy. I gave a class report on McTaggart's argument for the unreality of time. It was the beginning of a passionate love affair with the problem of time that fully occupied all of my thoughts for the next fifteen or so years and still continues to engage me. For every class I subsequently took, I managed to write a term paper on time—Aristotle's theory of time, Kant's theory of time, Husserl's theory of time, etc., etc. Thus, by the time I finished my course work, I already had worked through much of the important literature on time. I really began to work on my PhD thesis, which was on *The Concept of Time in 20th Century Analytic Philosophy*, from my very first semester in graduate school. This extra time enabled me to publish several spin-off articles from it in various journals. The director of the dissertation was Milton K. Munitz, a saintly man whose egoless love of philosophy was inspiring. He has always remained my role model of what a philosopher should be.

I began seeking a job in January of 1961, just a few months before I received my PhD. If there was a way to blow a job interview or campus visit, I would find it. I had an intense, aggressive quality that scared off people. I remember Sidney Hook excitedly telling me that he had just gotten off the phone with Gail Kennedy and that I was going to be invited to visit Amherst. He informed me that this was a wonderful prospect, since Amherst is the Harvard of the Little Three. Naturally, I said all the wrong things during my visit and was not offered the job. Two weeks later Hook excitedly told me that he just got off the phone with Virgil Aldrich and that Kenyon was going to invite me out. He informed me that this is a great opportunity because Kenyon is the Amherst of the Midwest. And so it went until I was invited in April (I was in a panic by then) to visit Vassar. For the first time I brought my wife, Maya, along, and was offered the job on the spot and accepted.

Anyone who has ever met Maya can understand why this happened, for people are instantly attracted to her. Of all the people I have ever known she is the one whom I most admire and aspire to be like. I don't want to be like Mike: I want to be like Maya. From the first moment we met by the sheerest of accidents at a party in New York City on the night of June 27, 1957 (I was still in the music business), she has been my moral and spiritual vitamin pills, the center of gravity for my life. The most heartfelt words I ever wrote were in the Acknowledgments section of my 1999 book, *The Divided Self of William James*. "Most of all I thank Maya, Celeste Maya, whose inspiring presence during the past forty-two years has taught me what life is all about." She is a remarkable combination of strength, courage, loyalty, spirituality, and a sweetness that comes from a sympathetic appreciation of all living creatures and nature at large. It is no accident that animals and birds are attracted to her. They know something. Maya had just graduated from Nihon University in Tokyo as a fine arts major and was planning on spending two years in the States to study interior design. After keeping company for two and a half years, we married on December 11, 1959 and soon after started to have a family. Andrew was born January 30, 1961, Laurence August 5, 1963, and Julia July 4, 1965.

I took up my duties as an instructor at Vassar in the fall of 1961. From the first day I hit the campus, I became restive to relocate. Although the students were quite good and my colleagues pleasant enough, I knew that I needed to get to a top graduate department where I would have colleagues and graduate students who would beat on me and from whom I could learn. Having succeeded in marrying a woman who was a much better person than myself, I now aspired to join a department that had much better philosophers than myself. Toward this end I gave first priority to my work, knowing that I had to publish my way out of Vassar. The place was crawling with "great teachers," who thought that if you published, it proved you didn't love your students. Although I had a rather heavy teaching load, three courses in each of the fall and spring semesters, I managed to spend almost all my time preparing articles for publication on the philosophy of time. Naturally, I had to cut some corners in my teaching, especially in the two-semester history of philosophy that every member of the department had to teach.

I remember in particular having to teach Spinoza's *Ethics*. I tried to read it, but realized that I would have to give it my full attention if I were to have a proper grasp of it and thus stop working on my own stuff. So I culled my lectures from Stuart Hampshire's Penguin book on Spinoza and an icky sentimental chapter on Spinoza in Will Durant's *Story of Philosophy*. This, of course, didn't stop me from assigning the entire *Ethics*, which the students dutifully read. In the middle of one of my lectures an especially hard-working student raised her hand and said, "Doctor Gale, your lectures are so clear and elegant but I can't locate the things you attribute to Spinoza in any one of his theorems or corollaries," to which I responded that Spinoza's deductive method of philosophizing was a sham and that you had to learn how to read between the definitions, postulates, and theorems. She replied that she wasn't able to and would like to get some help from secondary sources. This caused a panic attack in me, since I feared she might find out where I was getting my lectures from. I responded that I could recommend two secondary sources that shouldn't be read since they were trash—Hampshire and Durant. Immediately after my lecture I raced to the library and checked out all the copies of their books. Subsequently, I have developed more integrity as a teacher, but not that much more.

I targeted specialists in the philosophy of time and made a point to send them off-prints of my articles and critical comments on their work. I haunted the mail room, checking my mailbox every hour, even though there was only one mail delivery a day at Vassar. If you are looking for a miracle, the fact that you would get a letter when there was no mail delivery would be only a minor part of the miracle. My anxiety about the mail was heightened by the fact that Vassar College was physically isolated from the outside world. The external world was a logical construction out of the contents of my mailbox. My form of the "cogito" argument was: I got a letter, therefore I exist. There was a small window on my mailbox. Whenever I saw an envelope of the size that you would receive from a department, my hopes would soar, only to be dashed when I opened the box. My friends knew about my nuttiness and made a point to send me only postcards. Sometimes a student would call me and ask, "Is this Professor Gale?," to which I would respond, "Put him on," thinking she was a long-distance operator or secretary in one of my targeted departments. And when the student would say, "This is Sally Jones in your logic class and I want to know what our assignment is for the next class," I would berate her for sounding like an out-of-town operator.

Things started turning in my direction in the fall term of my third year at Vassar. The National Science Foundation informed me that I was going to be awarded a fifteen-month fellowship to work on time but that I had to resubmit my application so that it was clear that my home institution was sponsoring the project, since the grant is made to the institution, not the individual. This required that I secure a cover letter from the president of Vassar, Sarah Gibson Blanding, a hard-drinking old hag, a Kentucky horse-trader type, who was great at raising funds and nothing else. (She once announced at a faculty meeting that some recently deceased alum had left $1,000,000 to Vassar but it was money down the drain since it was earmarked for faculty salaries.) I went to see her with a prepared letter for her to sign. She immediately told me that she didn't know whether or not she was willing to sign it. Like a dying man, I saw my whole life passing in review. She was loaded and slumped back in her chair with her legs somewhat apart. This triggered some wild free association, making me think about what Goldie Goldmark, a typical oversexed music business crazy, used to say to me before he sent me off on a song-plugging trip. "Richard, many of the stations you will be going to will have a middle-aged record librarian who programs the shows for all the disc jockeys. You must do whatever it takes to get her to schedule our records. I don't want to hear any excuses why our song isn't being played. Go down on her if you must. Remember that no greater love hath a man than to put his body on the line for the firm." Suddenly I burst out laughing because I was identifying Sarah Gibson Blanding with one of these record librarians. She asked me what was so funny, and I said, "Nothing." Finally, I got her signature on the paper without having to resort to nonorthodox methods of inducement.

I was beginning to get calls from real out-of-town operators. Good job offers were coming in. In early January of 1964 I visited Santa Barbara to give a talk and accepted an offer. But before the contract reached me, I visited the University of Pittsburgh in late January. It was love at first sight. I had landed in the space-time capital of the world. I accepted their offer and withdrew from Santa Barbara. Adolf Grünbaum was instrumental in bringing me to Pittsburgh. I greatly admired his monumental work on the scientific concept of space and time. We struck it off when we first met at a conference at New York University in 1960. We kept in touch with each other, exchanging off-prints and criticisms of each other's work. Wilfrid Sellars, whose work I also admired, especially his piece on "Time and the World Order," also pushed to get me at Pitt. I brought my National Science Foundation grant along and, in addition, was given an Andrew Mellon Post-Doctoral Fellowship during my third year at Pitt, thus freeing me from teaching for two of my first three years at Pitt. Every week Sellars, Grünbaum, Rescher, Belnap, and myself would get together to talk about time. I was amazed and awed by the excellence of the graduate students. In my second year I taught a graduate seminar on time that was the most exciting experience of my life. It was loaded with hot shots who pushed me to the wall. I was beginning to compose my first book, *The Language of Time*, during the class meetings. Pitt graduate students really put the fear of God into me. No more "Blessed Spinoza!" schtick for me. Even though I overprepared for every seminar meeting, I still had panic attacks on my way to the classroom. I found an effective way to calm myself down. I would say to myself, "What is the worst thing that can happen? I'll go into the class and be totally embarrassed and humiliated professionally. So what am I worrying about?" By some strange reverse psychology, this worked for me.

During my first two years at Pitt I enjoyed stimulating discussions with Bruce Aune, and John Robison, both members of the department, and visitors Jim Cornman, Ed Gettier, and Charles Chihara. We hung out together and often had lunch at the Clock Restaurant, where to our consternation all of the waitresses would fall all over Ed, who was a Richard Widmark look-alike with dreamy bedroom eyes. Ed, being the all-time great counterexample man, made most of my arguments disappear and kept me from publishing some really bad stuff. Bruce was a very driven, hard-working philosopher with whom I competed. When I would leave my office at 5 p.m. and would hear his Adler portable typewriter going as I walked past his office, I would go back to my office and work some more. One late afternoon I was standing with Bruce in his office looking out of his window at the Cathedral of Learning across the street when in walked old man Oliver Reiser, the only hold-over from the bad old days prior to 1960, when Pitt was one of the worst departments around. Oliver was the sweetest of men but his philosophy was what you would write if you were really high on something, what today would be called "New Age." He stood between us and joined us in staring out at the cathedral. Out of the blue he said to us, "You know, boys, the students just aren't interested in pantheism any more." Bruce and I looked at each other and had to bite our lips to keep from bursting out in laughter. Oliver stayed for what seemed to be an interminable time and continued to lay such lines on us. Finally, mercifully, he left. We heard his footsteps in the hallway, the opening and closing of the elevator doors, the elevator going down, and then we started rolling on the floor. Suddenly this sobering thought occurred to me: Some day I will be Oliver Reiser and I will attempt to engage some of the young Turks in my department in conversation by saying, "You know, boys, the students just aren't interested in ordinary language philosophy any more," and they will barely be able to control themselves. The "king must die" legend is alive and well in philosophy.

I received a continuing education at Pitt, certainly the equivalent of a second PhD in philosophy. Just as I had succeeded in marrying a woman who is a much better person than myself, I managed to join a department containing much better philosophers than myself. I audited courses by Adolf Grünbaum, Nick Rescher, Kurt Baier, Alan Ross Anderson and Nuel Belnap, and Wilfrid Sellars. Most inspiring were Adolf's courses, since they presented me with a paradigm case of a consummate professional in action. I have greatly valued his friendship and mentoring over the years. Sellars's undergraduate classes were especially helpful in enabling me to get into the Sellarsian system, since, unlike his graduate seminars, he lectured and showed the historical roots of his leading ideas, which made them more accessible. Like the Shadow, he had the ability to cloud men's minds and make them see what he wanted them to see. He was the master tease. A typical Sellars undergraduate lecture would consist in thirty minutes of brilliant excursions into the history of ideas, followed by twenty minutes of brilliant criticisms of some central concept. Now it was his turn to give you the truth about the matter, and you were convinced that he had it, but just then the damn bell would ring ending the class. He would issue a promissory note that never got cashed. In later years, I audited classes by Carl P. Hempel, Wesley Salmon, Clark Glymour, and John Earman. I also spent a good deal of time at Pitt's great Center for the Philosophy of Science listening to lunch-time talks by visiting fellows from all over the world.

I was especially intrigued by Sellars's linguistic nominalism, which attempted to give an adverbial or cognate accusative analysis of indirect discourse so as to avoid referring to abstract propositions. I had written the piece on "Propositions, Sentences, Judgments, and Statements" for the 1966 *Encyclopedia of Philosophy*. No sooner did it appear than it became obsolete. In addition to the Sellars analysis, there was the adjectival analysis of indirect discourse by Scheffler and Davidson's paratactic analysis.

My continued hard work on time was beginning to reach fruition. In 1967 I published a widely used anthology on *The Philosophy of Time* with Anchor Books with lengthy introductions to the five sections of the book. I requested that the river of time be put on the cover, replete with the observer on the bridge shining his spotlight of presentness onto the water, illuminating one of the events in his history floating on the river's surface. I was completely floored by a brilliantly astute query from the publisher's art department: "What age should the observer be?" This brings out the sense in which the observer is some kind of a transcendent spook, similar to Vonnegut's Tralfamadorians. I asked if they could give a Picasso-like multidimensional depiction of the observer so that he would be of every age in his life. They replied that their artist wasn't up to it so they put a pocketwatch reflected in several mirrors on the cover. This anthology sold well and went through several reprintings and new editions. It helped to clarify and popularize the clash between the *A*- and *B*-Theories of time.

A year later my book, *The Language of Time*, was published by Routledge & Kegan Paul in their International Library of Philosophy and Scientific Method series. This book gave an impassioned defense of the *A*-Theory of time. According to the *B*-Theory, time is nothing but a temporal series of events running from earlier to later, the distinctions of past, present, and future being reducible in some way to temporal relations between these events. The *A*-Theory denies that such reductions are possible. But even if the *A*-Theory is right about this, as is argued for in the included essay, "McTaggart's Analysis of Time," many *B*-Theorists are ready to argue that these tensed distinctions are *subjective* in the sense of being ontologically dependent upon a *subject* as either a language-user or a perceiver, which I have challenged in the included essay on "The Egocentric Particular and Token Reflexive Analyses of Tense." *B*-Theorists often argue for the subject-dependency of now or the present, and thus of past and future as well, by an analogy between now and here. Since it is granted that there is not an objective here, the same should be said about now, given how similar they are in their logical grammar. The included papers on "Disanalogies Between Space and Time" and "God Eternal and Paul Helm" attempt to counter this argument by showing deep disanalogies between now and here that speak for now being objective in a way that here is not. They concern our temporal indexical perspectives being imposed on and shared by us in ways that our spatial indexical perspectives are not. Furthermore, there are agency-based asymmetries between past and future that have no spatial analogues. The included essay, "Why Causation Cannot Go Backwards," which is a chapter of my book, *The Language of Time*, argues that many of these asymmetries are rooted in an asymmetry in our concept of causation in that we can bring about events in the future but not the past.

In arguing for the objectivity of the perspectives of past, present, and future, I am not arguing for the objective reality of a queer entity, the present or now, the transcendent spotlight of presentness in the River of Time representation, which inexorably shifts to ever later times. Such a view of "temporal becoming" or "passage" quickly leads to a contradiction. "The present" and "now" are rigid designators in that the proposition expressed by "now (or the present) might not be now (or the present)" is necessarily false. But if the present shifts to later times, then now will not be now—this very moment of time—at some later time, in violation of the necessity of identity between individuals designated by rigid designators. My early essay in this volume, "Is It Now Now?," makes this point in a different way. But that you will never run into Mr. Now at a party is consistent with the objectivity of the perspectives of past, present, and future. Entiative theories about the present confound the *what* with the *how* of reference. There is nothing queer about *what* is denoted by a use of "now," it being a moment of time, whatever that might turn out to be upon further analysis, but there is a mysterious *how* in such a reference in that we are prisoners of time who have a unique temporal perspective imposed upon us.

An important issue hangs in the balance in the disputes between *A*- and *B*-Theorists, namely, whether there is bifurcation between man and nature. The *B*-theorists advocate an error theory of tensed temporal perspectives according to which we illicitly project onto the objective world peculiarities of our own psychological states of mind. Smart and Grünbaum have the scientistic intuition that what science does not take note of is not. And since science intentionally abstracts from our personal indexical perspectives, they are merely subjective. This is an argument that only has to be stated clearly to be refuted.

With the publication of my two books on time, I felt free to explore other topics in metaphysics, as well as aesthetics. In particular, I became fascinated by issues in negation and nonbeing. The skills that I had honed in my work on time found a fruitful application in this area. For in both areas there is an attempt to eliminate or ontologically downgrade some puzzling type of fact by reducing it to some favored type of fact. Just as the dispute between *A*- and *B*-Theorists over the translation or reducibility of *A*-propositions, i.e., propositions that report an event's temporal position through the use of a sentence that can express propositions differing in truth-value when used at different times, into *B*-propositions, i.e., propositions that report a temporal relation between individuals through the use of a freely repeatable sentence, would not get resolved until adequate criteria were found for *A*- and *B*-propositions, the dispute between the friends and foes over the translation or reducibility of negative to positive propositions would not get resolved until adequate criteria were devised for these two type of propositions. This is what I attempted to do in the included article on "Negative Statements." My criteria made use of the primitive notion of *being of the same quality as* and held that an atomic property is negative just in case it is logically compatible with every atomic property of the same quality, otherwise positive. Armed with these criteria, it can be shown that otherness and incompatibility analyses fail to reduce negative to positive propositions, in which the otherness analysis renders "This is not green" as "Every positive property of this is other than greenness" and the incompatibility analysis as "There is some positive property of this that is incompatible with greenness."

Although the incompatibility analysis fails to make good on its reductive boast, it does serve the salutary purpose of demystifying negative events. From Plato on up through Quine, what has worried philosophers about negative events is that we do not seem to have adequate criteria of identity for them, there being no nonarbitrary answer, for example, to the question, "How many forest fires did not occur yesterday?" In the included essay "On What There Isn't," it is shown how the incompatibility analysis gives nonproblematic extensional criteria of identity for negative events. It, along with the otherness analysis, also satisfies Parmenides' dictum against referring to that which is not, since both analyses quantify over only positive properties and existent individuals. I published an essay on "Bergson's Analysis of Nothingness" in which I showed how these analyses apply to the issue of whether there could have been Nothing—an absolute nothingness in which all positive properties go uninstantiated—rather than something. Another way of approaching this issue arises out of the question in Wittgenstein's *Tractatus* as to whether every atomic proposition could be false. This is explored in the included essay on "Could Logical Space Be Empty?" Another aspect of the problem of nonbeing concerns the role played by a receptacle comprised of an amorphous space-time in grounding the individuation of empirical particulars, which is explored in the included essay on "Nonbeing and the Receptacle." This is me at my wildest, most speculative phase.

I am happy to have this opportunity to republish these essays, which were the core of my monograph, *Problems of Negation and Non-Being*, that was published as Monograph 10 in 1976 by *The American Philosophical Quarterly*. It came stillborn from the press, in part because it went unreviewed. There is, I believe, a definite niche for this book, since it still is the only thorough, book-length treatment of these issues that is both historical and systematic.

I managed to produce this book, and all of my subsequent books, while teaching fulltime, enjoying only a one-semester sabbatical leave every seventh year. Ever since 1967 I have applied to the different foundations for research leaves, only to be rejected. I remember asking my friend and colleague, Nick Rescher, who is very knowledgeable about getting grants, to help me with my application to the NEH for my work on negation and nonbeing. In my description of the project I used Santa Claus as an example of a nonexistent being, but Nick thought it too frivolous and suggested I change it to the Anti-Christ. Even the Anti-Christ didn't help. I mention my lack of success in securing a grant to give encouragement to young people who suffer a similar fate that you can still turn it out, provided you forego reading Spinoza's *Ethics*, of course. Your ego may take a beating, but it isn't the end of the world.

My next major research interest was the philosophy of religion. It gradually snuck up on me through my teaching, which shows the value of teaching material outside your current fields of interest. Not since I was a teenager did I have any personal involvement with questions about God. But I do love to argue and no area is more loaded with foxy arguments than the philosophy of religion, mainly due to the brilliant work by the analytically oriented contemporary defenders of theism—Alvin Plantinga, William Alston, Robert M. Adams, and Richard Swinburne. I made it my business to be the fly in their ointment, and included in this volume are a number of such efforts. Just to prove that I am an equal-opportunity arguer, I even devised a new version of the cosmological argument that I presented at a conference on Faith and Christianity in Munich in 1999. The argument came to me in a flash, all thirty-two steps of it, while I was swimming laps, as I do every day. I skipped my shower and raced home to get it down on paper to see whether it would hold water. That evening I called Adolf, an atheist's atheist, and told him of my great new argument for God's existence. He asked, what's the catch, and I answered that there isn't any: it works. After a very long silence Adolf asked, "Why did you do it, Richard?" I had the feeling that if Adolf were my superior in the order of Pythagoreans, I would have been set adrift sans supplies. I told him that I did it because I could, because I was clever enough to come up with this new argument. In philosophy, as in life, we do what we can, not what we ought to do.

The argument was printed in the proceedings of the conference, *Faith and Christianity*, under the title, "A New Argument for the Existence of God: One That Works, Well Sort of." Subsequently, my student, Alexander Pruss, showed me how to simplify and strengthen the article, and we jointly published this revised version in *Religious Studies* for 1999 under the title "A New Cosmological Argument." It has attracted a good deal of critical attention and is included in this volume, along with our published responses to criticism by Oppy, Davey, and Clifton. Working with Alexander has been my most exhilarating experience in philosophy. Nothing could please me more than to have a student who can wipe the floor with me. He is a rare combination of technical brilliance, having earned a PhD in mathematics by the time he was 22, and great philosophical depth, being an exceedingly devout Polish Catholic. At one point we were intensely engaged in finding responses to our critics, and I said to Alex that this is the first time in my career I have had a personal involvement in one of my arguments, to which he responded that it is because this is the only argument that I have given that has a true conclusion. We coauthored a number of pieces. Recently we coedited *The Existence of God* in the International Research Library of Philosophy series, for which we contributed a mammoth introduction.

Around 1990 I found my interests reverting reverting back to my old flames, the ones through whom I entered philosophy, William James and John Dewey. I fell madly in love with William James again and worked my way up gradually to a book on him by publishing many articles along the way. I received invaluable critical feedback from a voluminous e-mail correspondence with most of the leading James interpreters. The book worked out very well because I held it at least two years longer than I had planned to, which gave me time to get even more criticisms and continue to rewrite in the light of them. As a result I managed to communicate successfully. I was very pleased with the reviews, not just because they were very laudatory, but even more because they fully understood what I was trying to put across. Another important factor in the book's success is that I managed to counterbalance my natural proclivity to be overly critical, the all-destroyer from New York City, with a very sympathetic positive interpretation of James. James is a perfect target for a hostile critic since his writing abounds in tensions and inconsistencies. I decided that, come what may, I was going to make James into a hero; and thus I found ways to counterbalance my withering objections with a positive effort to make something really interesting and important out of the text. For the first time in my life I felt good about something I published, even after six months, for I knew in my heart that I had done the best I could. *The Divided Self of William James* appeared in 1999 with the Cambridge University Press, which also published my 1991 *On the Nature and Existence of God*, under the superb editorship of Terence Moore.

Currently, I am working on a book on John Dewey. Over the years I have had a love/hate relationship with Dewey. Sometimes I see Dewey as a messiah and find all sorts of depth and inspiration in his writings; at other times I find myself alienated by his preachiness and one-idea fanaticism, it being inquiry all the way on down. It will be much more difficult for me to make a hero out of Dewey, and I fear that the book will fail because its harsh criticisms will not get properly counterbalanced with an attractive positive take on his philosophy. It will turn out that the same tension between prometheanism and mysticism that was so prominent in my interpretation of James also underlies Dewey's philosophy. Whereas James is an experiential mystic, stressing the salvific nature of conceptless intuitions of the Bergsonian musing together of things, Dewey is within the Parmenidean-Hegelian tradition of intellectual mysticism. One can see in both men the schizophrenic nature of New England culture in the latter half of the nineteenth century, which involved the attempt to become the master of nature through applied science and also to achieve spiritual intimacy with it through unifying experiences.

As I look back upon my career, I am impressed that I have done by far my best work during my sixties. There are many causes of this. First, I am in remarkable physical condition, because I have worked out every day of my life and lived a very healthy life. So much of one's success in any endeavor is having enough gas. A second factor is that my children had grown up and were happy off on their own, which meant that I could focus all my attention on my work. Third, and most important, is that my love of philosophy is a pure one and thus grows greater with time, like in a good marriage. Philosophy has never entered into my personal life. That is why I could give an argument for God's existence and defend it in the last ditch and yet remain a nonbeliever. If one asked me whether I was a theist, atheist, or agnostic, my response would be, none of the above. For in my real life I never feel the need to deal with such questions. If one needs to ask what is the meaning and purpose of life, it is a sign that one has lost one's way. The examined life isn't worth living, in my opinion. The value of doing philosophy professionally is that it enables one to live unphilosophically. My student, Mitch Green, perfectly captured my essence in some remarks he made at my retirement dinner. "Richard Gale is a counterexample to Harry Frankfurt's claim that to qualify as human one must engage in second-order reflection on what sorts of reasons should be determinative of one's will." I am incapable of that kind of self-reflection. The one thing that always shall be and always should be a mystery to us is ourselves. Each of us is like a spotlight or index finger that can illuminate or touch everything but itself. (I know, unless it is shining in a mirror or the person has a bad case of arthritis.)

GOD

I

ON THE COGNITIVITY OF MYSTICAL EXPERIENCES

I begin by summarizing my previously published objections to the argument for the cognitivity of mystical experiences based on their being analogous to sense experiences. Then I respond to published objections to my position from Alston, Gellman, Wainwright, and Plantinga. Finally, I revise my original position so as to meet some new objections of my own.

Are mystical experiences cognitive, a basis on which knowledge is gained of an objective reality that transcends the world accessed through the ordinary five senses? No doubt they have an overpowering noetic phenomenological quality that leaves their subjects sweating with conviction that they are. But appearing noetic and actually being noetic do not always coincide, as witnessed by the equally overwhelming noetic quality possessed by various noncognitive experiences, such as dreams, and drug-induced experiences. Plainly, arguments are needed to support the cognitivity claim. Fortunately, there has been no shortage of arguments in recent years to show that mystical experiences, understood as direct nonsensory perceptions of the presence of God, are cognitive.[1] This paper will critically evaluate them.

I. ARGUMENTS BASED ON AN ANALOGY WITH SENSE EXPERIENCE

Most of these recent arguments are based, explicitly or implicitly, on an analogy with sense experience, the generic version of which goes as follows:

1. Mystical experiences are analogous to sense experiences in cognitively relevant respects.
2. Sense experiences are cognitive.
3. Therefore, mystical experiences are cognitive.

Since sense experiences are taken by all but complete skeptics to be cognitive, if mystical experiences should prove to be sufficiently analogous to them, they should be accorded all the epistemic rights and privileges thereunto appertaining to sense experiences.

Analogical arguments vary with respect to how strong they take the analogy to be. The weakest is a version of language-game fideism based on the greatest story ever told—that the language-game is played. But that both types of experience are included within an ongoing normative rule-governed linguistic practice is too thin an analogy to support the inference of 3 from 2. For there have been numerous language-games, such as witchcraft and astrology, that their participants took to be cognitive of an objective reality that plainly are not, given that their belief outputs clash with those of more deeply entrenched and well supported language-games. Furthermore, there are language-games in which belief outputs are based on subjective experiential inputs, such as those for making avowals of pain on the basis of introspective experience. In these subjective language-games the experiential verb takes a cognate accusative, "I pain (or feel painfully)" being the perspicuous rendering of "I feel a pain."

A language-game can count as cognitive only if it supplies checks and tests for distinguishing between its veridical and unveridical experiential inputs. Thus, the analogy between sense and mystical experiences can be supportive of the inference of 3 from 2 only if there are tests for distinguishing between veridical and unveridical mystical experiences. But they cannot be just any tests, for this would allow cultist type language-games, in which the only test is based on what the cult leader says, to count as cognitive. The tests must be sufficiently analogous to those for sense experience.

Among the analogical arguments that require analogous tests, there is a distinction between the retail and wholesale versions. The former, which was advanced initially by William James in *The Varieties of Religious Experience* and more recently by Richard Swinburne, draws the analogy between individual sense and mystical experiences, whereas the latter, which has been championed by William Alston and William Wainwright, draws the analogy between the sense experience doxastic practice (SP) and the mystical experience doxastic practice (MP), in which a doxastic practice is a normative rule-governed social practice for forming existentially committed objective beliefs from a certain type of experiential input, subject to defeating overriders. This is the wholesale analogical argument:

4. The MP doxastic practice is analogous to the SP doxastic practice in cognitively relevant respects.
5. The SP doxastic practice is reliable in that most of its belief outputs are true.
6. Therefore, the MP doxastic practice also is reliable.

Both doxastic practices are based on an a priori, framework-constituting rule that holds the occurrence of the experiential input in question to constitute both evidence and a prima facie warrant for the belief that reality is the way in which it is represented in this experience. The rule is a priori because any justification of it will have to assume that experiences of this type usually are reliable, thereby falling prey to vicious epistemic circularity. The warrant for believing is only prima facie, because it is subject to defeat by overriders consisting in flunked tests. The wholesale version is superior to the retail one, since the needed tests must be part of a social practice, given that a rule requires the possibility of public enforcement, which is just what a doxastic practice supplies.

In Richard Swinburne's argument this rule takes the form of the "Principle of Credulity" (PC), according to which if it epistemically seems to a subject that x is present, then probably x is present, unless there are defeaters, in which an epistemic seeming serves as a basis for a subject to believe that the apparent object of the seeming exists and is as it seems to be (254). Since Swinburne gives full generality to PC, he does not have to present an analogical argument to justify extending it from sense to mystical experiences. His argument goes as follows:

7. It epistemically seems to the subjects of mystical experiences that God is present.
8. If it epistemically seems to a subject that x is present, then probably x is present, unless there are defeaters.
9. Therefore, God probably is present, unless there are defeaters.

Swinburne thinks that the only possible defeater for 9 is a powerful argument for the nonexistence of God, and it is the purpose of his global probabilistic argument for God's existence, based on an agglomeration of the premises of all the empirical theistic arguments, to defeat this potential defeater.

My interpretation of Swinburne's argument as an analogical one, in which PC is initially applied to sense experience and then extended to mystical experiences on the grounds of their being analogous to sense experience, is a well-intentioned anachronistic interpretation of his text.[2] For the unrestricted version of PC is not acceptable. A person's nonperceptual epistemic seemings are notoriously subject to all kinds of irrationalities. The best that can be said for a nonperceptual epistemic seeming that a proposition p is true is that it increases p's probability over its prior probability, but this watered down version of PC is too weak to enable Swinburne to infer 9 from 8. That it is pragmatically, as contrasted with epistemically, rational for subjects to trust their epistemic seemings is plausible, but this version of PC will not enable 9 to be derived from 8 but only 9'.

9'. It is pragmatically rational to believe that God probably is present, unless there are defeaters.

II. OBJECTIONS TO THE ANALOGICAL ARGUMENT

It now will be argued that the analogy between sense and mystical experiences is far too thin to support the inference of 6 from 5 in the wholesale version of the analogical argument. My argument is two-pronged: It is argued, first, that the tests for the veridicality of mystical experiences are not sufficiently analogous to those for sense experience and, second, that mystical experiences, on purely conceptual grounds, fail to qualify as perceptions and thus are radically disanalogous to sense experiences. In addition to rehashing some of my previously published criticisms,[3] I will respond to objections that have been made to them and also will try to correct some blunders I made.

The major tests for the veridicality of sense experience include agreement among observers, successful predictions, and being caused-in-the-right-way by the apparent object of the experience. The agreement test requires the observers whose testimony counts as confirmatory or disconfirmatory of the veridicality of a person's sense experience to be normal and in the right sort of epistemic circumstances. With respect to the former, they must not be subject to any psychological disorder that would distort their perception and their sensory faculties must be functioning in a normal, healthy manner; and, with regard to the latter, they must be properly positioned in space and time and the causal chain linking the experience with its object be of the right sort.

The mystical analogue to this agreement test is woefully weak. In the first place, whereas there are objective, agreed-upon tests for determining when a person's sensory faculty is not functioning properly, there are no such tests for determining when a person's mystical faculty is not functioning properly. Furthermore, there is no mystical analogue to a sensory observer being properly positioned in space, since God does not stand in any spatial relations. That there is no mystical analogue to normality of observer and circumstances results in a pernicious evidential asymmetry in that the occurrence of mystical experiences are taken to be confirmatory but the failure to have them, even when the mystical way of meditating, fasting, and the like is followed, is not taken as disconfirmatory. Thus the mystical agreement test is one that can be passed but not flunked and thus no test at all. It is like a heads I win, tails you lose sort of con game.

There is no mystical analogue to the caused-in-the-right-way test, because there are no supernatural causal chains or processes linking God with worldly events. Another disanalogy is that whereas we can determine on the basis of sense experience alone that a given sense experience is caused in the right way by its apparent object, we cannot determine on the basis of mystical experience alone that a given mystical experience is caused in the right way. Furthermore, the defenders of the cognitivity of mystical experiences cannot agree among themselves whether there are any limitations on what is the right way for God to cause a mystical experience. At one extreme there are those like Wayne Proudfoot who require that a veridical mystical experience be directly caused by God sans any worldly proximate cause. And, at the other extreme, there are those like Walter Stace and Houston Smith who allow for a veridical mystical experience not only to admit of a worldly cause but any worldly cause, even ingestion of LSD.

It is only the prediction test that seems to have any application to mystical experiences. All of the great mystical traditions have taken the subject's favorable spiritual and moral development and the beneficial consequences for her society to count as confirmatory of the veridicality of her mystical experience. They reason that if one is in direct experiential connect with God, no less realizing partial or complete unification with him, it should result in these favorable consequences. Thus, these good consequences are confirmatory of the experience's veridicality in virtue of categoreal link between them and God's omniperfections.

There are two difficulties with the mystical analogue to the prediction test. The less serious difficulty is that the predicted good consequences are just as likely to occur whether the mystical experience that is being tested is veridical or not, that is, the probability that there will be these good consequences relative to background knowledge, k, and that the experience is veridical is about the same as it is relative to k alone, the reason being that k contains facts about the naturalistic causes and consequences of mystical experiences. No doubt, these good consequences are more likely to occur if the subject believes that her experience is veridical, but this gives only a pragmatic, not an epistemic, justification for her so believing. The more serious difficulty is posed by the existence of equally viable rival doxastic mystical practices within the great extant religions, with their different conceptions of what constitutes desirable moral and spiritual development, revealed truths that the experience must not contradict, and ecclesiastical authorities and past holy persons.

Another way that the prediction test is appealed to is that it is more probable that mystical experiences will occur if God exists than if he doesn't, that is, the probability that mystical experience will occur relative to the existence of God and background knowledge k is greater than the probability that mystical experiences will occur relative to k alone. But this is dubious, again, because k contains facts about the naturalistic causes of mystical experiences. This stands in stark contrast with sense experience, for which it unquestionably is the case that it is more probable that sense experiences will occur if there are physical objects than if there are not, assuming that k in this case contains neither that there are physical objects nor any evil demon–type hypothesis. What this shows is that a prediction test is confirmatory of the veridicality of an experience of an O-type object only if the existence of an O-type object has both explanatory value and prior probability with respect to O-type experiences. Mystical experiences of a God-type object have been seen to have neither. The theist might argue at this point that it is more probable that there will exist creatures of sufficient complexity to be subject to these causes if God exists than if he doesn't. This greatly complicates the case for the cognitivity of mystical experiences, but it might be, as Alston, Wainwright, Gellman, and Swinburne contend, that we must consider the global or agglomerative case for theism in determining whether mystical experiences are cognitive. If it could be established that God exists, this would greatly increase the probability that mystical experiences are reliable indicators of objective reality.

III. RESPONSES TO OBJECTIONS

The defenders of the cognitivity thesis have ready responses to all of the preceding objections to the mystical analogues to the veridicality tests for sense experience. Both Alston and Wainwright stress that disanalogies between how these tests apply to sense and mystical experience are not damaging to their analogical argument if these differences are a result of a conceptual difference between the respective apparent objects of these experiences—physical objects and God. Because it is a conceptual truth that God is a completely free supernatural being whose behavior and linkage with the world is not nomically based, the analogical arguer should not be bothered by the fact that the agreement and caused-in-the-right-way tests work in radically different ways for the two types of experience. But to show the conceptual basis for a disanalogy between them does not explain away the disanalogy, just as explaining why one has a disease does not eliminate the disease. Furthermore, a conceptually based disanalogy is the most damaging sort there can be.

Alston contends that the disanalogy between the way in which the agreement test applies to sense and mystical experiences would be damaging if it resulted from an ad hoc requirement that this test can serve only as confirmatory for mystical experiences, thus being a test that can only be passed, whereas it serves as both confirmatory and disconfirmatory for sense experience. Since the evidential asymmetry in the way in which the agreement test works for mystical experience results from the theistic creed, with its claim that God freely bestows grace on someone whom he permits to directly perceive him, no harm is done to the analogical premise. But, again, to explain why there is a disanalogy does not lessen the harm it does to the analogical premise.

I had argued that the challenge posed by religious diversity to the mystical prediction test is especially virulent: Because these rival mystical traditions have opposing consequentialist criteria of veridicality, they are more deeply divided than if they accepted the same criteria but differed with respect to how they applied to specific cases. In response, Alston wrote the following: "If there is no neutral procedure for settling the dispute, each party is in a better position to stick by its guns than they would be if there were such a procedure. This is because in the latter case the most reasonable course would be to suspend judgment until that procedure is deployed. In the other case, since there is nothing analogous to wait for, there isn't the same reason to deny the rationality of each contestant's holding firm."[4] This shows only that when the disputants do not agree upon a decision procedure for settling their disagreement, each is pragmatically justified in holding firm in their rival beliefs. But Alston is supposed to show that each is epistemically justified in doing so. And herein the fact that they cannot agree upon a method for settling their difference more seriously divides them than would a disagreement about the facts, thereby discrediting the epistemic credentials of each of their claims. A better way for Alston to meet the challenge of religious diversity is to pursue the ecumenical route by showing that there are important commonalities between the mystical traditions of the great extant religions and that their differences do not amount to any incompatibility between their different reality-claims.

Another defensive strategy pursued by the analogical arguer is the divide-and-conquer one in which each of the preceding alleged disanalogies is discussed separately and shown not to be alone decisive. This is clearly seen in Wainwright's criticisms of my attack on the analogical premise.[5] With regard to the agreement test, he contends that "Gale *overstates* his case when he claimed that are no [mystical experience] analogues to the sense experience agreement test's requirement that the observer and circumstances be normal" (116; my italics). No doubt, I am guilty of overstating my case, both here and elsewhere, given that before I entered philosophy I worked as a song plugger for a music publishing firm and became adept at the great art of the "hype-job." But, nevertheless Wainwright does concede some force to my charge of disanalogy when he writes that the connection between the condition of the observer and her having an M-experience "is admittedly *looser* than it is in the case of sense perception." (116; my italics). Another example of his giving ground but denying that this alone is sufficient to wipe out the analogical argument is: "Admittedly, failures of agreement like these differ from those counting against the veridicality of an apparent sense perception. Even so, the 'evidential asymmetry' Gale alludes to *isn't great enough* to make 'the mystical use of the agreement test look like a heads I win, tails you lose sort of con game'" (120; my italics).

The same is said in response to my charge that there is no mystical analogue to the caused-in-the-right-way test for sense experience. "While these points are important, they aren't *sufficient* to *totally* undermine the caused-in-the-right-way test. For example, diversity [among different religions] is, as Gale says, 'a cognitively invidious disanalogy.' Whether it is *sufficient* to 'destroy' the relevant analogy is another matter" (122; my italics). The tests, in general, "aren't *as dissimilar* as Gale thinks." In response to another alleged disanalogy he counters that it "is [not] *as devastating* as [Gale] thinks" (124; my italics). And when Wainwright summarizes his discussion of the alleged disanalogies he concludes, "I don't think that the contents of the tests are *totally* dissimilar although the disanalogies as well as analogies are striking" (128; my italics).

The italicized parts of these quotations clearly bring out Wainwright's piecemeal, divide-and-conquer strategy for neutralizing the force of the disanalogies. Although he shows that each disanalogy is not alone sufficient to destroy the analogical argument, he fails to consider whether they are when agglomerated. Obviously, the issue of how close the analogy must be between the tests for the veridicality of sense and mystical experiences for the argument to work is a vague one; for, as my laid-back Canadian good old boy, Bob, who made a prominent appearance in my *On the Nature and Existence of God*, said, "Everything is just aboot like everything else." As I see the agglomerative case, Wainwright has unwittingly given away almost the entire family farm acre by acre, leaving him, at best, with only a tiny vegetable garden, to which Bob would counter that a vegetable garden is just aboot the same as a farm. I guess we'll always have Bob with us, damn him! But one thing is for sure: the agglomerative case is far stronger than one based on taking each disanalogy in isolation.

The same sort of divide-and-conquer strategy runs rampant in Alston's great, classic book, *Perceiving God*. He does grant that the unresolved problem of religious diversity "does have *significant* adverse consequences for the epistemic status of CMP [Christian mystical doxastic practice] and other forms of MP" (275; my italics). But this candid admission of *significant* epistemic discreditation is counterbalanced by the claim that "although this diversity reduces somewhat the maximal degree of epistemic justification derivable from CMP, it leaves the practitioner sufficient prima facie justified in M-beliefs [mystical beliefs] that it is rational for her to hold those beliefs, in the absence of specific overriders" (279). (Are these two claims logically compatible?!) Similar concessions of lessened epistemic creditability are made at many other places in his book in response to ways in which MP is SP's epistemic inferior. That MP's agreement test is a pale shadow of SP's agreement test "shows that [MP] is epistemically inferior to SP" but it does not go so far as to show "that [MP] is unreliable" (220). Other ways in which he concedes that MP is SP's epistemic inferior is that SP is far more well established than any version of MP (283), that everyone must participate in SP whereas only a small minority participate in MP, and, moreover, we have the option of not doing so. But, like Wainwright, he never considers whether he has given away the whole family farm acre by acre when all of his concessions are agglomerated. Again, we run up against Bob, and again it might well be that how one is impressed by the analogies and disanalogies depends on one's background belief concerning the overall case for theism.[6]

Jerome Gellman's defensive strategy in his *Mystical Experience of God* also treads on this ineliminable vagueness but with a twist that brings his position perilously close to a language-game fideism with any old tests:

> There is no good reason to make physical-object claims our evidential standard.... Our ordinary physical-object beliefs are way overjustified by confirming evidence. We have extremely luxurious constellations of confirming networks there. Hence it does not follow that were mystical claims justified to a lesser degree than that, or not by similar procedures, that they would be *un*justified. All that follow would be that they enjoyed less justification than belief in physical-object statements, but perhaps be justified nevertheless. (27)

Herein Gellman appears to be making epistemic warrant and justification internal to a doxastic practice, each being given carte blanche to

IV. MY "KILLER ARGUMENT"

The second prong of my attack on the analogical argument is to show that mystical experiences, on purely conceptual grounds, cannot be perceptual. That they are taken to be perceptual by their subjects doesn't settle the matter, since mystics can be mistaken in what they say about their experiences, as witnessed by their mistaken claim of ineffability. If they were ineffable, how come mystics keep writing about them and, moreover, do such a good job of describing their experiences, even for the straight community of nonmystics? Recall that we did not want to give mystics privileged authority as to whether their experience is noetic. That the apparent object of their experience is given independently of their will is consistent with their experiences not being perceptual: an experience of a pain has such a givenness but its apparent object is only a cognate accusative. What I hope to do is to unearth a conceptual truth about a perceptual experience that mystical experience fails to satisfy, thereby showing that,

> A. It is conceptually impossible to perceive God.

This would totally devastate the analogical premise. What follows is a reformulation of my argument in *On the Nature and Existence of God* (326-43) that I hope will escape the published objections that were made to it by Gellman, Plantinga, and Wainwright. Their objections are based on a misconstrual of the argument, but the fault is mine for not having more clearly formulated it, which fault I hope to rectify now.

The first step in my argument is to point out that it is a conceptual truth that

> B. A type of experience can qualify as perceptual only if it is possible its object (i) can exist when not actually perceived, (ii) be

the common object of different experiences, both by a single person at different times and by two persons at the same time, and (iii) be such that a distinction can be made between perceptions that are of numerically one and the same rather than qualitatively similar objects of that type.

It must be stressed that B gives only a necessary condition for an experience being perceptual. There is no doubt that the object of a sense perception satisfies requirements (i)–(iii). But it is equally clear that the object of a mystical experience also satisfies (i)–(iii). Requirement (i) is met with flying colors, since God is the most objective, independent type of being there could be, given his absolute aseity. Not only can (ii) and (iii) be satisfied, we can have overwhelming empirical evidence that they are. Consider this possible course of experience. The heavens become completely dark across the world as a voice from above the clouds says, "I am the Lord thy God, and I assure you that these persons (or the same person at different times) had veridical mystical experiences of me. And, in case you doubt me, I will now bring about miracles M, N, and O," all of which immediately follow. To strengthen the case we could imagine that the same message appears over the internet and that there is lightning and snow that have the sign design of "I am the Lord...." This would make a believer out of me!

The sought-for conceptual disanalogy, therefore, is not to be found in B but in the manner in which B's requirements must be satisfied. First, it will be shown how B is satisfied by sense perception and then it will be asked whether there is an analogous way in which mystical experience could satisfy B. With regard to sense perception, it is a necessary truth that the perceivers and the objects of their perceptions are housed in a common space-time receptacle in which these objects serve as the common cause, via the different causal chains that link them with these perceivers, of the, for the most part, nomic-type coherence among the contents of these perceptions. This receptacle account explains how objects can exist when not perceived by supplying the needed dimensions in which to house them, thereby satisfying (i). These objects are ultimately individuated by their position in this receptacle, it being a necessary truth that objects of the same kind cannot be spatiotemporally coincident. In order to perform this individuating function for these empirical objects, these dimensions of space and time must not themselves be empirically determined.[7] The receptacle account also explains how (ii)'s requirement that an object can be perceived by more than one person is met by the different causal chains connecting it with these persons within the receptacle.

The receptacle account also satisfies requirement (iii). The receptacle creates the possibility of there being counterexamples to the principle of the identity of indiscernibles when restricted to fully general properties. Any such property admits of the possibility of multiple instantiations at different regions within the receptacle. And, as a consequence, we are able to distinguish between perceptions that are of numerically one and the same object and those of objects that are only qualitatively similar. In the latter case there are noncoincident objects that are hooked up with different perceptions via different causal chains.

Let us call the receptacle explanation of how requirements (i)–(iii) are satisfied a "dimensional explanation." So far it has been established that it is a necessary conceptual truth that

> C. For an experience to qualify as a sense perception it is required that a dimensional explanation can be given of how its object satisfies requirements (i)–(iii) of B.

It would be an egregious piece of linguistic imperialism to require that a mystical experience satisfy C if it is to count as perceptual. For the dimensional account in terms of the receptacle's dimensions invokes space, and the object of a mystical experience, God, is not in space. What must be done is to genericize C so that it is not required that the dimensions of the receptacle be those of space and time. They can be analogues of space and time that perform the same function that space and time do in explaining how (i)–(iii) are satisfied. This genericized version is

> D. For an experience to qualify as a perception it is required that a dimensional explanation or an analogue to a dimensional explanation can be given of how its object satisfies requirements (i)–(iii) of B.

I think it is pretty clear that there is no analogue to a dimensional explanation of how the object of a mystical experience satisfies (i)–(iii) of *B*. As a consequence, mystical experiences fail to be perceptual. And this is the demise of the argument from analogy.

My argument has been subject to many objections. I will attempt to show that they rest on a misunderstanding of it, although the fault is mine for not having written more clearly. Alvin Plantinga, in his *Warranted Christian Belief*,[8] has referred to my argument, tongue in cheek, as Gale's "killer argument." What Plantinga refutes is not my argument for

A. It is conceptually impossible to perceive God

but an extended version of my argument for the stronger conclusion

A'. It is conceptually impossible to perceive or experience God.

He gratuitously burdens me with having the onus of proving *A'* when he writes that Gale "seems to believe or assume that any experiential awareness of God would have to be like *perceptual* awareness of God ... [and] he therefore concludes, I think, that it is not possible to have knowledge of God by way of experience" (336). It is not a great feat to refute an extended version of an argument, since every argument admits of such refutation. I make it quite explicit in both the introduction to my argument and the concluding summary that it is an argument only for *A*. "It now will be argued that it is conceptually impossible for there to be a veridical perception of God," (*On the Nature and Existence of God* [326]) and "Even though it is impossible to have a veridical experience, that is, nonsensory *perception* of God, it does not follow that an of-God experience could not be caused in the right way and thereby qualify as some kind of *nonperceptual* apprehension of God"(343). In fairness to Plantinga, it must be pointed out that I do make a couple of careless remarks, about which more will be said, that support his strong interpretation of me.

Because he interprets me as defending *A'* rather than the weaker *A*, Plantinga interprets me (on p. 339) as defending not

D. For an experience to qualify as a perception it is required that a dimensional explanation or analogue to a dimensional explanation can be given of how its object satisfies requirements (i)–(iii) of *B*.

but the stronger

D'. For an experience to qualify as a perception it is required that a dimensional explanation or an analogue to a dimensional explanation can be given of how its object satisfies requirements (i)–(iii) of *B* and no other sort of explanation can be given of how its object satisfies these requirements.

The crucial difference between *D* and *D'* is that *D'* precludes any nondimensional explanation of how requirements (i)–(iii) are satisfied whereas *D* allows for it.[9] I did point out that a nondimensionality-type explanation could be given of how God satisfies requirements (i)–(iii), and thus Plantinga and Wainwright are running through open doors in their refutation of me. God can be individuated by his fully general properties, such as being the only creator of the world, and a theistic explanation can be given for how he causes there to be by his supernatural will multiple experiences of himself. Furthermore, we could even find out that the latter is the case by the preceding example of hearing the voice from above the clouds.

It seems to me that the most reasonable way to challenge my argument is to deny that *D* is a necessary conceptual truth. Although it is obvious that sense perceptions satisfy *D*, it is not clear that all perceptual experiences must satisfy *D*. I am afraid that the best that I can say in response to this denial of the necessity of *D* is, "Isn't it?" It looks like I am again mired in the modal intuition bowl, in which opponents with rival modal intuitions go back and forth endlessly saying "Tis!" and "Tisn't!"

Even if my argument turns out not to be a "killer argument," it at least has the power to maim, for it significantly deepens the disanalogy between sense and mystical experience by showing that only the former has an object for which there could be a dimensional explanation or an analogue to a dimensional explanation of why its object satisfies requirements (i)–(iii) of *B*. It is yet another acre of the family farm that is given away by the analogical arguer; and, when it is added on to the other acres that have been given away as a result of there being only quite weak mystical analogues to the sensory tests for veridicality, the analogical premise is acceptable only by Bob.

V. NONPERCEPTUAL EXPERIENCES OF GOD

So far I have argued only that it is impossible or, at least, very dubious that there can be veridical *perceptions* of God. But, what about other types of experience? Could one of them give us a cognitive apprehension of God and thus be a source of knowledge of God's existence? Before considering this, I need, for the good of my soul, to point out a terrible blunder that I made in some of my previous publications. On the one hand, I contended that "even though it is impossible to have a veridical... nonsensory perception of God, it does not follow that an of-God–type experience could not be caused by God in the right way and thereby qualify as some kind of nonperceptual apprehension of God" (343). But, on the other hand, I argued that these experiences, like painings, take only a cognate accusative, as witnessed by: "It is the aim of this chapter to supply just such a criterion of objectivity and thus for a verb taking an objective rather than a cognate accusative" (314; see also 326 and 341); and "In order for MPs to qualify as *objective*, not just reliable, it is necessary that their [mystical experience] inputs really be perceptual as advertised" ("Why Alston's Mystical Doxastic Practice Is Subjective," 869). These two claims are incompatible, and it is the latter that must go. I wrongly inferred from the fact that mystical experiences are not perceptual that they are subjective because I operated with a bogus dichotomy that holds every experience to be either perceptual or subjective, that is, to have a cognate accusative. Mystical experiences might be neither, especially since their accusative, God, is not a cognate accusative. Maybe they could serve as a warrant for the existential beliefs based on them concerning the existence and actions of God in accordance with Plantinga's extended Aquinas/Calvin model of basic warrant. This model, as Plantinga makes clear in his criticism of my argument (336), is not confined to perceptual experiences.

Plantinga had argued with considerable force in *Warrant: The Cur-*

rent *Debate* and *Warrant and Proper Function* that what warrants a "basic belief," a belief that is not based on or inferred from another belief, is that it results from the proper functioning of one's cognitive faculties in the right sort of epistemic environment according to a design plan successfully aimed at truth. In these books he confined himself to beliefs based on the "standard package" faculties of sense, memory, introspection, sympathy, and a priori reason. In his monumental *Warranted Christian Belief,* Plantinga argues that it is possible that theistic and, in particular, Christian beliefs have warrant in an analogous way to that in which these standard package beliefs do.[10] If theism is true, then God would want to reveal himself to created persons. Toward this end he implanted in them as part of their original cognitive equipment, along with the cognitive faculties in the standard package, a *sensus divinitatis* that would enable them to form true noninferential beliefs about God's presence, nature, and intentions upon having certain experiences, both perceptual and nonperceptual. Plantinga also introduces a special supernatural process involving the internal instigation of the Holy Spirit by which one is directly caused by God, without any intervening worldly causes, to believe the great things of the Gospel concerning the incarnation, resurrection, and atonement.

Plantinga does not argue that people are in fact warranted in their basic Christian or theistic beliefs by this model—to do so he would have to argue for the existence of God and our possession of a sensus divinitatis—only that it is possible that they have basic warrant for these beliefs. Furthermore, they can have such warrant even if the believers are not able to give any evidential or arugmentative backing for these beliefs. His argument is based on a rich analogy between the sensus divinitatis and the standard package faculties and goes as follows.

10. The sensus divinitatis is analogous to the standard package faculties.
    11. Some beliefs based on the standard package faculties are basically warranted.
    12. Therefore, it is possible that theistic and, in particular, Christian beliefs based upon the sensus divinitatis also are basically warranted.

The astute reader, at this point, knows just what moves I am going to make against this argument—attack its analogical premise in just the same way I did the analogical premise 4 of the doxastic practice version of the analogical argument. The heart of Plantinga's analogy is that we can say of both standard package faculties and the sensus divinitatis faculty that they are "functioning properly," as contrasted with suffering from a "disease," being "dysfunctional," "malfunctioning," suffering from a "pathology," or being in "disorder."

Now either we predicate these terms in the same sense of both types of faculties or we do not. On both alternatives the argument fares badly. If these terms are predicated in the same sense, the analogical premise fares badly, suffering from all the disanalogies that were seen to undermine the analogy between SP and MP. There are agreed-upon objective tests for the standard package faculties being in a state of dysfunction, pathology, disorder, or malfunctioning. But there are no sensus divinitatis analogues to these tests. In regard to basic religious beliefs that are internally instigated by the Holy Spirit, it is obvious that the notion of proper functioning could have no application to them since they are supernaturally caused directly by God. Such instigation, furthermore, is not a faculty but a process, and this cannot be said to have any function and therefore cannot be said to malfunction or be subject to a pathology.

Plantinga continually talks about the sensus divinitatis in natural law terms; but, whereas for Aristotelian natural law theorists questions concerning an individual's nature and proper mode of functioning are to be answered, at least in part, by empirical inquiry, there is nothing analogous in regard to determining the nature and proper function of the sensus divinitatis or for what constitutes a proper way for the internal instigation of the Holy Spirit to occur.

There are further damaging disanalogies between Plantinga's Aquinas/ Calvin experience and those in the standard package. Whereas there is universal participation in the very same doxastic practices based on the experiences in the standard package, this is not so for sensus divinitatis–based experiences. Plantinga has an explanation for this disanalogy based upon the serious damage that was done to the sensus divinitatis as a result of Original Sin, a damage that is repairable only by the supernatural intervention of the Holy Spirit. But to explain why there is this disanalogy does not explain it away. Another damning disanalogy is that there is no standard package analogue to religious diversity, which issue has already been treated.

The multivocalist horn of my dilemma argument fares no better than did the univocalist one. Plantinga now is to say that these terms ("pathology," etc.) are predicated with a different sense of the two kinds of faculties. This precludes Plantinga's making use of the results established in his two earlier *Warrant* books in his argument for the possibility of having a warranted basic belief that God exists. Thus, basic sensus divinitatis–based beliefs can be said to admit of the dysfunction-proper function distinction just as do standard package beliefs, only the tests for the former will be radically different from those for the latter. Whereas the latter are based on empirical tests that are grounded in what is vouchsafed by science, the former will be based on criteria that are internal to the different religious doxastic practices and thus will vary across these practices. And this is language-game fideism, a most vile doctrine and one that Plantinga's ardent theological realism rightly rejects.[11]

In conclusion, it must be stressed again that it is possible that there be veridical nonperceptual experiences of God's presence, only they could not give warrant to the beliefs based on them so that they would constitute knowledge. There is a very powerful William James–style will-to-believe argument for it being pragmatically rational for the subjects of mystical experiences to believe both that their experiences are veridical perceptions and that MP is a reliable objective doxastic practice, but this is a story for another paper.[12]

NOTES

1. See in particular: William Alston, *Perceiving God: The Epistemology of Religious Experience* (Ithaca, NY: Cornell University Press, 1991); William Wainwright, *Mysticism, A Study of Its Nature, Cognitive Value, and Moral Implications* (Madison: University of Wisconsin Press, 1981); Gary Guting, *Religious Belief and Religious Skepticism* (Notre Dame, IN: University of Notre Dame Press,

1982); Jerome Gellman, *Experience of God and the Rationality of Theistic Belief* (Ithaca, NY: Cornell University Press, 1997), and *Mystical Experience of God* (Aldershot, UK: Ashgate, 2001); Richard Swinburne, *The Existence of God* (Oxford: The Clarendon Press, 1991). References to these books will be made within parentheses in the body of the essay.

2. Jerome Gellman's argument in *Mystical Experience of God* (17) is based on Swinburne's Principle of Credulity, but it is unclear whether he gives it full generality and thus whether his argument is analogical.

3. The publications in question are: Chapter 8 of *On the Nature and Existence of God* (Cambridge: Cambridge University Press, 1991); "Why Alston's Mystical Doxastic Practice Is Subjective," *Philosophy and Phenomenological Research* 4 (1994), along with Alston's response; "The Overall Argument of Alston's *Perceiving God*," *Religious Studies* 30 (1994), along with Alston's response; "Swinburne on Religious Experience," in *Reason and the Christian Religion: Essays in Honour of Richard Swinburne*, ed. A. Padgett (Oxford: Clarendon Press, 1994); A Critical Study of Keith Yandell's *The Epistemology of Religious Experience, Faith and Philosophy* (1995); and "A Response to My Critics," *Philo* 6 (2003).

4. "Response to Critics," *Religious Studies* 30 (1994), pp. 174–75.

5. "Gale on Religious Experiencce," *Philo* 6 (2003).

6. For an insightful account of this see William Alston, "The Distinctiveness of the Epistemology of Religious Belief," in *The Rationality of Theism*, ed. G. Bruntrup and R. Tacelli (Dordrecht: Kluwer Academic Publishers, 1999).

7. For the full details on this see my *Problems of Negation and Non-Being*, *The American Philosophical Quarterly*, Monograph 10 (1975), reprinted in this volume.

8. Oxford: Oxford University Press, 2000, p. 335.

9. Wainwright also so interprets me: *Mysticism*, p. 160. Gellman, on the other hand, when he lists the key propositions in my argument, fails to mention *D*: *Mystical Experience of God*, p. 40.

10. For a detailed account of exactly how his argument is analogical see my "Alvin Plantinga's *Warranted Christian Belief*," *Philo* 4 (2001).

11. See Plantinga's trenchant objections to fideism in his "Reason and Belief in God," in *Faith and Rationality*, ed. Plantinga and Wolterstorff (Notre Dame, IN: University of Notre Dame Press, 1983), pp. 87–89.

12. For the full details I refer the reader to my *The Divided Self of William James* (Cambridge: Cambridge University Press, 1999), and an abridged version, *The Philosophy of William James: An Introduction* (Cambridge: Cambridge University Press 2004).

2

THE PROBLEM OF EVIL

The greatest epistemic challenge to the rationality of theistic belief is based on the widespread existence of evil, much of which appears to be gratuitous or unjustified. There are two types of atheistic arguments from evil—the deductive and the evidential. The former is an atheological argument that attempts to deduce an explicit contradiction from there being both evil and a God who is omnipotent and omnibenevolent. The evidential argument, of which there are many different versions, uses the known evils of the world to infer the improbability of God's existence or the irrationality of theistic belief. Each will be discussed in turn.

I. THE DEDUCTIVE ARGUMENT

Before we get down to considering various atheistic arguments from evil, it is necessary to say something about what evil is and to distinguish between different types of evil. An evil is something that, taken by itself in isolation, is an ought-not-to-be, an "Oh, no!" Examples are physical and mental suffering by a sentient being, including lower animals; immoral action; bad character; and a privation in which something fails to measure up to what it ought to be, such as a human being born blind. The qualification "taken by itself" is important, since some evils are not gratuitous because they are a so-called blessing in disguise, being necessary for the realization of an outweighing good or prevention of an even greater evil. As members of such a larger whole they are not an ought-not-to-be, although taken in themselves they are. A distinction that will play a crucial role in our discussion of evil is between justified and unjustified evils. A justified evil is one for which God, were he to exist, would not have a morally exonerating excuse for causing or permitting it. An evil can be both justified and gratuitous, as for example a merited punishment that is not necessary for the realization of an outweighing good or prevention of an even greater evil.

Another important distinction is between natural and moral evil, the latter, unlike the former, being attributable to the misuse of free will by finite creatures. Examples of natural evils are floods, earthquakes, typhoons, and famines. It is possible that we are mistaken in so classifying them, since, for all we can know with absolute certainty, they might result from the free evil doings of very powerful but finite creatures, such as the Devil or ETs, or some of them might have been prevented had we properly exercised our free will in discovering their causes and ways of preventing them. Some theists refuse to call anything but moral evil or wickedness an evil, thereby eliminating natural evils as challenges to theism. This linguistic maneuver, however, accomplishes nothing, for the problem still remains as to how God could be justified in permitting suffering that is not attributable to the misuse of free will by finite creatures. To accommodate this redefinition of "evil," natural evils could be called "schmevils," the problem now being how God could be justified in allowing there to be schmevils.

With these preliminaries out of the way, we can consider the deductive or atheological argument from evil as presented by J. L. Mackie, who is to be credited for being the first person to give an explicit mounting of this age old argument. The initial set of propositions is:

1. God is omnipotent;
2. God is omnibenevolent; and
3. Evil exists.

From 1 and 2 it is deduced that

4. Evil does not exist.

This yields the contradiction that

5. Evil exists and evil does not exist. From 3 and 4

Whereas certain Eastern religions would deny 3, Western theism cannot since it is based on the Bible, which abounds in descriptions of every imaginable type of evil.

It is plain that 4 does not follow immediately from 1 and 2. Some additional premises are needed and they must be either necessarily true or accepted by the theist. Mackie supplies the following two additional premises that are supposed to be necessarily true in virtue of linguistic rules:

5. An omnipotent being can bring about anything;

and

6. An omnibenevolent being prevents or eliminates every evil it can.

Clearly, these additional premises are neither necessary truths nor acceptable by the theist. 6 must be restricted as follows:

6'. An omnipotent being can bring about anything that it is consistent for it to bring about.

And 7, in the light of the distinction between a justified and unjustified evil, must be restricted so as to yield:

7'. An omnibenevolent being prevents or eliminates every unjustified evil it can.

From the initial set of premises, in conjunction with 6' and 7', it can be deduced only that

4'. Unjustified evil does not exist
but 4' is consistent with
4. Evil does not exist.

This manner of rebutting Mackie's argument, however, leaves us with the resident problem of explaining how a being who is both omnipotent and omnibenevolent possibly could be morally justified in bringing about or permitting an evil. What sort of a morally exonerating excuse could be available to this being, remembering that it is supposed to be God and thus omniscient and sovereign as well? The excuses that we are familiar with are applicable to human beings but do not seem applicable to God. The lack-of-power excuse for failing to eliminate or prevent an evil (I wasn't strong enough to lift the car that you were pinned under) cannot be available to an omnipotent being. And the excusable-ignorance excuse (How could I have known that saying "Niagara Falls" would send him into a homicidal rage) could not apply to an omniscient being. And since God is sovereign over everything, he cannot be excused because of a lack of opportunity (I couldn't have saved him from dying from the rattler's bite because I did not have the needed antivenom, or, I wasn't there). That no excuse that we know of seems applicable to God should worry the theist.

The theist could respond that it is unacceptably anthropomorphic to demand that at least some of the excuses that apply to us human beings are applicable to God; for he is infinite and we are finite. This is the message of the book of Job, about which a lot more will be said later. This raises the problem of what is required of a *personal* God and just how anthropomorphic our conception of this God should be. Be that as it may, it would help the cause of theism if we could at least spell out some excuse that it is at least logically possible for God to have. To do this is to create a *defense*, which is a description of a possible world containing both God and evil and thus a world in which God has a morally exonerating excuse for permitting evil. A *theodicy* is a defense plus an argument to show that this exonerating condition or possible world actually obtains or at least that it is not implausible that it does in the light of what we know.

There is the compensation-in-an-afterlife defense for God permitting or even causing an evil, regardless of how horrendous it is. It is not enough that God awards the sufferer with heavenly pleasures that far outweigh the suffering underwent by the creature in this life, for this would not justify his allowing the suffering. Why not just create the pleasures sans the suffering? Why not plug everyone in to an ecstasy machine that would produce in them the greatest pleasurable state, say a combination of an orgasm and a mystical state? It is necessary that the evil is an intrinsic organic or aesthetic part of the pleasurable heavenly outcome so that the value of this outcome depends upon the earlier evil. For a compensation-in-an-afterlife defense to be effective it needs to spell out what this would be like. Furthermore, this defense, even when properly filled in, leaves a lot of work to be done if it is to be upgraded to a theodicy, since adequate evidence or arguments would have to be given for the existence of God, as well as an after-life, no easy undertaking. An attempt will be made to come up with better defenses, ones that are based upon what obtains on this side of the vale.

II. FREE WILL DEFENSES

The free will defense (FWD) attempts to show how it is possible for God and moral evil to coexist by describing a possible world in which God is morally justified or exonerated for creating persons who freely go wrong. There are several different versions of it. The following is a generic brand FWD that captures what is common to them.

1. It is God's intention to create the best overall situation or the best world that he can. (Intention premise.)
2. A world containing free persons who freely perform both right and wrong actions, but for the most part go right, is better than any possible world devoid of free persons. (Normative premise.)
3. God cannot cause or determine in any way what a created person freely does. (Incompatibilist premise.)
4. It is logically possible that God is contingently unable to create free persons who always go right. (God-could-be-unlucky premise.)

What happens to premise 1, the intention premise, if, as seems reasonable, there is no uniquely best of all possible worlds in a way that is analogous to there not being a largest positive integer (a world with 1,001 happy egrets in it is better than one that contains only 1,000 happy egrets, and so on ad infinitum)? In that case God will create a world that is overall worth having and, moreover, one that is devoid of any unjustified evil. It has been brilliantly argued by Robert M. Adams that even if there were a uniquely best of all possible worlds, God would not be morally obligated to actualize it, since by actualizing less good creatures than he could have he is bestowing grace upon them, that is, bestowing a benefit without consideration of merit, and grace is recognized by the theist as a virtue of God. This seems plausible when confined to nonmoral goodness such as beauty, athletic ability, and the like, but is highly dubious if it is moral goodness that is in question. But one thing is for sure: there cannot be any morally unjustified evil in a world that God actualizes.

The incompatibilist premise, 3, requires that a free action be determined wholly by the agent and thus not by something external to the agent, such as prior causes or even the will of God, which can be explicitly formulated as

L. A free act is not sufficiently caused by anything external to the agent.

Without this premise the proponent of the FWD would have no response to the objection of the causal or theological compatibilist who contends that God could have determined that every created free person always freely goes right by either, respectively, a suitable determination of the initial state of the universe and the causal laws or simply willing in his own inimitable supernatural way that they do.

Each version of the FWD will tell a different story about how the God-could-be-unlucky premise, 4, could be realized, of how it is possible that God be frustrated in his endeavor to create a universe containing moral good (good that results from the use of creaturely free will) sans moral evil. According to the normative premise, 2, the value of free will is supposed to be so great that God is morally exonerated under such circumstances for creating the Mr. Rogers–type persons—you know, the very same people who are good sometimes are bad sometimes.

We will begin our survey of different versions of the FWD by considering the one that was formulated by Alvin Plantinga, who has a very ingenious story to tell about how God could be unlucky. We know from L that God cannot both create free beings and determine what they freely do. What he must do, therefore, is to create persons who are free with respect to certain actions and then leave it up to them what they freely do. This requires that God does not instantiate or actualize a *possible free person* but rather what I will call a *diminished possible free person*. The former is a maximal and composible set of abstract properties that could be instantiated by a single person and contains the property of being free with respect to at least one morally significant action, A, that is, the property of either freely doing A or freely refraining from doing A. You can think of it as a set of abstract propositions that completely describes the life of such a free person, everything that she does and undergoes. The set is composible in that it admits of the logical possibility of coinstantiation by a single concrete individual, and it is maximal because for every property that could be possessed by a person either it or its complement is included in the set, the complement of the property P being non$P$. Each possible free person contains a *diminished possible free person*, which is its largest proper subset of properties that is such that for any action A it neither includes or entails freely doing A nor includes or entails freely refraining from doing A, in which a property H includes or entails another property G just in case it is logically impossible that H be instantiated and G not be. The property of being red, for example, includes or entails the property of being colored since it is impossible for an object to be red but not be colored. A diminished possible free person is a "freedom-neutral" set of properties. Each property included in a set of properties could be freedom-neutral in that it does not entail for any action, A, freely doing A and yet the set as a whole not be, for the set could contain the properties (either freely doing A or freely refraining from doing A) and doing A. The conjunction of these two properties entails freely doing A.

For every possible free person containing the property of freely doing A there is a numerically distinct possible person that includes all of the same properties save for its including freely refraining from doing A instead. Let us call such a pair of possible free persons an "incompatible pair." Whenever you freely perform an action you instantiate one member of such a pair to the exclusion of the other. For any incompatible pair God will be contingently unable to actualize one person in the pair. Let our specimen incompatible pair be P and P_1, who include all of the same properties save for P's including freely doing A and P_1's instead including freely refraining from doing A. The question is what would result if God were to instantiate DP. Would the concrete instantiator of this diminished person or set of freedom-neutral properties freely do A or freely refrain? Plainly, it must do one or the other, since it has the disjunctive property of either freely doing A or freely refraining from doing A. Thus, it is either true that

> F. If DP were instantiated, the instantiator would freely do A.

or true that

> F'. If DP were instantiated, the instantiator would freely refrain from doing A.

Let us call a subjunctive conditional whose antecedent reports the instantiation of a diminished possible free person and consequent the performance of a free action by the instantiated person a "free will subjunctive conditional," for short an "F-conditional." If F is true, then were God to instantiate DP, it would result in P being actualized; whereas, if F' is true, were God to actualize DP, it would result in P_1 being actualized. Since F and F' are logically incompatible, it follows that if F is true God is unable to actualize P_1, and if F' is true God is unable to actualize P. But necessarily one of them is true and therefore necessarily true that God cannot actualize P or cannot actualize P_1.

This proof assumed that the law of conditional excluded middle holds for F-conditionals. Herein the necessarily true disjunction is formed not from the disjunction of an F-conditional with its negation, as is the case when the weaker law of excluded middle is applied, but from the disjunction of an F-conditional with an F-conditional containing the same antecedent and the denial of the former's consequent, as is the case above with the disjunction of F and F'. Plantinga gives an alternate proof that applies only the law of excluded middle to F-conditionals. It begins with what Plantinga calls "Lewis's lemma," which, when translated into my terminology, says that God can actualize a possible person P containing the property of freely doing A only if it is true that if God were to actualize its diminished person DP, the instantiator would freely do A. It next is claimed by appeal to the law of excluded middle that it is either true or false that F. If it is false, then, given Lewis's lemma, God cannot actualize P; and, if it is true, then he cannot actualize P_1.

At the outset let us confine ourselves to possible persons that include the property of being free with respect to only one action, such as persons P and P_1 above. What we establish then can be generalized to more complex possible persons. Any incompatible pair of such simplified persons is a Dr. Jekyll and Mr. Hyde pair, the former being the one that contains the property of freely doing A (which we'll suppose is the morally right thing to do), the latter the property of freely refraining from doing A (which is the morally wrong thing to do). God might not be able to actualize P, the Dr. Jekyll member of the pair, since F could be false. But what could be true for this particular Dr. Jekyll and Mr. Hyde pair could be true for all of them. Every incompatible pair of this sort could be such that it is true that if God were to instantiate the diminished possible person common to both, the instantiator would freely do the morally wrong alternative. Under such unfortunate circumstances, God can actualize only Hydes, and therefore will not attempt to instantiate any of these simple possible free persons, assuming that his brand of benevolence requires that there be a favorable balance of moral good over moral evil.

The result can be generalized so as to apply to more rich possible persons that contain the property of being free in respect to more than one action. It could still be the case for every such person that it is true that if God were to actualize its diminished person, the instantiator would freely go wrong with respect to at least one of these actions, which shows that it is possible that God cannot actualize a possible world in which all free persons always freely go right.

At this point Plantinga can complete his FWD by claiming that in the possible world in which the truth-values of the F-conditionals preclude God from actualizing any Dr. Jekylls or, more generally, possible persons containing the property of always freely doing what is right, he is excused for creating persons who sometimes freely go wrong provided that for the most part they freely go right. This completes my rough sketch of Plantinga's FWD account of the possible world in which God is unlucky and thereby morally exonerated for allowing moral evil.

There are three salient theses in Plantinga's version of the FWD that must be stated explicitly, since they are challenged by other versions of the FWD, namely:

I. Every F-conditional has a contingent truth-value, that is, is contingently true or contingently false.
II. God knows the truth-value of all F-conditionals prior, either in the order of time or explanation, to his creative decision.
III. God does not determine the truth-values of F-conditionals.

Theses *I* and *II* together comprise the doctrine of God's "middle knowledge," about which a lot more will be said when we consider alternative versions of the FWD. Thesis III is required by the Libertarian incompatibilist premise L, since if God were to *both* determine the truth-value of an F-conditional and create the instantiator of its antecedent, he would be assuring that this created person freely does the action reported by the the F-conditional's consequent, and, thus, *pace* what is said in the consequent, this action is not free. And this is a contradiction since this action is both free and unfree. This contradiction is avoided by having God do only half the job, being the determiner of which F-conditionals get their antecedent actualized but not their truth-values.

If God does not determine the truth-values of the F-conditionals, who or what does? There is an answer to this that is implicit in the Platonic ontology employed in Plantinga's FWD. Since possible persons, including diminished possible persons, are sets of abstract properties, they exist in every possible world. Abstract entities have both essential and accidental properties. The number two has the property of being even in every possible world but has the property of being Igor's favorite number in only some. Our old friend, diminished possible person *DP*, being a set of properties, has the same essential properties in every possible world, such as containing the property of being free with respect to action *A*. However, it also has some accidental properties, among which is the following: containing the property of being-such-that-if-it-were-instantiated-its-instantiator-would-freely-do-*A*. In some worlds it has it and in others not. It is all right to call this funny property of *DP* a "dispositional property" provided we are clear that it is not a disposition of *DP* to freely perform *A* if instantiated (abstract entities, with the possible exception of God, cannot perform actions) but rather a disposition to have its instantiator freely do *A*.

But what, it will be asked, determines whether a diminished person has one of these funny dispositions? As they used to say in the Bronx, "Don't ask!" Here's where the regress of explanations hits the brick wall of brute, unexplainable contingency. There are no further elephants or tortoises upon whose back this contingency rests. Let us now consider some objections to Plantinga's FWD.

According to its Story of Creation the *F*-conditionals are God's kryptonite, limiting his power in a similar way to that in which fate limits the powers of the Greek gods. In both cases there is a force or power above and beyond the control of the individual that limits its powers to do what it wants. The idea that God must be lucky, that he must be dealt a favorable poker hand of *F*-conditional facts, if he is to be able to create a universe containing moral good sans moral evil, strikes some as blasphemous, as a radical distortion of the orthodox concept of God's omnipotence. While Plantinga's account of omnipotence is not every theist's cup of tea, certainly not that of the great medieval theists, it might be the cup of tea that will prove most digestible and healthy for theism in its effort to construct an adequate defense for God's permitting moral evil. We should not allow ourselves to be intimidated by orthodoxy in designing the concept of God.

Numerous objections have been made to Plantinga's FWD, but each one admits of a response. The first claims, contra the normative premise, that it would be better for God to create a world containing conscious automata who are programmed by God always to go morally right than a world containing the Mr. Rogers–type free persons. Plainly, this is not the normative intuition of the theist, who places a much greater value upon free will than does this objection. And since it is the internal consistency of theism that is challenged by the deductive argument from evil, it should be the theist's normative intuition that is operative. And, by the way, it is a normative intuition that is shared by numerous nontheists, some being willing to go so far as to hold that a world containing free creatures who go wrong for the most part is better than a world devoid of free creatures.

There are a number of objections of the "God-can-do-more" variety. One version maintains that God could ensure that all created free persons always freely go right by a selective use of his power of grace: for example, when Mayor Curley is deliberating about whether or not to accept a bribe God could cause Curley to have conscious experiences that would aid him in rejecting the bribe, say by having him hear a menacing voice, in a southern accent of course, say, "Do you want to be the husband or the wife?" The key question is whether having this auditory experience would frighten him enough so that he would reject the bribe. If God determines that it will, he exercises a freedom-canceling control over Curley, since it is God, not Curley, who determines Curley's choice. And if God does not determine that it will, he leaves open the possibility that it won't, in which case God's bestowal of grace upon Curley would not realize its intended objective.

Another version of the God-can-do-more objection portrays God as an enabling foreknower. If you hire a person who you know will do a good job and then leave her alone so that she does a good job on her own, you do not cause her not to freely do a good job as you would if you hired her and then caused her to do a good job. You merely create a situation in which she can exercise her free will. Similarly, if God creates a person who he foreknows will always do right, he does not negate her freedom in so acting, as he would if he created her and then rode herd on her to insure that she always does right. But this solution faces the same problem as did the bestowal of grace objection. Can God be assured that if he were to create her, she would always do right? If he determines that this subjunctive conditional proposition is true, he has gone too far and assumed a freedom-canceling controlling over the created person. And if he doesn't determine that it is true, he leaves it open whether it has a favorable truth-value so that his creation of this person insures that she will always do right. He could be screwed by its contingent truth-value so that he is unable to create her and have her always do right.

Yet another objection is based on God having the power to step in just in the nick of time when he foresees, on the basis of his middle knowledge, that someone will freely go wrong, by either preventing this wrong choice or causally quarantining the culprit from the surrounding world so that no innocent persons are harmed. In the first case, when he foresees on the basis of his middle knowledge that persons will freely go right he leaves them alone, but when he foresees that they won't he cancels their free will just in the nick of time, thereby assuring that all created persons always freely make the right moral choice. The response is that if he adopts this policy of selective intervention, the created persons aren't really free, since to be free with respect to an action is to be free to do it as well as free to refrain from doing it. In the second case, God intervenes after the morally wrong choice is freely made so as to prevent any innocent persons from being harmed. The response to this is that God has bestowed an insignificant sort of free will on his creatures, not the sort of freedom that the theist prizes. It is not enough to have freedom of the will—the freedom to make choices—it also is required that one has freedom of action—the freedom to carry out one's choices and effect one's world for good or ill.

There are two versions of the God-can-do-more variety that are directed against the incompatibilist premise. The first comes from the theological compatibilist who holds that God can determine a free human action, and, moreover, as is the case with Augustine, hold the person morally responsible for the action. The second is that of the soft determinist who contends that a free action can be causally determined, and therefore, God could determine that every created person always freely does right by a proper selection of the scientific laws that obtain and the initial state of the universe, everything that follows, including free actions, being causally determined by the conjunction of these two factors. Both of these compatibilist objections will be responded to in the later discussion.

It is interesting to press an opposite objection to the God-can-do-more variety, namely, that God cannot consistently do as much as is required by Plantinga's FWD. It could be argued that God, in virtue of having middle knowledge, has a freedom-canceling control over created persons. And because these created middle-men aren't free, the buck of moral blame for seeming moral evils cannot stop with them but must reach through to God, which destroys the FWD's attempt to show how God can escape blame, although not responsibility, for these evils. I will begin by marking the distinction between blame and responsibility.

In general, one is responsible for an occurrence that she was fully able to prevent, that is, had the power, opportunity, and necessary knowledge to prevent. God, for example, is responsible for moral evil, since he could have prevented it by electing not to create any free persons. An especially pertinent case is that in which one person delegates some of its power to another but retains the power to revoke the delegated power. In a dual-control student driver car the instructor can throw a switch that gives the student control over the car but still retain the power to regain control over the car by flipping the switch the other way. If the car should be involved in some foreseeable untoward incident while the student is in control, the instructor, along with the student, is responsible, but it could be that only the student is blameworthy. Whether the instructor shares blame will depend on whether she has a good reason for not having retaken control of the car, for example, the resulting harm was minor and the student can best learn by being left free to make mistakes. The relation of God to created free persons is similar. By creating free persons God delegates some of his power to them, but he still retains the power, called "overpower" by Nelson Pike, to rescind their power, either in part or wholly. Because God can withdraw his gift of free will—flip the big switch—he is responsible along with created free persons for the moral evil they cause. But, like the driving instructor, he might have a good excuse that frees him from sharing the blame with those to whom he has delegated some of his power. The FWD supplies such an excuse. God can be responsible but not blameworthy for the evils caused by created beings only if they are free. But, I will now argue, they are not according to the Plantinga Story of Creation. He never succeeded in flipping the switch that gave them the power to freely control their own lives.

The first stage of the argument establishes that God causes the actions of created free persons according to the FWD by virtue of creating them with knowledge of what will result. Consider this stochastic or indeterministic machine. When its button is pressed, a stochastic or indeterministic process, such as the decay of a radioactive element, is instigated, the outcome of which determines whether a poisonous gas will be released into a crowded stadium that will result in the deaths of fifty thousand innocent people. When the button is pressed, either this outcome will ensue or it won't. Therefore, either it is true that if the button were to be pressed, this horrendous outcome would ensue or it is true that if the button were pressed, this outcome would not ensue. Let us assume, furthermore, that we mortals cannot discover by any discursive methods which of these subjunctive conditional propositions is true, any more than we can for similarly matched F-conditionals.

Imagine the case in which I chance on the scene and inadvertently press the button, resulting in the horrendous outcome. Given that I did not have "middle knowledge" of what would result from pressing the button and did not intend to bring about or even risk bringing about this outcome, I am blameless for the resulting evils. Furthermore, I do not even cause these evils.

Let us change the circumstances so that I now have "middle knowledge" via some ESP faculty and press the button so as to bring about the deaths. In this case my action is a sufficient cause of the deaths, and is so in spite of the interposition of a stochastic process, which shows that causation can reach through an intervening stochastic process. Furthermore, I am blameworthy for the deaths, unless I have got a mighty good excuse, such as, "They were not innocents but terrorists."

Although there is no doubt that this is what people on the street would say, it might be objected that their concept of causation is confused, for the only difference between the two cases is my psychological state, what I know and intend, and how can this determine whether or not I cause the deaths? If what was at issue was the physicist's concept of causation, this would be a powerful objection. But this is not the concept of causation in question. Rather, it is the forensic one that concerns the assignment of moral and legal responsibility and blame, which is the very concept that figures in the FWD, since it is concerned with the assignment of responsibility and blame to God and man for moral evil.

It might be urged by Plantinga that while both God and created free persons were fully able to have prevented moral evil, only the latter are to blame for it, since only God could have a morally exonerating excuse for not doing so. God, not they, is the creator of the universe, and thus he alone could say that his allowing such evil was the price that had to be paid for there existing any free persons at all. The evil in question was necessary for the realization of an outweighing good.

Notice that the response that has been made on Plantinga's behalf does not claim that God does not cause moral evil, only that he is not blameworthy for it since he has an excuse that cannot be available to created free middlemen, and thus they alone take "the fall" for the existence of moral evil. This excuse collapses if these middlemen are not free, since then the buck of blame could not stop with them. And this is just what will now be argued.

Since God creates free persons with middle knowledge of what will ensue, he sufficiently causes the free choices and actions of these persons. This alone does not negate the freedom with which these acts are done, for one person can cause another to act without thereby rendering the act unfree. As a rule, the more the external event only triggers a deep-seated character trait or natural disposition of the agent, the less difficulty there is in treating it as not abrogating the free will of the affected agent. When I induce a person of amorous nature to call Alice for a date by telling him that she is desirous of going out with him, I cause him to act but do not usurp his free will in doing so since prominent among the causes of his action are his own deep-seated character traits, which were not imposed on him by me. I didn't have to "work on him"—drug, hypnotize, brainwash, etc. him—to call Alice. Unfortunately, God's way of causing created persons to act is not of this innocent sort. It is freedom canceling.

The argument for this is anthropomorphic in that it applies the same freedom-canceling principles that apply to man-man cases to the God-man case. Whether it is impermissible, as the theological compatibilist would contend, to reason in this anthropomorphic manner will be considered subsequently. Obviously, any analogy between man and God will be an imperfect one, since there are such striking disanalogies between the two. For this reason this argument hardly is conclusive. At best, it might make a Free Will Defender have second thoughts. I will try to derive these freedom-canceling principles by examining paradigm cases in which one man or finite person has a freedom-canceling control over another.

Imagine the case of the Sinister Cyberneticist, a *Stepford Wives*-type situation in which a cyberneticist operates on his wife's brain or replaces it with a preprogrammed computer-analogue so that he can inculcate in his wife the desired psychological make-up comprised of various desires, wants, dispositions, etc. As a consequence, she is always amorous, anxious to cook and clean, etc. To an uninformed observer her actions will appear free and voluntary, since they emanate from and are explainable by her own psychological make-up. But her cyberneticist husband has imposed this make-up on her. Her lack of freedom of the will is not due to the fact that this make-up has been determined by factors external to herself (No man is either an island or a *causa sui*.) but rather to the manner in which it has been determined, namely, through the machinations of another person for the purpose of controlling her responses to stimuli. The case of the Insidious Hypnotist and *Manchurian Candidate*-type Barbaric Brainwasher who have gained an habitual ascendancy over the will of another by inculcating in them a certain psychological make-up are similar.

Our intuitions about these cases suggest the following freedom-canceling sufficient condition for man-man cases:

C_1. If M_1's actions and choices result from psychological conditions that are intentionally determined by another man M_2, then these actions and choices are not free.

Under these circumstances, M_2 has a freedom-canceling control over M_1, not in virtue of determining M_1's actions and choices, but rather causing M_1 not to have a mind or will of her own. It isn't so much M_1's actions and choices that are not free but M_1 herself; and, in virtue of M_1's lack of global freedom, her specific actions and choices are not free. There are good arguments for not taking C_1 alone to be sufficient in every case, but even those who so argue grant that satisfaction of it is at least freedom lessening, which, it will turn out, is enough for my objection.

Consider another case, that of the Evil Puppeteer. Stromboli has poor Pinocchio wired up in such a way that he controls his every movement. An observer who fails to notice the wires might falsely believe that Pinocchio's behavior was fully free and voluntary. Stromboli controls Pinocchio, not via having imposed on him an inner network of dispositions, motivations, intentions, etc., but by exerting a compulsive force over him that renders such inner factors irrelevant. There need not be actual wires connecting the controller with the "puppet." It could be a wireless radio hookup such as exists between a controller and a remote-control toy airplane or between the Horrible Dr. Input and a brain in a vat that in turn has a radio-control hookup with a shell body.

By a coincidence that rivals that of the preestablished harmony of Leibniz it could be the case that every time the external controller causes the "puppet" to perform some movement the "puppet" endeavors on its own to perform this movement. This is a case of causal overdetermination in which there is more than one sufficient cause of a given occurrence. Although the puppet's action is unavoidable in that it would have made this movement even if it had not endeavored to, there are those, like Locke, who would still call it free. Locke's intuition in this matter is quite dubious.

What is it about these cases that makes us say the controller, be it the Evil Puppeteer or the Horrible Dr. Input, has a freedom-canceling control? It is that most of the "victim's" behavior is caused by and subject to the whim of the controller. This suggests that

C_2. M_2 has a freedom-canceling control over M_1 if M_2 causes most of M_1's behavior.

Is God's relation to created persons in the FWD such that it satisfies C_1 and/or C_2? If it satisfies either, no less both, the FWD is in trouble. There is reason to think that it satisfies both. It is clear that it satisfies C_1, since according to the FWD God intentionally causes a created free person to have all of her freedom-neutral properties, which include her psychological make-up. The Free Will Defender will make the Libertarian claim that these inner traits only "incline" but do not causally determine the person to perform various actions or act in a certain regular manner, but this does not make the God-man case significantly disanalogous to the man-man cases. For even if we imagine that our intentional psychological-trait inducers could render it only probable according to various statistical laws that their victims would behave in certain characteristic ways, they still would exercise a global freedom-canceling control in which the person is rendered nonfree due to her not having a mind of her own.

The God-man relation in the FWD also satisfies C_2, for when God instantiates diminished possible persons or sets of freedom-neutral properties he does have middle knowledge of what choices and actions will result, and thereby sufficiently causes them. And he does so quite independently of whether or not he is blameless for the untoward ones among them.

It might be objected that for M_2 to have freedom-canceling control over M_1 it is not enough that M_2 cause most of M_1's behavior: M_2 also must have counterfactual control over M_1 in virtue of which M_2 can cause M_1 to behave in ways other than those in which M_1 in fact behaves. Whereas Stromboli and Dr. Input have this additional counterfactual control over their victims, God does not have it over created persons. For while God causes the instantiator of DP to do A, he does not have the power to cause this instantiator to do other than A, given that it is true that if DP were instantiated, its instantiator would freely do A. God could have prevented the instantiator from doing A by not instantiating DP, but this is not causing the instantiator to do other than A—nonexistent persons do not act.

Granted that there is this disanalogy between God and our finite controllers in that only the latter have this sort of counterfactual control, what follows? Not that God does not have freedom-canceling control over created persons in virtue of satisfying C_2 (as well as C_1), but that there is a stronger sufficient condition for having freedom-canceling control that he does not satisfy, namely,

C_3. M_2 has a freedom-canceling control over M_1 if M_2 causes most of M_1's behavior and also has the counterfactual power to cause M_1 to act differently from the way in which M_1 in fact acts.

In general, to satisfy one sufficient condition for being X does not require satisfying every sufficient condition for being X. The objector might retort that having counterfactual control is necessary for having freedom-canceling control: the "if" in C_3, accordingly, is to be replaced by "only if." This is not particularly plausible for two reasons. First, if C_3 is turned into a necessary condition, it follows that C_1 is unacceptable and that therefore the Insidious Cyberneticist, etc. do not have freedom-canceling control, which is not what we want to say. Second, God, although lacking counterfactual control, has an additional C_1-type power over created persons that Stromboli and Dr. Input do not have in that he both creates and determines the psychological make-up of his "victims." This additional power of God's, even if it is not freedom canceling but only freedom lessening, should at least counterbalance his lack of counterfactual power and thereby make him at least as good a candidate as our finite controllers for having freedom-canceling control.

Furthermore, it should be obvious by now that the FWD's gambit of having something other than God determine the truth-values of the F-conditionals does not succeed in showing that God does not cause the free acts of created persons. Stromboli and Dr. Input were not excused from being the cause of their victim's behavior because they did only "half the job" since they determined the causally relevant instantial conditions but not which causal laws hold. Analogously, God is not excused from being the cause of the free acts of created persons because he did only half the job by determining which diminished possible persons get instantiated but not the truth-values of the relevant F-conditionals. If this does not convince you, try these counterfactual thought-experiments. Our finite controllers do only half the job by determining which causal laws hold after they come upon their victim in some instantial state, and God does only half the job by determining the truth-values of the F-conditionals after he comes upon concrete instantiations of various diminished possible persons. Certainly, we want to say of both God and the finite controllers in these thought-experiments that they cause their "victim's" behavior and have a freedom-canceling control in virtue of C_2 alone.

So far, it appears that God's relation to created persons satisfies both C_1 and C_2 (but not C_3) and that he thereby has a freedom-canceling control over them. But there still remain some disanalogies between the God-man and man-man cases that have not been explored. One of them concerns the fact that the finite controllers in our type 1 and 2 cases were a sinister bunch who meant no good for their victims, whereas God is benevolent and intends the best for his created beings. This makes no difference in regard to having freedom-canceling control but only in how the movie is titled. One is titled "The Horrible (Sinister, Insidious, Barbaric) Dr. Input (Cyberneticist, Hypnotist, Brainwasher)" while the other is titled "The Incredible (Fabulous, etc.) Supernatural Predeterminer." One is a horror movie and the other is not; but neither involves free persons.

Another tack is to argue, as would the theological compatibilist, that God's relation to man is so disanalogous to man's relation to man as to render our freedom-canceling principles, C_1 and C_2 that hold for the latter inapplicable to the former. It is not just that God is quite different from men, but that he is different in just those respects that make these principles inapplicable to his relation to created persons. He literally is out of it, not a part of the universe. No insult intended, but he is as unnatural as you can get; in fact, he is supernatural. He does not cramp our elbow room in the way in which finite men do. Unlike these universe-mates who block our path and physically compel and coerce us, God is not pushing, elbowing, or kneeing anyone in the subway, goosing someone on a crowded elevator, or putting a gun to anyone's head ("Your money or your salvation!"). In these respects he is crucially unlike our bevy of sinister finite controllers. These people ride herd on their fellow man. God does not do so. This is not an epistemological point concerning our being unaware of God's causal efficacy in bringing about things in the world, but an ontological one having to do with the radical difference in the way his causal efficacy works from that in which a finite controller's does.

It is just such antianthropomorphic considerations that are at the foundation of theological compatibilism. There is much merit in this, but, unfortunately, Plantinga cannot avail himself of this strategy for averting the objection that God assumes a freedom-canceling control over created persons in his FWD. The reason is that his FWD must take the anthropomorphic route in its rejection of theological compatibilism. For it claims that God cannot determine the free acts of persons without negating their freedom. And the only basis for this claim is that if one man were to do this to another, it would be freedom canceling. In other words, God cannot get away with determining the free actions of men, because this would violate C_1 and/or C_2—the very principles that operate in man-man cases.

We cannot allow Plantinga to be a good-time anthropomorphist: to reason anthropomorphically when warding off the objection of the theological compatibilist and then refuse to do so for the purpose of rebutting the charge that God has assumed a freedom-canceling control over created persons. Thus, Plantinga is caught on the horns of a dilemma. If he reasons anthropomorphically, his FWD collapses because it imputes to God a freedom-canceling control over created persons. And if he does not reason anthropomorphically, again his FWD collapses, this time because it has no reply to the objection of the theological compatibilist. But either he reasons anthropomorphically or he does not. Therefore, his FWD collapses.

The God-cannot-do-as-much objection has considerable force against the Plantinga version of the FWD, since it imputes middle knowledge to God. Without it, God's instantiating the antecedent of a true F-conditional no longer would count as a case of his causing the instantiator to do what the consequent reports, since he now does not know in advance what this person will do. Created persons, then, could serve as suitable scapegoats for moral evil. This naturally gives rise to the question whether a viable version of an FWD can be constructed that denies middle knowledge to God, that is, that God knows the contingent truth-value of every F-conditional prior to his creative decision and thus foreknows for every diminished possible person what free actions would be performed if that person were it to be instantiated.

It will be recalled that God's middle knowledge is comprised of these two theses:

I. Every F-conditional has a contingent truth-value, that is, is contingently true or contingently false.
II. God knows the truth-value of all F-conditionals prior, either in the order of time or explanation, to his creative decision.

Tenet *II* is entailed by *I* because God's omniscience requires him to know every true proposition. Since God's middle knowledge is comprised of the conjunction of theses *I* and *II*, there will be two ways of constructing an FWD sans middle knowledge. The first version, which is ably championed by Robert M. Adams, denies *I* and thereby *II*, since not even an omniscient being can know what isn't true. This renders God blameless for permitting moral evil, since he could not have known in advance the moral evils that would result from his creation of free persons. The second version accepts *I* but denies *II*, again rendering God blameless in virtue of an excusable lack of knowledge. Unlike the first version, there was something to be known but there was no way in which God could have known it. God winds up watching the unfolding of the history of the universe containing free persons in just the way parents watch their child play in a hockey game. In both cases, there are a lot of grimaces and groans as they observe unforeseen errors and transgressions.

Because both versions have God instantiate the antecedent of F-conditionals without foreknowledge of what the created persons will freely do, they face the objection that God is acting in a recklessly immoral way by shooting crap at our expense. No red-blooded theist would accept the wimpy moral intuition underlying the Reckless objection, and would give God's creation of free persons in both versions as a counterexample. The objection also faces an ad hominem–type rebuttal in that no existent person, except for a few grippers, are apt to make it; for, if God hadn't elected to roll the dice, they wouldn't even exist, and, supposedly, they are glad that they do.

Although both versions make the same lack-of-knowledge excuse available to God, they differ significantly in their epistemological and metaphysical underpinnings, and thus require separate consideration. Adams develops his version in the course of defending the attack on middle knowledge by certain late sixteenth-century Dominicans against their Jesuit opponents, Molina and Suarez. Adams's denial of I is built upon the Libertarian account of F-conditionals, according to which the act reported by the consequent is not causally determined by prior events, being determined instead by the instantiator's free, causally undetermined choice. Given this account, he does not see how an F-conditional could possibly be true. Thus, it appears to be logically or conceptually impossible for it to be true and therefore it necessarily lacks a truth-value. Unlike Lukasiewicz's "neuter" or "indeterminate" propositions reporting future contingents, it does not become true or false with the passage of time. Adams says that he doubts if they ever were, or ever will be, true. This means that even if the antecedent should be instantiated and the instantiator subsequently perform the action reported by its consequent, the F-conditional does not become true. And a fortiori this sequence of events does not show that the F-conditional was true all along, for there is no present truth to cast a backward shadow. Adams gives us a choice between F-conditionals being necessarily false and being necessarily neither true nor false. The common denominator of these options is that F-conditionals necessarily are not true.

Adams's argument for the denial of I is not made fully explicit. One who denies I typically is a warranted-assertibility theorist who holds a proposition to be true only if it is in principle epistemically supportable. But this isn't Adams's line, for he says that a proposition reporting a future contingent, although in principle not warrantedly assertible, can be true by *correspondence to* the actual occurrence of the event it predicts. This suggests that for Adams a necessary condition for a proposition being true is that it have an external correspondent. The "external" qualification precludes the correspondent of the proposition that p being the fact that p; for, given that a fact is a true proposition, this would make that p the correspondent of that p.

In the above discussion of III it was suggested that for Plantinga the external correspondent of the true *F*-conditional, that if *DP* were instantiated its instantiator would freely do *A*, is the abstract diminished possible person *DP* having the funny dispositional property of being-such-that-if-it-were-instantiated-its-instantiator-would-freely-do-*A*. *Pace* Adams, it seems clear that if *DP* were to be instantiated and its instantiator were to do *A*, we would say that *F* was true. Moreover, if *F* were not true, it would not be possible for God to instantiate *P*, as Lewis's lemma states.

It would be a mistake, however, to say that *DP*'s instantiator doing *A* makes *F* true. For this makes it appear as if the instantiator's freely doing *A* is a sufficient *truth-condition* for *F*, being that thing in the world that makes *F* true, in answer to Adams's puzzlement about how an *F*-conditional could be true. But this way of construing the truth-conditions of *F* clashes with the account of its truth-condition based on a diminished possible free person, *DP*, which is an abstract entity, having the funny contingent dispositional property of being-such-that-if-it-were-instantiated-its-instantiator-would-freely-do-*A*. A consequence of this account is that an *F*-conditional can be true even if it is counterfactual because its antecedent goes unactualized; and, even when not counterfactual, it is true prior to the occurrence of the instantiator's action.

The action of the instantiator of *DP* is only a *verifying-condition*, not a *truth-condition*, for *F*. A verifying-condition is what enables us to discover the truth of a proposition but need not coincide with what makes it true. Think in this connection of how you go about indirectly verifying a proposition about the past or about another mind. What makes a proposition about a past event (or another person's conscious state) true is not the future effects of the past event or (the person's overt behavior) by which we indirectly verify it, but the past event (or conscious state) itself.

This way of distinguishing between the truth-conditions and verifying-conditions for *F*-conditionals escapes a reductio ad absurdum argument against Plantinga's FWD that I owe to Dean Zimmerman. The argument attempts to unearth a vicious circularity in the order of explanation or causation in it. The argument goes as follows. Prior to God's decision to instantiate *DP*, be it in the order of time or that of explanation, God knows that F is true. That F is true is part of the explanation for his decision to instantiate DP, which in turn explains DP's instantiator freely doing A, given that it causes his very existence and thus is a necessary cause of A. But DP's instantiator freely doing A is the truth-condition for F and thereby explains why F is true, which completes the vicious circle. This vicious circle is broken when DP's instantiator freely doing A is downgraded to a verifying- but not truth-condition for F, since DP's instantiator freely doing A no longer explains why F is true, only how we come to know that F is true. According to this version of the excusable ignorance FWD, what God cannot know prior to his decision to instantiate DP is that the worldly verifying-conditions for F obtain: For, necessarily, before an agent decides, she knows neither what she will decide nor of the occurrence of an event that is dependent on how she decides. Whether the verifying condition for F will occur depends upon whether God chooses to actualize DP.

The other version of the excusable ignorance FWD accepts condition I for middle knowledge, that every F-conditional has a contingent truth-value, as well as Lewis's lemma, but rejects condition II, that God knows the truth-value of all F-conditionals prior to his creative decision. God's morally exonerating excuse for permitting moral evil is that he could not have known in advance what would result from his instantiating various diminished possible persons, and, as it sadly worked out, he got screwed by the contingent truth-values of the relevant F-conditionals.

It is plain that in accepting I and rejecting II, the second version rejects the traditional definition of God's omniscience according to which God knows all and believes only true propositions, since there are true F-conditionals that he does not know, at least before he chooses to actualize their antecedents. One way to attempt to escape this problem, which Swinburne espoused, is to work with a definition of God's omniscience that is modeled on the definition of his omnipotence. Just as God can bring about anything that it is consistent for him to bring about,

> K. God knows every true proposition that it is logically consistent that God knows.

Since it is an essential property of God that he is able to create free persons and he cannot do so if he knows the truth-values of the F-conditionals in advance of his creative choices, it is inconsistent for God to know their truth-values in advance.

This restriction on God's omniscience has the consequence of excusing a timelessly eternal God from having to know true tensed propositions, given that it is logically impossible for a being who is not in time to know such a proposition. But this gives God a second-class type of omniscience, and, most important, seems to render him religiously unavailable to working theists since it precluded his having meaningful personal interaction with them. Whereas it is important that God knows true tensed propositions, it is important that he *not* know true F-conditionals prior to his creative choices. How can God's omniscience be restricted so that it requires him to know true tensed propositions but not true F-conditionals? The following is one way of doing this:

K_1. God knows every true proposition that it is logically consistent for him to know and have the ability to create free creatures.

This definition will not appear to be objectionably ad hocish once it is realized that it is an essential property of God that he is able to create free persons but highly dubious that it is an essential property of God that he is timeless and immutable. Notice that the God of my FWD must be temporal, for he changes over time; prior to his creative decision he does not know any F-conditional but after he creates diminished possible free persons he comes to know some F-conditionals in virtue of coming to know their verifying-conditions. By placing God in time and denying him prior knowledge of the F-conditionals, we make it possible for God to react to our actions as he is reported to do in the Bible. In a meaningful personal relation there is an element of otherness and mystery. We don't know what the other person will do and therefore have not already made up our minds as to how to act toward the other. There is a processual unfolding of new and unpredictable actions that call for each member in the relation to readjust their behavior toward the other. Given that God essentially is both capable of personal interaction, which requires that he know true tensed propositions, and capable of creating free persons, which requires that he does not know F-conditionals in advance, definition K will suffice.

III. THE EVIDENTIAL ARGUMENT FROM EVIL

Everyone has been personally touched at some time in their life with a seemingly pointless evil—the premature loss of a loved one, a hideous disease or devastating loss from a natural disaster, and, of course, the horrendous evils that we are bombarded with every time we open a newspaper or turn on the TV. We ask "Why?" but are unable to come up with a satisfying answer. It is the rare person who can say, *and mean it*, "It's God's will and therefore for the best." Most believers find their faith challenged, in many cases lessened or even destroyed. This is a normal human, maybe all too human, reaction. But the question is whether this normal psychological reaction is rationally justified. Are there any good arguments to show that it is? A number of such arguments will be presented and then responded to.

William Rowe has presented an inductive argument that has triggered a flurry of critical responses and counterresponses and thus is a good place to start. His argument is built on two examples of horrendous evils. One is the case of a five-year-old girl, Sue, who is raped, brutally beaten, and then strangled to death; the other a deer, Bambi, who dies a hideously painful death over a period of three days from a forest fire. These cases will be referred to respectively by "S" and "B." Rowe chose to work with these cases because they are the most difficult cases for the theist to find a God-justifying reason for. The argument is based on induction by enumeration and goes like this:

    1. No good we know of justifies God, were he to exist, in permitting S and B;

        2. No good justifies God, were he to exist, in permitting S and B. (From 1 by inductive enumeration.)

        3. Gog does not exist. (From 2.)

The reason why 3 follows from 2 is that 2 reports an unjustified evil, an evil that God, were he to exist, would not have a justification for permitting, and, by definition God and an unjustified evil cannot coexist. Step 2 is inductively derived by simple enumeration from 1, in which we exhaustively consider every good that we know of to see if it could justify God permitting S and B and find that it cannot. This is similar to examining exhaustively each and every marble in a box and finding that it is not blue and then inferring that no marble in the box is blue.

This exhaustive enumeration goes as follows. Evils S and B, based on what we know, are completely gratuitous in that they are necessary neither for the realization of an outweighing good nor the prevention of a greater evil. Sue and Bambi are not going to develop higher-order character traits as a result of their struggles against the evils that have befallen them nor are they going to acquire faith in God because of the realization that pointless evils can randomly happen to anybody. Certainly, Bambi's demise from the natural disaster cannot be attributed to misuse of free will by herself or anyone else, and, in Sue's case, her attacker exercised his free will but God should not have permitted him to have free will with respect to attacking Sue in the first place; the value of his being free in this regard does not outweigh the harm done to Sue. But not all justified evils are nongratuitous. They could be merited or deserved as punishments for transgressions or be consequences of them and thereby are justified even if they do not serve to reform the wrongdoer or deter others from performing similar untoward acts. But certainly both Sue and Bambi are innocent of any crimes that would call for such harsh punishment.

The search for a God-justifying reason, however, is not as straightforward as looking for a blue marble in a box; for there is a real possibility that we failed either to exhaust all of the justificatory reasons or to see how they might possibly apply in the Sue and Bambi cases. Maybe what is called for is a weaker, probabilistic version of the induction by simple enumeration argument, namely:

1'. No good we know of justifies God, were he to exist, in permitting S and B;

2'. It is probable that no good justifies God, were he to exist, in permitting S and B;

3'. It is probable that God does not exist.

There is an even weaker version of the evidential argument that begins with a premise listing all the known cases of evil (call them E):

A. There are evils E;
B. The probability that God exists (G) relative to that there are evils E and background knowledge (K) is less than the probability that God exists relative to this background knowledge alone, that is, $P(G/\text{There are evils } E \text{ and } K) < P(G/K)$.

The background knowledge K includes everything that we know that is not relevant to determining the truth of either G or that there are evils E. It is not inferred from the proposition that that there are evils E that the probability of G is less than ½, only that that there are evils E lowers the probability of G over what it is relative to K alone. Let us call this version of the probabilistic argument the "modest probabilistic argument" and the preceding one the "strong probabilistic argument."

There is a theistic response to both of these probabilistic arguments that is based on the fact that a proposition's probability can vary relative to different propositions. The probability that Feike can swim relative to the proposition that he is Swiss is quite low, say .1, but relative to the proposition that many people believe that they have seen him swim quite high, near 1, given that seeing is believing. Similarly, the proposition that God exists relative to the conjunction of K and that there are evils E could be quite low but quite high when all of the arguments for the existence of God are added to this conjunction. And, if it is probable that God exists relative to the agglomeration of these arguments, then it also is probable that for each evil specified in E there is a God-justifying reason. In fact, if among them is a knock-down ontological argument, we can be certain that there is and thus that there are evils E does not even lower the probability that God exists, as the modest probabilistic argument contends. It was because Leibniz thought he had such an argument that he confined himself in his misnamed book, *The Theodicy*, to sketching some possible *defenses* for God's allowing evil without making any effort to give evidence for their actually obtaining. Saint Augustine did likewise.

Plantinga believes that we are possessed of a God-implanted sensus divinitatis that works in an analogous way to the cognitive faculties of perception and memory in that it too is a source of warranted beliefs that are not based on any evidence or arguments. Because of the sensus divinitatis we find ourselves forming the warranted belief that God exists upon reading the Bible, hearing the choir sing, seeing a beautiful sunset, and the like. The probability that God exists relative to the conjunction of this sensus divinitatis–derived knowledge and K remains the same when the proposition that there are evils E is added to the conjunction. This completely neutralizes the challenge that E poses for theism IF it is true that God exists and implanted this sensus divinitatis in us. But without adequate argumentative support for this, the challenge of evil is still alive and well.

There is another version of the evidential argument from evil in addition to the inductive and probabilistic ones that is based on abduction or inference to the best explanation. It has its roots in Hume's *Dialogues Concerning Natural Religion*. After savaging the teleological argument at length, Hume suddenly has his spokesman in the dialogue, Philo, concede, maybe just for the sake of argument, that there is considerable force to this argument if it is taken to establish only the existence of an intelligent designer-creator of the world, leaving its goodness unresolved. What, he asks, is the most reasonable hypothesis to form concerning its moral nature—that it is all-good, all-bad, morally indifferent, or that there is both a good and bad god, as in Manicheanism. Given that the world is a mixed bag of goods and evils, he claims that the morally indifferent god hypothesis offers the best explanation of the known facts.

Paul Draper has refined Hume's abductive argument. He begins with a proposition, O, that reports the observations one has made of humans and animals experiencing pain or pleasure and the testimony one has encountered concerning the observations others have made of sentient beings experiencing pain or pleasure. Draper then contends that O is better explained by the hypothesis of indifference

HI. Neither the nature nor the condition of sentient beings on earth is the result of benevolent or malevolent actions performed by nonhuman persons. than it is by the incompatible theistic hypothesis (*T*).

HI amounts to the anything-but-theism hypothesis, and it is preferable to *T* because *O* is more to be expected on *HI* than it is on *T*, that is, $P(O/HI) < P(O/T)$. This expectation is based on the theistic God being omnipotent and omniscient. As will be seen at the end of this chapter, lessening God's power or knowledge provides an easy way for the theist to neutralize the challenge of evil. But at what expense?

William Alston has raised two objections to the Draper argument. First, the argument makes the illicit slide from a proposition being probable relative to another proposition to the latter explaining the former. That a marble that was drawn from a box is green has a very high probability relative to the proposition that almost every marble in the box is green, but the latter hardly explains the former. Furthermore, the adequacy of an explanation depends crucially on the prior probability of the explaining proposition. That I hear rumbling noises in the attic is highly probable on the hypothesis that there are gremlins there; however because the latter is highly improbable, it does not afford an adequate explanation of the noises. Second, contrasting the hypothesis of indifference explanation of the known pleasures and pains of animals with the theistic one, which says *only* that God caused them, is unfair because it gives too anemic a theistic explanation, omitting the crucial features of it that speak about God's purposes and values, which are the very features that are employed in a theodicy.

IV. THEODICIES

The theist has a battery of responses to all of these evidential arguments, ranging from giving a not implausible God-justifying reason for whatever evil is in question to a skepticism about our being cognitively up to giving such a reason because of the inscrutability of the divine mind and our limited knowledge of the world. The former is an effort at giving a theodicy, the latter a reason for why no theodicy is needed. First, we will consider efforts to give a theodicy.

It must be stressed at the outset that it is not required that any one theodicy alone do the whole job. What is required is that for every *type* of evil there is some plausible theodicy that applies to it. It might be demanding too much to require that every *instance* of evil be so justified. But unless this latter task is accomplished, the challenge posed by evil to theism is not completely neutralized. Theodicies vary widely with respect to how they conceive of God's goodness and the evidential standards for a theodicy, some requiring only that it not be implausible, others that it is probable relative to the available evidence.

The task of giving a theodicy is greatly lessened if one does not require much of an omnibenevolent being, thus the point of the bumpersticker, "God exists. He just doesn't want to get involved." Richard Swinburne, for example, understands by God's being perfectly good that he does no morally bad action and does any morally obligatory action. Requiring of an omnibenevolent being only that it keep its nose clean, not that it also perform acts of supererogation, plainly sets the bar too low, for many an SOB satisfies this duty-based requirement.

An example of a theodicy that might set this bar too low is Peter van Inwagen's fundamentalist theodicy in which all of the evils reported by E are a result of the first generation of humans freely rebelling against God, with their ruin being inherited by all of their descendants. There is no attempt to show that the descendants are in any way blameworthy or morally responsible for these sins, and yet they are the victims of this hereditary ruin. But this seems unfair in just the same way as it is to keep in the whole class for the misdeeds of a single person. The whole idea of a deity who is so vain that if his children do not choose to love and obey him will bring down all sorts of horrible evils on them and their innocent descendants elicits horror from many who would ask what we would think about a human father who treated his children in this way. Like Iago's "Credo" in Verdi's *Otello*, van Inwagen seems to believe in a cruel and vengeful god. His theodicy, by the way, even if successful, does not do the whole job, since it doesn't account for animal suffering, as in the Bambi case, unless we include forest fires as another instance of hereditary ruin, along with all the other natural evils. Another deficiency in this theodicy is that it is empirically implausible, thereby being at best only a defense.

The fundamentalist theodicy of Peter van Inwagen is based on another sort of moral horror. One of the ways in which God makes it clear that man cannot live apart from him is to create a system of chance evils, the victims of which can be and often are innocent persons, such as Sue. Among the natural consequences of the Fall is the following evil state of affairs: Horrors happen to people without any relation to desert. They happen simply as a matter of chance. It is a part of God's plan of atonement that we realize that a natural consequence of our living to ourselves is our living in a world that has that feature. Van Inwagen papers over the problem of fairness by the following referential equivocation. *We* complain that some of us—quite often the good and wise and innocent—fall into the pits. God's response to this complaint is this: "*You* are the ones who made yourselves blind," in which the pits represent chance evils and our being blind represents our being defenseless before these evils as a result of hereditary ruin. The use of "we" refers to the innocent descendants of the original culprits who are doing the complaining, but the use of "you" by God refers to the original perpetrators. Herein God is depicted as confounding the perpetrators with their innocent descendants, which is surprising given his omniscience. (I suspect that the equivocation is the fault of Van Inwagen rather than God.)

Eleonore Stump has espoused a theodicy that is a close cousin to van Inwagen's in that it too is based on original sin. God brings about natural evils so as to help us achieve salvation, which we do by entering into the proper relationship to him. Our wills have been damaged by original sin and have turned away from God. Natural evils help to realign our wills so that they will again be directed toward serving God by reminding us that we are unable to make it on our own. They humble us by reminding us of how vulnerable and fragile we are, which will aid our coming back to our Lord. They are, however, mere aids; for, if they alone were enough to determine that our wills would become directed toward God, this turning of our wills would not be done freely, which is not what God wants. He wants us to freely elect to return to him. Again, the problem is whether a god who has these moral attributes is eminently worthy of love and worship although not unfit to be eminently worthy of being feared and obeyed—a supernatural Al Capone.

Axiological problems with theodicies concern not only the type of goodness attributed to God but also the relative values given to wordily goods. Here are some examples of a greater-good theodicy that flagrantly overvalues certain types of worldly goods. It is good that there is consumption, for if there weren't, Verdi never would have written *La Traviata* and Puccini *La Boehme*. Only someone possessed of an Oscar Wilde–type mentality who makes aesthetic values the summum bonum would find this plausible. If he hadn't burned down his house in a drunken stupor killing his wife and five children, he never would have given up drinking. Only a member of the Women's Christian Temperance Union would find this at all plausible. My personal favorite example of the if-it-wasn't-for–type theodicy concerns the emergence of good, cheap Asian restaurants in Pittsburgh after the end of the Vietnam War. When I moved to Pittsburgh in 1964 there were only three Asian restaurants in the whole city, all of which served bland Cantonese cuisine. In 1980 I was munching on some delicious satay chicken that I had purchased from a curbside vendor for $3.50, when suddenly it occurred to me that if it weren't for the perverse foreign policy of the United States in Southeast Asia during the 1960s and 1970s, I would not have this satay chicken available to me now: it all happened for the best. (The problem with the United States' incursions into Afghanistan and Iraq is, who wants to eat their food? What must be done is to find a nation with good ethnic food that is underrepresented in the States and then bomb the hell out of them.)

Almost as ludicrous as these parodies of the greater-good theodicy are some of the theodicies that Richard Swinburne devised in his *Providence and Evil*. One example is his attempt to convert the free will *defense* into a free will *theodicy*. To be free with respect to an action having moral significance, one must be tempted to choose the morally wrong alternative. Swinburne attributes such great value to persons having this sort of freedom that it justifies God in allowing, for example, Sue's attacker to have the temptation to rape, beat, and strangle her or for persons to be tempted to enslave others. This flies in the face of the moral intuitions that guide our social policies and practices, for we do our best to reform persons who face such temptations and prevent others from having them, thereby preventing them from being free with respect to such actions that can bring great harm to innocent persons. Another example of dubious axiological intuitions is found in Swinburne's deployment of the being-of-service-to-others theodicy to the Bambi case. It is quite possible that Bambi's dying a hideously painful death in he forest fire served as a lesson to other animals as to how to avoid such a fate in the future (or Sue's murder in helping to spur the passage of stronger laws against sexual predators), and this would justify God's permitting this to happen. This looks like more satay chicken for $3.50.

Not all theodicies suffer from dubious axiological assignments either to God or worldly states. Some of them appeal to distinctively Christian values, but that alone should not render them nonstarters. An example is the Redemptive Suffering theodicy of Marilyn McCord Adams. It is based upon the value of martyrdom, which then is extrapolatable to some but not all other types of suffering. Through being successfully tested in her faith, the martyr builds a closer relation of trust with her God. Furthermore, through suffering one gets a vision into the inner life of God incarnate on the cross. This theodicy has a limited application, doing nothing to address the cases of Sue and Bambi.

The most impressive theodicy is John Hick's free-will-cum-soul-building one. It is based on the reasonable axiological intuition that it is better to achieve some desirable state through one's own free endeavoring than to be in this state from the very beginning or have it imposed on one by some external power. This is a version of a causal theory of value that values a state in terms of how it is brought about. It also is based on an axiological asymmetry between past and future, which is captured by the saying, "All's well that ends well," as opposed to all's well that begins well. If it is better to be a philosophy professor then a loan shark (a big assumption), then it is better first to be a loan shark and then a philosophy professor rather than vice-versa, provided one is the right sort of free, active cause in bringing about this "desirable" development. God could have created human beings in a state of perfection, but it is better that he created them in an imperfect state so that they could freely bring about their own moral progress in approximating this ideal state, which, for the Christian, is union or a communal relation with God. God does not merely allow but actually causes natural evils so as to give persons the opportunity to freely develop certain desirable character traits, such as sympathy, charity, courage, patience, and the like. If it be objected that this would license a finite father breaking his son's legs so as to afford him an opportunity for soul building, the reply is that this confounds the role of God as the designer of the entire scheme of things with that of created person, which is that of promoting good and fighting evil. Thus, the fact that God is permitted to do things that a human being is not does not result from his being subject to a different moral code than are humans, but to the different roles they play.

There are severe limitations in Hick's theodicy, even if its underlying axiological intuitions are accepted. First, it doesn't apply to the vast majority of the known evils, beginning with animal suffering. Often the victim of an evil is so devastated that she is unable to put it to the positive use of aiding her moral development, as for example Sue or the child who succumbs to leukemia at the age of one. That the parents of Sue or the leukemia victim are afforded an opportunity for soul building hardly suffices to justify the evils in question. To handle these recalcitrant cases, Hick has supplemented his theodicy with a compensation-in-an-afterlife one. But the latter is nothing more than a defense, since the evidential credentials for it are very thin.

In addition to the limited range of application of Hick's theodicy, there is a problem about the cases to which it does apply in that they seem to involve more evil than is required for the sake of spurring soul building. One can develop sympathy and charity in response to a single person's suffering from hunger or disease; it doesn't require one million. The response is that the objector commits the slippery slope fallacy when she charges that any evil, however slight, is not justified since it is possible for God to further his soul-building project with an even smaller evil. An objection that can be raised no matter what the circumstances are is not a legitimate objection. The God-could-have-done-better objection has been raised against the widely offered significant-contrast theodicy that justifies God's allowing evil because we could not appreciate the good without a contrast with evil. Supposedly he could have achieved this objective without allowing as much evil as he did. Again, it is an objection that can be raised no matter how small the quantity of allowed evil is. There is a more telling objection to this theodicy that contends that God could have created us with a different psychological makeup that would have enabled us to appreciate the good without having in our experience any significant contrast with evil.

There is a very fanciful theistic response to the God-could-do-more objection that I owe to Donald Turner. Traditional theism assumed that God elected to actualize one and only one of the infinitely many possible worlds. But a case can be made out that God's omnibenevolence requires him to create as much good as possible—let the good times roll, the more the merrier—which would result in his actualizing every possible world in which there is a favorable balance of good over evil. It should not surprise us, therefore, that the world we inhabit contains some evil. All that we should expect if we are theists is that it is overall a world worth having, because it contains a favorable balance of good over evil. There aren't many takers for this many-world theodicy, no doubt because it deflates our ego, just as did the Copernican discovery that we are not geographically the center of the universe or the news that a baby brother has just been born so that our parents will love us less. Are these good reasons?

There is yet another way of blocking this God-could-do-more objection. If God were to have created us with a different psychology than we in fact have, the causal laws of science would have had to be different, but van Inwagen has questioned whether this is possible. He refers to some respected physicists who claim that the causal laws that hold for the actual world are the only possible ones. He defends a doctrine of modal skepticism about possibility and necessity claims that transcend our ordinary, everyday experiences. It is okay to have such modal intuitions. He himself has them, since as a committed theist he believes that it is possible for there to be a creation ex nihilo. What we are not permitted to do is to employ one of these dubious modal intuitions as a premise in an argument; for then the onus falls on us to justify it, and this cannot be done. For example, we cannot justify the claim that God could have created water that would not drown, fire that would not burn, and wild tigers that would not be carnivores, or at least some reasonable facsimiles of them, since to do so we would have to be able to design the causal structure of a universe in which these things obtain. And this we cannot do.

Van Inwagen fails to notice that many theodicies, including some that he gives, violate his modal skepticism, since they employ a dubious modal premise or a premise that entails a dubious modal proposition, such as that it is possible that original sin caused hereditary ruin and that it is possible that humans will survive death in a Christian type of heaven. Furthermore, the manner in which van Inwagen defends and deploys his modal skepticism is quite dubious. It seems obvious to most physicists that a different law of gravity could have obtained, for example, one that has a different value for the gravitational constant. They would view his opposing modal intuition as qualifying him for nonvoluntary commitment to the EMIDS (Extreme Modal Intuition Deficiency Syndrome) Foundation hospital. Van Inwagen, of course, has rooms in his own EMIDS hospital that await the involuntary commitment of his rivals. It is interesting to note that if the causal structure of the universe is necessary, van Inwagen's God winds up as a limited God that is in the same fix as the Demiurge in Plato's *Timaeus* who is limited by the principle of necessity inherent in the stuff—the Receptacle—that he is given to work with. This solves the problem of evil, but at what price?

V. THEISTIC SKEPTICISM

So far only theodical responses to the evidential arguments from evil have been considered. But by far the most favored response among sophisticated contemporary theorists, most notably Alston, Plantinga, Wykstra, and van Inwagen, is that of theistic skepticism. Because our imaginative and cognitive powers are so radically limited, we are not warranted in inferring that there are not or probably are not God-justifying reasons for evils E. Theistic skepticism involves our inability, first, to access the divine mind so as to determine the different sorts of reasons that God could have for permitting evil and, second, to determine whether some purported God-justifying reason applies to a given case of evil. The former will be called "reason skepticism" and the latter "application skepticism." Defenders of theistic skepticism invariably supplement it with some speculation about possible defenses or theodicies for E. This is fitting, since the believer must have some target for her faith, however sketchy and evidentially unsupported it is.

Rowe's argument based on exhaustive enumeration mistakenly assumes that we are up to divining every possible God-justifying reason for permitting evil. As Stephen Wykstra has put it, God's reasons are no-see-ums for us. If you carefully inspect a room and fail to detect a zebra, it is reasonable for you to inductively infer that there is no zebra in the room. But if you were trying to detect an ammonia molecule in the room, your failure to find it by unaided observation would not justify your inference that no ammonia molecule is in the room. The divine mind is the ultimate no-see-um for us, regardless of what instruments of detection we employ. Our minds are to God's as a one-month-old baby's is to an adult's mind. It is contended that a universe created by God would likely have great moral depth in that many of the goods below its puzzling observable surface, many of the moral causes of God's current allowings and intervenings, would be "deep" moral goods. Alston develops an analogy between the physical world and morality in respect to their having a hidden nature that is gradually brought to light by painstaking investigation.

This analogy appears strained. To discover the hidden nature of gold, its molecular structure, required a long-term, sustained inquiry. But no analogous inquiry was required to unearth the hidden nature of morality, for a hidden morality is no morality. The "discovery" that love is better than hate because it is more affectionate is quite different from the discovery that gold has a certain atomic weight and number. To be sure, some of our primitive progenitors in the evolutionary process did not recognize any moral rules and principles, but that no more shows that we had to perform inquiries over a long period of time analogous to those employed by scientists to discover the inner nature of morality than does the fact that they blew their nose on the ground while we use Kleenex show that we had to inquire deeply into the nature of nose blowing. No doubt we have a heightened moral sensitivity relative to them, but that is not due to our having unearthed the deep, hidden nature of morality.

That morality be on the surface, common knowledge of all, is an empirical presupposition for our engaging in our social moral practices, the purpose of which is to enable us to modify and control each other's conduct by the use of generally accepted rules and principles of moral evaluation, thereby effecting more satisfactory social interactions. It also is required for our entering into relationships of love and friendship with each other. Such relationships require significant commonality of purposes, values, sympathies, ways of thinking and acting, and the like.

Many objections have been lodged against theistic skepticism. One is that it precludes the theist from employing teleological arguments, although not ontological and cosmological arguments; for, if the bad things about the world should not be evidence against the existence of God, the good things should not count in favor of his existence. Teleological arguments turn into two-edged swords. Maybe the good aspects of the world that these arguments appeal to are produced by a malevolent deity so as to highlight evil or because they are necessary for the realization of an outweighing evil, and so on for all the other demonodicies.

The most serious problem for theistic skepticism, which is raised by Bruce Russell, is that it seems to require that we become complete moral skeptics. Should we be horrified at what happened to Sue? Should we have tried to prevent it or take steps to prevent similar incidents in the future? Who knows?! For all we can tell it might be a blessing in disguise or serve some God-justifying reason that is too "deep" for us to access: For example, it might be a merited divine punishment for some misdeed that Sue will commit in the afterlife. The result of this moral skepticism is paralysis of the will, since we can have no reason for acting, given that we are completely in the dark whether the consequence of our action is good or bad.

Another objection concerns whether theistic skepticism allows for there to be a meaningful personal love relation with God. The problem concerns whether we humans can have such a relation with a being whose mind so completely transcends ours, who is so inscrutable with respect to his values, reasons, and intentions. Not all kinds of moral inscrutability preclude a love relationship. It is important to distinguish between the moral rules and principles employed by a person and the manner in which she applies them to specific cases based on her knowledge of the relevant circumstances, this being a casuistic issue. A distinction can be made between moral principle inscrutability and casuistic inscrutability. That another person is casuistically inscrutable to us need not prevent our entering into a communal love relationship with it, provided it is far more knowledgeable than us about relevant worldly conditions, as is God, an omniscient being. But moral principle inscrutability of a certain sort does rule out such a relationship. Although we need not understand all of the beloved's moral reasons for her behavior, it must be the case that, *for the most part*, we do in respect to behavior that vitally affects ourselves. One thing, and maybe the only thing, that can be said in favor of the theodicy favored by fundamentalists according to which all the evils reported by E result from the Fall and are messages from God to show us how lost we are without him, is that it does not run afoul of this requirement. We can hardly love someone who intentionally hurts us and keeps his reasons a secret unless for the most part we know his reasons for affecting us as he does and moreover know that they are benevolent. The answer to Plantinga's rhetorical question that if God did have a reason for permitting evil, why should we be the first to know, is that we should be for those that vitally concern us, at least for the most part. No doubt, the theistic skeptic will respond that this is being too anthropomorphic in its likening of a man-God personal relation to a man-man personal relation. Again we are confronted by the question of how anthropomorphic our concept of God should be.

Making God so inscrutable also raises a threat that theism thereby will turn out to be falsified or, if not falsified, rendered meaningless. Several atheists, including Michael Scriven and Theodore Drange, have used the hiddenness of God as the basis for an argument against his existence. There is, they say, a presumption of atheism so that no news is bad news. Numerous quotations from the Bible are assembled in which it is said that God's intention in creating men was so that they would come to know of his existence and worship, obey, and enter into a communal loving relation with him. Thus, if we do not have good evidence that God exists because he has chosen to remain hidden, this constitutes good evidence against his existence.

Swinburne has an answer to this atheistic argument that is based on God wanting created persons to come to know of his existence and enter into a communal relation with him of their own free will. If he were to make his existence too obvious, this would necessitate their doing so and thus be freedom canceling. If God's existence, justice, and intentions became items of evident common knowledge, then man's freedom would in effect be vastly curtailed. An ontological argument would do even greater violence to the traditional Christian view of God as wanting men to come to know, love, and obey him of their own free will. If someone were to come up with a really convincing version of the ontological argument, Swinburne might not be crushed if we followed the example of the Pythagoreans, who set adrift sans supplies the person who demonstrated the existence of irrational numbers. Again, we see Swinburne radically overestimating the value of free will. A consequence of his position is that we should not raise our children in a religion, since then their subsequent religious belief will not have been acquired freely. Swinburne has mislocated the point at which free will enters into the religious life. It is not in regard to one's believing that God exists, but how she lives up to this belief in her life.

By not allowing known evils E to count against God's existence, not even allowing it to lower the probability that he exists, the skeptical theist might be draining the theistic hypothesis of all meaning. E is itself a staggering array of evils, many of the most horrendous sort. If E is not the least bit probability lowering, then it would appear that for theistic skeptics no amount of evil would be. Even if the world were a living hell in which each sentient being's life was one of unrelenting suffering of the worst sort, it would not count as evidence against God's existence, would not lower the probability of his existence one bit. This seems highly implausible and calls into question the very meaningfulness of their claim that God exists. And this is so whether or not we accept the notorious verifiability theory of meaningfulness, which Plantinga likes to have die the death of self-reference by pointedly asking whether it is applicable to itself. We can recognize that something has gone wrong even if we cannot come up with a good theoretical explanation of why it is wrong.

That E is not probability lowering will come as news to the working theist who sees the evils reported by E as counterevidence to God's existence that tries her faith. The response of defensive skeptics such as Plantinga is to make a distinction between the pastoral and epistemic problem of evil. What this amounts to, though they wouldn't want to put it this bluntly, is that the working theist whose faith is strained or endangered by the evils that directly confront her is emotionally overwrought and not able to take the cool stance of the epistemologist of religion and thereby see that these evils, however extensive and seemingly gratuitous, are really no challenge to her theistic beliefs. Since she is unable to philosophize clearly at her time of emotional upset, she needs the pastor to hold her hand and say whatever might help her to make it through the night and retain her faith in God.

There is a problem here; however, it is not a pastoral problem but a problem with the pastor and the theistic skeptic who runs such a line. Her crisis of faith, although rationally explainable in terms of psychological causes, is not rationally justified because it rests upon the epistemically unwarranted belief that the evils confronting her probably are gratuitous or, at least, counterevidence to God's existence. It also follows that her emotion of horror at the evil of the Holocaust, for example, is equally irrational because it is based on the epistemically unwarranted belief that the apparent gratuitousness of this evil lessens the likelihood that God exists. Rationally speaking, she ought not to feel horror at the Holocaust!

Theistic skepticism appears to be an ivory tower invention of the detached epistemologist of religion who is completely out of touch with the grimy realities of everyday religious faith and experience. By neutralizing the dramatic bite of evil, it makes it too easy to have religious faith, as Kierkegaard might say. There are responses to all of the objections that have been raised against theistic skepticism, but because of space limitations we will exit the tennis match here, bearing in mind that the rally has not come to an end, nor will it ever.

We have yet to consider one rather obvious way for theists to meet the challenge of evil—go with a finite God, as do process theologians like Alfred North Whitehead and Charles Hartshorne. There are many ways to achieve this, since God has many omniperfections that can be tinkered with. No theist wants to downgrade his omnibenevolence, since this would preclude God from playing the role of an eminently worshipable being. It has already been seen how tinkering with his omniscience can create a defense of God for permitting moral evil.

Here is a fanciful, never-before-given way of playing with his omniscience that would give him an excuse for allowing evils E. God's omniscience does not extend to knowing metaphysical truths. Assume that Bishop Berkeley's metaphysical theory of matter is right. Material objects are nothing but coherent congeries of ideas in different minds, including God's. Berkeley's gloss on the account of divine creation in Genesis is that God creates the heavens and earth by coherently ideating in a heavenly and earthlike manner. Imagine that God is in the process of deliberating about what world to create and innocently imagines a quite defective world, namely ours, without having any intention to create it. Being unaware of metaphysical truths, he fails to realize that he is thereby creating this world. Upon learning that, he said, "Oops, sorry about that."

This story at least holds on to his omnibenevolence. The only thing wrong with it is Berkeley's idealist theory of matter. The most obvious omniperfection to downgrade is omnipotence, which brings us back to the Demiurge of Plato's *Timaeus*. Like a sculptor who is given a block of marble to work with that limits what he can create because it has a nature of its own, this God is given stuff to work with that limits what he can create. But if God is not all-powerful, how powerful is he? Does not this account of God's excuse for allowing evil run into the same unfalsifiability-in-principle problem as did theistic skepticism? No matter how much evil there is, the response is that he is just not *that* powerful, which resembles the punch-line of the famous shaggy dog joke, "Yes, he was a shaggy dog, but he wasn't *that* shaggy."

3

GOD ETERNAL AND PAUL HELM

I am honored to have been afforded this opportunity to pay tribute to Paul Helm upon his retirement. We rarely feel good about ourselves in philosophy, but Helm has earned that right through his many valuable contributions to the philosophy of religion and religious studies. Especially noteworthy is his probing, sensitive, and vigorous defense in his *Eternal God: A Study of God without Time* of the view of God as timelessly eternal—not subject to any temporal distinctions or determinations—rather than omnitemporally eternal—enduring in time without beginning or end.[1] Whether you are a friend or foe of divine timelessness, you cannot fail to find this book a valuable springboard for developing your own position. I am still a foe, but my position has changed and, I hope, become more defensible as a result of my encounter with Helm.[2] Through a critical analysis of his views I will develop this new view.

The long-standing and seemingly endless dispute between the friends and foes of divine timelessness is typical of perennial philosophical disputes. Equally intelligent and knowledgeable people are lined up on both sides, neither being able to convince the other; for there is no agreed-upon decision procedure for resolving their disagreement. In philosophy we do not know how to keep score and thus cannot determine who wins and who loses. If it matters to you to be able to find out who wins, take up pingpong instead of philosophy.

These disputes often are intractable because the disputants have different sentiments of rationality or paradigms of explanation, in other cases because their rival accounts have different purposes or goals. I believe, as a result of my confrontation with Helm's book, that the dispute over divine timelessness is of the latter sort. Put in a nutshell, the foes of divine timelessness want a God who is religiously available to agents whereas the friends of divine timelessness want a God with whom they can mystically commune. The latter will have the features of the content of a unitive mystical experience—timelessness, immutability, ineffability, and simplicity—while the former will be of a kind with which worldly agents can interact. We want both of these Gods and the challenge to the theologian is to find some way to unify them, as, for example, by some mystical doctrine like that of the Trinity. The mistake made by Helm and other friends of divine timelessness is to argue that the God of agency is amenable to the same analysis as is appropriate for the mystic's God and thus will be timelessly eternal like the latter.

God is that than which none greater can be conceived (a GCB for short). Attempts to deduce that God is timeless from this conception of God as a GCB are unconvincing. Typical of them is Anselm's claim that a GCB must be timeless for if it were in time it would have at least the possibility of beginning or ending and thereby fail to qualify as a GCB. A foe of timelessness will reject this argument because it makes use of a hasty generalization from ordinary temporal beings. The deep source of the failure of all such deductions is that they fail to relativize the concept of a GCB. For when *great* and *good* are used to characterize something, it must be specified in which respect it is great or good. This holds also for comparative evaluations employing these words. Helm correctly points out that we cannot ask whether an individual "is better than another if we are not allowed to ask better *for* what, or better *than* what.... The difficulty of operating with 'better than' at [Anselm's] level of abstraction casts doubt" on his whole procedure. (13) Thus when we say a being is the greatest conceivable one, we must specify the respect in which it is the greatest.

The next step in establishing my thesis, which also is located in Helm's text, is that the friends and foes of timelessness relativize the greatness of the GCB in different ways. The book's opening quotation from John Duncan's *Colloquia Peripatetica* hints that their dispute results from their different attitudes toward mysticism. "When at the Grammar School in Aberdeen, I got hold of a volume of George Campbell, in which he ridicules, as lamentable folly, the notion that to God there is no past, present or future—to Him all are one. I remember how well I abhorred George Campbell for that. I thought it the most magnificent thought I had ever met with." (x) This hint at a mystical basis for the differences between the manner in which the friends and foes of timelessness relativize the concept of greatness is developed further when Helm writes, "The idea of God as timeless, as the changeless ground of all that changes, has profound implications for the character of human spirituality, for the focusing of faith, hope, and love in what is unseen and eternal rather than what is visible and transient. John Milton gave expression to such spirituality when he wrote of the prospect of triumphing over death and chance and time." (xiv–xv)

The timeless God, although appealing to those of a mystical bent, is ill-fitted to perform the roles that are required of him by those who want a God of action who will effectively engage with them in their endeavors. For them, God should be, as William James put it, our ideal social self—that being to whom we look to for inspiration and guidance and by whom we want ultimately to be judged. Since it is required that agents temporally interact with this God, it must be a God in time. Helm takes note of this when he writes, "If God were timelessly eternal ... the character of God, particularly the God of Christian theism who judges and redeems, is radically compromised." (43) "One of the main reasons that certain philosophers have for maintaining that God is in time is that only so is it possible to think of God reacting to human choices. The idea of a responsive divine life, and of divine and human freedom, are closely intertwined in their thinking." (109)

Whether or not there even was available to the authors of the Bible a conception of timeless eternity, they give numerous reports of God interceding in human history. Periodically he is back in town, even more pissed off than he was on previous occasions because of our sinful ways. Whereas it is plausible to give a metaphorical interpretation of depictions of God as having bodily parts, it is not reasonable to do so for the numerous accounts of God as temporally interacting with creatures. The Bible abounds in descriptions of Alstonian-type apparent direct nonsensory perceptions of God in which God warns, comforts, counsels, and chastises his creatures. The phenomenology of these experiences is of a God who acts and endures in time.

Helm briefly sketches a way in which a devotee of divine timelessness can accommodate these phenomenological appearances of God as temporal: "Just as a tree can be thought of as made up of a collection of objects which we cannot observe without thereby making reference to the tree as a palpable physical object impossible, so the God to whom we refer as acting in time and space in fulfillment of his own purposes and in reaction to human needs can be thought of, albeit with difficulty, as transcending space and time. The difficulty is real enough, but it need be no more intellectually embarrassing than is talk of unobservable electrons." (107. See also p. 23) This analogy between God and the theoretical entities of science needs to be filled out further with respect to the ontological status of their phenomenal appearances. Either they are mere appearances, having no objective reality, or they are not. This disjunction can serve as the basis of a dilemma argument against Helm's timeless God.

The first horn, which denies objective reality to God's temporal phenomenal aspects, is the divine analogue to the scientifically based bifurcationism in which it is claimed, to use Sellarsian terminology, that the *manifest image* of physical objects based on sensory experience depicts the world in a way in which it isn't. The *scientific image*, which employs concepts of unobservable entities, alone depicts things as they really are. (Bruce Aune, whom Helm gives as the source of his analogy, defends this Sellarsian error theory of the manifest image.)

This horn of the dilemma has the unwanted consequence that the *Biblical* apparent direct nonsensory perceptions of the temporal presence of God are erroneous, unveridical, because they depict God in a way in which he isn't. This troublesome consequence gives rise to an even more troubling one. That God would produce this plethora of unveridical experiences of himself as temporal makes him a deceiver and seems incompatible with his essential benevolence. Descartes tried to ward off this objection to his scientific bifurcationism by using a free will defense of God for allowing us to freely form erroneous beliefs about the world based on our senses. A similar defense of God for permitting erroneous beliefs about his nature based upon apparent direct perceptions of him is far more difficult to sustain. Unlike our sensory-based beliefs about physical objects, it is God himself who is the immediate cause of our apparent direct nonsensory perceptions of him. And, furthermore, whereas we have some power to resist believing that physical objects are as they perceptually appear to be, we do not seem to have the freedom to resist forming beliefs about God's nature upon having an apparent direct perception of him because of the overpowering nature of such an experience.

Things fare even worse for Helm's *exclusively* timeless God on the second horn. Now we are to take the manifest image based on phenomenal appearances as objective features of reality. This can be combined with a compatibilist account that accords objective status also to the scientific image, or one that denies it any objective status, such as would an instrumentalist account. Either way God turns out to have temporal features, which is inconsistent with Helm's view of God as devoid of any temporal features. It would best fit "the two aspects of God" (or maybe "the two Gods") thesis of this essay to opt for the compatibilist alternative and thereby ascribe to God both temporal and timelessly eternal features. While it is difficult enough to combine the manifest and scientific images of the physical world, it is even more difficult to do so with respect to the temporal and timelessly eternal God. How can a single God manifest himself under such different, and apparently incompatible, guises? As suggested earlier, something like a doctrine of the Trinity is needed. Traditional mysticism faced this problem, because it held that the Eternal One becomes, via some sort of emanations, a temporal many, only to be unified back into the Eternal One.

Helm, holding that God is *exclusively* timeless, must opt for the first horn of the dilemma and thus take his chances with showing that God really is no deceiver. Helm never recognizes this problem, but, being the extremely honest philosopher that he is, recognizes problems aplenty with his doctrine of divine timelessness and, no doubt, would include this one among them. However, Helm argues throughout his book that these problems are far less severe than those that arise for a temporalistic God, thereby resembling the baritone, who after being thoroughly booed by the notoriously tough Parma audience for his opera-opening aria, responded, "If you think I stink, wait till you hear the tenor." Two of the most prominent objections to a timeless God that Helm attempts to lessen hold that a timeless God can be neither a person nor omniscient. Each will be considered in turn.

Personhood Objection. All parties to the dispute agree that God must be a person; and, even though they disagree about the niceties of the analysis of the concept of personhood, which is not surprising given that the concept is largely a forensic one, they agree that at a minimum a person have reason, which involves being conscious, having memories, knowledge and beliefs, as well as the capacity to act intentionally. In other words, a person must be a rational agent. The friends and foes of divine timelessness have opposed intuitions about whether it is conceptually possible for a timeless being to have these rationality and agency properties. The foes appeal to "ordinary language" to support their modal intuitions, for the beings of which we ordinarily predicate these properties are temporal. For example, the foes would reject on conceptual grounds the imputation of purposeful action to a timeless God, since ordinary, familiar cases of purposeful action have the fulfillment of the purpose come later than the action, but for a timeless God there is no temporal relation between his timeless act and its worldly fulfillment.

But we must be on guard against the fallacy of "the legislativeness of ordinary language," according to which the ordinary use of a word is legislative for all uses of it.[3] For the fact that we have never had the occasion to so speak does not show that it would be conceptually wrong, violate a "rule" of language, so to speak. For example, it is dubious to infer from the fact that all the causal relations we know of involve a temporal relation between cause and effect that it is conceptually impossible for God to timelessly bring about effects in time. This needed jump from what we actually say to what it is conceptually correct to say is the bane of ordinary language philosophy or conceptual analysis. And, since God is such an extraordinary being—*the* extraordinary Being—it is not surprising that the dispute over whether it is conceptually possible for a timeless being to be a person is a seemingly intractable one. The best that the disputants can do is to snipe at each other's arguments, bearing in mind that no one is going to win a decisive victory; for we do not know how to keep score in philosophy.

To begin with, consciousness, at least of the more developed sort that is required of a person, is a process, something that goes on, and therefore is temporal. Helm never considers this basic objection, but this is not a serious omission, since he does attempt to show that his timeless God can have specific forms of consciousness, such as memory and belief and purpose, which would entail being conscious. Having memory certainly is essential for any more developed sort of consciousness, and Helm attempts to show how a timeless God can have memory. Ordinarily, we say that someone remembers only if what is remembered is earlier than the remembering. Helm's timeless God cannot have such ordinary memories and thus cannot be conscious. To meet this difficulty Helm concocts a timeless analogue to ordinary temporal memory that God can have. Whereas ordinary remembering is "knowing that p and having not forgotten that p...a timeless being remembers p when he knows p and it is impossible for him to forget p." (59)

This contrived timeless analogue to ordinary memory is suspect. The only part of Helm's definition that specifically concerns memory is the clause that "it is impossible for God to forget p." But it is true also of the number seven that it is impossible for it to forget p. Are we then to say that there is a number analogue to memory? Seven "remembers" being odd just in case seven is odd and it is impossible for it to forget being odd.

Another thing required of a person is that it have a life, though not necessarily in the honorific sense ("Go and get a life!") or the biological one. It was for this reason that Augustine and Boethius spoke respectively of all of God's years standing together and his life being an illimitable one had all at once. Unfortunately, it is contradiction in terms to speak of a timeless duration and all of one's years standing together. Helm analyzes Humpty Dumpty style God's having an illimitable life in terms of each of his essential attributes being illimitable. (39) That there are no limitations on God's attributes, however, is totally irrelevant to his life being illimitable. These objections to the possibility of there being a timeless person are put forth tentatively, since I fear they may rest on the fallacy of the legislativeness of ordinary language. But the friends of divine timelessness should be at least as cautious in advocating their blatant departures from ordinary usage.

For the purpose of establishing my thesis, what matters is not whether the timeless God is a person but whether he is the right sort of person for playing the role of our ideal social self, the one with whom agents have intimate action-guiding interactions. It was baldly claimed that Helm's timeless God cannot play this role, and, surprisingly, it is the issue of the divine omniscience that best reveals why it cannot.

Omniscience Objection. An omniscient being must know every true proposition. But among the true propositions are temporal indexical ones, to be called *A-propositions*. An *A*-proposition makes a temporal determination and is expressed by the use of a sentence that is not freely repeatable in time in that successive tokenings of it could express propositions that differ in truth-value.[4] A *B-proposition* reports a temporal relation and is expressed by the use of a sentence that is freely repeatable in time in that successive tokenings of it could not express propositions that differ in truth-value. Sentences that are freely repeatable in time are *B-sentences* and those that are not are *A-sentences*. These definitions leave it an open question whether for every *A*-proposition there is a *B*-proposition that is identical or at least logically equivalent with it. The omniscience of a timeless God is challenged by his apparent inability to know true *A*-propositions, since it would seem that only a being in time could have such knowledge. Helm exerts considerable ingenuity in his attempt to neutralize this problem for his timeless God. Toward this end he employs these three strategies: (1) appeal to degrees and importance of omniscience; (2) reduction of *A*- to *B*-propositions; and (3) refutation by parody based on an analogy with spatial and personal indexical propositions.

(1) Initially, Helm *seems* to accept the claim of the enemies of divine timelessness that God cannot know an *A*-proposition.[5] "If the omniscient being were timeless, he would necessarily not know that it was raining now, since being timeless, he could not be temporally present on the occasion on which it is raining." (40. See also p. 80) "The significant fact about ... [*A*-propositions] is that they can only be known to be true when they are true." (42) Thus the reason why a timeless God could know an *A*-proposition, such as that event *E* is happening now, or that it is now time *T*, is that only a being who exists at the time referred to—now or this time—could know the proposition. But why is this the case? Two answers might be given. The first is that a being who does not exist now cannot *understand* this proposition; the second, that he cannot express it. The second answer might appear more helpful; for, when it is asked just why this being cannot know the proposition, it would seem that the only answer is the he cannot express it. But a lot depends on what is meant by *express*. A timeless being can timelessly bring it about that an *A*-sentence is tokened at a certain time. Think of a parallel case involving a spatial indexical sentence containing "here." A being who is not here, or maybe not even in space at all, could cause it to be the case that a tokening of "The treasure is here" occurs at a certain place, that is, the sound of the tokening appears to come from a certain place. Think of a ventriloquist. Why couldn't there be a temporal ventriloquist? It might be countered that although he causes a tokening of an *A*-sentence at a certain time, he does not *express* the *A*-proposition because he cannot understand it, since he doesn't exist at the time in question. But this is the first explanation and thus brings us full circle. Maybe the second answer can be bolstered by analogy with the personal indexical proposition that I am Richard Gale. Even if some ventriloquist were to cause it to be the case that the sounds made by a tokening of the sentence "I am Richard Gale" were to emanate from my mouth, he would fail to express the very same proposition that would be expressed by my uttering the sentence. Whatever the right answer is, I think we can agree with Helm that an improperly positioned person cannot know these different temporal, spatial, and personal indexical propositions.

Granted, at least for the sake of argument, that a timeless God cannot know an *A*-proposition, what are theists to make of it? What importance should it have for them? Should it bother them? These are the right questions to ask, given that the concept of a GCB cannot be understood without connecting it up with a context of human concern and endeavor. Where I differ from Helm is over how he answers these questions, for I think it should greatly bother the theist, as will emerge from my discussion in (3) of the parody refutation, whereas he does not.

Helm's response has two prongs. First, it is claimed that the timeless God's failure to know *A*-propositions is of little importance, because for every event truly reported by an *A*-proposition God knows of this event under a different description, namely via a *B*-proposition that reports the very same event. For example, while God cannot know that it is raining now, he can timelessly know that rain occurs (tenselessly) at T, provided that now=T. The second prong, which has Helm's timeless God play baritone to the omnitemporal God's tenor, argues that the timeless God's omnitemporal rival also fails to be omniscient. For in order to know any *A*-proposition, it must exist at the appropriate time; but by virtue of having this unique temporal perspective, it will be denied knowledge at that time of those *A*-propositions that are truly expressible at earlier and later times. (81) He also will be unable to know those *A*-propositions that are true at that very time that predict future contingents, such as creaturely free actions, thereby further lessening its omniscience. (82) Another disadvantage of placing God in time is that he loses his required immutability; for, not only does he grow older, he must continually change his mind about what time it is and the like. (85ff.)

So far Helm's a plague-on-all-your-houses strategy has argued for a tie between a temporal and a timeless God's omniscience: both are restricted. He now argues that there is a respect in which the latter's omniscience is superior to the former's. "If it is granted that there are expressions of propositions which a timeless omniscient being could not use [namely, *A*-sentences], this must be balanced against the fact that a timeless omniscient being knows the future, our future, something which other accounts of divine omniscience find difficulty in accommodating." (85) So the baritone isn't as bad as the tenor! The reason for a temporal God having to be ignorant of future contingent propositions is due to Boethius's and Pike's arguments for fatalism.[6] Another respect in which a temporal being's knowledge is inferior to that of a timeless being is that the latter but not the former can know *B*-propositions. "But even if [a temporal being] knew the truth of all temporal indexicals at the times when they were true, he would know nothing timelessly. So while an omniscient being in time would know more than a timeless omniscient being, he would also know less."(78) Helm gives no support to this implausible claim, implausible because we seem to know many *B*-propositions, such as that the Civil War begins (tenselessly) in 1861.

(2) *A*-propositions have been a breeding ground for conceptual puzzlements and perplexities. They seem to ontologically commit us to a queer entity—now or the present—that mysteriously shifts to ever-later times or events at the rate of one time unit per time unit, which is the basic problem with the river of time depiction of temporal passage. *A*-propositions, as we have seen, also muck things up for God's omniscience. The "propositional *B*-reduction" helps us flies to escape from the bottle by showing that every *A*-proposition either is identical with or entailed by a *B*-proposition. There also is the more radical "ontological *B*-reduction" that attempts to show that there are no *A*-propositions in the traditional, abstract *Fregean de dicto* sense—a unity comprised of both the sense of the subject and the predicate expressions. Rather, an *A*-proposition, such as that now is when event *E* occurs, is an ontological mixed bag, being an ordered pair comprised of the real life referent of the tokening of "now" and the concept of being the time when event *E* occurs. Helm inconsistently defends both the propositional and ontological forms of the *B*-reduction; for an *A*-proposition cannot be identical with or entailed by a de dicto *B*-proposition unless it too is a de dicto proposition.

The Propositional B-reduction. The identity version of this reduction runs up against the problem that a person can have a propositional attitude toward an *A*-proposition (*B*-proposition) without having that attitude toward the *B*-proposition (*A*-proposition) that is *coreporting* with it, even when she understands both propositions. (Propositions are coreporting just in case their participial nominalizations are coreferring; assuming that now=T, that now is when E occurs is coreporting with that T is when E occurs because now being when E occurs is identical with T being when E occurs. In various publications I had defended a criterion of propositional identity that required of identical propositions that it is impossible for someone who understands both propositions to have a propositional attitude toward one of the propositions that she does not have to the other. By this criterion, no A-proposition is identical with any B-proposition because it always is possible for someone who understands both propositions to believe one of them, for example, without believing the other—to believe that it is raining now without believing that rain occurs (tenselessly) at time T. Prior's well-traveled "thank goodness that's over" example rests on this criterion.

Helm is well aware of this consequence of my criterion and accordingly attempts to undermine it: "a and b both express the same proposition if it is impossible to believe—and not to believe b, or vice-versa. The basic problem with such a criterion is that for it to operate in the case of a timeless God such a God must be able to adopt a propositional attitude, to believe, temporal indexical expressions [A-propositions], when manifestly this is impossible." (77) This objection to my criterion misses the mark because Helm's formulation fails to specify that the person who performs the thought experiment of seeing if she could believe a but not believe b understands both a and b. The viability of my criterion does not require that every subject who is capable of having a propositional attitude is a suitable subject for the thought experiment. The results that are obtained from the thought experiments of those who have sufficient understanding of both a and b hold true for everyone, even those who cannot perform the thought experiment because of limitations in their understanding. Helm's God will just have to take our word for it. Helm has unwittingly unearthed yet another limitation on the omniscience of this being.

There is another way in which Helm can challenge my criterion: produce a counterexample to it, which could be done via a good argument for an A-proposition being identical with a B-proposition.[7] And this is just what Helm attempts to do on the basis of D. H. Mellor's *Real Time*, in which it is argued that for every A-proposition there is a B-proposition that has the same truth-conditions as and therefore is identical with it. "A sentence such as 'It is raining now' uttered by A on

30 July 1987 has the same truth-conditions as the sentence 'It is raining on 20 July 1987', and so expresses the same proposition. So a timeless God knows that it is raining now if he knows its dated equivalent." (78) By the same appeal to truth-conditions it can be shown that the appropriate use of differently tensed counterpart sentences express one and the same proposition. "If one says that what counts as sameness of fact is sameness of truth-conditions, then 'It is raining now' uttered on 24 September and 'It was raining then [yesterday]' (uttered on the 25th) have the same truth-conditions, namely that it is raining on 24 September." (82) The only difference between a timeless God and time-bound creatures with regard to *A*-propositions concerns not the fact or true proposition that is known, it being the same in both cases, but only their *ways* of knowing or expressing them. "For though there are ways in which an eternal being cannot represent certain facts to himself he can still know those facts, or at least he knows facts that entail the facts that he cannot represent to himself, and he knows that this entailment holds." (85) This is the entailment version of the *B*-reduction and relies on the principle, not that knowledge is closed under entailment, which it isn't, but rather that if a person knows p and that p entails q, then she knows that q.

The Mellor-Helm criterion for propositional identity fails because it confounds the truth-conditions for propositions with those for sentences. This is patent when it says, "A *sentence* such as 'It is raining now' uttered by A on 30 July 1987 has the same truth-conditions as the *sentence* 'It is raining on 30 July 1987', and so expresses the same *proposition*." (78. My italics.) The truth-conditions for a proposition are the worldly verifiers or truth-makers for the proposition. The truth-conditions for the proposition that S is F is S's F-ing (or being F). Thus, when I say that E occurs now, the proposition that I express has as its truth-conditions the worldly event of E's occurring now. What I say, the proposition that I express, does not entail that E occurs at the date on which I say or token the sentence in question. The truth-conditions for the sentence "E occurs now" are the rules for correctly tokening it so as to express a true proposition, namely that a tokening of "E occurs now" expresses a true proposition if and only if it is tokened simultaneously with an occurrence of E.

Whereas the truth-conditions for an *A*-sentence make reference to a temporal relation between a tokening of it and the event it reports (the one referred to by its participial nominalization), this is not the case for the truth-conditions for an *A*-proposition. The *A*-proposition that it is raining now does not entail that any token occurs, and thus it is not contradictory, only pragmatically self-falsifying, to say that it is raining now although no tokens occur. Helm's token-reflexive analysis of *A*-propositions runs afoul of this point. "The question 'What does God (timelessly) know now?', is equivalent to 'What does God (timelessly) know at the time this utterance is being made?'" (103) "If truth is applied strictly to a tensed sentence, it is being applied to something which has some of the logical characteristics of an *event*. ... [The] event in question is necessarily either an uttering or inscribing, something datable." (135. See also 52 and 136) But it is only the truth-conditions for an *A*-sentence, not an *A*-proposition, that refer to a tokening event.

The Ontological B-reduction. Helm says some things that speak for this elimination form of the *B*-reduction. He does not reduce *A*-propositions to the ontological mixed bag *de re* propositions of Russell and Perry, but instead to an event. *B*-propositions are abstract entities that are timelessly true or false, but *A*-propositions are events, tokenings of *A*-sentences, as was the case with Helm's above token reflexive analysis of them. Furthermore, when we predicate truth and falsity of an *A*-proposition it is the tokening of a sentence, not an abstract proposition, that is the subject of our predication; and the same *A*-sentence can vary in its truth-value over time. Propositions are said, by Helm, to be immutable in that "if it is true that I am at my desk on 1 March 1987 then it always was true that I am at my desk on 1 March 1987, for though sentences can change their truth value, propositions cannot." (133) The verb in this *B*-proposition is tenseless, being "no more about the future than it is about the past. ... To be about the future the expression would itself have to be regarded as an event occurring at a particular time." (136)

Helm's reduction of an *A*-proposition to a sentence tokening flies in the face of ordinary usage. For when we translate the sentence, "The man in the corner believes that it is raining now," into a foreign language, the entire sentence, including "it is raining now," gets translated.

But if the intentional accusative of this man's belief were a sentence tokening, as in "The man in the corner believes the tokening of the sentence 'It is raining now,'" the mentioned sentence "it is raining now" would remain untranslated. Furthermore, *pace* Helm, when we predicate truth of an *A*-proposition we do so of an abstract proposition and in a tenseless manner. We say that it is (tenselessly) true that it is raining now. We do not say that the tokening of the sentence "It is raining now" is now true. For it is only a contingent fact that the mentioned sentence is used to express the proposition that it is now raining; and thus it is possible that it is true that it is true that it is now raining and false that the tokening of the sentence "It is raining now" is now true. Truth is tenselessly predicated of the abstract *A*-proposition that it is raining now. For if the predication were tensed, it would make sense to say that it was true that it is raining now. What does make sense is to say that it was true that "it is then raining," in which "then" functions as a Castaneda quasi-indicator.[8]

(3) *Refutation by Parody.* It is this response to the challenge posed by *A*-propositions to the omniscience of his timeless God that Helm primarily relies on. Thus, he would not be crushed if his attempted *B*-reduction did not succeed, for he is willing to bet the family farm on his refutation of this challenge by a reductio ad absurdum parody. It goes as follows. (41–55)

(i) There are exactly parallel or analogous arguments based on spatial and personal indexical propositions against a timeless God's omniscience to the one based on *A*-propositions.

(ii) These parallel arguments have absurd consequences by the standards of traditional theism, and thus should be rejected by the theist.

(iii) The argument against a timeless God's omniscience based on *A*-propositions also should be rejected by the theist. (From (i) and (ii) by the principles of analogical reasoning.)

Premise (i), at first glance, looks right; for, just as *A*-propositions are expressed through the use of sentences that are not freely repeatable across times, spatial and personal indexical propositions are expressible by sentences that are not freely repeatable respectively across places and persons. Furthermore, just as one must exist now in order to know the *A*-proposition that it is raining now, one must exist here and be identical with me to know respectively the propositions that the treasure is here and that I am Richard Gale. But it would be absurd, according to traditional theism, to say that God is numerically identical with his creatures or that he occupies some place. Thus, theists must excuse God from having to know spatial and personal indexical propositions; and, given the strong analogy between these propositions and *A*-propositions, they should do likewise for *A*-propositions. Helm challenges those who think it is important for God to know *A*-propositions but not these other indexical propositions to produce relevant disanalogies between them. I accept this challenge.

It must be granted to Helm at the outset that it is impossible for God to know every true indexical proposition of any one of the three types—temporal, spatial, and personal. But this leaves open whether this God must know at least some true indexical propositions, and, if so, of which of the three types must he have this knowledge. And if he must have this knowledge for any given type, he must have the indexical perspective that is required for having this knowledge. It would be a howler to infer from the fact that God cannot know every true indexical proposition of a certain type that he cannot know any one of them, or even, that it is not required that he know some of them. It will be argued that God must know some temporal and personal indexical propositions but need not and cannot have knowledge of any spatial one. And thus there is a very significant disanalogy between temporal and personal indexicals on the one hand, and spatial indexicals on the other.

It is obvious that God, being a person, must be capable of making a firstperson indexical reference to himself, as for example by tokening "I am God" or whatever sentence in Deitiese has the same meaning. And thus God will know at least some true personal indexical propositions. If he is a purely spiritual being, then he is barred from having any spatial indexical perspective and therefore from knowing any spatial indexical proposition. This does not hold if God bcomes incarnate.

There is another reason why it is crucial to the role played by the personal God of the Bible, the one that interacts with men, that he have a personal indexical perspective. This is a requirement for his being able to have relations of intimacy with them. He must be able to you our I and we, turn, *you* his *I*. While God cannot know the very proposition I express when I say "I am Richard Gale," he can know a different indexed counterpart proposition that entails the former, namely "He is Richard Gale," said as he ostends me. This mutually *I-you*-ing, or, as some would say, *I-thou*-ing, is necessary for personal dialogue.

Must God also have a unique spatial perspective for him to have intimate dialogue with men? No, for we can imagine having an intimate relation with a purely spiritual being. This is just what a séance is attempting to achieve. *Here* and *I*, therefore, are disanalogous with respect to our concept of intimacy, thereby undermining the analogical premise, (i), in Helm's parody reductio. A individual's not being in space does preclude some forms of intimate interaction, with their attendant thrills and tingles, such as was achieved when Jack and Jill's index fingers touched as they each said "this water pump." And zing went the strings of their hearts. But, if we are to trust the reports of the medieval nuns who, on the basis of their mystical experiences, claimed to be the "bride of Christ," maybe not having a body did not cramp God's style.

Here also is disanalogous with *now* with respect to intimacy, which further undermines (i). For you can have an intimnate dialogue or interaction with someone only if you assume that your temporal perspectives coincide—that she is speaking to you when you hear her (assuming for the sake of brevity that there is no time lapse between the speaking and hearing) and that she, in turn, hears your response and subsequently reacts to it, and so on back and forth. Each "moves" the other. This sort of intimate interaction cannot be achieved if you know that your correspondent timelessly knows everything you say in the course of the "conversation" and timelessly causes you to hear his "responses" at certain times, as would Helm's timeless God. Think in this connection of conversing over the phone with a tape recording that was made in advance by some prescient individual who knew just what you would say. Once you learn of this fact, there no longer is any sense of intimacy between you and this being. The *Biblical* apparent direct perceptions of the presence of God are good examples of the sort of intimate dialogue that is so central to the working theist. Job would be very upset if he learned that he was "talking" with a tape-recorded message.

Just as a personal God could *you* our *I*'s and thereby know differently personally indexed counterpart propositions to the ones we express by using "I," a temporal God can, at any given time, know different temporally indexed counterpart propositions to those that are truly expressible at earlier and later times. And since the former entail the latter, his failure to know every true *A*-proposition and personal indexical proposition is significantly lessened. For example, that S was F yesterday entails that yesterday S is then (quasi-indicator) F. Through the entailment relations between the *A*-propositions expressed by persons at different times a sort of temporal "intimacy" is achieved across these times, but it is quite limited because a conversation could take place between differently temporally positioned persons only if causation, *per impossible*, could go backwards.

There is yet another reason why a conversation requires that the communicants share the same temporal but not the same spatial perspective that rests on a very deep disanalogy between *here* and *now* with respect to the concept of objectivity, further undermining premise (i), the analogical premise, in Helm's reductio by parody.[9] After this disanalogy is unearthed, it will be employed in showing why there cannot be a conversation between a person existing now and one existing earlier than now, whereas there can be a conversation between a person existing here and one existing in front of (to the rear of, etc.) here. The link between the concept of a conversation and that of objectivity is that a conversation requires that the communicants agree in their judgments of objectivity, that there is an objective reality that they share in common.

A determination is objective only if it is not be subject to choice and is common to or agreed upon by other observers. *Now* satisfies these two requirements for objectivity, but *here* neither. They are conceptually disanalogous in these respects in that the spatial (temporal) analogue to a given proposition containing a spatial (temporal) indexical term differs from it in its modal status. A spatial (temporal) analogue to a given proposition is formed by replacing every spatial and temporal term in it respectively with a suitable temporal and spatial term. "Here" is to be replaced with "now" and "earlier than" by "in front of," though "to the rear, or right, or left of," would work equally well. Thus, the spatial analogue to the proposition that an object cannot now wholly occupy two different places is that an object cannot here wholly occupy two different times. This brings out a conceptual disanalogy between *here* and *now*, since the former is necessary and the latter impossible, which is due to the fact that an object has spatial but not temporal parts.

Whereas the use of *now* is not subject to selection or choice, the use of *here* is. This can be brought out clearly by the following pair of analogues.

(T1) A tokening of "now" now denotes a time but this very tokening could have denoted a time other than that time.
(S1) A tokening of "here" here denotes a place but this very tokening could have denoted a place other than that place.

At first glance, there appears to be no disanalogy, since both (T1) and (S1) seem to be impossible. But, far from being impossible, (S1) is necessary. The reason is that a tokening of "here" can be accompanied by an act of pointing and thus denote a different place than the one occupied by the speaker: I say to the movers, "Put the table here [as I point to a place in front of myself]." Since I could have pointed in a different direction than I in fact did, that very tokening of "here" could have denoted a different place than it in fact did. Obviously, there cannnot be an analogous type of selectivity with the use of "now." Our only choice is when to token it, but once we have made that decision there is no further choice as to what time is denoted. But, with "here," even after I decide where to token it, I have a choice as to what place will be denoted by my tokening.

The response to this alleged selectivity-based disanalogy will be that a naked use of "here," one unaccompanied by any act of ostension, cannot refer to any place other than the one occupied by the speaker, thereby making (S1) impossible when restricted to naked uses of "here." The reply is that even with a naked use of "here" there is choice, for the speaker has chosen whether or not to use it nakedly. But, disanalogously, a use of "now" must be naked, and thus the speaker has no choice in the matter.

There is another respect in which "here" is selective and "now" is not. Even if a tokening of "here" were in no way selective, it still would be the case that

> (S2) A tokening of "here" later than now both could refer to a place in front of here and could refer to a place to the rear of here,

whereas

> (T2) A tokening of "now" in front of here both could refer to a time earlier than now and could refer to a time later than now.

It is clear that (S2) is necessary, since it is possible for the speaker to be spatially free and rangy, and thus be able to change her spatial perspective at will in any direction in space. But (T2) is not necessary, because a speaker is not analogously able to change her temporal perspective at will in any direction in time. The reason is that it is impossible for a speaker who exists now to bring it about that a tokening of "now" denotes a time earlier than now, for causation cannot go backwards in time although it can go in any direction in space.

The other, and more important, objectivity-involving disanalogy concerns the agreement-injudgment-among-normal-observers test for the objectivity or veridicality of a perceptual experience. Whereas these relevant observers must be copresent with the perceptual experience, they need not occupy the same place as does the perceiver. This gives rise to the following conceptual disanalogy.

> (T3) To test a perceptual claim made now appeal is made to the noninferential perceptual claims only of observers who exist now.[10]
>
> (S3) To test a perceptual claim made here appeal is made to the noninferential perceptual claims only of observers who exist here.

These propositions differ in their modal status since (T3) is necessary and (S3) is not. In testing the objective truth of a percetual claim made here we do not confine ourselves to the testimony of observers who are here, for someone who is not here can have just as good a view, often better, of what is happening here. But we do not elicit the noninferential perceptual judgments of past or future observers with regard to what exists or is happening now. Their testimony as to what they then noninferentially perceive is irrelevant. If we were able, *per impossible*, to converse with Plato we would not ask him what time it is now; for what he says after consulting his sun dial would be totally irrelevant.

We want those with whom we enter into intimate dialogue to share our view of objective reality and thus they must be copresent with us and share our temporal indexical perspectives of past, present, and future. A timeless God could not have these perspectives and thus could not share our sense of objective reality. These perspectives are essential to our lives as agents in which we deliberate and intentionally carry out our decisions. If we want a God who is available to us as agents, a God who will warn, direct, and comfort us in our worldly endeavors, it cannot be the timeless God of Helm. But if, on the other hand, we want a God with whom to mystically commune, he would be the one that we want. Most theists want both Gods, and the challenge is to find a way to synthesize them.

NOTES

1. Oxford: Clarendon Press, 1988. All references to this book will be included in the body of the essay.

2. My earlier view is developed in my *On the Nature and Existence of God* (Cambridge University Press: Cambridge, 1991).

3. There is the corresponding scientisitic fallacy of "the legislativeness of scientific concepts," according to which the manner in which a concept is used in scientific contexts is legislative for all proper uses of it.

4. For a full account see my *The Language of Time* (London: Routledge & Kegan Paul, 1968).

5. I say "seems" advisedly, because it is not clear whether Helm is

speaking for himself or is merely expounding the view of others. That Helm subsequently attempts to reduce *A*- to *B*-propositions speaks for the latter way of interpreting Helm.

6. Helm repeats on pages 98 and 180 the *de re-de dicto* modal fallacy that infects their arguments. For a reconciliation of God's foreknowledge with human freedom based on the hard-soft core fact distinction that neutralizes the objections of John Martin Fischer, see my "Divine Omniscience, Human Freedom, and Backward Causation," *Faith and Philosophy 19 (2002)*.

7. There is an alternative, trivializing startegy for undermining my criterion. It could be charged that we must appeal to our preanalytic intuitions about when propositions are identical in determining whether a person is a suitable subject for its thought experiment. For if her claims do not match these intuitions, we rule her out for not having the needed proper understanding of the propositions in question. Thus, the application of my criterion presupposes that we already can determine when propositions are identical.

8. On page 80 and 135 Helm confounds quasi-indicators with temporal indexicals.

9. For a full discussion of this disanalogy see my "Disanalogies between Space and Time," Process Studies and "Time, Temporality, and Paradox," in the *Blackwell Guide to Metaphysics*, ed. R. M. Gale (Oxford: Blackwell, 2002).

10. For the sake of simplicity, the time lapse between what is perceived and the perceiving of it will be ignored.

4

A NEW COSMOLOGICAL ARGUMENT

Coauthored with Alexander Pruss

We will give a new cosmological argument for the existence of a being who, although not proved to be the absolutely perfect God of the great medieval theists, also is capable of playing the role in the lives of working theists of a being that is a suitable object of worship, adoration, love, respect, and obedience. Unlike the absolutely perfect God, the God whose necessary existence is established by our argument will not be shown to *essentially* have the divine perfections of omnipotence, omniscience, omnibenevolence, and sovereignty. Furthermore, it is not even shown that he is *contingently* omnipotent and omniscient, just powerful and intelligent enough to be the supernatural designer-creator of the exceedingly complex and wondrous cosmos that in fact confronts us.[1] Hopefully, his benevolence can be taken to be unlimited.

I. THE ARGUMENT

The argument makes use of certain technical notions that need to be defined and explained at the outset. A *possible world* is a maximal, compossible conjunction of abstract propositions. It is maximal in that, for every proposition p, either p is a conjunct in this conjunction or its negation, not-p, is, and it is compossible in that it is conceptually or logically possible that all of the conjuncts be true together. Let us call the maximal, compossible conjunction that a given possible world is identical with the "Big Conjunctive Fact" of that world.[2] The Big Conjunctive Fact for a given world comprises all the propositions that would be true if this world were to be actualized. The actual world comprises all the propositions that are actually true. (If this were intended as an analysis of actuality, it wouldn't be much help!) A *contingent* proposition (or *being*) is one that possibly, in the broadly conceptual or logical sense, is true (or existent) and possibly is false (or nonexistent). A being is a *necessary being* (or has necessary existence) if and only if it is necessary that it exists. Such a being is a self-explaining being in that there is a successful ontological argument for its existence, even if we aren't up to giving it.

Let us look more closely at a world's Big Conjunctive Fact. Some of the conjuncts in this Fact will be necessary propositions, assuming there are such propositions, as for instance, a proposition that reports the existence of a necessary being, e.g., the number 2, or some necessary relation between abstracta, e.g., that 2+2=4. Since these sort of propositions are necessary, they will appear as conjuncts in every world's Big Conjunctive Fact, and thus they will not serve to individuate or distinguish between worlds. In addition to these necessary propositions, every world's Big Conjunctive Fact will include as a part of itself a Big Conjunctive Contingent Fact comprised of all the contingent propositions that are true in that world. These propositions report the existence of a contingent being, as well as the occurrence of a contingent event or states of affairs. A Big Conjunctive Contingent Fact perhaps could have a conjunct that reports what some necessary being contingently does, for example, that a necessarily existent God freely elects to actualize a certain possible world.

Possible worlds are uniquely individuated by their Big Conjunctive Contingent Facts. This is because a possible world, according to our definition, is identical with a *maximal*, compossible Big Conjunctive Fact. From this it follows that a world's Big Conjunctive Contingent Fact will be maximal with respect to contingent propositions. Thus, for every contingent proposition, *p*, either *p* is a conjunct in this Fact or not-*p* is. And from this it follows that no two worlds have the same Big Conjunctive Contingent Fact. For since these worlds share the same necessary propositions, it is their Big Conjunctive Contingent Fact that serves to individuate them. This will serve as the first premise in our argument:

1. For any possible worlds, w and w_1, if w is not identical with w_1, then there is a Big Conjunctive Contingent Fact such that w contains this fact but w_1 does not. (True by definition.)

Our argument will consider the actual world, which is fitting since the intent of our argument is to establish that there exists in the actual world a very powerful and intelligent supernatural designer-creator of this world's universe, where a world's universe is what verifies or makes true all of the conjuncts in this world's Big Conjunctive Contingent Fact. (A universe is a maximal concrete aggregate of contingent beings.) Let us call the actual world's Big Conjunctive Contingent Fact "*p*." *p* will not only report the existence of every contingent being and event in the actual world but also the contingent acts of any necessary beings that there might be in this world. The second premise of our argument states that

2. *p* is the actual world's Big Conjunctive Contingent Fact. (True by hypothesis.)

Is there an explanation for *p*? According to the strong version of the Principle of Sufficient Reason (PSR), namely,

S-PSR. For every proposition, *p*, if *p* is true, then there is a proposition, *q*, that explains *p*.

there actually is an explanation. It would be imposing on the atheistic opponents of our argument to baldly ask them to accept S-PSR, as do all traditional cosmological arguments. For the strong version of PSR occupies almost as high an echelon in one's wish book as does the existence of God. Our new cosmological argument far outstrips traditional cosmological arguments in that it can make do with Duns Scotus's very weak version of PSR that requires only the possibility that there be an explanation for any true proposition, that is, for any proposition, p, if p is true, then it is possible that there exist a proposition, q, such that q explains p. When recast in terms of a possible worlds semantics, this says:

> 3. **W-PSR.** For any proposition, p, and any world, w, if p is in w's Big Conjunctive Fact, then there is some possible world, w_1, and proposition, q, such that w_1's Big Conjunctive Fact contains p and q and the proposition that q explains p.[3]

Whether or not w_1 is identical with w is left open by W-PSR. Whereas the atheistic opponents could have been justified in not granting PSR to traditional cosmological arguers, it would seem unreasonable for them not to grant us W-PSR. More will be said about this in the Objection Section.

The next step in our argument involves applying the principle of Universal Instantiation to W-PSR. By substituting the constants or proper names p, the actual world, and q respectively for the variables p, w, and q in W-PSR, we get

> 4. If p is in the actual world's Big Conjunctive Fact, then there is some possible world, w_1, such that w_1's Big Conjunctive Fact contains p and q and the proposition that q explains p.

This enables the derivation of

> 5. There is a possible world w_1 and a proposition q, such that w_1's Big Conjunctive Fact contains p and q and the proposition that q explains p. (From 2 and 5 by modus ponens.)

What now must be shown is that w_1 is identical with the actual world. To do so, appeal must be made to the premise that holds a world's Big Conjunctive Fact to be unique to it and thereby individuative. Since, as premise 2 says, p is the actual world's Big Conjunctive Fact and, as 5 has it, p is in w_1's Big Conjunctive Fact, it follows that

6. w_1=the actual world.

And given that identicals have all their properties in common, it follows from 5 and 6, by substituting the actual world for w_1 in 5, that

7. There is in the actual world a proposition q, such that the actual world's Big Conjunctive Fact contains p and q and the proposition that q explains p.

What kind of a proposition is q? It is the burden of the remainder of our argument to flesh out q. We already know from 7 that q explains p. But just how does q explain p? The only sort of explanations that we can conceive of are personal and scientific explanations, in which a personal explanation explains why some proposition is true in terms of the intentional action of an agent and a scientific one in terms of some conjunction of law-like propositions, be they deterministic or only statistical, and one that reports a state of affairs at some time. Thus,

8. q is either a personal explanation or q is a scientific explanation. (Some sort of a conceptual truth.)

It cannot be the case that q gives a scientific explanation of p. The reason is that q must contain some law-like proposition, as well as a proposition reporting a state of affairs at some time, but such propositions seem to be contingent, especially the latter. And, since they are contingent they are members of the Big Conjunctive Contingent Fact. But then they would have to explain themselves, since q must explain each and every contingent proposition in this Fact, as well as the Conjunction as a whole. But law-like propositions and propositions reporting a contingent state of affairs cannot explain themselves. Therefore,

9. q is not a scientific explanation. (Premise.)

From 8 and 9 it follows by the principle of the Disjunctive Syllogism that

10. q is a personal explanation.

Since q is a personal explanation, q will explain p in terms of the intentional action of either a contingent or a necessary being. (There is no need to consider an impossible being, since such a being cannot explain anything.) Thus,

11. q reports the intentional action of a contingent being or q reports the intentional action of a necessary being. (Premise.)

It is impossible that q reports the intentional action of a contingent being. The reason is that if it did, there would be in the Big Conjunctive Contingent Fact a proposition reporting the existence of the contingent being in question. But q itself is not able to explain why the contingent being it refers to exists, since a contingent being's intentional action evidently must presuppose, and hence cannot explain, that being's existence. Thus, it can be inferred that

12. It is not the case that q reports the intentional action of a contingent being. (Premise.)

And from 11 and 12 it follows by the principle of Disjunctive Syllogism that

13. q reports the intentional action of a necessary being.

Notice that there will not be in the Big Conjunctive Contingent Fact a proposition reporting the existence of the necessary being in question, since this proposition is necessary, given that a being has necessary existence only if it is necessary that it exists.

Proposition q stands in need of further fleshing out. q is true in the actual world by 7. But, firstly, is q contingent or necessary? And, secondly, is the intentional action of the necessary being that is reported by q done freely or not? We will argue for the first disjunct in each of these two questions.

Regarding the modal status of q, it might appear at first glance that it would be contradictory to hold q to be contingent. The reason is as follows. Since a necessary being is such that it is necessary that it exists, q is equivalent to the proposition that it is necessary that there exists a being who intentionally brings it about that p. But then a contradiction results from holding q to be contingent, since it results in the apparently contradictory proposition that it is contingent that it is necessary that there exists a being who intentionally brings it about that p. Appearances, however, deceive in this case. If this proposition is contradictory, then so is any proposition that results from an existential instantiation of it. But the existential instantiation of this proposition is not contradictory. For example, when we existentially instantiate this proposition with the constant or proper name G, it results in the proposition that it is contingent that (it is necessary that G exists and G intentionally brings it about that p). The latter is contradictory only if its second conjunct also is necessary, but that does not appear to be the case. An independent argument would have to be given for its necessity in order to claim that we have a contradiction.

Spinoza and Leibniz would argue that q is necessary, because they take G to be God and believe, on the basis of their ontological argument, that God is essentially benevolent and thus required by his nature to intentionally actualize the best of all possible worlds, which happens to be the actual world. It will not do for us to argue against Leibnoza that the necessary being that is referred to by q, since it is not subject to any possible kind of coercion, freely brings it about that p; and, because a necessary condition for acting freely is being able to do otherwise, this being could have done other than intentionally bring it about that p, thus establishing the contingency of the proposition that it is necessary that G exists and G intentionally brings it about that p. For we have not shown that this necessary being, G, is omnipotent and thereby not subject to any form of external coercion. And even if we could establish its omnipotence, Leibnoza could charge our argument with begging the question against their theory of freedom, since they take a free act to be one that accords with the nature of the agent, thereby not requiring a could-have-done-otherwise condition for a free action.

A more effective argument for q's contingency is the following reductio ad absurdum argument from the assumption that q is necessary. If q is necessary, q is a conjunct in every possible world's Big Conjunctive Fact. But q entails p, since that a necessary being intentionally brings it about that p entails that p, and thus p also is a conjunct in every possible world's Big Conjunctive Fact. Given that p is the actual world's Big Conjunctive Contingent Fact and that a possible world is individuated by its Big Conjunctive Contingent Fact, it follows that every possible world is identical with the actual world. Therefore, there is only one possible world. And this, surely, is absurd. Thus, it can be inferred, in conjunction with 13, that

> 14. q is a *contingent* proposition that reports the intentional action of a necessary being.

That there is only one possible world for Leibnoza has the consequence that he cannot make use of our argument. For him, every true proposition is necessary, and therefore, there is no Big Conjunctive Contingent Fact, and thus premise 2 fails for want of a suitable explanandum.

The next issue that must be resolved in our fleshing out of q is whether the intentional action of the necessary being is free or not. As will be seen in the Objections Section, unless the action is free, q will not terminate the regress of explanations and thus will not serve to explain p. The question, then, is whether q is to be fleshed out as:

> q_1. There is a necessary being who freely intentionally brings it about that p,

or as:

> q_2. There is a necessary being who unfreely intentionally brings it about that p.

If q is understood as q_2, there is a proposition, r, not identical with q_2, that explains q_2. r will report that something, perhaps something psychological or perhaps an external force, compels the necessary being mentioned in q_2 to bring it about that p. There are two possibilities: either r is necessary or r is contingent. It is to be argued that if r is necessary, a contradiction results, and, if r is contingent, a vicious circularity in the order of explanation results. r, therefore, is neither necessary nor contingent. r must be one or the other because if an action is coerced, then it is true that something internal or external coerces the action.

Let us first assume that r is a necessary proposition. r entails q_2, because the proposition that something coerces q_2's necessary being to bring it about that p entails the proposition that q_2—that there is a necessary being who unfreely brings it about that p. But given that $[L(P \supset Q)$ and $LP)] \supset LQ$ is a valid argument form, it follows that from Lr and $L(r \supset q_2)$ that Lq_2; however, q has already been proven to be contingent, and since q is assumed to be the same as q_2, the contradiction that q_2 is both necessary and contingent results.

Things fare no better if we assume that r is contingent. r explains q_2, since r explains how it is that q_2's necessary being is coerced into bringing it about that p. And q_2, in turn, explains p. But, since r is contingent, r is a conjunct in p, and this results in a vicious circularity of explanation—r explains q_2, while q_2 explains r since q_2 explains p and therefore every conjunct in p, including in particular r. Since q is either q_1 or q_2, and q_2 leads to either a contradiction, if taken to be necessary, or a vicious explanatory circle, if taken to be contingent, it follows that q is to be understood as

q_1. There is a necessary being who freely intentionally brings it about that p.

Since the Big Conjunctive Contingent Fact reports the existence of the actual world's universe, it follows from q_1 that:

15. q_1 is a contingent proposition that reports the *free* intentional action of a necessary being that explains the existence of the actual world's universe.

Considerably more fleshing out of q_1 is required before its necessary being can be shown to be capable of playing the role in the lives of working theists of a being that is a suitable object of worship, love, respect, and obedience. Because this being is necessary it is not included in the universe, which is the maximal aggregate of contingent beings, and thereby qualifies as supernatural. But that this being is supernatural is not alone enough for the working theist, since it is left undetermined how powerful, intelligent, and good this being is. For, although our argument shows that in every possible world there exists a necessary being who freely brings about its Big Conjunctive Contingent Fact, there are possible worlds that are so cruddy that nothing very admirable can be inferred about the qualities of their necessary explaining beings. Is our world one of them? At this point in the argument, we must avail ourselves of the whole battery of teleological arguments to establish that:

16. The actual world's universe displays a wondrous complexity due to its law-like unity and simplicity, fine tuning of natural constants, and natural purpose and beauty. (Premise.)

Herein we see the need to make out a global case for theism.

Given these facts about the universe, there are some grounds for inferring that

17. q_1 is the contingent proposition that there exists a necessary supernatural being who is very powerful, intelligent, and good and freely creates the actual world's universe.

Since q_1 has been proven to be a member of the actual world's Big Conjunctive Contingent Fact, and any member of this Fact is actually true, it follows from 17 that

18. It is contingently true that there exists a necessary supernatural being who is very powerful, intelligent, and good and freely creates the actual world's universe. (QED.)

II. OBJECTIONS

Even if our argument has avoided committing any non sequitur, there are numerous objections that could be raised. By considering these objections, we hope to deepen the reader's understanding of our argument, making clear just what it does and does not accomplish.

The Explanation Is Agglomerative Objection. A crucial step in the argument was the claim that the Big Conjunctive Contingent Fact in a given world is explainable only by the free action of a necessary being. It could be objected in the name of Hume that if the conjunction were infinite, with each conjunct being explained by another conjunct, the entire conjunction would thereby be internally explained. This assumes that explanation is agglomerative, meaning that it is closed under conjunctive introduction: if there is an explanation for P and another explanation for Q, there is an explanation for the conjunction $(P \& Q)$. We have both argued elsewhere at length that Hume's objection fails.[4] For instance, it could be a mere coincidence that P and Q are true together, even when each of them has some explanation. It also is possible that there is a common cause that explains their conjunction—their being true together.

The Taxicab Objection. Our argument proved that the Big Conjunctive Contingent Fact is explained by a contingent proposition that reports the free action of a necessary being. But this contingent proposition goes unexplained. And, since we are willing to countenance an unexplained proposition, why should we not have accepted as a brute, unexplained fact the Big Conjunctive Contingent Fact with which our argument started? Is not our argument, to paraphrase Schopenhauer's objection to the cosmological argument, like a taxicab that we hire and dismiss when it suits our purpose?

Pace what this objection contends, our explanation for The Big Conjunctive Contingent Fact is in terms of a proposition that ends the regress of explanations. The proposition that there is a very powerful and intelligent necessary being that freely causes the existence of the actual cosmos (or brings it about that the Big Conjunctive Contingent Fact is true) is a self-explaining proposition (and thus not unexplained) in spite of it being a contingent proposition. The reason for this is that a necessary being is one whose existence can be explained by an ontological argument, even if we cannot give it, and that a being *freely* performs an action, such as freely causing the actual cosmos to exist, stands in need of no further explanation, at least on the Libertarian Theory. Thus, the proposition that some necessary being freely does action A is a regress-of-explanation ender. Hence, it is possible that a conjunct could explain a conjunction of which it is a member without vicious circularity, provided the proposition is a self-explaining one that explains why all of the other conjuncts in the conjunction are true together. And this is just what our proposition q does for the Big Conjunctive Contingent Fact, p, of which it is itself a conjunct.

It might be objected that the Libertarian explanation of an action is not a *full* explanation and thus not a regress-of-explanation ender. Explanation is highly context-sensitive, since it is an attempt to answer someone's 'why' question, and thus is relative to the interests and purposes of this person. There are contexts in which the simple Libertarian explanation, 'She did it of her own free will,' is a *full* explanation in that it fully satisfies the interests and needs of the questioner. There could be other contexts in which this explanation will need further fleshing out if it is to fully satisfy the questioner. For example, our Libertarian explanation for God's creating the actual world's universe in terms of His freely doing so, permits a more detailed explanation that would specify His reason for doing so, if that should be what the questioner requires.

The Unintelligibility of Theistic Explanations. Scientistically inclined philosophers find unintelligible the notion of a purely spiritual being freely causing there to exist a cosmos by his will, because there is not the required relation of statistical relevance between his free effort of will and its effect, the resultant cosmos. We cannot in this essay do full justice to this objection, since a proper response to it would have to defend the coherence of theism against this and many similar types of objections, such as that the theistic explanation for the existence of the cosmos does not enable predictions to be made and thus is no explanation. Of course, in effect, this objection would necessitate the denial of even the Duns Scotus's Weak PSR, since it would imply that the universe as a whole with all its natural laws *cannot* have an explanation. This is a priori implausible.

The general strategy for a response to the incoherency-of-theism objection is to charge it with employing a question-begging scientistic premise, which we will call the "Legislativeness of Scientific Contexts" principle. This principle holds that the features that inform the use of a concept in a scientific context are legislative for the use of this concept in every context, any use that does not incorporate them being unintelligible. Thus, the scientistic objector finds through his analysis of the use of the concept of causation in scientific contexts that it involves a relation of statistical relevance between the cause and its effect, and thereby demands on the basis of the principle of the Legislativeness of Scientific Contexts that every use of the concept of causation have this feature. Since theistic uses of the concept of causation do not, he charges them with being unintelligible. One has only to state this principle in order to defuse the unintelligibility-of-theistic-explanations objection that is based on it. For the principle is not one that is vouchsafed by science. Rather it is a metaphysical thesis that fails to find adequate argumentative support and can rightly be charged by the theist with begging the question.

It would be dogmatic for the scientistic objector to dismiss the Libertarian Theory of freedom that is involved in q's explanation of p. Our argument has established that if it is possible, as W-PSR requires, that there is an explanation for p, it must be in terms of a necessary being's libertarian-type free action. Thus, to reject the Libertarian Theory is, in effect, to reject W-PSR, and this doesn't seem reasonable.

The Unintelligibility of a Free Necessary Being. One might charge our concept of a God who is both a necessary being and a free agent with being unintelligible. We assume that the problem is not concerned with the concept of a necessary being nor that of a Libertarian free agent but with the conjunction of them. Given that the latter concept is employed in some extant religious creeds, the onus rests with those who find this conjunctive concept to be an impossible one to give some good argument to support their modal intuition; for a concept that is employed in actual language games should be assumed to be innocent until proven guilty. We know of no such argument. Moreover, our argument shows that a free necessary being exists, and hence a fortiori is possible. Furthermore, we gave a reductio ad absurdum argument against the existence of the Leibnozian God, who is a necessary being determined by His nature to actualize the best of all possible world, which showed that then there is only one possible world and that every true proposition is necessary.

The Nonpersonal God Objection. Phil Quinn, in correspondence, has questioned our claim that the only type of explanation that we can imagine or conceive of for the Big Conjunctive Contingent Fact, p, in the actual world, given that it cannot have an explanation whose explanans contains at least one contingent proposition that does not report the action of a necessary being, is a personal one in terms of the intentional actions of a necessary being. He writes:

> I agree that the necessary being cannot be a number or Platonic form. Nor, I would add, can it be the Plotinian One, from which the cosmos emanates of necessity. I also agree that it cannot be without power. But I think it can be without intelligence or will. I can conceive of explaining [the Big Conjunctive Fact] in the following way: There is an impersonal necessary being, rather like the Brahman of advaita Hinduism, that generates the cosmos by means of blind but indeterministic mechanical causation.

There are several ways of attempting to meet this interesting objection. First, we could concede the objection and work with a more generic-brand Deity who is a common denominator of the different cosmos-explaining necessary supernatural beings. My argument, then, would prove the existence of a necessary supernatural being of considerable power who is the cause, though not necessarily in a personal manner, of the cosmos. This is no mean feat; however, we don't think we have to concede to Quinn's objection. In the first place, the Brahman of the advaita is not a necessary being in the sense that is relevant to our argument, namely, a being the concept of which explains its existence. Furthermore, it is dubious that the purported explanation of the cosmos in terms of the blind, indeterministic activity of this impersonal force is any better explanation of the existence of the cosmos than that in terms of a mystical One out of which the actual cosmos emanates. This cosmos displays considerable lawlike regularity and simplicity, as well as remarkable fine-tuning of its physical constants, all of which goes unexplained by an impersonal "explanation." Moreover, there is a dilemma argument possible. Either the impersonal force acts deterministically or not. If it acts deterministically, then we end up in a universe that could not be other than it is. In such a case, e.g., that there exist humans will be a logical necessity. This seems highly implausible. On the other hand, if the impersonal force acts indeterministically then we still do not have an explanation of why it acted as it did, and so the objection contradicts the conclusion of our argument that there is an explanation of the actual universe, since any such explanation will have to be a self-explainer. For an indeterministic action is a self-explainer only if it is a *free* action.

The Our-Argument-Doesn't-Do-Enough Objection. One of the aims of our argument was to escape the closing of the gap problem that has infected past cosmological arguments, the unwarranted move from a conclusion that there exists a first mover (cause, etc.) to the claim that this being is God, that is, has *all* of the divine perfections. This yawning chasm was papered over by St. Thomas's glib remark that "*et hoc dicimus Deum.*" So as to avoid the difficult problem of closing the gap, we chose to have the more modest conclusion that there necessarily exists a very powerful and intelligent supernatural being who is the free cause of the actual world's universe. But in avoiding the Scylla of the gap problem we may have wrecked on the Charybdis of proving the existence of a being who falls far too short of the divine mark.

So far we have done nothing to show that our God is one. It is reasonable, however, to infer that our God is one because of the law-like regularity and simplicity of the universe. Moreover, Ockham's razor should come into play: multiple Gods are not to be posited where one will do.

Another aspect of the problem concerns whether our argument proves "God" to be powerful and intelligent enough to be a suitable object of worship and adoration for the working theist. But given the incredible complexity and wonderfulness of the actual cosmos, any being who is capable of designing and causing this cosmos is sufficiently awesome in his power and intelligence to be a suitable object of worship and adoration by the working theist. That this "God" has not been proved either to be omnipotent or omniscient, no less essentially so, should not render the argument entirely unserviceable for the needs of ordinary believers. We do not claim that the conclusion of our argument gives all theists, in particular theologians of a scholastic bent who seek the absolutely perfect God (the one who essentially has all of the omniperfections), everything they want. Our claim is only that it gives the average working theists, who do not have the conception of logical or metaphysical necessity, everything *they* want.

The most serious problem concerns the moral attributes of our "very powerful and intelligent supernatural necessary being that freely causes the existence of the cosmos in the actual world." If we cannot show that this being is at least a very good being, our argument may very well have created a Frankenstein's monster, for this being will not be a suitable object of worship and thus will not meet the needs of the working theist.

To begin with, our creator God is not shown to be such as to have the essential property of always having to do the best. For some theists, this has the advantage of saving God's freedom, which was required to meet the taxicab objection. Moreover, our God was not even shown to be perfectly good in every possible world, and for this reason the God of our argument's conclusion will not fully satisfy the hopes and wants of all theists. What matters foremost to the working theist, however, is not whether it is *logically* possible (which is a concept that she does not have) that God do what is morally wrong, but whether God is capable of doing so in the actual world, in which *capable* is understood in terms of what a being has the capacity, knowledge, and opportunity to do. God could be said to be incapable in the *actual* world of doing wrong in the sense that he could not get himself to do so, that he is above temptation, that we can place absolute confidence in him.

The most serious problem with our argument is not whether its God is essentially benevolent but whether he is *actually* benevolent. And this is of primary concern to the working theist. It is here that our argument becomes quite vulnerable. To meet this problem we'll have to marshal all of the extant theodicies for God's permitting all of the known evils of the world. This battery of theodicies will still leave countless apparently gratuitous evils, and it is at this point that faith must enter in that God has morally exonerating reasons for permitting these evils, even if we cannot access these reasons.

The Objection to Our Principle of Sufficient Reason. Our argument employed a weak version of the Principle of Sufficient Reason, namely:

> **W-PSR.** For any proposition, p, and any world, w, if p is in w's Big Conjunctive Fact, then there is some possible world, w_1, and proposition, q, such that w_1's Big Conjunctive Fact contains p and q and the proposition that q explains p.

Our atheistic opponent might have initially been willing to grant us this premise, but after it is seen what results from this acceptance, it no longer will be granted. The opponent might charge W-PSR with begging the question. When confronted with a valid deductive argument for the existence of God, the atheist can always charge one of its premises with being question begging. The problem with this facile move is that it lays the foundation for charging every valid deductive argument with begging the question in one or more of its premises.

The concept of begging the question is based on a historical context that has to do with the background beliefs and assumptions that the disputants have *before* the argument is presented. Many atheists would be willing to grant W-PSR *before* we gave our argument, but once they see what follows from it in conjunction with some other seemingly innocent premises, they will no longer grant it to us and will charge it with begging the question. This move looks dogmatic, unless they can muster some grounds for doubting W-PSR. It appears as if they are dogmatically committed to rejecting any deductive theistic argument by rejecting some one of its premises.

There are, however, cases in which atheists are well within their rights in leveling the charge of begging the question against a theistic argument. A good case in point is the possibility premise of the S5-based modal ontological argument, which states that it is possible that it is necessary that there exist a being who essentially has every divine perfection. Whereas the Biblical Fool gladly consented to the possibility premise of Anselm's ontological argument in chapter 2 of the

Proslogion, in which what was at issue is the plain old existence of a being who essentially has all of the divine omniproperties, he would rightly reject the souped-up possibility premise of the S5 argument. He is a fool but not a complete schmuck. This means that he will not consent to a proposition that he does not understand. A consent to this possibility premise can be informed only if the consenter understands what is meant by its nested modal operators, it is possible that it is necessary that. But to understand this requires understanding the S5 axiom (that what is possibly necessary is necessary) to which it is subject. Thus, the properly informed fool will not only withhold his consent but will charge it with begging the question.

But our argument's use of W-PSR is far less subject to the charge of begging the question, since the existence of God is not an immediate consequence of it, in the way in which it is in regard to the possibility premise of the S5 argument. We are not omniscient and thus cannot always know all of the deductive consequences of propositions that we accept. The deductive powers of the opponent of an argument are another feature of the historical context that determines whether there is a begging of the question.

Still, it might be felt that W-PSR leads too quickly, with too few steps, to the highly controversial and amazing proposition that there *actually* is an explanation for the actual world's Big Conjunctive Contingent Fact, which would be an immediate consequence of S-PSR. Not only is there no general answer to the question of how many steps are required in a deduction for an argument not to be question-begging, but it is wrong-headed to even try to find an answer to it. The reason is that much of an argument consists in its stage-setting—the concepts and distinctions that it employs. It is like laying seige to a city. Much of the success of such an operation depends upon assembling just the right weapons and properly positioning them. Once this is accomplished the siege might require only a short time to get the city to capitulate. Similarly much of the originality and power of our argument consists in the background concepts and distinctions that we forge, concerning possible worlds and their Big Conjunctive Facts, and the manner in which we assemble and deploy them.

Even if our atheistic opponents reject W-PSR, our argument represents an advance over traditional cosmological arguments that had to appeal to S-PSR in that the atheists must pay a greater price, run a greater risk of being wrong, for rejecting our argument than a traditional cosmological argument. For our argument manages to use weaker premises than do these other cosmological arguments and thereby runs a lesser chance of having a false premise.

But how much does our argument justify theistic belief? There is room here for widespread disagreement, especially because of the gap problem that could be closed only by appeal to a battery of teleological-type arguments and theodicies. We believe, however, that it goes quite some way, maybe even making it more likely than not that God exists. Especially when combined with other arguments, like that from religious experience, the case may become quite compelling.

NOTES

1. Richard Gale sees this as a desirable feature of our new argument, for he has argued at length in his book *On the Nature and Existence of God* that a necessarily existent God who essentially has all of the divine perfections is an impossible being. His reason is that since such a being exists in every possible world and is at its greatest greatness in every one of them, given that it essentially has all of its omniproperties, in no possible world is there an instance of a purely gratuitous or unjustified evil; but, plainly, it is possible that there be such an evil, thereby engendering a contradiction. Alexander Pruss is not convinced by this ontological disproof, because he is inclined to be a modal skeptic about such alleged possibilities.

2. There will be no truth-functional repetitions in a world's Big Conjunctive Fact, such as (p and p) or (p or p), both of which are to be replaced with plain old p. This restriction is necessary in order to avoid the absurdity of a conjunction being one of its own conjuncts.

3. The authors are indebted to Jerome Gellman for suggesting to us this way of formulating W-PSR. Helpful comments were made also by Graham Oppy and Peter van Inwagen.

4. Richard M. Gale, *On the Nature and Existence of God*, chapter 7; and Alexander R. Pruss, "The Hume-Edwards Principle and the Cosmological Argument," *International Journal for the Philosophy of Religion* 43 (1998): 149–65.

5

A RESPONSE TO OPPY AND TO DAVEY AND CLIFTON

Coauthored with Alexander Pruss

We are gratified that our "A New Cosmological Argument"[1] has elicited some excellent discussion. First, there was Jerome Gellman's ingenious extension of our argument[2] to show that the necessary being that we proved to be the very intelligent and powerful creator of the universe is omnipotent and moreover essentially so, thereby helping to narrow the gap between this being and the God of traditional Western theism. There still remains a gap with respect to the goodness of this being that, given the severity of the inductive problem of evil, is not easily closed. Graham Oppy[3] and Kevin Davey and Rob Clifton,[4] however, have advanced objections to our argument. While not questioning its validity, they argue that the nontheist opponent of the argument is well within her rights to reject one of its premises, in particular the one that holds that for every true contingent proposition it is logically or conceptually possible that it has an explanation. First, the objections of Oppy will be considered and then those of Davey and Clifton.

I. OPPY

We advertised our new cosmological argument as being an improvement upon traditional cosmological arguments. Whereas they employ a strong version of the Principle of Sufficient Reason, namely,

> S-PSR. For every contingent proposition, p, if p, then there is an explanation for p.

our argument can make do with the following weaker version,

> W-PSR. For every contingent proposition, p, if p, then it is logically possible that there is an explanation for p.

thereby making it more difficult for the nontheist opponent to reject the PSR premise of our argument. It is Oppy's contention that our W-PSR is just as unacceptable to our nontheist opponent as was S-PSR, thus occasioning the same charge of being question begging as was leveled against cosmological arguments employing S-PSR. From this Oppy concludes that "their new argument is no better than the more familiar arguments which they take as their benchmark." (1)

The basis of Oppy's contention is that it is possible to deduce S-PSR from W-PSR, and he gives a very beautiful Fitch-style deduction (5). The following argument, which is due to Pruss, is about as simple and straightforward a deduction of S-PSR from W-PSR as one could hope for, and is essentially the same as the Oppy-Fitch proof.

THE PRUSS DEDUCTION

1. For every contingently true proposition, p, there is a possible world w that contains the propositions p, q, and that q explains p. (W-PSR.)
2. p is contingently true and there is no explanation of p. (Assumption for indirect proof.)
3. There is a possible world w that contains the propositions (p

and there is no explanation of p), q and that q explains (p and there is no explanation of p). (From 1 and 2.)
4. In w q explains p. (True because explanation distributes over a conjunction [is dissective in Oppy's terminology].)
5. In w proposition p both does and does not have an explanation.
6. It is not the case that p is contingently true and there is no explanation of p. (From 2–5 by indirect proof.)
7. It is not the case for any proposition p that p is contingently true and there is no explanation of p. (From 6.)

Oppy realizes that the fact that S-PSR is deducible from W-PSR is not alone sufficient to justify the charge of begging the question, for it could be contended that the deduction is far from being obvious. And that certainly seems to be the case for both Oppy's and Pruss's deductions. Oppy himself seems to grant this when he writes that "Fitch credits the argument to an anonymous referee for a paper which he sent to the *Journal of Symbolic Logic* in 1947, but never published.... It would be nice to know the identity of that referee" (endnote 5). Why would it be nice to know the identity of this referee if the argument were obvious or trivial? What counts as obvious or trivial is relative to the epistemic powers of an individual. An omniscient being would find every valid deductive argument to be such. We were negligent in not stating that our argument is not directed at such a reader, as well as those who have an Oppy-level understanding of logic. Whether an argument begs the question is relative to the epistemic circumstances of its opponent before the argument is given, not after it has been given.

This response will not silence Oppy, since he has more to say in support of his charge of begging the question. He claims that "once you understand W-PSR *properly*, you can see that it entails S-PSR; and S-PSR is something which non-theists have good reason to refuse to accept.... Those non-theists who were 'willing to grant W-PSR' before they heard the argument which Gale and Pruss give should then say that they didn't *fully* understand what it was to which they were giving assent" (8. Our italics). Herein Oppy is demanding that *proper* or *full* understanding be closed under deduction. This demand is completely contrived and has the unwanted consequence that every valid deductive argument, when its premises are *fully* understood, can rightly be charged with begging the question.

Although Oppy's demand is unacceptably strong, it still is true that to have an adequate understanding of a proposition one must know some of its entailment relationships. One would not understand, for example, the proposition that this is a material object unless one were prepared to deduce from it that this occupies space. (Please no Castenada-type counterexamples of the "I went to kiss Mary but her lips were not extended" sort!) But, plainly, one can understand that this is a material object without being aware of the very complex propositions that it entails within mereological theory.

No one has yet given a precise criterion for distinguishing between those entailment relations that are constitutive of understanding a given proposition and those that are not, since the concept of understanding is a pragmatic one and thus context sensitive. But this does not mean that we cannot identify clear-cut cases of someone understanding a proposition and those in which she does not. *Pace* what Oppy says on page 9, there is a very significant difference between the possibility premise of our argument—W-PSR—and the possibility premise of the S5 ontological argument—that it is possible that it is necessary that there exists a being who essentially has every divine perfection. There can be no doubt that one cannot understand the latter without understanding its nested modal operators, which requires in turn knowing that the proposition that it is necessary that it is possible that p entails that it is necessary that p. But it would be wildly implausible to say that one cannot understand W-PSR without knowing that it entails S-PSR; for, given that this entailment is far from obvious and was not discovered until recently, it has the consequence that before this discovery no one understood the proposition that every proposition possibly has an explanation, or any proposition that makes use of the concepts of possibility and explanation, for that matter. One can understand a proposition that uses a modal concept without knowing every theorem of modal logic, just as one can understand a proposition employing geometrical concepts without knowing every theorem in a system of geometry.

To understand a universally quantified proposition of the form

for all x, $F(x)$

it is sufficient to understand the formula $F(x)$ and to understand what the scope of the quantifier is. It is certainly not necessary to understand what every substitution instance $F(a)$ of $F(x)$ entails; otherwise, the categorical syllogism would always be question begging. In the case of the W-PSR, the formula $F(x)$ says that x possibly has an explanation and the quantification is over the class of all propositions. Now, we only get the implication from the W-PSR to the S-PSR if we consider some special substitution instances, such as the Big Conjunctive Contingent Fact (BCCF) in our original argument or the conjunctive proposition that p and p has no explanation in the Fitch-Pruss proof. But we can understand the force of $F(x)$ in general without explicitly considering these special substitution instances.

There is yet another ground on which, according to Oppy, the non-theist could be justified in rejecting W-PSR: "If non-theists have strong independent ground for refusing to accept theism, then the discovery that W-PSR entails theism will surely be good grounds for rejecting W-PSR" (8). Supposedly, the "strong independent ground" is not unique to the irreligious language-game; for, if it were, this would be language-game fideism since what is rationally accepable would be relative to a given language-game. Oppy does not go into what this "strong independent ground" might be, but no doubt it will be either an inductive argument from evil or a materialistic metaphysical theory. If it is the former, it is not a ground for rejecting W-PSR, since, *pace* Oppy, W-PSR, unless the admitted gap problem with our argument over the goodness of the designer-creator of the universe can be solved, does not entail theism. It is instead a ground for rejecting the claim that our necessarily existent designer-creator of the universe is omnibenevolent, and thus fails to be God. But if it is a metaphysical argument for materialism it does challenge our argument, since our designer-creator is a supernatural and thereby immaterial being. It is our contention, though it cannot be argued here, that any argument for materialism will employ premises that have less plausibility than does W-PSR.

There is another way in which materialism can be used to challenge our argument, which Oppy does explore, though very briefly (12). Our argument conceives of a possible world as a maximal compossible conjunction of abstract propositions and thus is ontologically committed to Platonic abstracta, which clashes with the nominalistic commitments of materialism. (A noun "that"-clause—"that Mary is baking pies"—refers to something that cannot be located in space or time, unlike Mary's baking pies.) Oppy certainly is right that materialism, with its denial of nonspatiotemporal objects, be they Platonic abstracta or immaterial persons, is a challenge to our argument. Again, we are prepared to argue that any argument for nominalism, such as an adverbial, cognate accusative or paratactic account of indirect discourse, employs premises that are less plausible than W-PSR. Furthermore, it is not clear that our argument could not accommodate a nominalistic rendering of propositions. There still would be the actual world's Big Conjunctive Contingent Fact, only it would be more impoverished than the one based on a realist theory of proposition, for whereas the latter thinks there are many things that are not said, the nominalist is committed to denying that there are any propositions that do not actually get expressed or thought.

Oppy also raises the problem of what an atomic proposition is—a really nasty problem—because we say that the actual world's Big Conjunctive Contingent Fact is a maximal compossible conjunction of propositions, the latter supposedly being atomic ones. For the purpose of our argument we can accept an account of atomicity that is relativized to a given language or context of inquiry. A singular positive proposition counts as atomic if it either is not further analyzable relative to a given language or does not require any further analysis for the purpose for which it is being used in some inquiry.

II. DAVEY AND CLIFTON

The first objection of Davey and Clifton (hereafter DC) is that there is no Big Conjunctive Contingent Fact, and thus our argument cannot get started for lack of a suitable explanatory target. In fact, DC attempt to produce a logical counterexample to the W-PSR.

The DC counterexample proceeds as follows. If p is a proposition, then let $E(p)$ be the proposition that p has an explanation. The W-PSR then states that for all contingent p, if p is true, then possibly $E(p)$. Now some formulae, such as the infinite formula

$$1=1 \text{ and } (1=1 \text{ and } (1=1 \text{ and } (1=1 \text{ and } (1=1 \ldots))))$$

figure as proper subformulae of themselves. In this example, the second conjunct is itself the same as the whole formula.

Now let a^* be the conjunction of all contingent true propositions p such that p is not a proper subformula of itself. Since the conjunction of contingent true propositions is contingently true, a^* is contingently true. According to the W-PSR, thus, possibly $E(a^*)$. But now we get a contradiction. Either $E(a^*)$ is a proper subformula of itself or not. If $E(a^*)$ is a proper subformula of itself, then $E(a^*)$ must in fact be a subformula, proper or not, of a^*, since the only proper subformulae of $E(a^*)$ are the subformulae of a^*. In fact, because $E(a^*)$ is not itself a conjunction, it follows that $E(a^*)$ must be a subformula of one of the conjuncts, say p, of a^*. But p is a subformula of a^* and hence a proper subformula of $E(a^*)$. Therefore, p is a proper subformula of $E(a^*)$, which in turn is a subformula of p, hence p is a proper subformula of p. But if p is a proper subformula of p then it is not one of the conjuncts of a^*, and hence we get the absurdity that p is both a conjunct of a^* and not a conjunct of a^*. On the other hand, if $E(a^*)$ is not a proper subformula of itself, it will be one of the conjuncts of a^*, and hence will be a proper subformula of itself, which is absurd. Thus, whether $E(a^*)$ is a proper subformula of itself or not, a contradiction ensues.

However, there is a crucial premise in this argument, namely, that a^* is a proposition. If a^* is not a proposition, then the W-PSR will not apply to it. In fact, a^* is not a proposition. For any proposition p, let $T(p)$ be the proposition that p is true. Suppose that a^* is a proposition. Then, a^* entails $T(a^*)$. But now $T(a^*)$ is a proper subformula of itself or not, and exactly the same argument as in the previous paragraph but with "T" in place of "E" shows that a contradiction ensues in either case. Therefore, a^* is not a proposition, and hence is not a counterexample to the W-PSR.

DC, however, explicitly say that if the BCCF is a proposition, so will a^* be. For, the BCCF is the conjunction of all contingent true propositions (minus truth-functional redundancies) and if the conjunction of all contingent true propositions is a proposition, the subconjunction of all those that are not subformulae of themselves will also be a proposition. However, the collection of all contingent true propositions is not a set. This follows from the fact shown by Pruss that the collection of all possible worlds does not have an upper cardinality bound.[5] But if the collection of all contingent true propositions is not a set, why should we think that we can blithely form a subcollection of all of these propositions that are not proper subformulae of themselves, and then form a conjunction of that supposedly existing subcollection? After all, the formation of subcollections can be problematic when dealing with nonsets.

However, DC can make the following response. Once one has admitted that there are some properties P of propositions, e.g., *being contingently true and not a subformula of itself*, such that there is no conjunction of all propositions having P, why should one think there is a conjunction of all propositions having the property of *being contingently true*? One answer to be made here is that a given candidate for a proposition should be innocent until proven guilty. We have proved above, relying on DC's own argument, that the conjunction of all contingent true propositions that are no subformulae of themselves is guilty, that is, is not a proposition. But DC have not offered any paradox starting merely with the BCCF, and so the BCCF is still innocent.

But even if these answers to the DC objection fail, as DC themselves note, we can still get all we need by restricting the propositions making up the BCCF. How exactly we would do that would depend on ontological issues. For instance, if one's ontology were one that included true atomic propositions, then we might let BCCF* be the conjunction of all of the following:

- all true contingent atomic propositions,
- a "that's all clause" that says that any true contingent atomic proposition is one of these ones (this clause will involve an infinite disjunction such as in: "for all p, if p is a true contingent atomic proposition then p is a_1 or a_2 or..."),

- all true propositions appearing in the explananda of basic propositions or of conjunctions thereof,
- all true basic propositions reporting causal relations,
- a "that's all clause" that says that all the actual explanatory relations supervene on the facts reported in the above conjuncts.

Assuming there are enough atomic propositions to individuate worlds, we could then run our whole argument with BCCF* in place of BCCF, making any other changes that might be needed, and perhaps throwing in some other conjuncts should we need them.

The next objection of DC is a very profound one that pushes us against the wall. Their strategy is to find a proposition that is strongly incompatible with W-PSR, in that if either is true in any possible world the other is true none, and which is at least as plausible a candidate for being logically possible as is W-PSR. Their candidate for such a proposition is that there is a contingent proposition that lacks an explanation in the actual world. "W-PSR without restriction runs counter to other modal intuitions at least as deeply entrenched as those concerning possible explanations about cosmology and cats. Consider events which are taken to be genuinely random, such as the flip of a coin that comes up heads, or a quantum measurement of an electron that returns a value of 'spin up'. Our intuitions suggest it is possible that the specific results of these experiments cannot be explained" in the actual world (5). They could have just as well picked out any contingently true proposition that in fact has an explanation and contended that it nevertheless is at least logically possible that it lack an explanation, that is, that there is some possible world in which it is true and has no explanation in that world.

That it is logically possible for there to be a contingent proposition that has no explanation is strongly incompatible with W-PSR, the reason being that W-PSR, given it entails S-PSR, entails that in no possible world is there a contingently true proposition that has no explanation in that world. This clash puts us in a bind, for many philosophers are initially inclined to accept both modal intuitions. Are there any grounds for choosing between them, for showing that one of them is more creditable than the other? The strategy that will be adopted for breaking this tie is to show that one of the two rival modal intuitions coheres better with another of our background modal intuitions.

To begin with, our belief in W-PSR coheres better with our proclivity to seek an explanation for any contingently true proposition. That we seek such an explanation shows that we probably do accept W-PSR, for we would not be likely to seek an explanation if we did not believe that it is at least logically possible that there is one. Second, we know what it is like to verify that a given proposition has an explanation, namely, by discovering an explanation for it, but we do not know what it is like to verify that a given proposition does not have an explanation: negative facts are notoriously difficult to verify. It is beside the point to respond that we know how to falsify the latter but not the former, since a proposition's truth-conditions are directly tied to its conditions of verification, not those for its falsification. Thirdly, observe the deep resistance of scientists like Einstein to the idea that some contingent events do not have an explanation. This deep resistance adds fuel to the idea that the possibility of something not having an explanation is more murky than the possibility of its having an explanation. These three considerations lend credence to the claim that, in the epistemic order, W-PSR is more deeply entrenched than is the DC claim that it is possible that a given contingent proposition has no explanation. From this conclusion it is reasonable to infer that, in the logical or conceptual order, W-PSR is a better candidate than is the DC proposition for being possible. For our only access to logical or conceptual modalities is through epistemic ones. To be sure, we cannot rest content with our original modal intuitions, since they often prove to be inadequate upon further inquiry. But after we have inquired into a modal issue as best we can, what else can we do but accept the modal intuition that emerges victorious? The best we can do is the best we can do.

DC has a response to this. They might, just for the sake of argument, concede that for any given contingently true "atomic" proposition it is possible that it have an explanation but deny that this holds for a world's Big Conjunctive Contingent Fact, call it p. There is an epistemic argument to show that it is logically possible that W-PSR applies to this fact.

THE EPISTEMIC ARGUMENT

1. It is logically necessary that (God exists ... there is an explanation for p). (A necessary truth.)
2. It is epistemically possible that God exists. (Premise.)
3. It is epistemically possible that there is an explanation for p (From 1 and 2 by a modalized version of modus ponens.)

And, given that it is reasonable to derive logical or conceptual modalities from epistemic ones after we have done the best we can in investigating the matter, it is reasonable to infer from 3 that

4. It is logically possible that there is an explanation for p.

DC cannot give a parallel epistemic argument for the proposition that it is logically possible that there is no explanation for p, such as:

1A. It is logically necessary that (God does not exist ... there is no explanation for p);
2A. It is epistemically possible that God does not exist;
3A. It is epistemically possible that there is no explanation for p.

For it is obvious that 1A is false, since p could have an explanation even if God were to not exist. This could be the case if the universe reported by p were an horrendous one, thereby showing that its designer-creator falls far short of being God.

But this does not put an end to the mischief that DC can create for our argument. They have a clever refutation by parody of the Pruss deduction of S-PSR from W-PSR (5–6). They give the same deduction that Pruss did, only they replace its "explains" with "someone truly believes" and thereby deduce from the proposition that for every contingently true proposition, p, it is possible that someone truly believes p the proposition that for every contingently true proposition, p, someone truly believes p. Obviously, we shouldn't be able to deduce the latter from the former; and thus, by parallel reasoning, neither should we be able to deduce the proposition that for every contingently true proposition, p, there is an explanation of p from the proposition that for every contingently true proposition, p, there is an explanation for p.

This clever parody refutation, however, fails because of destructive disanalogies between "explains" and "truly believes." In the first place, for those who do not believe that there is a necessarily existent person, there is an obvious counterexample to their initial premise in their deduction that for every contingently true proposition p it is possible that someone truly believes p—the proposition that there are no believers—but there is no obvious counterexample to W-PSR. This proposition could be true but it is impossible that someone truly believe that there are no believers. This is because the sentence, "There are no believers," is pragmatically self-falsifying in the sense that necessarily every intentional tokening of it expresses a contingently false proposition. There is another damning disanalogy between "truly believes" and explains." Whereas it is prima facie possible that there is an explanation for there being no explanation of some contingently true proposition, q, it is not possible that someone truly believes that no one truly believes a contingently true proposition, q. The former would be true if there is an explanation based on the nomic structure of the universe as to why q lacks an explanation. Because of this disanalogy, it is illegitimate to subsitute "truly believes" for "explains" in the Pruss deduction.

There is yet another analogically based objection to accepting W-PSR. Appeal is made to Aristotelian essentialism in which it is up to science to discover through inquiry what properties are essential to a given kind of entity (6). Herein we cannot trust our scientifically untutored modal intuitions as to whether it is possible for an individual of this kind to have (or not have) a certain property, for we lack an adequate epistemic ground for such an intuition. A person who is ignorant of chemistry does not have epistemic grounds for determining whether or not it is possible for this piece of gold to have a certain atomic weight. DC suggests that analogously we lack adequate epistemic grounds for determining whether it is or is not possible for the actual world's Big Conjunctive Contingent Fact to have an explanation, as well as for whether every true contingent proposition possibly has an explanation.

Again, DC's analogically based objection suffers from a crucial disanalogy. In the case of Aristotelian essential properties, it is science that is to determine what properties are essential to a certain type of entity. But patently it is not the prerogative of science to determine the sort of modal issues that enter into our argument, such as whether it is possible that every contingently true proposition, including the actual world's Big Conjunctive Contingent Fact, possibly has an explanation.

DC concludes on a note of scepticism about whether W-PSR is true based on the fact that it is so radically different from the contingent conjuncts that comprise it. "The sceptic can quite correctly suggest that GP [Gale and Pruss] have applied W-PSR to cases too different from those that motivated him originally to assent to it" (7). This sceptical doubt has little force unless it can be backed up with some Kantian-type paralogism that results from making a collective use of a principle to the totality that admittedly has a legitimate distributive use. DC attempted to show that a paralogism of reason breaks out when we form the Big Conjunctive Contingent Fact for a world, but that effort was shown to fail. We eagerly await the production of a good such paralogism of reason, but until it is produced we shall not lose any sleep over it.

NOTES

1. "A New Cosmological Argument," *Religious Studies* 35 (1999): 461–76.
2. Jerome Gellman, "Prospects for a Sound Stage-3 of Cosmological Arguments," *Religious Studies* 36 (2000): 195–201.
3. "On 'A New Cosmological Argument'," *Religious Studies* 36 (2000): 345–53.
4. "Insufficient Reason in the 'New Cosmolological Argument'," *Religious Studies* 37 (2001): 485–90.
5. *Technical Note:* To see this implication, suppose for a reductio that there is a set S of all contingent true propositions, and let n be the cardinality of S. Then, for any world w, let $N(w)$ be the subset of S containing all the propositions of S that are false at w. Thus, $N(w)$ is the set of all propositions false at w but true at the actual world. Observe that if $w_1 \uparrow w_2$ then $N(w_1) \uparrow N(w_2)$. To see this, suppose that $w_1 \uparrow w_2$. First assume w_1 is the actual world. Then $N(w_1)$ is the

empty set while $N(w_2)$ is not, since $N(w_2)$ contains at least the proposition that w_2 is nonactual, which is false at w_2 but true at w_1 and hence actually true. Thus, $N(w_1) \uparrow N(w_2)$. Now, suppose w_1 is not the actual world. Then, the proposition that w_1 is nonactual is false at w_1, true at the actual world, and true at w_2. Hence, the proposition that w_1 is nonactual is a member of $N(w_1)$ but not of $N(w_2)$, so that $N(w_1) \uparrow N(w_2)$. Therefore, if $w_1 \uparrow w_2$ then $N(w_1) \uparrow N(w_2)$. But $N(w)$ is always a subset of S. This shows that the number of worlds cannot exceed the number 2^u of subsets of S, which contradicts the fact that there is no upper cardinality bound on the number of worlds (see Alexander R. Pruss, "The Cardinality Objection to David Lewis's Modal Realism," *Philosophical Studies* 104 [2001]: 167–76).

6

THE ECUMENICALISM OF WILLIAM JAMES

What the world desperately needs now, given that it is about to be blown apart by warring exclusivist religious beliefs, is a good shot of just the sort of ecumenicalism that William James's *The Varieties of Religious Experience* delivers so effectively.[1] Ecumenicalism is not only the ultimate message of this book but is of the very warp and woof of William James's philosophy as a whole, finding support in its most basic doctrines and tenets. At the bottom of the pyramid of supporting doctrines is that of a moral democracy based on what is revealed when we enter most intimately into the conscious interiors both of ourselves and of others through an I-Thou experience. This, in turn, supports a democratic metaphysics, as well as the Sentiment of Rationality. The Will-to-Believe can be extended in a thoroughly Jamesian manner to show that we are morally forbidden from having nonecumenical exclusivist religious beliefs. This, in turn, supplies a powerful motive to seek to discover a vital common denominator among the great extant religions, which task is assigned to the Science of Religions in *Varieties*, this being the ultimate culmination of James's quest for ecumenicalism. Although James eschewed writing philosophy in a systematic way, these doctrines will be shown to be a highly integrated and effective defense of ecumenicalism.[2]

I. THE QUEST FOR INTIMACY

William James's distinction between the tough- and tender-minded set the stage for the subsequent schism in the twentieth century between respectively analytic and phenomenological-existential philosophers. The former take the stance of an external observer intent on giving an objective account of reality, in contrast to the latter who attempt to achieve intimacy with reality by entering into its interiors through acts of sympathetic intuition. If reality were a delicatessen with a staggering variety of enticing goodies laid out in its glass cases, the externalist would analyze the composition of the various cold cuts, as might an inspector for the department of health—"This corned beef has a 5 percent phosphate content"—but the internalist would want to achieve a deep existential appreciation of them by eating them. James, being the ultimate inside man, wanted to eat the universe at large and everything in it. His philosophy is a desperate quest for intimacy that begins with the introspection of his own consciousness and then attempts to achieve a similar sort of intimacy with the conscious interiors of *everything* else, which includes other persons, both natural and supernatural, as well as animals and fishes, even the universe at large. If James were to have placed an ad in the Personals it would have read:

> Harvard University professor. Equally comfortable in a Norfolk jacket or a woodsman's outfit, doing science or leading the morally strenuous life. Desperately seeking to penetrate to the inner consciousness of other beings: animals and fish okay. No kooks please.

Given how threatened James's contemporaries felt by the dehumanized, impersonal world depicted by science, over half of Boston, and all of Cambridge, would have responded to the ad.

James's quest for intimacy begins with the introspection of his own psyche since

> the only form of thing we directly encounter...is our own personal life. The only complete category of our thinking...is the category of personality, every other category being one of the abstract elements of that. And this systematic denial on Science's part of personality as a condition of events, this rigorous belief that in its own essential and innermost nature our world is a strictly impersonal world, may...be the very defect that our descendants will be most surprised at in our own boasted Science. (EPR 136)

This passage reveals the most fundamental assumption of James's philosophy—that the true nature of reality is to be ascertained not through the employment of symbols or concepts but rather through personal experience. "So long as we deal with the cosmic and the general [as does Science], we deal only with the symbols of reality, but as soon as we deal with private and personal phenomena as such, we deal with realities in the completest sense of the term" (VRE 393). "Individuality is founded in feeling; and the recesses of feeling, the darker, blinder strata of character, are the only places in the world in which we catch real fact in the making, and directly perceive how events happen, and how work is actually done"(VRE 395).

Through introspective analysis James discovers that he is a bundle of different selves competing with each other for actualization:

> I am often confronted by the necessity of standing by one of my empirical selves and relinquishing the rest. Not that I would not, if I could, be both handsome and fat and well dressed, and a great athlete, and make a million a year, be a wit, a *bon-vivant*, and a lady killer, as well as a philosopher; a philanthropist, statesman, warrior, and African explorer, as well as a "tone-poet" and saint...But to make any one of them actual, the rest more or less be suppressed. (PP 295)

More serious than the lack of time and opportunity to actualize all these selves is that there are serious conflicts between their different perspectives or takes on what the world is like. His scientific self, for example, accepts determinism, epiphenomenalism, and the bifurcation between man and nature, but his moral-agent self believes that there are undetermined acts of spiritual causation in a world that has human meaning. Furthermore, whereas both selves use concepts as teleological instruments for gaining power to control the world, his mystical self eschews concepts altogether so as to penetrate to the inner core of a cotton-candyish reality through an act of sympathetic intuition. How James neutralized these intra-personal conflicts will be considered shortly.

The next challenge to James's quest for intimacy is to penetrate to the conscious interiors of other beings through a type of I-Thou experience, the outcome of which is that the sort of wondrous complexity that he finds within himself characterizes reality at large. Through an act of sympathetic intuition Jack realizes his beloved Jill concretely, to use James's beautiful example from "What Makes a Life Significant" (TT 151). He comes to realize what it is like to be Jill. Just how this I-Thouing of another person occurs is best left to Tin Pan Alley: "I Took One Look at You and Zing Went the Strings of My Heart," "It's Magic," "I've Got You Under My Skin," "You're My Everything." James's romanticism comes to the fore in his ecstatic descriptions of the marvelous wondrousness of the inner life that one grasps through the I-Thou experience of another. He speaks of its "vital secrets, "zest," excitement," mysterious inwards," and "mysterious sensorial life" (TT 132, 135, 137, 149), along with its "acutest internality" and "violent thrills of life" (ERM 99). To miss the joy of this inner consciousness in another person is to miss all, for it is this that makes her life significant, provided it is coupled with the requisite strength of character to see to it that it gets properly expressed in her overt behavior. James prizes this inner life so highly that he holds that "in every being that is real there is something external to, and sacred from, the grasp of every other" (WB 111).

II. A MORAL DEMOCRACY

James deduces from this "sacredness" of an individual's inner life a principle of moral democracy enjoining us to respect other persons, even nations, and adopt a live-and-let-live, hands-off policy. This is a deontological moral principle and clashes with the exclusively consequentialist casuistic rule of "The Moral Philosopher and the Moral Life" that requires us always to act so as to maximize desire-satisfaction over desire-dissatisfaction (WB 155). He calls this "respect for the sacredness of individuality...the outward tolerance of whatever is not itself intolerant." James did not stop with I-thouing his fellow humans. He even wanted to I-Thou the beasts and fishes, as well as nature. In a letter of 1873 he writes: "Sight of elephants and tigers at Barnum's menagerie whose existence, so individual and peculiar, yet stands there, so intensely and vividly real, as much as one's own, so that one feels again poignantly the unfathomableness of ontology, supposing ontology to be at all."[3] Not to slight the fishes, in a letter of 1899 to his wife, he says: "four cuttle-fish in the Aquarium. I wish we had one of them for a child—such flexible intensity of life in a form so inaccessible to our sympathy."[4]

James wanted to go all the way and I-Thou the entire universe, as nature mystics have traditionally done. James is personalizing the universe when he writes: "The Universe is no longer a mere *it* to us, but a *Thou*, if we are religious; and any relation that may be possible from person to person might be possible here" (WB 31). Taking a religious stance to the world "changes the dead blank *it* of the world into a living *thou*, with whom the whole man may have dealings" (WB 101). Whereas the I-Thouing of other persons leads to a deontological moral democracy, the I-Thouing of the universe supports an ecological doctrine of the reverence for nature or natural piety. Ecumenicalism, therefore, applies across the board, giving equal legitimacy and value to *every* individual's inner life and perspective.

III. A DEMOCRATIC ONTOLOGY

James wants to have a democratic ontology that will be supportive of this ecumenicalism by giving equal reality to all of these many different ways of depicting or experiencing reality. Since each of them finds expression in the way in which one of his many selves experiences the world, the problem is how is achieve an ontological ecumenicalism among the world-views of his many selves. This he achieves by his doctrine of ontological relativism. It has the interests of each of his many selves directed to its own world of interrelated objects, among which are the worlds of scientific theoretical entities, the medium-sized dry goods of common sense, platonic heavens of abstracta, and fictional and mythical worlds. "*Every object we think of gets at least referred to one world or another.* ... It settles into our belief as a common-sense object, a scientific object, an abstract object, a mythological object, an object of someone's mistaken conception, or a madman's object" (PP 922). There is a democratic equality among these worlds, no one of them winning the coveted title of "*the* actual world *simpliciter*" for there is no such title to be won. For what qualifies one of these worlds as the actual world is relative to the passing interests and needs of persons. "Reality means simply relation to our emotional and active life. This is the only sense the world ever has in the mouths of practical men. In this sense, whatever excites and stimulates our interest is real" (PP 924–25). "Actuality" is not the one-place predicate that it grammatically appears to be but rather is the disguised three-place predicate, "World x is actual (real, existent) for person y at time t." Through this ontological relativism James gives carte blanche to each of his selves to see the light of day, provided that they democratically take turns with the other selves thereby providing an ecumenical solution to the apparent clash between these many selves. The result of this taking-turns solution is a kind of temporal schizophrenia: on weekdays from nine to five I am scientist and in the evenings I lead the morally strenuous life; on weekends I'm a mystic.

The doctrine of ontological relativism makes a prominent appearance in *Varieties*:

> The experiences which we have been studying during this hour (and a great many other kinds of religious experiences are like them) plainly show the universe to be a more many-sided affair than any sect, even the scientific sect, allows for. What, in the end, are all our verifications but experiences that agree with more or less isolated systems of ideas (conceptual systems) that our minds have framed? But why in the name of common sense need we assume that only

> one such system of ideas can be true? The obvious outcome of our total experience is that the world can be handled according to many systems of ideas, and is so handled by different men, and will each time give some characteristic kind of profit, for which he cares, to the handler, while at the same time some other kind of profit has to be omitted or postponed. (VRE 105)

James's "conceptual systems" are the many "worlds" that are the objects of the different interests and needs of his many selves.

IV. THE SENTIMENT OF RATIONALITY

The ecumenicalism that is achieved by ontological relativism is reinforced by James's Sentiment of Rationality doctrine, which explains the ultimate parting of the ways among philosophers in terms of differences in their psychological make-up, their rival predilections as to what constitutes a rationally satisfying explanation. Some philosophers, for example, find an explanation rational when it reduces a subject matter to a collection of externally related atoms, whereas others want a unifying explanation that has these atoms lose their distinct identities by merging or fusing together. Just as no one of James's many selves could claim to have the absolute truth about the nature of reality, no philosophy can make this claim.

Psychological diversity not only makes for an irreducible pluralism in philosophy; it also does for the spiritual life:

> The whole outcome of these lectures will...be the emphasizing to your mind of the enormous diversities which the spiritual lives of different men exhibit. Their wants, their susceptibilities, and their capacities all vary and must be classed under different heads. The result is that we have really different types of religious experience. (VRE 94)

Given this diversity, James asks rhetorically, "Ought all men to have the same religion?...Are they so like in their inner needs that, for hard and soft, for proud and humble, for strenuous and lazy, for healthy-minded and despairing, exactly the same religious incentives are required?" (VRE 267). That these questions are rhetorical becomes manifest later when James answers, "'No' emphatically," to the questions "Ought it...to be assumed that the lives of all men should show identical religious elements?" and "Is the existence of so many religious types and sects and creeds regrettable" (VRE 384). Underlying James's ecumenical answer is his denial that there is an ideal man. "According to the empirical philosophy, however, all ideals are matters of relation" to our different interests and purposes (VRE 297).

The sort of psychologically based diversity among the religious lives and experiences of different persons also produces an irreducible diversity among the theologies and philosophies of religion that they develop:

> The logical reason of man operates...in this field of divinity exactly as it has always operated in love, or in patriotism, or in politics, or in any other of the wider affairs of life, in which our passions or our mystical intuition fix our beliefs beforehand. It finds argument for our conviction, for indeed it *has* to find them. It amplifies and defines our faith, and dignifies it; it cannot now secure it." (VRE 344–44)

One of the important grounds for the ultimate disagreements among theologies and philosophies of religion, as well as among philosophies in general, is differences in aesthetic predilections. People have a need to intellectualize their religious experiences, and the manner in which they do so will be based on aesthetic considerations. Although the scholastic theology of Cardinal Newman is not James's personal aesthetic cup of tea, he appreciates its aesthetic value for persons of a certain type of mindset:

> The eloquent passage in which Newman enumerates [the attributes of the deity] puts us on the tract of it. Intoning them as he would intone a cathedral service, he shows how high is their aesthetic value. It enriches our bare piety to carry these exalted and mysterious verbal additions just as it enriches a church to have an organ and old brasses, marbles and frescoes and stained windows. (VRE 361)

There is a counterpart in religion to the clash between the sentiments of atomism and monism in philosophy. "Although some persons aim most at intellectual purity and simplification, for others richness is the supreme imaginative requirement. When one's mind is strongly of this type, an individual religion will hardly serve the purpose" (VRE 362).

V. THE WILL TO BELIEVE

There is a more direct and forceful support for James's religious ecumenicalism than the ones that have so far been considered, all of which involved highly speculative considerations. It is based on an extended use of his famed doctrine of the Will to Believe. Although James did not himself make this extension, he supplied all of the premises that are needed for it. The basic idea of the Will to Believe is that one is morally permitted to believe (or retain a belief in) an epistemically nonwarranted proposition when doing so will help to produce good consequences overall, be they understood deontologically or in terms of James's casuistic rule.[5] Speaking about believing at will is elliptical for intentionally doing that which will help to self-induce (or retain) a belief (such as acting as if you believe), since one cannot, except in rare cases, believe at will, voluntarily, on purpose. Whereas James's Will to Believe doctrine concerns only cases in which one is morally *permitted* to believe (or continue believing) without sufficient epistemic warrant, it quite plausibly can be extended to cases in which one is morally *forbidden* to believe (or continue believing) without sufficient epistemic warrant, namely, cases in which believing (or continuing to believe) without sufficient epistemic warrant will have bad consequences overall. It will be shown that James firmly believed that the case of an exclusivist religious belief is a suitable target for this extended version of the Will to Believe, in which an exclusivist religious belief is one that entails that *all* religious creeds other than the one of which it is a creedal part are mistaken in some of their fundamental creedal beliefs. An example of such a belief is that God is triune and that only those who believe this will find salvation. For reasons that will become manifest, I will restrict the discussion to exclusivist religious beliefs that get publicly promulgated, which is not much of a restriction since almost invariably they do.

The following is an extended Will to Believe–type argument for one being morally forbidden to believe (or continue to believe) an exclusivist religious proposition.

A WILL TO BELIEVE ARGUMENT AGAINST RELIGIOUS EXCLUSIVISM

1. For any proposition, p, if one cannot show that p is epistemically warranted and the consequences of believing p are worse than they would have been if one were not to have believed p, then one morally ought not to believe p. (Premise.)
2. An exclusivist religious proposition cannot be shown to be epistemically warranted. (Premise.)
3. The consequences of believing an exclusivist religious proposition are worse than they would have been if one were not to have believed it. (Premise.)
4. One morally ought not to be believe an exclusivist religious proposition. (From 1, 2, and 3 by modus ponens and universal instantiation.)

This hardly is a decisive argument. Its premises call for further clarification and support.

The use of "epistemically warranted" in premise 1 and 2, for the sake of argument, will recognize two species of epistemic warrant. One is the familiar notion of Lockeian *evidential warrant* and the other the reformed epistemology's notion of *basic warrant*, according to which a belief is basically warranted if it is not based on or inferred from another belief and results from the proper functioning of one's cognitive faculties in the right kind of epistemic environment according to a design plan successfully aimed at truth. The very same arguments that James gave for our being morally permitted, in certain special circumstances, to believe upon inadequate epistemic warrant apply mutatis mutandis to 1 and will not be repeated here.

Premise 2 is highly controversial, since there are those, such as Richard Swinburne, who argue that exclusivist Christian beliefs are evidentially warranted. It is the purpose of the chapter on "Philosophy" in *Varieties* to show that this isn't so. Although this chapter's attack on natural theology is much too quick and shoddy, I believe that it can be strengthened and extended so as to work. Contemporary reformed epistemologists, such as Alvin Plantinga, argue only that it is possible that we have basic warrant for believing an exclusivist religious proposition, not that we actually have. To prove the latter requires showing that God exists and has instilled in us a *sensus divinitatis* as part of our original cognitive equipment and directly causes beliefs in us about the great things of the Gospel through the internal instigation of the Holy Spirit.

Premise 3 does not admit of any straightforward verification. In the first place, it is very difficult, if not impossible, to total up the goods and evils that have actually resulted from exclusivist religious beliefs; however, given that most of the evils in the present world result from religious exclusivism, it intuitively seems that the evils of such beliefs outweigh the goods. I say "intuitively" because we are unable to quantify good and evil. But even if the evils "outweigh" the goods, this does not settle the issue in favor of 3; for we might have a Hobson's Choice with respect to having an exclusivist religious belief, the consequences of each alternative being overall bad. Thus, we must consider what would have happened in the counterfactual situation in which there are no exclusivist religious beliefs. Would things have gone better or worse than they did in the actual world? Again, a strain is put on our verificatory capacities.

James would not be phased by these verificatory complications, since he makes it quite clear in *Varieties* that he fully and passionately accepts premise 3. In fact, James's basic intention in writing the *Varieties*, to show that the essence of religion consists in personal religious experiences rather than in religious institutions and their creeds, is driven by his abhorrence of what results from institutionalized exclusivist religions, as is amply borne out by the following quotations:

> Certainly the unhesitating and unreasoning way in which we feel that we must inflict our Civilization upon "lower" races, by means of Hotchkiss guns, etc., reminds one of nothing so much as of the early spirit of Islam spreading its religion by the sword. (VRE 69)

> A survey of history shows us that, as a rule, religious geniuses attract disciples, and produce groups of sympathizers. When these groups get strong enough to "organize" themselves, they become ecclesiastical institutions with corporate ambitions of their own. The spirit of politics and the lust of dogmatic rule are then apt to enter and to contaminate the originally innocent thing; so that when we hear the word "religion" nowadays, we think inevitably of some "church" or other; and to some persons the word "church" suggests so much hypocrisy and tyranny and meanness and tenacity of superstition that in a wholesale undiscerning way they glory in saying that they are "down" on religion altogether. (VRE 268–69)

James locates the cause of this institutional exclusivizing and dogmatizing what were originally vital personal religious experiences in our "spirit of corporate dominion." And when this is combined with our "spirit of dogmatic dominion" it leads to horrible evils, such as

> the baiting of Jews, the hunting of Albigenses and Waldenses, the stoning of Quakers and ducking of Methodists, the murdering of Mormons and the massacring of Armenians, [which] express much rather that aboriginal human neophobia, that pugnacity of which we all share the vestiges, and that inborn hatred of the alien and of excentric and non-conforming men as aliens, than they express the positive piety of the various perpetrators. Piety is the mask, the inner force is tribal instinct. (VRE 271)

It should now be clear why my Will to Believe argument against exclusivist religious beliefs was restricted to those that get publicly promulgated, for it is through their publicity that repressive, exclusivist religions get founded.

VI. THE SCIENCE OF RELIGIONS

The stage is now set for James to develop a viable ecumenical alternative to exclusivist religions. This is accomplished through his science of religions, which is an empirical study of the great extant religions for the purpose of extracting from them a significant common denominator. James is not interested in off-beat cults or merely possible religions, for they have not passed the pragmatic test of time. All too often ecumenical efforts suffer shipwreck on either the Charybdis of being contentfully too thin or the Scylla of being contentfully too thick and thereby giving pride of place to some pet religion. It will be shown that James manages to steer a viable course between these undesirable extremes.

Initially, it appears as if he passes too close to the contentless Scylla. There are some unsettling, careless remarks that make it appear as if James's ecumenicalism is to suffer the same disastrous fate as does John Hick's, which is based on an unknowable and indescribable *ding an sich* as the common denominator among religions. This is disastrous because it strips religious belief of all content and winds up being indistinguishable from atheism. James expounds Kant's doctrine that religious ideas, although devoid of any significance, are pragmatically meaningful in our moral life. He concludes this exposition by saying that "we have the strange phenomenon, as Kant assures us, of a mind believing with all its strength in the real presence of a set of things of no one of which it can form any notion whatever" (VRE 53). Two pages later, James characterizes the religious feeling as "*a feeling of objective presence*," and then goes on to add that "so far as religious conceptions were able to touch this reality-feeling, they would be believed in spite of criticism, even though they might be so vague and remote as to be almost unimaginable, even though they might be such non-entities in point of *whatness* as Kant makes the objects of his moral theology to be" (VRE 55). In spite of James's slide from "can form no notion whatever" to the last quotation's weaker "almost unimaginable," James seems to give in too much to Kant.

But when James actually gets down to the task of extracting his religious common denominator, he does manage to give a reasonable amount of positive content to religious belief, so much so that he comes close to giving too much content and thus wrecking on the Charybdis of provincialism. He describes himself as engaged in "a laborious attempt to extract from the privacies of religious experience some general facts which can be defined in formulas upon which everybody may agree" (VRE). This will have a desirable ecumenical upshot, since it "can offer mediation between different believers, and help to bring about consensus of opinion" (VRE 359. See also 402.). The contentful, as contrasted with psychological, common denominator that James discovers is summarized as follows:

1. That the visible world is part of a more spiritual universe from which it draws its chief significance;
2. That union or harmonious relation with that higher universe is our true end;
3. That prayer ... is a process wherein ... spiritual energy flows in and produces effects ... within the phenomenal world. (VRE 382)

James then attempts to supply further content to the conception of the "more spiritual" or "higher" universe, also called the "More." The aim is to find a generic account of the More that will be neutral between rival "over-beliefs" or philosophical theories about its nature. Among the many contentful things James says about the More is that it is a supernatural spiritual entity that is "of the same quality with our own higher self" (VRE 401). Furthermore, it has "exteriority" to us (VRE 400) but we can achieve "union with it" (VRE 402).

But just how exterior is it and how complete is our union with it? James is well aware that monistic and dualistic mystics give incompatible answers to these question, the former, unlike the latter, denying that there is any numerical distinction between the subject and object of a mystical experience. "Religious mysticism ... is much less unanimous than I have allowed.... It is dualistic in Sankhya, and monistic in Vedanta philosophy" (VRE 336–37). James attributes these differences to the "various theologies and various personal temperaments" of the individual mystics (VRE 401), though he personally favors the dualistic over-belief about what mystical experiences reveal.

More can be done to achieve ecumenical harmony between individuals and religions holding apparently incompatible over-beliefs. One way James does this is to assert that you must look to feelings and the conduct as being the very essence of religion and then point out that "the feelings ... and the conduct ... are almost always that same, for Stoic, Christian, and Buddhist saints are practically indistinguishable in their lives" (VRE 397). This is supposed to show that their over-belief differences are not of much moment and should not be allowed to be divisive. Echoing the very words by which he described his moral democracy—"the outward tolerance of whatever is not itself intolerant"—we should treat rival over-beliefs "with tenderness and tolerance so long as they are not intolerant themselves" (VRE 405).

There is another strategy for neutralizing the clash between rival over-beliefs that harks back to that well-known group of blind men simultaneously feeling up the same elephant and making apparently conflicting claims about the nature of the beast, such as would be made by the one who has him by the balls and the one who has him by the trunk, and so on. One and the same More can appear under different guises to differently circumstanced individuals. Each of their descriptions of it can be true as far as it goes, provided that it is not intolerant by denying some modicum of truth to all the other descriptions. Even though the analogy with the elephant limps on all four hoofs, I think something worthwhile can be made of this multiple-guises idea.

There is an apparent inconsistency in *The Varieties of Religious Experience* that I would like to neutralize, if possible. Briefly, it consists in an apparent clash between the underlying thesis of *Varieties*, that religious experience is the essence and life-blood of religion, and the claim that "the most interesting and valuable things about a man are usually his over-beliefs," an over-belief being a philosophical theory about the nature of the apparent object of a religious experience (VRE 405). Before an attempt is made to reconcile these apparently conflicting claims, it is necessary to bring this conflict into bold relief by expounding further on each of them.

By giving pride of place to religious experiences over religious institutions, with their creeds and theologies, *Varieties* supports a religious ecumenicalism that fits in with the overall ecumenical tenor of James's philosophy. Just as James, in *The Principles of Psychology*, refuses to give a privileged authority to the perspective of any one of his many selves, he refuses to make invidious ontological distinctions between the many worlds that are the objects of the interests and purposes of these selves. This democratic ontology reconciles the apparently conflicting perspectives taken by the moral agent, scientist, and mystic. The apparently conflicting revelations of different religious experiences, as for example between monistic and dualistic mystical experiences, admits of a similar type of ecumenical resolution. James's empirical science of religion attempts to extract a vital common denominator from the great extant religions. It is found to consist in three theses:

1. That the visible world is part of a more spiritual universe from which it draws its chief significance;
2. That union or harmonious relation with that higher universe is our true end;
3. That prayer or inner communion with the spirit thereof—be that spirit 'God' or 'law'—is a process wherein work is really done, and spiritual energy flows in and produces effects, either psychological or material, within the phenomenal world." (VRE 382)

An over-belief attempts to fill in the metaphysical details about the nature of this more spiritual universe. When these over-beliefs gain sufficient currency, they become embedded in the official creed of some religious institution. There is no doubt that James sees this as a great misfortune, since it is these institutionalized over-beliefs that create religious exclusivism, with all of its attendant horrors, as we clearly see in the world today. (See especially 270–71 of VRE.) There are two ways in which James defangs over-beliefs and thereby religious exclusivism. First, in the chapter on "Philosophy" he attacks the epistemic credentials of over-beliefs by attempting to show the impossibility of presenting good philosophical arguments concerning the existence and nature of God. Second, he claims that what really matters is one's feeling and conduct and people can agree in these respects although they have conflicting over-beliefs. "When we survey the whole field of religion, we find a great variety in the thoughts that have prevailed there; but the feelings on the one hand and the conduct on the other are almost always the same, for Stoic, Christian, and Buddhist saints are practically indistinguishable in their lives. The theories which Religion generates, being thus variable, are secondary; and if you wish to grasp her essence, you must look to the feelings and conduct as being the more constant elements" (VRE 397).

Given James's strong moral and philosophical motivation for de-emphasizing the importance and epistemic legitimacy of over-beliefs, it is surprising to find him suddenly saying that "the most interesting and valuable things about a man are usually his over-beliefs" (VRE 405). That a man's over-beliefs are usually the most *interesting* thing about him does not contradict James's claim that over-beliefs are of secondary importance or value in religion, since something could be interesting without being important or valuable. The consistency problem arises from James's claim that usually a man's over-beliefs are the most valuable thing about him.

How are these apparently conflicting claims to be reconciled? And reconciled they must be, since an interpretation that leaves an unresolved inconsistency in the text of a great philosopher is one of last resort. Probably the least satisfactory resolution is the one that holds James to be intentionally espousing inconsistent doctrines so as to stimulate his readers to think more deeply. This "solution" is not to be confused with one that interprets James's inconsistencies as his way of giving dialectical expression to the irreconcilable conflicting interests and needs of human beings. This particular inconsistency does not seem to be a case in point of this.

Dewey attributed James's inconsistencies to his "willingness to make concessions to his opponents in the hope of finding common ground beneath and to his large-minded indifference to minor details of his own former writings." Lovejoy saw them as due to his "enthusiasm and instinct for the effective and emphatic way of putting things," which led him to overstate a position, omitting the needed qualifications. The accounts given by Dewey and Lovejoy, at best, causally explain James's inconsistencies, but they fail to explain them away, in particular, the one in *Varieties*.

It also is surprising to find him saying "Although the religious question is primarily a question of life, of living or not living in the higher union which opens itself to us as a gift, yet the spiritual excitement in which the gift appears a real one will often fail to be aroused in an individual until certain particular intellectual beliefs or ideas which, as we say, come home to him, are touched. These ideas will thus be essential to that individual's religion—which is as much as to say that over-beliefs in various directions are absolutely indispensable, and that we should treat them with tenderness and tolerance so long as they are not intolerant themselves" (VRE 405).

On occasion, James charged critics who claimed to find an inconsistency in his philosophy, such as the lady whose doctoral dissertation attempted to unearth several of them, with failing to note the different contexts in which the apparently inconsistent claims were made. A case in point is his response (in footnote 10 of the 1904 "The Experience of Activity") to critics who claimed that he said inconsistent things about the nature of activity, espousing both naturalistic and supernatural views of it: "Single clauses in my writing, or sentences read out of their connexion, may possibly have been compatible with a transphenomenal principle of energy; but I defy anyone to show a single sentence, which taken with its context, should be naturally held to advocate that view." We should be suspicious of appeal to context, since experience has shown that it usually is the last refuge of a scoundrel. It is true that many of James's inconsistencies can be explained by differences in context, namely, the different audiences to whom he directed his inconsistent claims. For James, like a good barnstorming political candidate, wanted to please all of his constituents and often wasn't above playing both sides of the street so as to ingratiate himself with audiences that held conflicting beliefs. But this, again, gives only a causal explanation, not a reconciliation, of his conflicting remarks.

In correspondence, Felicitas Kraemer suggested that we interpret an over-belief in a broad, generic sense so that it includes not just metaphysical beliefs about the nature of the apparent object of mystical experience but in addition a "weltanschauung, vision, feeling for life, temper, attitude, and personal susceptibilities." Thus when James asserted the paramount importance of a person's over-beliefs he was thinking primarily about the latter type of philosophical beliefs, especially those that concern freedom and determinism. On this reading of "over-belief," there is no inconsistency in asserting that over-beliefs are of little importance to religion but are of importance in a person's life. Furthermore, James's ecumenicalism is not undermined by encouraging people to having philosophical beliefs about monism versus pluralism.

The problem with Kraemer's solution based on the generic interpretation of an overbelief, is that James initially introduces the term on p. 402 of *Varieties* as being a philosophical theory about the nature of the "more," which is defined as the apparent object of a mystical experience. This connection between an over-belief and the *more* gets retained on pp. 404–5. Herein an over-belief is only one among the many different species of philosophical beliefs that Kraemer mentions; and the fact that some of the latter species of belief are compatible with James's ecumenicalism does nothing to show that an over-belief is. Being a lion is not shown to be compatible with being noncarnivorous just because some other species of the genus animal are noncarnivorous. But in fairness to Kraemer's generic reading of over-belief, it needs to be pointed out that on pp. 407–8 James broadens the concept in the direction of her genus interpretation.

The following might be the best way to resolve the apparent inconsistency. The underlying thesis of *Varieties*—that over-beliefs are not important to *religion*—is not obviously inconsistent with the claim that over-beliefs are important to a man, since the subjects of these claims are different. Creedal beliefs, which include over-beliefs in the narrow sense, *are* the least important thing about religion, and, moreover, ought to be since they invariably lead to religious fanaticism with all of its attendant evils. Herein James is thinking of religion as an institution or widely shared social practice. But these narrow over-beliefs *are* the most important thing about an individual *qua* isolated individual. For many people are so constituted that how they conceive of God is determinative of much of their behavior. By allowing and even encouraging individuals to have over-beliefs about the nature of God, James is not comprising his religious ecumenicalism. The reasons are twofold. First, these beliefs are private matters, not creedal beliefs of an organized religion. Second, they must be held in a most tentative manner, given James's trashing of the epistemic credentials of such beliefs in the chapter on "Philosophy" in *Varieties*. Furthermore, an over-belief has a more specific reason for being held in a tentative way. It gives an interpretation of the apparent accusative of a mystical experience. But James relativizes the evidential force of a mystical experience for the objective existence of its apparent accusative to the subject of the experience. Thus an over-belief, in addition to being highly dubious in the way in which all statements about the existence and nature of God are, has the additional reason for epistemic modesty because of the failure of the mystical experience upon which it is based to constitute intersubjective evidence for its own veridicality. Because of their lack of epistemic support, they are suitable targets for a will-to-believe option, but this, again, is a private affair that is compatible with religious ecumenicalism.

NOTES

1. All James references are to the Harvard University Press editions of The Works of William James and will be included in the body of the paper using the following abbreviations: (VRE) *The Varieties of Religious Experience*, (EPR) *Essays in Psychical Research*, (PP) *The Principles of Psychology*, (TT) *Talks to Teachers on Psychology and to Students on Some of Life's Ideals*, (ERM) *Essays on Religion and Morality*, and (WB) *The Will to Believe and Other Popular Essays in Philosophy*.

2. Before I begin I want to stress that this is not the only account that can find textual support, for James is too profound, subtle, and suggestive a philosopher for any interpretation to lay claim to being *the* correct one. Any account that makes this claim thereby shows itself to be a wrong interpretation.

3. *The Letters of William James*, ed. Henry James. 2 vols. (Boston: Atlantic Monthly Press, 1920) 1: p. 224.

4. Quoted from Gay Wilson Allen, *William James* (New York: Viking Press, 1967), p. 309.

5. This is a radical oversimplification and for all of the gory details I refer the reader to chapter 4 of my *The Divided Self of William James* (Cambridge: Cambridge University Press, 1999).

TIME

7

IS IT NOW NOW?

This essay will attempt to exhibit three necessary conditions for successful tensed communication, i.e., for one person to inform another that some event is past, present, or future: first, the speaker must use, not just mention, a tensed sentence; second, the hearer must either, in the paradigm case, share the same context as the speaker—be standing face-to-face with him—or, in the nonparadigm case, be able to relate the speaker's temporal perspective to his own; and, third, both speaker and hearer must have a unique temporal perspective in the same time-series to which the event being designated as past, present, or future belongs. There are, of course, countless other necessary conditions for successful tensed communication, but these are the most interesting philosophically, the neglect of which has given rise to McTaggart's famed infinite regress of meta-time-series. A case of successful tensed communication does not require that the statement made by the speaker be true; it only has to be a case in which it would be redundant, and therefore pointless, for the addressee, upon seeing or hearing a tensed statement, to ask "Is it now now?" or "When are you?" In order to clarify the nature of cases of successful tensed communication, I shall consider certain unsuccessful ones in which such questions would not seem to be redundant to the addressee, even though, as we shall see, they would be meaningless since in principle unanswerable.

In his very penetrating discussion of time-language in *The Brown Book*, Wittgenstein points out that "now" is not a common or proper name of a moment of time, as are terms such as "five o'clock," "midday," and "July 4, 1776." He calls these latter terms "specifications of time" (p. 108). "Now" has a logic of its own that is quite different from that of a specification of time. This is seen by the fact that we can use a specification of time in such phrases as "It is now Valentine's Day," and "The Ides of March is now present" ; whereas, it makes no sense to say "It is now now," or "Now is now present."

Similarly, we can ask "Is it now five o'clock?" or "Is Valentine's Day now present?" to which an answer might be "It is now five o'clock," or "Valentine's Day is not present now"; whereas, in cases of successful tensed communication, it is pointlessly redundant to ask "Is it now now?" or "Is now now present?" I know what it is like for it not to be Valentine's Day now (or for the equator not to be here), but not what it would be like for now not to be now (or for here not to be here). The function of words such as "now" and "here" is not to describe or name something but rather to indicate or point to something in an indexical manner.

Imagine this paradigm case of tensed communication: A and B are standing face-to-face and A says to B, "She is on her way over now." To A's surprise B then asks "But is it now now?" or "When is she on her way over now?" The appropriate answer to B would be to inquire whether he understands English for he has just been told when she is on her way over, i.e., right now. Certainly we would not answer him by saying that it is now now or that now is now present or even that she is on her way over now at a moment of present time.

Because B's question is pointlessly redundant, McTaggart's analysis of "M is present" into "M is present at a moment of present time" is incorrect. For, according to his analysis, B's question would not be redundant, and the answer to it would be, "She is now on her way over *at a moment of present time.*" But in accordance with this analysis, we are justified in coming back with an identical question concerning the moment of present time—when is it present?—and so on to infinity.

However, this hopeless infinite regress of meta-time-series can be nipped in the bud when we see the pointless redundancy of B's initial question. There are some vernaculars, such as the current Beatnik one, in which a second "now" is sometimes put in for emphasis, e.g., "She is on her way over now: Man, like right NOW!" It is apparent that the "Man, like right NOW!" is redundant since a question concerning when she is on her way over has already been forestalled by the first clause.

In nonparadigm cases of tensed communication the hearer does not share the same context as the speaker—they are not standing face-to-face—but, due to certain additional information, he is able to relate the speaker's temporal perspective to his own, i.e., he can ascertain whether the sentence-token he sees or hears occurs virtually simultaneously with or so many time-units earlier than his seeing or hearing it. (I cannot, without logical absurdity, conceive of any case in which the sentence-token occurs later than the seeing or hearing of it; this is due to the fact that it is *logically* possible to have traces of the past through tape-recordings and photographs, but not of the future.) In the absence of such additional information there would be a case of unsuccessful tensed communication in which it would not seem redundant to the addressee to ask, "Is it now now?"

Consider the following case: A wealthy widow finds that the tape-recorder in her living room has been left on. Out of curiosity she starts the machine and hears her faithful butler, James, say to her cook, "I'll kill the old witch seven days from now," to which she replies, "But when is seven days from now?" or "Is it now now?" If she possesses additional information that makes it possible for her to ascertain how many time-units ago this sentence-token occurred, she would be able to make the same statement by suitably altering the time-determination of the original statement, e.g., if she knew the butler's statement was made two days ago, she would rephrase his statement as, "I'll kill the old witch five days from now." We would then have a nonparadigm case of successful tensed communication.

Cases in which the hearer is able to relate the speaker's context to his own through additional information are called nonparadigm cases. This is not just because they occur less frequently than the face-to-face ones, but rather because one could not understand a tensed statement made at some time other than the time at which it is heard unless one could first understand tensed statements made by a speaker with whom one is standing face-to-face.

Let us now consider a fantastic, yet nevertheless logically conceivable, situation in which it would be impossible in principle for the hearer to ascertain when the statement he hears is made. A group of philosophers who wish to converse with the great philosophers of old build a History of Philosophy Machine. Once the Machine is started, for every minute that is ticked off on their wrist-watches a clock on the wall, called the Counterclock, which lists the date as well as the time of day, is put back one hundred years. If the Machine runs for twenty minutes as measured by their wrist-watches the Counterclock will be put back two thousand years, so that at the end of the twenty minutes it will list the date as 39 BCE The Machine is equipped with a telephone on which they can converse with those philosophers and only those philosophers who existed at the date indicated by their Counterclock, *provided that the Counterclock has been put back the correct amount of time.* Before getting into the Machine they make a tape-recording of present-tensed sentences listing the telephone numbers at which different philosophers can be reached, e.g., "Aristotle is now at Lyceum 5-3200." This tape-recorder is synchronized with their Counterclock so that when they start the recorder it will play a present-tensed sentence listing the telephone number of a philosopher who existed at the date listed on the Counterclock.

Soon after they start the Machine their wrist-watches and Counterclock cease to work. Because the Counterclock is not being put back the proper amount of time this throws their tape-recorder out of gear so that it will not play the correct present-tensed sentence when they finally stop the History of Philosophy Machine and put it on. After an indeterminate lapse of time they stop the Machine and someone puts on the tape-recorder, which says, "Plato is now at Academy 2-6000," to which someone counters, "But is it now now?"

Let us now consider a more complicated case that involves not just the understanding of a tensed statement made by someone having a different temporal perspective but the possibility of conversing with such a person. Let us allow the people in the out-of-gear History of Philosophy Machine to make one telephone call to any philosopher of their choosing, regardless of whether or not he existed at the date listed on their Counterclock. The purpose of this call is to help them orient themselves so that they can readjust their Counterclock and tape-recorder. They get Plato on the phone and ask him, "What time is it now?" He looks at his sundial and calendar and replies "It is now December 28, 360 BCE." They then ask, "But is it now now?" or "When is December 28, 360 BCE now present?" to which Plato replies, "Right now." Still not satisfied, they come back with an identical question to which Plato gives an identical answer, and so on back and forth to infinity.

Suppose that instead of Plato they were talking with a member of the Academy named McZeno, who was a forerunner of McTaggart. If after being informed by McZeno that it is now December 28, 360 BCE they had countered with "But when is December 28, 360 BCE present?" he would have cheerfully replied that it is present at a moment of present time. This reply, of course, would be no more helpful than Plato's "Right now," since there is no way for the people in the out-of-gear History of Philosophy Machine to find out whether or not the tensed statements they hear on the telephone are made simultaneous with their hearing of them. In neither case could they readjust their Counterclock so that it would list the correct date.

McZeno's answer suggests that there is a second-order time-series composed of queer entities called moments of time at which events in the first-order time-series become present. This is to dive into the muddy waters of the River of Time Metaphor, the essence of which is to think of *the* present moment as some point or observer "outside" of the first-order time-series. Events in this first-order time-series receive the determinations of past, present, and future because of their relation to this transcendent point, and their change in respect to these characteristics is due to either the "movement" of the point along this time-series or the "movement" of this series past a stationary point. Events in this first-order time-series are then substantialized into things that exist both before and after they happen. McTaggart's analysis of "M is present" into "*M* is present at a moment of present time" suggests such a River of Time representation, since the "moment of present time" supposedly is some transcendent point, like the spotlight of presentness that plays along the line of thing-like-events or the transcendent observer on the bridge spanning the river of time who is always (!) watching the events of the first-order time-series flow past him.

What sense would there be to the question "When are you?" if asked of Plato by the people in the out-of-gear History of Philosophy Machine? While both "now" and "here" are indexical signs, there is nevertheless an important difference in their logical behavior. The question, "Where are you?" has a clearcut use in ordinary language but the question, "When are you?" seems queer since it has not.

We might attempt to give it a sense by first distinguishing between two different senses of the question, "Where are you?" and their corresponding answers and then seeing if we can give analogous senses to the question, "When are you?" by substituting temporal for spatial terms. "Where are you?" could have the following two senses:

(1) It could be a request for the addressee, assuming, of course, that he is within earshot of the speaker, to give an answer employing a *spatial indexical sign*, e.g., "I am *here*." A snort would do as an answer since it is the direction from which the voice comes that constitutes the answer.

(2) It could be a request for the addressee to give an answer employing *nonindexical spatial signs*, e.g., "I am at the North Pole." It is important to note that answers (1) and (2) employ the temporal indexical sign "am," which is a full-blooded present tense, since both answers tell where the utterer is at the time he utters his sentence-token.

Let us now see if we can give analogous senses to "When are you?" by substituting temporal for spatial terms:

(1) It could be a request for the addressee to give an answer employing a *temporal indexical sign*, e.g., "I am *now*." Unlike answer (1) to "Where are you?" the direction from which the voice comes does not constitute an answer—a snort will not do. Because the direction from which a voice comes indicates whether a person is here or over there, it is meaningful to ask, "Are you here or over there?" Since the direction from which a voice comes does not indicate whether the speaker is now or then, it is meaningless to ask, "Are you now or then?" If the commu-

nicants share the same temporal perspective, the question, "When are you?" is redundant; and if they do not, as in the case of the people in the out-of-gear History of Philosophy Machine conversing on the telephone with Plato and McZeno, it is meaningless since in principle unanswerable. Therefore, we are not able to give a use to "When are you?" which is the analogue of sense (1) of "Where are you?"

(2) It could be a request for the addressee to give an answer employing *nonindexical temporal signs*, e.g., "I *am (tenselessly) at December 28, 1961.*" We must distinguish this sense of "When are you?" from the meaningful and familiar question, "What time is it now?" which would be answered by employing both an indexical and nonindexical temporal sign, e.g., "It *is now December 28, 1961.*"

Because the answer to this question employs a *temporal indexical sign* ("is now"), it cannot be the analogue of sense (2) of "Where are you?" which employs no *indexical spatial sign* in its answer, and because it employs a *nonindexical temporal sign* ("December 28, 1961"), it cannot be the analogue of sense (1) of "Where are you?," which employs no *nonindexical spatial sign.*

"I am (tenselessly) at December 28, 1961," as an answer to sense (2) of "When are you?" does not tell us that the utterer is at December 28, 1961 at the time he utters his sentence-token, since a single person tenselessly occupies all those moments of time that fall within his lifespan. It is hard to conceive of any situation in which this question and answer would have any point. "I am at the North Pole," as an answer to sense (2) of "Where are you?" does tell us that the person making the statement is at the North Pole when he makes his statement. Therefore, we are unable to give a sense to "When are you?" that would be the analogue of sense (2) of "Where are you?"

The reason why we have not been able to give "When are you?" a sense analogous to either of the two senses of "Where are you?" is that the answers to both senses of "Where are you?" employed *temporal indexical signs*, while neither answer to "When are you?" employed *spatial indexical signs.* Thus a *precondition* for meaningfully asking, "Where are you?" is that the communicants share the same temporal perspective; however, they need not share the same spatial perspective, though, of course, they must belong to the same spatial system. That the communicants share the same temporal perspective is a precondition for asking *any* tensed question, such as "What are you doing now?" Obviously this precondition cannot itself be made the subject of a tensed question, as it is when we ask someone, "When are you?"

Such a question is either redundant or meaningless. To claim that there is no important difference between temporal and spatial perspectives is to overlook this important difference in logical behavior between "now" and "here."

The people in the out-of-gear History of Philosophy Machine are completely "out of it," i.e., are not in the same time-series to which the people belong with whom they converse on the telephone. They can hear people in this time-series, such as Plato and McZeno, uttering tensed sentences, but for them, as it likewise would be for a transcendent God, these sentences have the effect of being mentioned rather than used. When we mention, rather than use, a tensed sentence we do *not* assert that some event is now past (or present or future). That is why they always come back with the question, "Is it now now?" This shows the vital difference between mentioning and using a tensed sentence, and shows the inadequacy of any tenseless ideal language in which the tensed sentences used in everyday life are mentioned but not used. For example, if in a face-to-face situation the speaker mentions the tensed sentence, "It is now raining," by saying "Rain is (tenselessly) simultaneous with the utterance of 'It is now raining'," he has not forestalled the question of whether it is raining *now*. In such a case, the hearer, even though sharing the same context as the speaker, would be in the same position as the people in the out-of-gear History of Philosophy Machine talking on the telephone with Plato.

By considering cases of unsuccessful tensed communication, we have been able to establish the first two necessary conditions for successful tensed communication: first, the speaker must use a tensed sentence, and second, the hearer must either share the same context as the speaker or be able to relate his temporal perspective to his own. As a sort of corollary to this second condition, we showed that the possibility of tensed conversation, the asking and answering of tensed questions, requires that the speaker and hearer share the same temporal perspective, though they need not share the same spatial perspective. I shall now try to establish the third necessary condition, requiring that both speaker and hearer have some unique temporal perspective or now in the same time-series as the one to which the event being designated as past, present, or future belongs. This shall be established only for the speaker, it then following that the hearer, since he must belong to the same time-series as the speaker, would also have to have a unique temporal perspective in the same time-series to which the event being described belongs.

We must first distinguish a tensed statement from one that makes a time determination in a tenseless manner. There are, of course, countless grammatical techniques for tensing a statement, i.e., for indicating that the event being talked about is past, present, or future. What all of these different "usages" have in common, and what will serve as a criterion for being a tensed statement is this: A tensed statement makes a temporal determination through the use of a sentence that can be used only at a *certain time(s)* so as to make a true statement. A tenseless statement that makes a time determination is one that describes a timeless relation of either precedence or subsequence or simultaneity between two events, without asserting that either one is past, present, or future; therefore, the sentence used in a tenseless statement is freely repeatable in a way in which a tensed sentence is not, i.e., the truth-value of the statements formed from its use at *any time* is invariant.

The difference, then, between a tensed and tenseless statement is found in a difference in the rules controlling the use of the sentences employed in such statements. The rules or conventions controlling the use of tensed sentences for making true or false tensed statements, which I shall call "Rules for Tensed Assertion," state that *the present-tensed sentence is used to describe events virtually simultaneous with the describing of them, the past-tensed sentence to describe events earlier than the describing of them, and the future-tensed sentence to describe events later than the describing of them.* It is now apparent why the speaker (and ipso facto the hearer) must have a unique temporal perspective in the same time-series to which the event being described belongs, for in order to designate an event as either past, or present, or future his utterance must, according to the Rules for Tensed Assertion, be respectively either later than, or simultaneous with, or earlier than the event described.

It does not follow from the Rules for Tensed Assertion that when someone uses a tensed sentence he is *asserting* a relation of precedence, subsequence, or simultaneity between his utterance and the events it describes, as claimed by the token-reflexive theory of tenses. This attempts to pack the contextual requirements for the use of a tensed sentence, which are contained in the Rules for Tensed Assertion, into what is asserted by a use of this sentence. Nor does it follow that past, present, and future are "subjective." All that follows from the Rules for Tensed Assertion is that if no one uttered a tensed sentence then no one would designate an event as being past, present, or future and communicate this information. If no one asserts that an event is past, present, or future then no one *asserts* that an event is past, present, or future. If this is a reason for calling the pastness, presentness, and futurity of events "subjective" then every item of discourse is "subjective," for in order to say anything I must *say* something.

By distinguishing the Rules for Tensed Assertion from what is asserted by someone who uses a sentence governed by these rules, we are doing justice to the realistic intentions of common sense, which believes that events are past, present, and future quite independently of their relation to a language-user, or, for that matter, a perceiver. When we say, "The eclipse is present," we mean to assert that *the eclipse* is present, that is, present *simpliciter*. In other words, we mean just what we said. Earlier it was shown that in order for there to be a tensed conversation, the communicants must share the same temporal perspective though they need not share the same spatial perspective. Common sense assumes that this shared temporal perspective reflects nature's own temporal perspective in that the events described, like our acts of speaking and hearing, are themselves intrinsically past, present, and future.

We assume that our temporal perspective is objective in a way in that our spatial perspective is not. For when we say that an object is to the right or the front we *explicitly assert* to whose right or front it is, e.g., "The statue is to my right and to your front." However, when we say that something is past we do not *assert* that it is to my or your past or, for that matter, earlier than my utterance or your hearing of my utterance. We simply say *it* is past.

8

McTAGGART'S ANALYSIS OF TIME

McTaggart's famed argument for the unreality of time, first presented by him in 1908 in *Mind*, comprises both a positive and a negative thesis. The positive thesis, which is presented in the first part of the argument, contains an analysis of the concept of time, which McTaggart claims to be the only correct one. The negative thesis that is presented in the second part of the argument attempts to show that this analysis of the concept of time entails a contradiction. The assumption here is that any concept that is contradictory cannot be true of reality, and therefore time is unreal. It is vital to distinguish between these two theses, for, as we shall see, one group of analytic philosophers who answered his argument agreed with his positive thesis concerning the correct analysis of the concept of time, but they disagreed with his negative thesis that this analysis entails a contradiction. On the other hand, another group of analytic philosophers who refuted his argument disagreed with his positive thesis and claimed that time could be real even if his negative thesis is correct. Thus, while these two groups of philosophers are in agreement as to the unsoundness of McTaggart's argument, they adopt competing analyses of the concept of time in refuting this argument. The purpose of this paper will be to examine critically McTaggart's positive thesis and thereby bring into sharper focus the exact nature of the dispute between these two groups of analytic philosophers. But before doing this, a rough sketch will be given of McTaggart's argument as a whole.

In the first part of his argument McTaggart analyzes the concept of time in terms of two different types of temporal facts. First, there are facts about temporal relations of precedence and subsequence between events, and, second, there are facts about the pastness, presentness, and futurity of these same events. Corresponding to the first type of temporal facts is a series of events, called the "*B*-Series," which runs from earlier to later, its generating relation being *earlier (later) than*; while corresponding to the second type of temporal facts is a series of events, called the "*A*-Series," which runs from the past through the present and through the present to the future. While both of these series are essential for the reality of time, the *A*-Series is the more fundamental of the two, since the *B*-Series can be derived from it alone. The arguments advanced by McTaggart for the necessity and fundamentality of the *A*-Series will be examined shortly.

The second part of McTaggart's argument attempts to show that the *A*-Series, which has been shown in the first part to be essential for the reality of time, entails a contradiction and that therefore time is unreal. His main argument is as follows. Every event in the *A*-Series, assuming that there is no first or last event, has the mutually incompatible properties of being past, present, and future, which is a contradiction. The obvious reply to this seeming contradiction is to say that no event has two or more of these incompatible properties *at the same time*, but rather has them successively *at different moments of time*. But this reply will not do, since it involves either a vicious circle or a vicious infinite regress. What we have done is to explain away the contradiction of an event in the first-order time-series being past, present, and future by claiming that it has these determinations successively *at moments of time* in a second-order time-series. But since this second-order time-series is a time-series, the moments of time that are its members must have the properties of being past, present, and future.

Therefore, we have explained away the contradiction inherent in the first-order *A*-Series, brought about by the fact that every event in it has all three mutually incompatible determinations of past, present, and future, by introducing a second-order *A*-Series. And this is to reason in a vicious circle, since we must presuppose an *A*-Series to rid the first *A*-Series of contradiction.

If we should try to remove the contradiction inherent in this second-order *A*-Series because all the moments of time in it are past, present, and future, by saying that these moments are *successively* future, present, and past at moments of time in some third-order *A*-Series, we are merely transferring this contradiction to this third-order *A*-Series. We are launched on a vicious infinite regress because at any point in this regress at which we stop, we are left with a contradictory *A*-Series. The curse of contradiction pursues us down this long infinite regress, being a sort of baton that each *A*-Series passes on to the *A*-Series that is one-order higher than itself.[1]

There are two different type of answers given to McTaggart's argument by analysts: (1) the *B*-Series alone is sufficient to account for time—the *A*-Series being reducible to the *B*-Series—and therefore the *A*-Series is not essential for the reality of time; and (2) the *A*-Series alone is sufficient to account for time—the *B*-Series being reducible to the *A*-Series—but the concept of the *A*-Series does not contain a contradiction. Answer (1), to be called the "*B*-Theory Answer," attacks McTaggart's positive thesis by denying that the *A*-Series is essential for time. It supports this contention by arguing that, contrary to what McTaggart said, the *A*-Series is reducible to the *B*-Series.[2] Answer (2), to be called the "*A*-Theory Answer," basically agrees with McTaggart's positive thesis that the *A*-Series is both necessary and fundamental, but denies his negative thesis that the concept of the *A*-Series is contradictory.[3] We shall now critically examine McTaggart's analysis of the *A*-Series to show that there is a crucial obscurity in the concept of the *A*-Series that has gone unnoticed by proponents of both the *A*- and *B*-Theory Answers. Once the concept of the *A*-Series is properly clarified, it will be seen that the *A*-Series, *properly understood*, is primitive, the *B*-Series being reducible to it. However, this thesis is not nearly as exciting as the one that the defenders of the *A*-Theory

Answer thought they were espousing. While my clarification of the concept of the *A*-Series will tend to trivialize the *A*-Theory Answer's thesis of the primitiveness of the *A*-Series as opposed to the *B*-Series, what it will indicate about our concept of time is far from trivial, and, in fact, is of the highest importance.

Let us now scrutinize McTaggart's analysis of time. His analysis is phenomenological, being based on the way in which temporal positions *appear* to us, but everything he says could be recast, and for purposes of clarity needs to be recast, in a linguistic idiom that describes the different ways in which we *talk* about temporal positions. He begins by saying:

> Positions in time, as time appears to us prima facie, are distinguished in two ways. Each position is Earlier than some and Later than some of the other positions.... In the second place, each position is either Past, Present, or Future. The distinctions of the former class are permanent, while those of the latter are not.[4]

This can be rephrased linguistically as:

> There are two fundamentally different ways in which we make temporal determinations. First, we can say that one event *is* earlier (later) than some other event; and, second, we can say that some event is now past (present, future). The sentences employed in making claims of the first sort make statements having the same truth-value every time they are uttered, while the sentences employed in the second sort of temporal determination may make statements having different truth-values if uttered at different times.

These two different ways of experiencing or talking about time are supposed to determine two different time-series:

> For the sake of brevity I shall give the name of the *A*-Series to that series of positions which runs from the far past through the near past to the present, and then from the present through the near future to the far future, or conversely. The series of positions which runs from earlier to later, or conversely, I shall call the *B*-Series.[5]

McTaggart's concept of the *B*-Series is clear because we can see the connection between it and our use of the expression "earlier (later) than." This connection consists in the fact that *earlier (later) than* is the generating relation of the *B*-Series; that is, given any two nonsimultaneous events, x and y, either x is earlier (later) than y or y *is* earlier (later) than x. The relation *earlier (later) than* is connected in the set of all nonsimultaneous events.

Unfortunately, McTaggart's concept of the *A*-Series is not as clear, for while we can see the connection between the *B*-Series and talk about "earlier or later than," we do not see the connection between the *A*-Series and our use of the predicates "is present," "is past," and "is future." Since the *A*-Series is a series, it must have a generating relation. But what could it be?[7] We know only that the generating relation of the *A*-Series, whatever it might be, must contain a temporal index since there is a different *A*-Series at any two different moments of time. The *A*-Series that McTaggart describes cannot be generated by the unqualified temporal indices "past," "present," and "future" since the *A*-Series involves not only that the events comprising it are past, present, and future but also that they are past and future by varying degrees. The necessity for the latter is contained in McTaggart's description of the *A*-Series as one "which runs from the *far* past through the *near* past." The use of the unqualified predicate "is now past" cannot distinguish between events in the far and in the near past: it determines a "blob past." Past, present, and future, rather than being the generating relation of the *A*-Series, merely indicate the kind of elements in the *A*-Series, just as +, –, and 0 do not generate the series of integers but only indicate the kind of elements that belong to the series. Before attempting to answer the question as to what could be the generating relation of the *A*-Series, we shall consider McTaggart's arguments for the necessity and fundamentality of the *A*-Series.

McTaggart claimed that there could not be time without both a *B*-Series and an *A*-Series. His arguments in support of this are directed only to showing the necessity for the *A*-Series. Probably he thought that the necessity for the *B*-Series is so obvious as to require no further comment; for to conceive of a "time" that admitted of no distinctions between earlier and later times would be a conceptual absurdity.[8]

While philosophers have rarely doubted the necessity for there to be a *B*-Series if there is to be time, several of them, in particular those who defend the *B*-Theory Answer, have questioned the necessity of the *A*-Series. They have argued that although we always experience events as forming both a *B*- and an *A*-Series, the determinations of events as past, present, and future are delusory or purely psychological, so that only the *B*-Series is objectively real. Against this line of reasoning McTaggart advances two arguments, the first showing that change requires an *A*-Series and the second, which is also an argument for the fundamentality of the *A*-Series over the *B*-Series, showing that "earlier (later) than" can be defined in terms of "past," "present," and "future."

McTaggart's first argument for the necessity of the *A*-Series has as its basic premise that there cannot be time without change, which would be granted by proponents of both the *A*- and *B*-Theory Answers to his argument. The purpose of this argument is to show that there could not be change (and therefore time) without the *A*-Series. The argument proceeds by examining every possible candidate for the title of "change" other than changes in the pastness, presentness, and futurity of events, and showing that none of them is logically possible. Thus, by a process of elimination, it is inferred that the only change possible is a change in an event's position in the *A*-Series. If time consisted only of a *B*-Series, the following are the possible candidates for "change."

(i) It might be held that an event in the *B*-Series could change. Maybe the death of Queen Anne could somehow cease to be the death of Queen Anne. But this is absurd. Events can never cease to be just the sort of events they are.

> Take any event—the death of Queen Anne, for example—and consider what changes can take place in its characteristics. That it is a death, that it is the death of Anne Stuart, that it has such causes, that it has such effects—every characteristic of this sort never changes.[9]

Events remain just as sweet, young, and innocent as they always were for McTaggart. By the law of identity, each event must forever remain itself.

(ii) It might be contended that two events in the *B*-Series could merge so as to form a new event. But such conjugal union between events is logically unthinkable for the reason given in (i): it would require that the two events that merge would cease to be themselves. If the death of Queen Anne and the death of Stalin were somehow to merge to form a new event consisting of the death of Queen Stalin, then these events would no longer be the same events.

(iii) Events might be thought to have the ability to get in or out of a *B*-Series, and this could constitute the change we are seeking. But this sort of change also is logically impossible, for the *B*-Series is a sort of logically escape-proof prison. An event "can never get out of any time-series in which it once was." Nor can an event enter into a *B*-Series in which it is not a member, since positions in the *B*-Series are permanent.

(iv) Possibly could change arise from events shifting in their position in the *B*-Series? This also is logically impossible, for our concept of the generating relation of the *B*-Series—earlier than—is such that it is nonsensical to speak about events changing in their relations of precedence to other events or changing in the metrical features of these relations. "If N is ever earlier than O and later than M, it will always be, and has always been, earlier than O and later than M, since the relations of earlier and later are permanent." Events are not able to sneak up on each other.

From this McTaggart concludes that the *B*-Series cannot give us change, and therefore the *B*-Series, although necessary for the reality of time, is not sufficient. To get change and therefore time we must invoke the change in the position of an event in the *A*-Series. Such changes are the only logically possible ones. For there to be such change there must be an *A*-Series. Take away the *A*-Series and the *B*-Series ceases to be a temporal series.

A proponent of the *B*-Theory Answer would claim that McTaggart has overlooked one possible candidate for the title of "change," namely, that it is things, rather than events, that change, and such change consists in a thing having a different quality at one phase of its history than it has at an earlier or later phase; e.g., a poker changes in that it is at one time hot and at a later time cool. Such qualitative changes *in* things can be analyzed solely in terms of the *B*-relations of subsequence or precedence between qualitatively different states that comprise the history of a single thing. Moreover, these qualitatively different states of a single thing can be described in a tenseless language, which makes no references to the *A*-determinations, i.e., pastness, presentness, or futurity, of these states; e.g., "The poker *is* hot on Monday," and "The poker *is* not hot at times other than Monday."[10] McTaggart raised the following objection to this analysis:

> This makes no change in the qualities of the poker. It is always a quality of that poker that it is one which is hot on that particular Monday. And it is always a quality of that poker that it is one which is not hot at any other time. Both these qualities are true of it at any time—the time when it is hot and the time when it is cold. And therefore it seems to be erroneous to say that there is any change in the poker.[11]

McTaggart's reply fails because of an equivocation on the word "always." He argues that because the tenseless statement, "The poker *is* hot on Monday," is *always* true, i.e., true independently of time in the sense that the use of this sentence makes a true statement every time it is uttered, the state of affairs described by this statement must *always*, i.e., in the temporal sense of "always," be occurring or existent. Because statements describing events in a tenseless manner are *always* true it does not require that these events are sempiternal: to claim the opposite is an unwarranted addition of an eternalistic ontology to a tenseless (or token-reflexive free) logic.

McTaggart's other argument to show the dependency of the *B*-Series upon the *A*-Series fares no better than his first one. This argument, which is never stated explicitly, is that our understanding of the concept of "earlier (later) than" essentially involves reference to the concepts of past, present, and future. *Earlier than* is a temporal relation only because its relata have *A*-determinations. At one place he claimed that we could *define* "earlier than" in terms of the *A*-determinations of "past, present, and future."

> The term P is earlier than the term Q, if it is ever past while Q is present, or present while Q is future:[12]

If it is possible to define "earlier than" in terms of "past, present, and future," it will follow not only that there could be no *B*-Series without an *A*-Series but also that the *B*-Series is reducible to the *A*-Series, since the generating relation of the *B*-Series is definable in terms of *A*-determinations.

McTaggart's attempt to define the *B*-relation "earlier than" in terms of the three *A*-determinations fails because of circularity. The *definiens* of the definition contains the statements, "*P is* past while *Q is* present" and "*P is* present while *Q is* future," which mean the same as, respectively, "*P is* past at *Q*" and "*Q is* future at *P*." The predicates "... *is* past at ..." and "... *is* future at ..." are synonyms for "... *is* earlier than ...," in that all three are tenseless two-place predicates that, when non-indexical or non–token-reflexive event expressions are substituted for their blank spaces, express a timelessly true or false statement about a *B*-relation of precedence between two events.[13] "Is past (present, future) at some event or date," unlike "is now past (present, future)," does not contain a temporal index. But, as pointed out above, an *A*-determination must contain a temporal index, for two nonsimultaneous uses of the *A*-determinations of "past," "present," and "future" will determine different *A*-Series of events. The event(s) that is (are) present in one of them will not be in the other. Therefore, McTaggart is cheating by allowing "*is* past (future) at" to count as *A*-determinations. If the copulae of the statements in the *definiens* are taken to be tensed—"*P* is now past while *Q* is now present" and "*P* is now present while *Q* is now future"—then the *definiendum* is not logically equivalent to the *definiens*, for it might be the case that *P is* earlier than *Q* but be false that *P* or *Q* is now present, in which case the *definiendum* is true and the *definiens* false.

If we take the *A*-Series to be determined by an unqualified past, present, and future, i.e., a past, present, and future that do not admit of degrees, then it can be shown that the *B*-Series cannot be reduced to the *A*-Series, this being due to the fact that the *B*-relation "earlier than" cannot be defined in terms of an unqualified "past, present, and future." In the first place, it is fallacious to argue that *earlier than* can be analyzed in terms of *A*-determinations because there are *A*-determinative statements that imply a tenseless *B*-relation statement but no tenseless B-relation statement that implies an A-determinative statement; e.g., "P is present and is future" entails, but is not entailed by, "P is earlier than Q."[14] For the fact that a statement containing a term X entails, but is not entailed by, a statement containing Y does not show that Y is analyzable in terms of X. For example, "All *animals* are mortal" entails, but is not entailed by, "All *men* are mortal," but this surely does not show that men are analyzable purely in terms of the concept of an animal. Thus, while it is true that there is an asymmetry in information content between a pure B-relation language and a pure A-determinative language, in that everything sayable in the former is sayable in the latter but not vice-versa, it does not establish that B-relations are reducible to A-determinations, and therefore that the B-Series is reducible to the A-Series.

Another attempt to reduce the B-Series to a *pure A*-Series, i.e., an A-Series determined by the use of an unqualified "past, present, and future," which is also unsuccessful, involves giving a "definition in use" of "earlier than" in terms of the three unqualified A-determinations, taken together. By a *definition in use* of a term is meant one that gives an analysis of a statement containing this term: a necessary, though possibly not sufficient, condition for a successful analysis is that the *analysandum* and the *analysans* are logically equivalent. Let us try to analyze a tenseless B-relation statement in terms of a logically equivalent disjunction of A-determinative statements:

(I) P *is* earlier than Q ≡ P is past and Q is present *or* P is past and Q is future *or* P is present and Q is future

in which 'P' and 'Q' are expressions referring to an event or state of affairs. It is quite apparent that (I) is not a logical equivalence, for whereas it could not be the case that the disjunction of A-determinative statements in the *analysans* is true and the B-relation statement in the *analysandum* is false, it could be the case that the *analysandum* is true and the *analysans* is false. The reason for this, which has already been given in the above discussion of McTaggart's definition, is that if P and Q are either both past or both future, P being *more past* than Q or Q being *more future* than P, then each of the three disjuncts would be false. To give an adequate definition in use of a *B*-relation in terms of a disjunction of *A*-determinative statements, we must enlarge our concept of an *A*-determination so as to include "more past," and "more future" as well as an unqualified "past," "present," and "future." With this expanded concept of an *A*-determination we can add two disjuncts to the *analysans* of (I):

(II) *P is* earlier than $Q \equiv P$ is past and Q is present *or P* is past and Q is future *or P* is present and Q is future *or P* is more past than Q *or Q* is more future than *P*.

What is to be concluded from this discussion is that the *B*-Series cannot be reduced to a *pure A*-Series, but that it can be reduced to an *impure A*-Series, i.e., an *A*-Series that is determined not only by an unqualified past, present, and future but also by more past and more future.[15] Thus the thesis of McTaggart and the *A*-Theory Answer that the *B*-Series is reducible to the *A*-Series is correct, provided that we are speaking of an *impure A*-Series. This qualification greatly trivializes their thesis. Not only can the *B*-relation *earlier (later) than* be analyzed in terms of the *five A*-determinations, taken together, but the same is true for the relation *simultaneous with*. The latter can be classified as a *B*-relation for the following two reasons. First, the relation of *simultaneity* is needed to construct the *B*-Series. The *B*-Series includes the totality of events that make up the history of the world. The generating relation of this series—*is earlier than*—is not connected in this set of events, since some events are simultaneous with each other. The relation of *simultaneity* is needed in determining the classes of events that are ordered by the relation of *earlier than* to form the *B*-Series. Therefore, the relation of *simultaneity* is needed in the construction of the *B*-Series. Second, "… is simultaneous with …" has the same logic as "… *is* earlier than …" in that both are tenseless two-place predicates expressing a temporal relation that, when nonindexical event expressions are substituted for their blank spaces, make timelessly true or false statements. The following is a reduction of "is simultaneous with" to a disjunction of *A*-determinative statements:

(III) *P is* simultaneous with $Q \equiv$ (*P* is present and *Q* is present) *or* (*P* is past and *Q* is past and it is not the case that either *P* is more past than *Q* or is more past than *P*) *or* (*P* is future and *Q* is future and it is not the case that either *P* is more future than *Q* or *Q* is more future than *P*).

Once again, it was necessary to use "more past (future)" in carrying out the reduction.[16]

In summary, an impure, but not a pure, *A*-Series is also a *B*-Series, in that a statement describing the *A*-determinations of events entails a statement describing tenseless *B*-relations between these events. However, a *B*-Series is not also a specific *A*-Series, in that a statement describing *B*-relations between events does not entail a statement describing the specific *A*-determinations of these events, but only a disjunction of statements describing different possible combinations of the *A*-determinations of these events. Thus, an *A*-Series already is some specific *B*-Series, but a *B*-Series is not at the same time some specific *A*-Series. This conclusion helps us to see why McTaggart's attempt to derive the *B*-Series from a conjunction of the *A*-Series with a *C*-Series, i.e., a series whose generating relation is nontemporal, is either pointless or futile:

> We can now see that the *A*-Series, together with the *C*-Series is sufficient to give us time.... The *B*-Series... is not ultimate. For given a *C*-Series of permanent relations of terms, which is not in itself temporal, and therefore is not a *B*-Series, and given the further fact that the terms of this *C*-Series also form an *A*-Series, and it results that the terms of the *C*-Series become a *B*-Series, those which are placed first, in the direction from past to future, being earlier than those whose places are *further in the direction of the future.*[17]

If the *A*-Series referred to in this quotation is an impure *A*-Series, then it is already a *B*-Series; and therefore it is pointless, since unnecessary, to combine this *A*-Series with another series in order to derive the *B*-Series. But if the *A*-Series referred to by McTaggart is a pure *A*-Series, then it can be shown that his attempt to derive the *B*-Series in the manner described is futile. Consider the problem of correlating the infinitely denumerable members of a pure *A*-Series with the members of a *C*-Series, such as the series of integers. There is no problem in correlating the present event(s) in the pure *A*-Series with the number 0 in the *C*-Series of integers. But it is impossible to correlate the past and future events of this *A*-Series respectively with the minus and plus integers because this *A*-Series contains a "blob" past and future, i.e., one that admits of no distinction between more past and less past. To make this correlation we must import a structural order into the past and future of the *A*-Series by introducing the concept of more past and more future, which, incidentally, is exactly what McTaggart does when he speaks of terms that are "*further* in the direction of the future." We must say something like "the more past (or future) an event is in the *A*-Series the smaller (or larger) the integer with which it is correlated."

Having clarified McTaggart's ambiguous concept of the *A*-Series and shown that only the impure *A*-Series is a series, we can now answer our original question concerning the generating relation of the (impure) *A*-Series. The answer is that its generating relation is *earlier than*, which is also the generating relation of the *B*-Series. Since a *B*-Series must also be an *A*-Series, though not any specific *A*-Series, it follows that the generating relation of the *B*-Series must also generate an *A*-Series, though not any one specific *A*-Series. There is another way of answering this question. The *A*-Series is formed from a conjunction of two different series having a common member, which serves as the *terminus ad quem* of one and the *terminus ab quo* of the other. There is a series whose generating relation is *more past than*, and there is another series whose generating relation is *more future than*. These two series can be conjoined to form an (impure) *A*-Series because the *terminus ad quem* of the series of past events is the present event(s) while the *terminus ab quo* of the series of future events is also the present event(s).

Regardless of which answer we give to the question concerning the generating relation of the *A*-Series, we have to invoke the concepts of more past and more future. It might be objected, and not without plausibility, that these concepts involve a tenseless *B*-relation because a statement of the form, "x is now more past than y," must be *analyzed* into a conjunction of the *B*-relation statement, "x *is* earlier than y" and the *A*-determinative statement, "*y* is now past." And if this is so, then our reduction of *B*-relations to *A*-determinations by logical equivalence (II) is circular, since the final two disjuncts in the *analysans* (the ones using "more past" and "more future") contain *B*-relation statements. There are two ways of countering this objection. First, it could be argued that the statement, "*x* is more past than *y*," is an *A*-determinative or tensed statement because it employs a sentence that has the same temporal restrictions placed upon its use as are placed upon the use of sentences, such as "*x* is now past," which unquestionably are used to make an *A*-determinative statement.[18] The utterance of "*x* is more past than *y*" at different times may make statements having different truth-values, which could not happen with different utterances of a sentence used in making a *B*-relation statement, such as "*x* is earlier than *y*." This fact, however, is not decisive in showing that this statement cannot be analyzed into a conjunction of a *B*-relation statement and an *A*-determinative statement; for the conjunction of an *A*-determinative and *B*-relation statement will always make an *A*-determinative statement, just as, analogously, the conjunction of a contingent and a necessary statement will always make a contingent statement. A more effective way to meet this charge of circularity in our reduction of *B*-relations to *A*-determinations is to claim, as we do in (II), that "*x* is more past than *y*" *entails* "*x* is earlier than *y*" but deny that we must *analyze* "*x* is more past than *y*" into the conjunction of "*x* is earlier than *y*" *and* "*y* is now past." I know of no argument that can be given to show that we must accept this as an *analysis* of "*x* is more past than *y*."

I am not very happy with this reply to the charge of circularity. It might be thought that this rather indecisive result could be avoided by offering a different reductive analysis of *B*-relations to *A*-determinations than that given in (II), e.g., instead of "more past than" we would have used "preceded," "was earlier than," or "occurred a longer time ago than," etc., but they are just as susceptible to the charge of circularity as is "more past than." We might try and recast McTaggart's question about the relation between the *B*- and the *A*-Series by using the *connectives* "before" and "while" instead of the *relations* "earlier than" and "simultaneous with." The former take sentences as their arguments, unlike the latter that take only event, or state of affairs, expressions as their arguments. The question then is whether we can analyze a statement containing the connective "before" and tenseless statements for its arguments into a logically equivalent disjunction of statements containing "before" and "while" and only *A*-determinative statements for their arguments. This can be accomplished as follows:

(IV) *P* is *Q* before *R* is *S* ≡ (*P* was *Q* and *R* is *S*) or *P* was *Q* and *R* will be *S*) or (*P* is *Q* and *R* will be *S*) or (*P* had been *Q* while *R* was *S*) or (*P* will have been *Q* while *R* will be *S*).[19]

Since (IV) is the analogue of (II) in connective discourse, it should not surprise us to find that (IV) is haunted by the same specter of circularity as is (II). Once again the difficulty occurs in the final two disjuncts. Instead of the problem arising with "more past than," as it does with (II), it concerns the use of the compound tense "had (will have) been." One might claim that we must *analyze* "*P* had been *Q* while *R* was *S*" into the conjunction of the *A*-determinative statements, "*R* was *S*," with the tenseless *B*-relation statement, "*P* is *Q* before *R* is *S*," thus making the analysis circular. And once again the reply must be that there is no reason why we must accept this as an analysis. One thing is certain: by allowing, as we must, "more past (future) than" or a compound tense to count as an *A*-determination, we trivialize the thesis of McTaggart and the *A*-Theory Answer that the *B*-Series is reducible to the *A*-Series. But what this indicates about our concept of time is far from trivial. It shows that our concept of time involves not only the three unanalyzable concepts of past, present, and future, but also the notion of a structural order, and it was because of the latter that we had to introduce the concepts of more past and more future.[20]

NOTES

1. It is not the purpose of this paper to answer this argument. For a complete bibliography and summary of the answers given to this argument see L. Mink, "Time, McTaggart and Pickwickian Language," *The Philosophical Quarterly* 10 (1960): 254–63.

2. The most illustrious defender of this thesis is Bertrand Russell, and among his followers are R. B. Braithwaite, A. J. Ayer, W. V. Quine, N. Goodman, D. Williams, and J. J. C. Smart.

3. C. D. Broad is the leading exponent of this answer, and among his followers are J. Wisdom, S. Stebbing, D. F. Pears, and W. Sellars.

4. J. M. E. McTaggart, *The Nature of Existence*, vol. 2 (Cambridge: Cambridge University Press, 1927), pp. 9–10.

5. We will adopt the convention in this paper of italicizing tenseless verbs and copulae.

6. McTaggart, *Nature of Existence* p. 10.

7. Surprisingly, none of McTaggart's commentators and critics have asked this basic question. The explanation for this strange oversight might be due to the ease with which we can *picture* the *A*-Series, and often this picture involves a correlation between the events of the *A*-Series and the marks on the edge of a ruler. Having such a picture of the *A*-Series, we then think we understand it and forget to ask what is its generating relation. This is a good example of the danger of pictorial thinking.

8. H. Bergson's analysis of time, I believe, comes very close to committing this absurdity, for he denies that events are distinct from each other.

9. McTaggart, *Nature of Existence* p. 13.

10. Russell's analysis of change as arising from the fact that there are propositional functions (e.g., "The poker is hot at t," in which 't' is a free variable) that are true of some, but not all moments of time, is in *The Principles of Mathematics* (Cambridge: Cambridge University Press 1903), p. 472.

11. McTaggart, *Nature of Existence* p. 15.

12. Ibid., p. 271.

13. It is crucial to find a language-neutral criterion for distinguishing between an *A*-determinative, or tensed, statement and a *B*-relation, or tenseless, statement. The strategy in discovering this criterion is to begin with paradigm cases of *A*-determinative statements, such as "*S* is now (was, will be) *P*," or "There now is a *P*ing of *S*," and to extrapolate from these examples a set of rules of use for the sentences employed in making these statements. These rules of use are: a present-tensed sentence can be used to make a true state-

ment only if uttered simultaneously with the event described, and so on for the other tensed sentences. Thus, an *A*-determinative statement is one that is made by the use of a sentence that has temporal restrictions placed upon its use: its use at different times may make statements having different truth-values. A *B*-relation, or tenseless, statement is one that is made through the use of a sentence that has no temporal restrictions placed upon its use: the utterance of a tenseless sentence makes a statement having the same truth-value whenever it is uttered. For a detailed account of the logic of tensed and tenseless statements see my articles: "Endorsing Predictions," *The Philosophical Review* 70 (1961): 376–85; "Tensed Statements," *The Philosophical Quarterly* 12 (1962): 53–59; "A Reply to Smart, Mayo, and Thalberg on 'Tensed Statements,'" *The Philosophical Quarterly* 13 (1963): 355–56; "Is It Now Now?" *Mind* 73 (1964): 97–105; "The Egocentric Particular and Token-Reflexive Analyses of Tense," *The Philosophical Review* 73 (1964): 213–28; and "Existence, Tense, and Presupposition," *The Monist* 50 (1966).

14. I committed this fallacy in my paper, "Tensed Statements," and am indebted to Professor J. J. C. Smart for pointing this out in his paper, "'Tensed Statements': A Comment," *The Philosophical Quarterly* 12 (1962): 264–65.

15. It might be pointed out that the concept of more past (future) is not a metrical concept. Even if time has no intrinsic metric (due to there being no ultimately discrete events) and we have not laid down conventional coordinative definitions for the metricization of time, we can say that one temporal interval is more past (future) than another due to the fact that these intervals overlap, one of them containing the other as a part of itself. For an excellent discussion of this see A. Grünbaum, *Philosophical Problems of Space and Time* (New York: Knopf, 1963), chap. 1.

16. The thesis of the B-Theory Answer that the *A*-Series can be reduced to the *B*-Series obviously is false, since an *A*-determinative statement cannot be analyzed into a tenseless *B*-relation statement, or even a disjunction of such statements. "*P is* present and *Q is* future" certainly is not logically equivalent to "*P is* earlier than *Q*, or *P is* later than *Q*, or *P is* simultaneous with *Q*," for the latter is a tautology, assuming that '*P*' and '*Q*' refer successfully, while the former is contingent. And even if we make the latter nontautological by dropping one of its three disjuncts, it could still be true and the former tensed statement be false. "*P is* now present" can be analyzed into "*P is* simultaneous with this (or now)," in which "this" is a demonstrative referring either to some event experienced by the speaker when he makes his utterance or to the utterance-token itself, but the latter is a tensed or *A*-determinative statement according to the criterion given in n. 13 above.

17. McTaggart, "The Unreality of Time," *Mind* 1 (1908): 462. My italics. This article is reprinted in McTaggart, *Philosophical Studies* (London: Edward Arnold, 1934).

18. See n. 13 above.

19. "*S is P* while *R is T*" is logically equivalent to "*S* is *P* and *R* is *T or S* was *P* while *R* was *T or S* will be *P* while *R* will be *T*." This is the analogue in connective discourse to reduction (III).

20. This essay was written while the author was engaged in research on "The Logic of Time Language" under a National Science Foundation grant. The author is indebted to Professor Edmund Gettier and Mr. Jay Rosenberg for their critical comments on a draft of the essay.

9

THE EGOCENTRIC PARTICULAR AND TOKEN-REFLEXIVE ANALYSES OF TENSE

It has often been argued that there is something "subjective" about the temporal perspectives of past, present, and future; that there is no "now" in nature except in relation to the tensed utterances of human beings. This supposedly follows from the fact that tensed verbs (as well as other temporal demonstratives), by which we indicate these temporal perspectives, are "egocentric particular" or "token-reflexive" words. The main purpose of this essay is to evaluate this argument. To do this it will be necessary, first, to examine carefully the egocentric particular and token-reflexive analyses of tense and, second, to see just what follows from them in regard to the subjectivity of temporal perspectives.

Reprinted from the *Philosophical Review* 73, no. 2 (April 1964)

I

The Egocentric Particular Analysis of Tense. Russell called pronouns, tenses, and demonstratives "egocentric particulars,"[1] since what they denote is relative to the speaker. He attempted to reduce all such expressions to the egocentric particular "this," in which "this" is a "logically proper name" for a sense datum experienced by the speaker at the time he makes his utterance. For example, "I" means "the biography to which *this* belongs"; "now" means "what is compresent with *this*." "This" is a strange sort of a proper name because it applies to something different—a different sense datum—every time it is uttered. And yet on each occasion of its use it is unambiguous, applying to one and only one particular, though, of course, only the speaker can know its referent since it is a sense datum private to himself.

In accordance with Russell's theory we might give the following analysis of tensed statements:

Analysandum   **Analysans**

S is now P. S's being P is (tenselessly) simultaneous with *this*.
S was P. S's being P is (tenselessly) earlier than *this*.
S will be P. S's being P is (tenselessly) later than *this*.

In this analysis "this" is a logically proper name for a sense datum experienced by the speaker at the time he makes his utterance. Before presenting some decisive objections to this analysis, it must be pointed out that, although tensed verbs and tensed copulas are eliminated in the statements in the analysans, these statements are nevertheless tensed. For the sentences employed in making these statements are controlled by the same rules as control the sentences employed in the corresponding statements in the analysandum. These rules are as follows: the sentences "S is now (was or will be) P" and "S's being P is (tenselessly) simultaneous with (earlier than or later than) *this*" can be used to make a true statement only if uttered at the same time as (later than, or earlier than) S's being P.

The demonstrative "this" in the analysans functions as a temporal, rather than a spatial, indicator. The test for whether "this" functions as a temporal indicator is whether it makes sense, and is natural, to say "the *time* at which *this* occurs," as opposed to "the *place* at which *this* occurs." Since a temporal designation is being made by the above statements, "this" functions in them as a temporal indicator, being short for "the *time* at which *this* occurs"; it would make no sense in these statements to interpret "this" as meaning "the *place* at which *this* occurs," since that would result in our saying "*S*'s being *P* is (tenselessly) simultaneous with (earlier than or later than) the *place* at which *this* occurs." "This" has the same logic as "now" in these statements. On the other hand, in the statement "*S*'s being *P* is to the west of *this*," "this" functions as a spatial indicator, it making sense to say "*S*'s being *P* is to the west of the *place* at which *this* occurs" but not "the *time* at which *this* occurs."

One set of objections to the egocentric particular analysis concerns the role of the logically proper name "this." Russell claimed that all egocentric particulars could be defined in terms of an expression containing "this," in which "this" denotes a sense datum private to the speaker. But since sense data are mental events, occurring in time but not in space, how can the egocentric particular "here" be defined? According to Russell it would mean "the place at which *this* occurs"; but this is inadequate, for "this" cannot denote a position in space since it denotes a mental event. A more fundamental objection to Russell's analysis is that it renders communication impossible, not only between different persons, but even in respect to a single person at different moments in his history. Only the speaker can know the referent of "this," and thus the hearer cannot know what event *S*'s being *P* is simultaneous with (earlier than, or later than). Any analysis of language that entails the impossibility of communication is reduced to absurdity.

These objections can be easily met by making a slight alteration in the egocentric particular analysis: instead of "this" denoting a private sense datum, let it have as its referent a publicly observable event that the speaker experiences at the time he makes his utterance. Russell's claim that "this" must denote a sense datum is a result of his epistemological quest for certainty, and by making the above alteration we are separating the analysis of egocentric particulars from this dubious piece of epistemology. All future references to the egocentric particular analysis will refer to this revised version.

The Token-reflexive Analysis of Tense. An independent, though in some ways similar, analysis of egocentric words was given by Reichenbach, who called them "token-reflexive" words.[2] A word is defined as a class of similar tokens, a token being defined as a physical sign; for example, ink marks on paper, chalk marks on a board, sound waves produced in a human throat. By *similar* tokens Reichenbach means tokens that are equisignificant, rather than tokens that physically resemble each other. A token-reflexive word is one that refers to the corresponding token used in an individual act of speech or writing. Every token of a given token-reflexive word will refer to a different physical token, namely, itself. All such words can be defined in terms of "this token." For example, "I" means "the person who utters *this token*"; "now" means "the time at which *this token* is uttered." Every token of the phrase "this token" refers to a different token—a different set of ink marks or noises. A sentence containing a token-reflexive word will be called a token-reflexive sentence; every token of a given token-reflexive sentence will refer to a different sentence token.

In accordance with this treatment of token-reflexive words we could give the following analysis of tensed statements:

Analysandum Analysans

S is now P.	S's being P is (tenselessly) simultaneous with *this token*.
S was P.	S's being P is (tenselessly) earlier than *this token*.
S will be P.	S's being P is (tenselessly) later than *this token*.

In this analysis "this token" refers to the entire sentence token within which the token of the phrase "this token" occurs.[3] In the above table of equivalences there are three different tokens of the phrase "this token," each one referring to a different sentence token, namely, the one within which it occurs. As was the case with the egocentric particular analysis, the statements in the analysans of the token-reflexive analysis are just as much tensed statements as are the statements in the analysandum, in that the sentences employed in both sets of statements are subject to the same temporal restrictions in their use; that is, they can be used to make a true statement only if uttered at the same time as (later than or earlier than) *S*'s being *P*. Also, "this token," like the logically proper name "this" in the analysans of the egocentric particular analysis, functions as a temporal, rather than a spatial, indicator because it is meaningful to say "the *time* at which *this token* occurs" but not "the *place* at which *this token* occurs." It is meaningless to say "*S* 's being *P* is simultaneous with (earlier than or later than) the *place* at which *this token* occurs."

While the token-reflexive analysis is in general agreement with the egocentric particular analysis, it differs from the latter in making the referent of "this" the physical token occurring in the speech act, rather than some *other* event simultaneous with the occurrence of this token. By doing this, the token-reflexive analysis makes explicit the implicit reference made to the sentence token in the analysans of the egocentric particular analysis, in that "this" denotes an event experienced by the speaker at the time he makes his *utterance*. Since "this" is a logically proper name for an event occurring simultaneously with the occurrence of the token of "this," we must first be able to locate the token of "this" before we can know what its referent is. By making do only with the token of "this" occurring in a speech act, the token-reflexive analysis eliminates the need to bring in some event in addition to the occurrence of the token. Therefore this analysis is more economical than the egocentric particular one, which must make reference to two events—the occurrence of the token and of some event *other* than the token that is simultaneous with the token.

It may be doubted whether the copula "is" in the analysans of the egocentric particular and token-reflexive analyses really is tenseless.[4] I believe, however, that it can be shown that the copula *must* be tenseless. In some contexts the copula "is" is tenseless—for example, "two and two *is* four," "red *is* a color"—while in others it is tensed—for example, "the battle *is* raging." The test for determining whether "is" functions as a tenseless, rather than a tensed, copula is as follows: if the context permits the substitution of "was" or "will be" for "is" the copula is tensed, if not it is tenseless. It is meaningless, for example, to substitute "was" or "will be" for "is" in "two and two *is* four," whereas such a substitution is not meaningless (though it may result in a false statement) in "the battle *is* raging." Using this test it can be shown that the copula must be tenseless in "*S*'s being *P is* simultaneous with (earlier than or later than) *this*," in which "this" is either a logically proper name or token-reflexive, for when we substitute "was" or "will be" for "is" it results in the nonsensical utterance "*S*'s being *P was* (or will be) simultaneous with (earlier than or later than) *this*." But what exactly is wrong with saying this?

When a speaker says "*this token*" or "*this event*," although he does not explicitly assert it, nevertheless it is presupposed that the token or event denoted by "this" is present.[5] It is for this reason that it is logically redundant to say "*This* token (or event) is present." In fact, it is a dangerous logical redundancy since it makes it appear as if it would be meaningful to assert "*This* token (or event) is *not* present" or "*This* token (or event) *was* (or will be) present; that is, is now past (or future)." But these statements are contradictory, for each of them contradicts a statement that it presupposes, namely, the statement to the effect that the referent of "this" is present. It is contradictory to say of an event that it is both present and not present, or present and past (or future). For this reason it is contradictory to say that some event *was* (or will be) simultaneous with *this*, since it is presupposed that the token or event denoted by "this" is present, and any event simultaneous with this token or event is itself present and therefore not past or future. That would entail that some event that is past (or future) is also present, which is a contradiction. Therefore, when we say "*S*'s being *P is* simultaneous with *this* (or *this token*)," the "is" must be tenseless since the context does not permit the substitution of "was" or "will be" for "is." Similar reasons can be given for the tenseless nature of the "is" in "*S*'s being *P is* earlier than *this* (or *this* token)" and "*S*'s being *P is* later than *this* (or *this token*)" for it is contradictory to say "*S*'s being *P was* later than *this*" and "*S*'s being *P will* be earlier than *this*."

II

Having clarified what is involved in the egocentric particular and token-reflexive analyses of tense, we can now directly attack the main question of this essay: what follows from these analyses in regard to the subjectivity of temporal perspectives?

Those who believe in the subjectivity of past, present, and future deny that these characteristics are intrinsic to events. All times are claimed to be equally real. There is "no more a single rolling Now than there is a single rolling Here along a spatial line—a standing line of soldiers, for example, though each of them has his vivid presentment of his own Here."[6] Russell used the egocentric particular analysis of tense to justify this democratic way of conceiving time:

> I think it is extremely difficult, if you get rid of consciousness altogether, to explain what you mean by such a word as "this," what it is that makes the absence of impartiality. You would say that in a purely physical world there would be a complete impartiality. All parts of time and all regions of space would seem equally emphatic. But what really happens is that we *pick out* certain facts, past and future and all that sort of thing; they all *radiate out from* "this."[7]

What is revealing in this quotation is Russell's use of the phrase "pick out." He claims that all parts of space and time are equally real, there being no "here" or "now" in the physical world. No event or moment of time is present *simpliciter* any more than any point in space is here *simpliciter*, but what happens is that the speaker "picks out" or selects some event or moment of time by pointing to it and uttering the word "this." It would follow that what event or moment is denoted by "this" is arbitrary, being subject to the speaker's free choice, in the same way that the object in space denoted by "this" is subject to the free choice of the speaker. Just as the spatial object denoted by "this" is not more real than, does not exist in any different sense from, the objects that coexist with it in space, so too the event or moment of time denoted by "this" in the analysans of the egocentric particular analysis of tense is not more real than, does not exist in any different sense from, the events or moments preceding and succeeding it in time. Therefore past, present, and future are relative to the speaker, since he is free to choose what event or moment of time will be denoted by "this," and as a result be present. And for this reason these temporal perspectives are subjective.

Ayer has given an analysis of temporal perspectives that involves the same "picture":

> Events are not in themselves either past, present, or future. In themselves they stand in relations of temporal precedence which do not vary with time.... What varies is only the point of reference which *is taken* to constitute the present... the point of present reference, by which *we orient ourselves* in time, the point of reference which is implied by our use of tenses, is continuously shifted.[8]

What is revealing in this quotation is Ayer's use of the phrases "the point of reference which *is taken*" and "the point of reference, by which *we orient ourselves*." Ayer, like Russell, suggests that the speaker chooses what event or moment of time is present; and since it is only in relation to this chosen event that other events are past, present, and future, these tensed perspectives are subjective.

If the Russell-Ayer way of picturing the selectivity of "this" is correct, it would follow that there is something subjective, in the sense of being language-dependent, about temporal perspectives. But this way of picturing the use or function of the demonstrative "this" is incorrect and rests on a false analogy between a temporal series of events and a spatial order of objects. The crucial point is: the demonstrative "this" is *spatially* selective, picking out one object in the speaker's visual field from among other objects coexistent with it that could have been chosen or selected in its place, but it is never *temporally* selective, picking out one event or moment from among other events or moments earlier or later than it that could have been chosen in its place. For example, in my visual field there are now three objects—a lamp, a pencil, and a pen. I point to the lamp and say "this," thereby picking it out; I could, however, have chosen to point to the pencil or the pen and thus have picked it out instead of the lamp. But there is no temporal field of vision corresponding to a spatial field of vision, since events that are earlier and later than each other by definition do not coexist. While it is correct to say that "now," and "this" in the analysans of the egocentric particular and token-reflexive analyses function as temporal indicators or demonstratives, it would be wrong to say that they pick out, select, or choose a moment of time.

What is so misleading in the quotation from Ayer is the suggestion that we are free to *orient ourselves* in time the way we do in space. The Russell-Ayer view of "this" being temporally as well as spatially selective implies that we spatialize time by conceiving of events as quasi-substances that coexist and endure in a one-dimensional spatial order. The speaker on this view plays a role similar to that of the transcendent observer in the River-of-Time metaphor. He is outside this order and is free to "move" along it in any direction he chooses, as is a general inspecting a row of soldiers. He can pick out any soldier he chooses merely by walking up to him and saying "this." When Russell says that everything "radiates out from 'this'" he is treating the "this" as if it were the transcendent spotlight of presentness that plays along a line of coexistent substances, such as a row of soldiers.[9]

The basic common-sense belief that man is not temporally free to choose his "now," that he is finite and time-bound, is reflected in that fact that "this" or "now" is never temporally selective. While it is true that a token of "here" does not select a position in space, since there is no possibility of its denoting a place other than that occupied by the speaker, nevertheless the speaker can, within some limits, choose what place will be denoted by his next utterance of "here" by moving to a different place. But unfortunately we cannot "move" about in time and make any event or moment of time we choose present merely by pointing to it and saying "this"; we cannot alter our temporal perspective at will, as we can our spatial perspective. If we could choose our temporal perspective we could not have the concepts we do of planning, choosing, intending, causing something to happen, and so forth, all of which rest on the fundamental fact that there is an *imposed* temporal schema of past, present, and future that is not of our doing or choosing.

A parallel argument to that of Russell-Ayer for the subjectivity of temporal perspectives, but based on the token-reflexive rather than the egocentric particular analysis, would be the following. The token-reflexive analysis shows that when we say "S is now (was or will be) P" we really are asserting that "S's being P is (tenselessly) simultaneous with (earlier than or later than) *this token*," in which "this token" *refers* to the entire sentence token within which it occurs. Since events are past, present, and future only in the elliptical sense of being respectively earlier than, simultaneous with, or later than a given tensed sentence token, and since the speaker can choose or select which sentence token that shall be by his use of the token-reflexive phrase "this token," it follows that temporal perspectives are subjective in the sense of being dependent upon the speaker.

This argument suffers from the same defective premise as the Russell-Ayer argument—namely, that the speaker picks out or chooses the event, in this case the occurrence of a sentence token, which will serve as the point of orientation for the temporal schema of past, present, and future. When a person utters a word that by stipulation is token-reflexive, such as "you" or "this" in Reichenbach's analysis, he in no sense picks out or selects which particular token of "you" or "this" will be referred to. He has some choice, however, as to which person or object shall be denoted by his token of "you" or "this," assuming that there is more than one person or object in his immediate vicinity. "This," when interpreted in accordance with the token-reflexive analysis, is a very queer sort of demonstrative, for it involves no element of selectivity. In the ordinary use of the demonstrative "this" there is an element of spatial, but not temporal, selectivity. But if "this" is token-reflexive, even the element of spatial selectivity drops out; for an utterance of "this token," when interpreted in accordance with the token-reflexive analysis, does not pick out one token from among other tokens simultaneous with it that could have been chosen in its place. What would it be like for a person to utter a token of the token-reflexive phrase "this token" and not refer to the token he utters? It is impossible for a token of "this token" to refer unsuccessfully, that is, not to refer to some physical token. It is possible for "I" and "here" to be used unsuccessfully if uttered, for example, by a disembodied spirit, for they would merely prompt the question "Who?" or "Where?" Similarly, a person who utters a token-reflexive sentence does not pick out or select a sentence token. Since the speaker does not choose the token or sentence token that serves as the origin of his tensed temporal schema when he says "this token," the argument is destroyed for the subjectivity of temporal perspectives based on the token-reflexive analysis, which made it appear that there was something speaker-dependent about past, present, and future. Moreover, when I utter a token of "this token" I am certain that it is present *simpliciter*, while my other utterance tokens are past or future. Though I do not assert that this token is present, it is, as pointed out in Section I, presupposed; and for this reason it is logically redundant to say, "This token is present," just as it would be contradictory to say, "This token is not present."

In granting, for the sake of argument, that language could be token-reflexive, we may have conceded too much or, at any rate, may have overlooked the difference between the way in which a token-reflexive word, phrase, or sentence refers to itself and the way in which it refers to something other than itself. I shall argue that: (i) no word is token-reflexive in the radical sense that no token of any word is self-referring; (ii) no phrase or sentence is token-reflexive in the less radical sense that for any phrase or sentence we can find some token of it that is not self-referring; and (iii) in cases where a particular phrase token or sentence token is token-reflexive it does not refer to itself in the manner of picking out or selecting itself. In raising the question whether language can be token-reflexive, we must stress that our concern is with ordinary language. One could make any word, phrase, or sentence token-reflexive merely by *stipulating* that it shall be. We could stipulate, for example, as Reichenbach does, that any symbol is token-reflexive when written within what he calls "token-quotes": ↘ this ↙. By writing "this" within token-quotes we make it token-reflexive, but such a move is unilluminating and does nothing to show that the ordinary use of "this" or any other symbol placed within token-quotes is token-reflexive.

(i) In arguing that no word is token-reflexive, we shall concentrate on demonstratives, pronouns, and verbs, since they are the usual candidates for token-reflexive words. These words are used to refer not to themselves, but to something other than themselves, though they do so by the spatiotemporal connection between the token occurring in a speech act and its referent. When I say "you," I am referring to a person in my vicinity and not to the token of "you" that I utter, though in order to know the referent of this token one would have to know the spatiotemporal relation that it has to the person in question. When I point and say "this tree," no doubt I attract attention to myself and my utterance token; otherwise I could not refer successfully to the tree. But it would be wrong to say that I refer to myself or to the token I utter.

The demonstrative "this" is ordinarily used in connection with an act of pointing. When used alone it is a surrogate for an act of pointing: it is a stand-in for an index finger. An index finger is a necessary element involved in pointing to something, but for this very reason can never point to itself, any more than a hammer, which is an instrument used in hammering something, can hammer itself. If I want to refer to my index finger I must point to it with my other index finger, or I might just hold up the index finger and say "this index finger," but the "this" is a surrogate for my pointing to this finger with my other index finger. The only case in which an index finger might be said to point to itself is when a person uses his index finger to point to itself in a mirror. But then he points, not to his index finger, but to the image of his index finger in the mirror.

Since the demonstrative "this" is a surrogate for an index finger, it follows that a token of "this" is never self-referring any more than an index finger is. When "this" is used in conjunction with some other word(s)—for example, "this tree," "this token"—"this" can never refer to the token of "this" that occurs in the speech act, but always to something other than the token. If a perverse radio announcer should say, "The time will be five o'clock when you hear the next token of the word 'this.' ... This," it would not be correct to say that the token of "this" occurring at the end of his sentence token is self-referring, for he denotes or refers to this particular token by the definite description, "the next token of the word 'this,'" that immediately precedes it. Another possible counterexample would be to say "this room and everything in it," but here "this" refers not to itself but to a room, it not being essential that the token of "this" occur in the room referred to. It would not if the speaker were standing outside the room when he made his utterance. Similar considerations can be brought to bear against the counterexample "this phrase and every token in it"; for "this" refers to something other than itself—a phrase—and, moreover, it is not essential that the token of "this" occur within the phrase referred to.

(ii) So far we have argued that in ordinary language no *word* is token-reflexive in the radical sense that no token of any given word is self-referring. The token-reflexive theory does not, however, claim merely that certain words, when used alone, are token-reflexive, but also that their inclusion in a phrase or sentence renders that *phrase* or *sentence* as a whole token-reflexive. In attempting to answer the question of whether a phrase or sentence *as a whole* can be token-reflexive, we must repeat the definition of a token-reflexive expression that we gave in Section I. A token-reflexive word, phrase, or sentence is one that refers to the corresponding token used in an individual act of speech or writing. Therefore, *every* token of a given token-reflexive word, phrase, or sentence must refer to itself. I believe that it can be shown that no phrase or sentence is token-reflexive in this sense, because for any phrase or sentence we can find some token of it that is not token-reflexive. In this connection let us consider the sentences that are most often cited as being token-reflexive: "This sentence is in pica type," "This sentence contains five words," "This sentence token is short," "This sentence token is loud." Most tokens of these sentences are not token-reflexive because they are used to refer to a sentence token that immediately precedes or follows them; for example, "This sentence contains five words. 'The boy hit the ball.'" Tokens of these sentences are self-referring only in default of there being any other sentence token in their immediate vicinity for them to refer to; for example, if a token of the sentence "This sentence is in pica type" appears alone on a sheet of paper, we then assume that it is self-referring. There are some sentence tokens, such as "This sentence is false," which we would not interpret as being self-referring even in default of there being some other sentence token for them to refer to. Similar considerations apply to phrases, such as "this phrase," and so forth.

(iii) In cases where a particular phrase token or sentence token is token-reflexive, we must make two things clear. First, a token-reflexive phrase token or sentence token refers to itself *qua* physical token and not to the meaning or reference of this token, it being nonsense to say, "The meaning of this sentence is the meaning of this sentence" or "This sentence refers to what this sentence refers to." Second, the word "refer" is being used in a way different from when we say that a demonstrative such as "this," or a pronoun such as "you," refers to something, for only in the latter case is there an element of selectivity—the picking out of one thing from among other things that could have been denoted in its place. Since the argument for the subjectivity of temporal perspectives rests on confounding these two different senses of "refer," let us designate the latter as "refer$_1$" and the former as "refer$_2$." A token-reflexive phrase token or sentence token refers$_2$ to itself, but cannot refer$_1$ to itself because it does not pick out or select itself. In cases where it has been stipulated that "this" or "this token" is to be token-reflexive, we must be careful not to confuse the way in which such a word refers to the token used in an individual speech act and the way in which it refers to something other than the token used in a speech act. A token of a token-reflexive word refers$_2$ to itself and refers$_1$ to something other than itself. But unless it can be shown that a tensed sentence token refers$_1$ to itself, it will not have been shown that there is something subjective about tensed perspectives in the sense of being relative to a token sentence or word that the speaker selects.

While the token-reflexive analysis is misleading and encourages philosophers to place a wrong interpretation upon it, it still serves a valuable function in making explicit the truth conditions of tensed statements, which I shall call "the Rules for Tensed Assertion." They are:

> The present-tensed sentence is used to describe (report or record) events virtually simultaneous with the describing of them; the past-tensed sentence to describe events earlier than the describing of them; and the future-tensed sentence to describe events later than the describing of them.[10]

These rules show why the speaker must have a unique temporal perspective in the same time series to which the event being described belongs: for in order to designate an event as either past, present, or future his utterance token must, according to these rules, be respectively either later than, simultaneous with, or earlier than the event described. A being outside of this time series could not designate any event in it as past, present, or future.

All that follows from the token-reflexive analysis or the Rules for

Tensed Assertion in regard to the subjectivity of tensed perspectives is the harmless tautology that if no one uttered a tensed sentence, then no event would be earlier than, simultaneous with, or later than a tensed sentence token. And as a result no one would designate an event as being past, present, or future and communicate this information. If no one asserts that an event is past, present, or future, then no one asserts that an event is past, present, or future. It does not follow from the token-reflexive analysis of tense that events *would* or *could* not be past, present, and future *if* no one uttered tensed sentences about them, because the token-reflexive analysis is concerned only with *categorical* statements and entails nothing about the analysis of hypothetical statements, such as, "Events would be present, past, and future even if no one spoke about them through the use of tensed sentences." Tensed perspectives are not subjective in any of the familiar senses of this term. They are not: (1) dependent upon the selection or choice of a language-user; or (2) knowable only through private access, for that an event past, present, or future is open to public verification; or (3) incommunicable, for tenses are part of intersubjective communication. In regard to (3), it can be shown that successful tensed communication—that is, for one person to inform another that some event is past, present, or future—requires: first, that the speaker must use, not just mention, a tensed sentence; second, that the hearer must either, in the paradigm case, share the same context as the speaker—be standing face to face with him—or, in the nonparadigm case, be able to relate the speaker's temporal perspective to his own; and third, that both speaker and hearer must have a unique temporal perspective in the same time series to which the event being described belongs.

NOTES

1. Cf. Russell, *An Inquiry into Meaning and Truth* (New York: W. W. Norton, 1990), ch. 7. In "The Philosophy of Logical Atomism," *Monist* 28–29 (1918–1919), Lecture 4, Russell called egocentric words "emphatic particulars."
2. In *Elements of Symbolic Logic* (New York: Macmillan, 1947), pp. 284–87.
3. Reichenbach uses "theta" in place of "this token." He gave another

analysis of tensed statements in which the analysans is not itself token-reflexive. "*S* is now (was or will be) *P*" is translated into "*S*'s being *P* is (tenselessly) simultaneous with (earlier than or later than) *theta*," in which "theta" is a metalinguistic proper name for the tensed sentence token that immediately precedes it in this sentence. Someone who asserts this latter statement merely describes a timeless relation of simultaneity (precedence or subsequence) between *S*'s being *P* and the occurrence of the tensed sentence token named by "theta," but does not assert that either event is now present, past, or future. But it is for this very reason that there is an asymmetry in information between the former and the latter statement. If someone were told that *S* was *P* it would be pointlessly redundant for him to ask whether *S*'s being *P* is now past, whereas if he were told instead that *S*'s being *P* is (tenselessly) earlier than "theta" such a question would not be redundant. For a more detailed discussion of this point cf. my articles: "Tensed Statements," *Philosophical Quarterly* 12 (1962); "A Reply to Smart, Mayo, and Thalberg on 'Tensed Statements,'" *Philosophical Quarterly* 8 (1963); and "Is It Now Now?," *Mind* 72 (1964).

4. Philosophers who argued that the copula is tensed are: C. D. Broad, *Examination of McTaggart's Philosophy*, vol. 2, pt. 1 (Cambridge: Cambridge University Press, 1938), p. 306; and J. Wisdom, "Time, Fact and Substance," *Proceedings of the Aristotelian Society* 29 (1928–1929): 85.

5. We are concerned only with the demonstrative use of "this." In some of its nondemonstrative uses, such as referring to a person previously mentioned or named in discourse, it is not presupposed that its referent is present. E.g., in "Napoleon was a great general. *This* man shaped history," it is not presupposed that the referent of "this" is present.

6. D. Williams, "The Myth of Passage," *Journal of Philosophy* 48 (1951): 467.

7. Russell, "The Philosophy of Logical Atomism," *Monist* 28–29 (1918–1919), Lecture 4, 55–56. Italics mine.

8. A. J. Ayer, *The Problem of Knowledge* (Baltimore: Penguin Books, 1956), pp. 152–53. Italics mine.

9. It is interesting to note that at the time Russell wrote this he adopted a River-of-Time picture of temporal becoming. In "On the Experience of Time," *Monist* 25 (1915), he pictured physical events as being laid out in a permanent order, with the mind "moving" along it, thereby creating the psychological illusion of events being past, present, and future, and changing in respect to these characteristics.

10. One might question the legitimacy of my speaking about the *use of a sentence* and *rules of use*. While Ryle is right in claiming that the dictionary

includes words, not sentences, he is wrong in claiming that it is incorrect to speak of "using a sentence." The rules for the use of tensed sentences are concerned with a type or class of sentences, and not with specific sentences. Furthermore, they are more than just implicit rules or conventions that native speakers follow in making utterances and in correcting other people's utterances; they are recorded in grammar books and therefore have the same overtly prescriptive role as do the rules of chess.

10

THE IMPOSSIBILITY OF BACKWARD CAUSATION

The preceding Part* explored the logical connections between *A*- and *B*-expressions. It was established that the *A*-determinations of events are both ineliminable and necessary for these events having *B*-relations to each other: and these results hold even if our attempts to reduce *B*-relations to *A*-determinations were unsuccessful. In arguing for these theses many interesting features of the logic of *A*-expressions were uncovered—that *A*-expressions have an informative role but not that of indicating a sensible property, that *A*-expressions are unusual singular terms in that they are neither proper names nor definite descriptions. This Part will explore a different dimension of the logic of *A*-expressions concerning logical asymmetries between the past and the future. It will be shown that many of our fundamental

---

*"The preceding Part," "this Part," etc. refer to this chapter as published in Richard Gale, *The Language of Time* (London: Routledge & Kegan Paul, 1968), chapter 7: "The Impossibility of Bringing about the Past."

concepts, such as causality, action, deliberation, choice, intention, memory, knowledge, truth, possibility, and identification, logically presuppose an asymmetry between the past and future.

It will be recalled that the *A*-Theory held temporal becoming to be an objective property of all events and claimed that because of this the past and future differ ontologically, the future being open and the past closed. Since past events have become present, they have already won their ontological diplomas, unlike future events that still exist in a limbo of mere possibility. Our ordinary concept of time contains this view, as witnessed by such gems as, "Don't cry over spilt milk," "It's like locking the barn after the horse has escaped," and "What has been done cannot be undone." This common-sense distinction between the open future and the closed past can best be clarified by reference to certain logical asymmetries in our ordinary ways of talking about the past and the future: for example, it is meaningful to speak of causing, deliberating, deciding, and intending about a future, but not a past, event, while, on the other hand, it makes sense to speak of having a trace (such as a memory, photograph, or scar) only of a past event.

Any one of these logical asymmetries, when viewed in isolation from the others, will seem to be a rather unexciting tautology—hardly the sort of a thing we would want to get down on our hands and knees and worship. However, when a synoptic view is taken of them, they no longer will appear trivial or unimportant. It will then be seen that these logical asymmetries interlock and mutually support each other like the legs of a tripod, such that one of them cannot be jettisoned without giving up the others as well. Together these asymmetries form the basis of our common-sense conceptual system.

The *B*-Theory's assessment of these logical asymmetries would be as follows. There are no logical asymmetries between past and future because events are not intrinsically past and future, but only earlier than (past at) and later than (future at) some other chosen event(s). At best, certain of the above logical asymmetries can serve as criteria for distinguishing between earlier and later events relative to some chosen event. In other words, none of these criteria enable us to pick out some event as uniquely present, and therefore other events as past and future; since it is true of any time that only events later than (future at) that time could be deliberated about, etc., and that only events earlier than (past at) that time could be remembered, etc. Not only do these logical asymmetries not serve as criteria for determining what event(s) is uniquely present, but there are compelling reasons, based on the Linguistic and Psychological Reductions, for believing that the distinctions of past, present, and future are "subjective."

The *B*-Theory, however, cannot accept the two logical asymmetries above—namely, that some statements about the future are neither true nor false, and that no future individual can be identified—even when they are demoted to the status of mere criteria for distinguishing between an earlier and later time. The *B*-Theory cannot accept them because it countenances no ontological distinctions between events occurring at different times. All events comprising history are equally real and determinate, and can be completely described by timelessly true or false *B*-statements. By a parity of reasoning, it should also be true that all individuals, regardless of when they exist, are equally real and determinate, and therefore should be identifiable through the use of suitable referring expressions, such as proper names and definite descriptions.

We shall begin our articulation of the complex logic of the above family of interrelated logical asymmetries between past and future by first considering the concept of causality and the asymmetry between past and future that is built into this concept. The question that philosophers have asked is, "Could a present event cause a past event?"[1] It is true but unhelpful to reply that this is logically impossible since it is an analytic truth that a present cause cannot have a past effect. The reason why this reply is unhelpful is that it does nothing towards answering the question of whether or not we could alter this analytic truth by suitably changing the rules for the use of the word "cause" and still have a recognizable analogue of our present concept of causality so that while it still is required that a cause be uniformly connected with its effect and could be used to bring its effect about, etc., it is no longer required that a present cause cannot have a past effect. This question, then, is not whether there could be a counterexample to the analytic truth that a cause cannot have a past effect, which, of course, is logically impossible, but whether there could be a "counterstipulation-example" to this analytic truth, that is, a description of a constant conjunction between events (such as is given in paranormal psychology and science fiction) that is of such a sort so as to justify our giving up this analytic truth.[2] A counterstipulation-example usually involves a description of a case in which an agent, in ignorance of the past, performs some intentional action to bring about a past event and later discovers that this event did happen.

The aim of this chapter will be to try and show why there could not be any acceptable counterstipulation-example to this analytic truth. The overall strategy will be to articulate the conceptual centrality of this analytic truth by showing that a change in it will cause absurdities to break out in certain neighboring concepts with which the concept of cause has logical liaisons, such as action, possibility, intention, deliberation, memory, experimentation, responsibility, and punishment; and when we try to protect ourselves from these absurdities by altering these latter concepts as well, we will have twisted our concept of causality, along with these other concepts, out of recognition. In other words, it will be argued that to give up this analytic truth will require such a drastic overhauling of the basic concepts of our conceptual system that they will not be recognizable analogues of their former self. Obviously, I cannot give any precise criterion for just when an altered concept ceases to be a permissible analogue of its former self. While there is room for disagreement about these matters, we can reach agreement upon the logical connections between the concept of causality and these other neighbouring concepts, so that we can determine what changes must be made in the latter so as to accommodate a change in the former. Whether we then wish to say that these changes are so extensive that these concepts are not permissible analogues of their former selves is of secondary importance. However, I do believe that it can be shown that the extended concept of causality that permits a present event to cause a past effect requires such a drastic change in neighboring concepts that there will be little room for disagreement as to whether it is a legitimate analogue to the original concept of causality.

To bring out the conceptual centrality of the analytic truth that a present cause cannot have a past effect, we shall try to devise a counterstipulation-example to this truth and shall note what corresponding conceptual reforms it requires us to make. But before doing this it will be necessary, first, to make some preliminary remarks about causality, and, second, to lay down certain necessary conditions that must be fulfilled by any successful counterstipulation-example.

I. PRELIMINARY REMARKS ABOUT CAUSATION

Fortunately, for our purposes it will not be necessary to define or analyse causality, which probably cannot be done; but it will be essential to distinguish, on the one hand, between a proximate and a remote cause, and, on the other, between a cause and a mere condition. A proximate cause is a cause (in some undefined sense) that bears one of the following three temporal relations to its effect: (1) it can be simultaneous with its effect (to be called a "proximate cause$_1$"); it can be temporally contiguous with its effect (to be called a "proximate cause$_2$"); or (3) it can be temporally separated from its effect by initiating some process that in the normal course of things terminates in its effect (to be called "proximate cause$_3$"). The best way to bring out the differences between these three types of proximate cause is to consider some examples of each.

When a lead ball is released on a not-too-tightly packed sandbag, it immediately begins to indent this bag and continues to do so until the ball ceases to fall because of some counteracting force. The falling of the lead ball is a process that is the proximate cause$_1$ of the indenting of the bag since these two processes are coterminus. Similarly, the movement of the sculptor's hands is the proximate cause$_1$ of the changing in shape of the block of clay. In cases of proximate causation$_1$ it might seem arbitrary as to which event is designated as the cause and which as the effect. This, however, is not so; for only one of the two related events will have a prior cause (a proximate cause$_2$ or $_3$) that is independent of the other event, i.e., this prior cause could occur without this other event occurring. Thus the falling of the ball is said to be the cause since there is a prior cause for it, such as someone's releasing the ball or the ball being knocked off a shelf, which makes no reference to the indenting of the bag, but there is no prior cause for the indenting of the bag that makes no reference to the ball's falling on it. The movement of the locomotive is said to be the cause of the movement of the cars that are attached to it, since the movement of the locomotive alone can be accounted for in terms of prior causes, such as the manipulation of various levers in the locomotive or the stoking of its fire, etc. (We are ignoring the temporal lapse between the movement of the locomotive and the attached cars due to the elasticity of the connecting medium.)

We are concerned not only with the cause of the changing in shape of the sandbag and the block of clay but also with the proximate cause of the final or completed shape of the bag or clay. When we ask for the proximate cause of the final indentation of the bag (as opposed to the indenting of the bag, which is a process rather than a state), we want to know what event immediately preceded this state of affairs. We distinguish between a physical object or system changing because of some outside intervention and this object or system enduring in some manner, for example, having some enduring property or changing in some uniform manner. The being fully indented is an enduring state of the bag, which commences at the instant at which the outside intervention—the falling of the lead ball—ceases to operate on it. The falling of the lead ball is the proximate cause$_2$ of the fully indented state of the bag since it ends just when its effect begins. In Aristotelian terminology, we might say that the efficient cause consisting of the movement of the sculptor's hands ceases at the instant at which the form is embodied in the clay. Thus the movement of the sculptor's hands is the proximate cause$_2$ of the changing in shape of the clay and the proximate cause$_2$ of the completed shape of the clay.

Often when we inquire into the proximate cause, or, simply, *the* cause, of a puzzling or unusual event or state of affairs, we do not want to know either what happens simultaneously with this event or what is temporally contiguous with it, but rather what initiates some process that in the normal course of things terminates in this event. Here the proximate or immediate cause is temporally separated from its effect by the process that it initiates and that terminates in the beginning of the effect. The action of a man who poisons someone is the proximate cause₃ of his death, since this action initiates a process which *ceteris paribus* will terminate in the person's death. This requires that there not occur during the time in which this process goes on any abnormal event or voluntary intervention of a third party that, in the context under consideration, would be said to be the proximate cause of the person's death. For example, if A pushes B out of the 100th floor window of the Empire State Building, A initiates a process that in the normal course of things will terminate in B's death. But if C should shoot B dead (killing him instantaneously) as he passes the 50th-floor window, A's action is superseded as the cause of B's death because there has been a voluntary intervention of a third person that makes the situation nonstandard. In law, C's subsequent action is said to negative A's action as being the immediate cause of B's death; A can be tried only for attempted murder.[3]

A *remote* cause of an event is a cause that, like a proximate cause₃, is temporally separated from its effect, but that, unlike a proximate causes, is the proximate cause₃ of some sequence of causally related events one of which is, in the context under consideration, said to be the proximate cause (in one of the three senses given above) of the effect. While a proximate cause₃ initiates some process, or sequence of events, it is not the case that some phase of this process, or some member of this sequence of events, is, in the context under consideration, said to be a proximate cause of the effect. It is important to put in the phrase "the context under consideration" to emphasize that we must not shift contexts, because then it could be the case that in the initial context some event is the proximate cause₃ of an event *X* but in some new context there is some subsequent event to this cause that is the proximate cause of *X*. For instance, in a legal context A's shooting B might be said to be the proximate cause₃ of B's death, but in a medical context the proximate cause would be said to be the deprivation of his blood cells of oxygen, which occurs subsequently to his being shot.

It is a gross oversimplification to speak of causality as a relation between two events, since this omits reference to the situation or state of affairs that must obtain if this causal connection is to hold. While common-sense causal generalizations do not specify in any detail what this situation is, we are nevertheless able to recognize when the situation is nonstandard, and therefore the causal generalization does not apply. In a nonstandard situation some necessary condition for the occurrence of the effect is absent or some condition sufficient for preventing the effect is present. Mill claimed that the set of all necessary conditions constituted the sufficient cause of an event, but this fails to take account of the common-sense distinction between a cause and a mere condition. This distinction is based on the fact that a cause, as distinguished from a necessary condition, is usually either an intentional action and/or an abnormal occurrence in relation to the subject-matter under inquiry. Oxygen is a condition but not a cause of a combustion, since oxygen is usually present; but if the usual state of affairs is one in which oxygen is absent, as in a vacuum tube, then the presence of oxygen in this tube could be said to be the cause of a combustion in this tube. In the course of this chapter, when it is said that one event is a sufficient cause of another, this will presuppose that there is a standard situation in which these two events occur, though we cannot specify in detail every necessary condition that makes up this situation.

The distinction between a cause and a mere condition explains why it is that we never speak of a remote cause as being sufficient. A remote cause is a proximate cause of some sequence of causally related event, the final one of which is the proximate cause of the effect. If we were to try and specify the standard situation in which a remote cause is sufficient, reference would have to be made to this sequence of causally related events, along with the situations in which each of them is a sufficient proximate cause of the event following it. Not only would our specification of this situation be fantastically complicated and extend over a long period of time, but more important it would have to include reference to either an unusual event or an intentional action, viz., the final one in the sequence of causally related events. But by including an abnormal event or an intentional action as a condition that comprises a part of the standard situation, we are violating our distinction between a cause and a condition.

The situation or state of affairs in which one event is a sufficient proximate cause of another will cover the period of time from the beginning of the cause to the end of the effect. The reason for this is that the presence or absence of some condition during this time could prevent the effect from occurring. This consideration helps to answer the Russell-Taylor paradox concerning the seeming impossibility of a cause ever being earlier than its effect.[4] For all they show is that the *situation* must extend to the end of the effect, not that the cause cannot precede its effect. The burning of logs in a fireplace is the proximate cause$_1$ of the simultaneous warming of the room only if certain conditions obtain during the occurrence of these two events, such as the room being sufficiently well insulated, no refrigerator being left open in the room, etc. The falling of the lead ball on a sandbag is the proximate cause$_2$ of the fully indented state of the bag only if certain things obtain *both* while the cause occurs (e.g., the ball is not so heavy that it will break the bag) and while the effect occurs or obtains (e.g., there is no counteracting force, such as someone ramming his fist upward into the bag at the instant the ball ceases to fall). Similar considerations apply to cases of proximate causation$_3$, the only difference being that the cause is temporally separated from its effect.

II. NECESSARY CONDITIONS FOR A COUNTERSTIPULATION-EXAMPLE

Having said something about the distinction between a proximate and remote cause and between a cause and a condition, we are now able to specify certain necessary conditions that must be fulfilled by any successful counterstipulation-example to the analytic truth that a present event cannot have a past effect. In saying that these conditions are necessary it does not follow that satisfaction of them is sufficient for a successful counterstipulation-example; in fact, it will be argued in Section III that any alleged counterstipulation-example that fulfills these necessary conditions will fail because it will cause absurdities to break out in neighboring concepts. The conditions that must be satisfied by any successful counterstipulation-example of a present event L being a sufficient cause of a past event E are:

(1) The ordinary use of "past" and "future" must not be radically altered.

(2) It must be the case that every occurrence of an event of type L in a situation of type S has been preceded by an event of type E.
(3) L must be an intentional action.
(4) E must not be a proximate or remote cause of L.
(5) There must be no proximate cause of E that is earlier than L.

The meaning of, and necessity for, some of these conditions may not be readily apparent. Therefore, it is essential that each of these conditions be separately explained at some length, and its necessity justified.

(1) The necessity for this condition is that without it a counterstipulation-example might fail through equivocation. When a person claims that some example justifies our saying that a present event causes a past event, he must continue to use the words "past" and "future" in their familiar sense. The ordinary use of these words is based on certain logical and empirical criteria for distinguishing an asymmetry between the past and the future; an example of the former being that it is logically possible to remember the past and to anticipate the future, and an example of the latter being that our birth is in the past and our death in the future.[5] Any successful counterstipulation-example requires a background of normal causal sequences (e.g., in which a scar is later than the slashing, etc.) in which causes are not later than their effects, and in which it is the past that is remembered and the future that is anticipated. If we should decide to say that our birth is in the future and our death in the past, etc., and that we remember the future and anticipate the past, then we will have accomplished the trivial feat of merely interchanging the use of "past" and "future" in our language. This will require us to recast certain analytic truths, so that it now is an analytic truth that a present event cannot have a *future* effect. But then we would have to devise a new counterstipulation-example to our old analytic truth that would consist of a present event causing a *future* effect. Backward causality necessarily must be the exception. One might object here that one of our logical criteria for distinguishing between the past and the future is that a present event can have future, but not past, effects, and to give this up is ipso facto to change our use of "past" and "future." To meet this

objection let us say that we must continue to use in our counterstipulation-example a majority of both our logical and empirical criteria for distinguishing between past and future.

(2) The necessity for this condition is obvious. Part of the meaning of the claim that a concrete event L in a situation S causes another concrete event E is a generalization to the effect that if there is an occurrence of an event of type L in a situation of type S it will be accompanied by an event of type E. Thus data to the effect that numerous occurrences of events of type L in situations of type S are without exception accompanied by events of type E constitute evidence for the claim that a concrete event L in S causes a concrete event E. That a causal claim about two specific events entails a generalization about a class of events and a situation is perfectly consistent with the belief that there can be a causal connection between two unique events in a certain situation, that is, events that occur only once in the history of the universe.[7] If the counterstipulation is to show that L in S is a *necessary* cause of the earlier E, then the data required would be that events of type E in situations of type S without exception have been followed by events of type L.

But the data required by condition (2) are neutral as to whether L is a sufficient cause of E or whether E is a necessary cause of L. In fact, it does not even establish that there is a causal connection between E and L: their conjunction on numerous occasions could be due to chance. This shows that causality cannot be analysed solely in terms of logical sufficiency or necessity. To be a cause of is something more than to be a sign of. For this reason causal statements cannot be looked upon as Rylean inference tickets or as statements of functional correlation.

(3) In addition to events of type L in situations of type S never failing to be preceded by events of type E, it must be the case that L *brings about E* or *makes E* happen. This notion of *effectiveness* is an essential part of our ordinary concept of causality. The paradigm cases of causality are those in which an agent intentionally intervenes into some situation and brings about a change in it. The situation, for example, might involve a cart's being at rest, and then starting to move when an agent begins pushing it. These are paradigm cases of effectiveness—one

event being made to happen or brought about by another. Because of the deeply entrenched nature of the analytic truth that a present event cannot have a past effect, we shall require that a counterstipulation-example involve a paradigmatic case of causality; therefore, L must itself be an intentional action. If this strong condition is not fulfilled, there would be no compelling reason for saying that L in S is sufficient cause of E rather than that E in S is a necessary cause of L.

It is very difficult to find a case of a present event making something happen in the past because the concept of making involves that the process of making be temporally prior to its result, whether the result be a product or a state of affairs (or event). Just as a particular boat cannot be temporally prior to the process of making it, the state of exhaustion cannot be temporally prior to the process, such as running, that makes a person exhausted. Making some thing or making something happen involves the active control of some material or mechanism. Since ordinary verbs of making have built into them the posteriority of their results, we cannot say that we make something to have happened. However, there is available to us a weaker expression, "bringing it about", which does not require the active control of some material or medium by an agent. Given a suitable counterstipulation-example we might be justified in saying that someone brings it about that something has happened, even though he has not manipulated any levers, pulled any wires, or chiseled any marble. Even with this weaker sense of causing something to happen we run into difficulty, since most ordinary action verbs, which involve bringing something about, require the posteriority of their effect. To find a counterstipulation-example of an agent intentionally performing some action to bring it about that something has happened, we shall have to either invent some new action verb or modify one that we have. We shall allow our alleged counterstipulation-example to envisage any sort of bizarre counterfactual association of events and to invoke as many coincidental occurrences as required. While there is complete freedom to supply content to causal generalizations or laws, there must not be too radical a departure from the form of causal generalizations or laws: that is, a successful counterstipulation-example must retain most of the features of our present conception of a causal law or explanation.

It might be argued that in regard to any alleged counterstipulation-example it can be shown that there is an incompatibility between condition (3) and (2), requiring that L never occur in S without being preceded by E. The argument is based on the introduction of experimental control in which the agent who can do L at will waits for some occasion on which E does not occur and then tries to do L. If he is successful, condition (2) is violated, since there is an occurrence of L in S that is not preceded by E; and if he is unsuccessful after numerous attempts, it shows, in violation of condition (3), that L is not an intentional action, that is, one that can be done at will. This argument is easily countered, for from the fact that on numerous occasions on which E did not occur the agent was unsuccessful in his effort to do L it does not follow that L is not an intentional action. On each occasion on which he tried and failed to do L there might have been lacking some necessary condition for his doing L, the absence of which was not a result of the nonoccurrence of E. This may require us to introduce a number of unlikely coincidences to account for the agent's failure to do L on those occasions, but, as pointed out above, we allow our counterstipulation-example to invoke as many coincidental occurrences as it requires. For example, E might consist in Jones dreaming that Smith will play *Petrouchka* on the piano the following day (call this event L). Smith is able to play the piano and also knows *Petrouchka* by heart. Smith waits for some occasion on which E does not occur and then attempts to do L on the following day. On one occasion his piano is stolen and on another thieves enter his home and tie him up just as he is about to strike the keyboard, etc., and none of these coincidences is caused by the nonoccurrence of E. But from the fact that Smith did not do L on these occasions, it does not follow that he did not have the ability to do L on these occasions, for *ex hypothesis* he is able to play *Petrouchka* at will.

(4) This condition is necessary because it is an analytic truth that causality is asymmetric. Therefore, if E is a cause of L, L cannot be a cause of E. To give up this analytic truth along with the analytic truth that a present event cannot cause a past effect would depart too far from our ordinary concept of causality to count as a recognizable analogue. An example of an alleged counterstipulation-example that vio-

lates this condition would be one in which an agent makes L happen because of his knowledge that E occurred. E might be a mentalist predicting that a man will ride into the night club in five minutes on top of an elephant. His stooge, who is planted outside the club on top of an elephant, hears E on a walkie-talkie radio, and five minutes later rides triumphantly into the club whistling the march from *Aida* (call this event L). Plainly E is a remote cause of L since the stooge does L because he has previously heard E. If we should persist in calling L the cause of E it would entail that E is God. The reason for this is that E is a cause of L and L in turn is a cause of E, in which case E is a cause of itself and therefore is God. One might quibble here that E still is not God since E is only a remote cause of itself.

It might be argued that even when collusion is absent, and therefore L is not caused by E, it can be shown that there is an incompatibility between condition (2) and (4). This argument is basically the same as the one presented in our discussion of condition (3), which is based on exercising experimental control over L so as to make it happen in the absence of E, thus refuting the claim that L is a sufficient cause of E.[7] Whereas the above argument claimed that repeated failures to do L in the absence of E showed that L is not an intentional action, this new form of the argument claims that it entails, contrary to (4), that E is a cause of L. The first premise of this argument is that the data required by condition (2) is neutral as to whether L is a sufficient cause of E or whether E is a necessary cause of L. If E is a necessary cause of L then not-E is a sufficient cause of not-L. Therefore, if on occasions when E does not occur we are unable to make L occur, thus satisfying condition (2), it shows that not-E is the sufficient cause of not-L. And this violates condition (4) since it entails that E is a necessary cause of L.

The conclusion of this argument is a nonsequitur, for it is hardly not-E that is the sufficient cause of not-L. In fact it was not-E that was the cause of our trying to do L, and usually our effort to do something that we have the capacity to do is a positive, rather than a negative, causal factor in its happening. On each occasion when we fail to do L in the absence of E there could be a causal explanation, coincidental though it may be, for not-E that is independent of not-B. For example,

The Impossibility of Backward Causation 239

we wait for some occasion on which the mentalist does not predict that a man will ride into the club in five minutes on an elephant and then attempt to ride into the club on an elephant. On one occasion we fail to get an elephant because the Hertz-Rent-an-Elephant people are all out of elephants, due to the Shriners being in town, and on another occasion the person riding the elephant falls off just as he is about to ride into the club, etc.

(5) Why is it necessary that there be no proximate cause of E that is earlier than L? The reason is that if there were a proximate cause of E that is earlier than L then there would be no causal determining of E left over for L in S to perform. In other words, if we already have a complete causal explanation of E in terms of an event(s) earlier than or simultaneous with E there is no need to invoke some later event L to causally account for E.

A rather ingenious argument might be advanced to show that condition (5) can never be satisfied. L is an intentional action for which the cause might be certain psychological factors, such as the agent's desires, motives, etc., and, granted the principle of determinism, there can be no limit placed upon how far back we can trace the causal ancestry of this cause of L. But this entails that we can always find some causal ancestor of L that is either simultaneous with or contiguous with E. But then there is a proximate cause of E that is earlier than L. The following diagram, using "t" to represent an interval (rather than an instant) of time and ⌢ to represent *is a proximate cause of*, illustrates this:

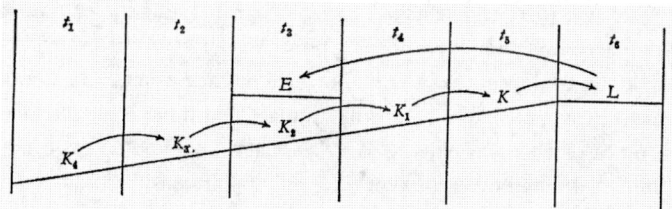

It is argued that in this diagram K_2 qualifies as a proximate cause$_2$ of E and K_3 qualifies as a proximate causes of E, thereby failing to satisfy condition (5). The reason for this is based on the definition that we gave of a proximate cause in section I. A proximate cause$_1$ is a cause (in some undefined sense) that is simultaneous with its effect, and a proximate cause$_2$ is a cause (in some undefined sense) that is temporally contiguous with its effect. Since K_2 is a cause of E and is simultaneous with E it is, by definition, a proximate cause$_1$ of E; and since K_3 is a cause of E and is temporally contiguous with E it is, by definition, a proximate cause$_2$ of K. It would be inconsistent with our definition of remote cause to say that K_2, as well as K_3, are remote causes of E, for a remote cause was defined as being both temporally separated from its effect *and* the proximate cause of some sequence of causally related events, one of which is the proximate cause of the effect. While K_2 and K_3 satisfy the second conjunct of this definition, they fail to satisfy the first conjunct, requiring that a remote cause be temporally separated from its effect. One cannot counter this argument by changing the definition of proximate cause so as to rule out the possibility of a proximate cause of an event being the proximate cause of some sequence of causally related events, the final one of which is the proximate cause of this event. For this gives us a circular definition, e.g. A proximate cause$_1$ is a cause that is simultaneous with its effect and is not the *proximate cause* of some sequence of causally related events, the final one of which is the *proximate cause* of this effect.

There is a way of meeting this argument. Let us assume that the concrete event K_2 occurred in a situation C. If the concrete event K_2 in C is a sufficient proximate cause of E, this entails, not that there are repetitions of K_2-type events in C-type situations accompanied by E-type events (there can be a causal connection between unique events), but that whenever (if ever) events of type K_2 occur in a situation of type C they are accompanied by events of type E. All our counterstipulation-example has to do in order to rule out the concrete event K_2 in C as a sufficient proximate cause of E is to stipulate that there is at least one occurrence of an event of type K_2 in a situation of type C that is not accompanied by an event of type E.[8] And similar considerations hold mutatis mutandis for K_3. To rule out in this manner any causal ancestor of L as being a proximate cause of E will require our counter-stipulation-example to make many stipulations concerning the way in which events occur, but we have agreed to allow complete freedom in the number and type of stipulations that are made concerning the de facto connections between events. Since there is no proximate cause of E earlier than L, it follows that any remote cause of E that is earlier than L, such as K_4 in the above diagram, cannot be a proximate or remote cause of any event earlier than L that is the proximate cause of E. Rather, K_4 can be a remote cause of E only because it is a remote cause of L. And note that K_4 is not a remote cause of L in virtue of its being a remote cause of E since, in accordance with condition (4), E cannot be a remote or proximate cause of L. K_4 must be the proximate cause of some sequence of causally related events that does not include E and one of which (in this case K) is the proximate cause of L.

Having done something to explain and justify condition (5), it can be shown why most of the counterstipulation-examples that have been offered, and, in particular, all of those offered by Dummett in his two articles, have failed to satisfy this condition. Dummett, in his article on "Bringing About the Past," gives an example of a tribe that has an initiation rite in which their young warriors go off on a six-day trip to prove their bravery. The young men are accompanied by elders of the tribe who act as witnesses. They spend the first two days journeying to the hunting area, on the third and fourth days the young warriors fight with wild animals and prove themselves brave or cowardly, and they travel homeward on the fifth and sixth days. The chief of the tribe dances during the entire six-day period to cause them to be brave. Now the brave conduct of the young men on the third and fourth days is the sort of event for which there are prior causes that together are a sufficient cause of this event, such as eugenics, education, wild-animal combat training, promises of rewards and punishment, etc. Dummett is conveniently silent as to how these young men are raised: a tribe would be most remiss if it relied solely on the chief's six-day dance marathon to bring about the men's bravery and paid no attention to the way in which these men were reared. On any occasion when the men's brave conduct can be satisfactorily accounted for by prior causes, there would be no need to invoke the chief's dancing on the fifth and sixth days as the cause, or even a part of the cause.

A similar objection can be made to another one of Dummett's examples:

> A man is observed regularly to wake up three minutes before his alarm clock goes off. He often does not know when he goes to sleep whether or not the alarm has been wound, nor for what time it has been set. Whenever the alarm has been set and wound, but fails to go off because of some mechanical accident, which is later discovered, he always sleeps till very late.[9]

Now a person's waking up is the sort of event for which there are known prior causes, such as being shaken violently. Dummett admits as much when he says that on occasions when the alarm fails to go off, the man oversleeps. But he nevertheless wakes up without the alarm going off three minutes later: he is not doomed to a possibly endless sleep that can be ended only by the arrival of a princely alarm clock that is about to go off in three minutes. On any occasion when there is a prior sufficient cause for the man waking up, we would not invoke the subsequent ringing of the alarm clock as the cause.

The objections that have been raised to Dummett's two examples could be met by stipulating that there are no proximate sufficient causes, for the brave conduct of the men and the waking of the man that are earlier than, respectively, the chief's dancing on the fifth and sixth days and the alarm clock ringing. This stipulation is in accordance with condition (5), which requires that there must be no proximate cause of E that is earlier than L. But condition (5) is ambiguous, admitting of a strong and a weak interpretation. The weak version, to be referred to as "(W_5)," states: On every occasion in which an event of type L occurs in a situation of type S there must be no proximate cause of E that is earlier than L. The strong version, to be referred to as "(S_5)," states: On every occasion in which an event of type E occurs there must be no proximate cause of it that is earlier than the subsequent occurrence of an event of type L in a situation of type S. The difference between these two versions of (5) is that (W_5) permits an occurrence of an event of type E for which there is a proximate cause that is earlier than or simultaneous with E, provided only that an event of type L does not subsequently occur in a situation of type S on that occasion; whereas, (S_5) rules out this possibility, since it requires that no occurrence of an event of type E can have a proximate cause earlier than the subsequent occurrence of an event of type L in S. It shall now be shown that (W_5) involves a departure from the ordinary concept of a causal explanation and law, and it shall then be shown that (S_5) is subject to the same difficulty, only not in as obvious a manner as (W_5).

In Section I it was pointed out that the situation in which a cause C is sufficient for its effect E will cover the period of time from the beginning of the cause to the end of the effect. The reason for this is that the presence or absence of some factor during this period of time could negative C as the cause of E either by *preventing* E from happening or *superseding* C as the cause of E (e.g., our earlier example in which the shooting of a man as he falls past the 50th-floor window supersedes his being pushed out of the 100th-floor window as the cause of his death). The description of the situation in which one event is a sufficient proximate cause of another must not refer to what does or does not obtain at any time *earlier* than the *beginning* of the cause or *later* than the *end* of the effect.[10] Obviously the temporal relation between a situation and two causally related events will be different when the cause is later than the effect, but we can derive the formula for the description of this situation by interchanging "earlier" with "later" and "beginning" with "end" in the preceding formula for the description of a situation in which a cause is not later than its effect. The description of the situation in which one event is a sufficient proximate cause of another (earlier event) must not refer to what does or does not obtain at any time *later* than the *end* of the cause or *earlier* than the *beginning* of the effect.[11] (W_5) violates this formula because it requires that our description of the situation in which L is a sufficient proximate cause of the earlier E make reference to what does not obtain *earlier* than the *beginning* of the effect E, namely, that there is no proximate cause of E that is earlier than E. If there is an earlier proximate cause of E it negatives L as the cause of E by superseding L. Thus the ringing of the alarm clock is the sufficient proximate cause of the man's waking up three minutes earlier only if this earlier event is not preceded by his being shaken violently, etc. This is analogous to describing the situation of a normal prior proximate cause by reference to what does not occur *later* than the *end* of the effect: shaking a man violently is the cause of his waking up only if in the situation there is not a ringing of his alarm clock three minutes after he wakes up.

It might be thought that this difficulty can be avoided by replacing (W_5) by (S_5). Since (S_5) stipulates that there must be no proximate cause of an event of type E other than L, and thus none that is earlier than E, we need not describe the situation in which L is a sufficient cause of E by reference to the nonoccurrence of certain other possible proximate causes of E earlier than E. If (S_5) is satisfied then there is *as a matter of fact* no proximate cause of E earlier than E, and therefore there is no event earlier than E whose occurrence must be ruled out in the description of the situation in which L is causally sufficient for E.

This superiority of (S_5) over (W_5) is, however, illusory. The question is not whether there is *in fact* any earlier proximate cause of E but what we would say if (as is logically possible) there were one. To understand the meaning of an expression we must elicit its rules of use, which permit us to use the expression on certain sorts of occasions and in certain sentential contexts, *but not in others*. The rules of use specify a set of permissible as well as prohibited moves. In eliciting the meaning that the word *cause* has in a counterstipulation-example that satisfies (S_5) we must discover its rules of use, and we discover these not only by noting on what sort of occasions it is used but also by seeing on what sort of occasions it would not be used. Thus, the question, "Would you call the concrete event L the cause of E if on that occasion there were a prior proximate cause of E?" is relevant to determining the meaning that *cause* has in a counterstipulation-example satisfying (S_5). That such a state of affairs does not in fact occur, which is what (S_5) stipulates, is irrelevant to how the word *cause* is being used. The fact that (S_5) requires us to answer that L is the cause of E only if on that occasion there is no proximate cause of E that is earlier than E shows that "cause" is being used in the same way as it is in an example that satisfies (W_5). And therefore the same difficulty that applies to the use of "cause" in a counterstipulation-example satisfying (W_5) holds for one satisfying (S_5).

A defender of a counterstipulation-example satisfying condition (W_5) or (S_5) might try to minimize the extent to which his use of "cause" departs from its ordinary use. He might argue that the reason why we do not have to characterize the situation in which an event is causally sufficient for a nonearlier effect by reference to what does not happen later than the end of the effect is due only to the contingent fact that we do not yet have any causal laws involving backward causation. But if such laws were to be established, then if a given event could have both a prior and a posterior cause, we would have to specify the situation in which some earlier event causes it by reference to the nonoccurrence of its posterior cause on that occasion. The difficulty with this reply is that it begs the question, for it attempts to eliminate the difficulty attendant upon a counterstipulation-example by presupposing that we already have, or could have, backward causal connections, which is the very thing to be proven by a counterstipulation-example. I do not know how serious a difficulty this is for a counterstipulation-example, for it is not clear whether the queer way in which the situation is described in such an example is so radical a departure from ordinary usage as to disqualify L as being the cause of E. We shall not linger on this difficulty, for we now hope to show that there are far graver conceptual difficulties connected with any counterstipulation-example satisfying conditions (1)–(5).

III. ABSURDITIES RESULTING FROM A COUNTERSTIPULATION-EXAMPLE

We shall now devise a counterstipulation-example satisfying conditions (1)–(5) for the purpose of showing that it involves a radical departure from the ordinary concept of causality. It will be shown that such an example causes absurdities to break out in certain neighboring concepts with which the concept of causality has logical liaisons, such as action, intention, deliberation, reason, memory, experimentation, responsibility, and punishment. These absurdities can be resolved only by radically altering these concepts. And since the meaning of "cause" depends upon its logical relationships with neighboring words in the language, the changes that we are forced to make in the meaning of the latter are ipso facto changes in the meaning of the former.

Let us devise a counterstipulation-example, which shall be called the *Case of the Retro-Warning*. On numerous occasions Jones learns that his friend Smith was in a dangerous situation at some earlier time. He learns of this in perfectly ordinary ways—records, testimony of observers, collation of disparate memories, etc.—but he does not know what was the eventuation of this dangerous situation nor whether Smith was warned of the danger by anyone. On each of these occasions Jones utters a "retro-warning" (call this event L); for example, he says, "Smith, this is Jones talking to you from your future. There's a time-bomb in the desk drawer!" And on each of these occasions it is the case that Smith has had a paranormal auditory experience in which he hears the exact words that Jones subsequently utters said in Jones's voice (call this event E). The present event L causes the past event E because it is reasonable, so it is argued, to say that Jones does L in order to bring about that E has happened. This example satisfies all of the five necessary conditions. (2) The use of "past" and "future" is not radically altered, for it still is the past that can be remembered, etc. (2) L never occurs without being preceded by E. (3) L is an intentional action. (4) E is not a cause of L. (5) E is called "paranormal" because it has no prior proximate cause, and, in fact, no proximate cause prior to L, thus satisfying (S_5).

It is apparent that the Case of the Retro-Warning requires that numerous conceptual changes be made. Since Jones can perform an intentional action so as to bring about a past event, it is necessary, for the sake of consistency, to alter our present concept of intention so that it is now possible for an agent to have intentions in regard to the past as well as the future. Moreover, we must also allow for *intentional knowledge* of the past as well as the future. An agent has intentional knowledge not solely on the basis of his intention to perform some action but also in virtue of possessing certain nonintentional knowledge. More precisely:

(i) An agent has intentional knowledge of one of his actions X if, and only if, he has an intention to do X and has non-intentional knowledge that he can do X.

(i') An agent has intentional knowledge of an event Y that is not one of his actions if, and only if, he has intentional knowledge of one of his own actions X and knows that X is sufficient to bring about Y.

In the Case of the Retro-Warning, Jones can have intentional knowledge not only of his action L but also of E, since he knows that L is sufficient to bring about E.

An agent gives up an intentional knowledge claim under one of two conditions: *(a)* he finds out either that he cannot carry out his intention to do X or that X is not sufficient to bring about Y; or, more commonly, *(b)* he finds good reasons for not doing X or for not bringing about Y. The "good reasons" have to do with the desirability of $X(Y)$ and its consequences as contrasted with the desirability of other possible courses of action. A peculiarity of intentional knowledge, due to the fact that an agent ceases to have intentional knowledge when he gives up his intention, be it under condition *(a)* or *(b)*, is that that an agent has intentional knowledge that X will occur does not entail that X will occur. Some would question the propriety of speaking of intentional "knowledge" as knowledge, while others might say that this is a counterexample to the claim that that X knows that p entails that p.

To allow for the possibility of backward intention it is necessary that our concept of deliberation be altered so that it is possible to deliberate about the past as well as the future. The necessity for this conceptual reform is due to the analytic truth that an intentional action is one that can, although it need not, be preceded by a period of deliberation about whether to perform this action.

At this point it might be asked, "Granted that we must permit backward intention and deliberation so as to accommodate backward causation, but what is so conceptually absurd about backward intention and deliberation?" What I shall try to show is that this change in our concept of intention and deliberation *radically* alters our ordinary concept of the past, which is in violation of condition (1) for a successful counterstipulation-example. Before doing this it is necessary to articulate a crucial analytic truth about our concept of the past. It is:

(ii) An event is past if, and only if, it is logically possible for any person who is neither in doubt about the occurrence of this event nor believes that it did not occur to have a trace of it.[12]

For a person to have a trace of an event it is required that the person both be in possession of a trace of this event and know on the basis of this trace that this event occurred: a person does not have a trace of an event if he merely has, unknown to himself, a photograph of this event stuck in his back pocket. On the basis of a trace a person can make a noninferential knowledge claim about what happened. It is because of the intentional nature of the concept of *having a trace of* that it is necessary to restrict the conditions under which it is logically possible for a person to have a trace: it is not logically possible for a person to have a trace of an event and also either be in doubt about its occurrence or believe that it did not occur.

I have stated analytic truth (ii) about our concept of the past in terms of the generic concept of trace, rather than the more determinate concept of memory, since it could plausibly be maintained, Plato and Bridie Murphy not withstanding, that it is not logically possible for a person to have a memory of an event occurring prior to his birth, although he could have a trace (such as a photograph) of this event.

There is an important analytic truth about our concept of having a trace of, which could not be given up without *radically* altering our concept of trace and as a consequence our concept of the past. It is:

> (iii) The only logically relevant reason for challenging or giving up a knowledge claim based on an ostensible trace is evidence that indicates that the ostensible trace is unveridical.

If an agent claims to have a trace of X we could legitimately challenge his claim by producing evidence that X did not in fact occur. A person gives up or begins to doubt a claim based on his ostensible memory when he finds new evidence that indicates that his ostensible memory is unveridical.

I shall now try to show that permitting deliberation and trace to work the same side of the street requires us to give up analytic truth (iii), thereby radically altering our concept of the past and rendering the Case of the Retro-Warning unacceptable as a counterstipulation-example. Let us suppose, as is logically possible, that Jones along with several other persons were eyewitnesses on some occasion to the nonoccurrence of E (E being Smith's paranormal auditory experience of being retro-warned): they were standing in the room with him and saw the bomb detonate in his face. Subsequently they remember the nonoccurrence of E and also have other traces of this negative event, such as motion pictures and a tape-recording. Jones certainly is in a position to say that he knows that E did not occur; for he has more than ample traces to backup his knowledge claim. However, all of a sudden Jones begins to deliberate about whether to do L so as to bring about E in the past. At the moment Jones begins to deliberate, he is logically required to give up his knowledge claim based on his ostensible memory and to call into question the knowledge claims of others based on ostensible traces of not-E. The reason for this is due to the following analytic truth about the concept of deliberation:

> (iv) It is not logically possible that an agent deliberate about whether to do X and at the same time either know that X will occur or know that X will not occur.

A corollary to (iv) is:

> (iva) It is not logically possible that an agent deliberate about whether to do X and at the same time know of the nonoccurrence of some event of which X is a sufficient cause.[13]

It would be absurd for Jones to say that he is now deliberating about whether to do L but already knows that L will (will not) occur or that he is now deliberating about whether to do L so as to bring about E but already knows that E does not occur. If Jones already has such knowledge, he is engaging only in a mock deliberation.

What has happened is that Jones has had to give up his knowledge claim based on ostensible traces of not-E, not because he has discovered any new evidence to indicate that E did occur and that therefore these ostensible traces are unveridical, but merely because he has begun to deliberate about doing L so as to bring it about that E did occur. This is in violation of analytic truth (iii) that the only logically relevant reason for challenging or giving up a knowledge claim based on an ostensible trace is evidence that indicates that the ostensible trace is unveridical. To see exactly why this is in violation of (iii) it is necessary to make explicit the following analytic truth about the concept of deliberation:

> (v) An agent's deliberation about whether to do X so as to bring about Y is concerned with reasons for doing X so as to bring about Y and not with evidence that Y in fact will occur.[14]

To deliberate about whether to do X is not to try and discover evidence that X will in fact occur; rather it is concerned with reasons for doing X, based on the desirability of the consequences of X over other possible courses of action. It would be absurd for someone who has just been deliberating about whether to do L so as to bring about E to say that he has made up his mind to do L because he has found conclusive evidence to the effect that E in fact will occur. Deliberating is not trying to infer what one will do. "What ought I to do?" is not a request for a prediction of what I shall do but for good reasons for doing one thing rather than another. Therefore, Jones's giving up his knowledge claim (based on ostensible traces of not-E) in the face of his beginning to deliberate about the desirability of bringing E about is due to his consideration of *reasons* and not *evidence* for these ostensible traces of not-E to be unveridical. Examples of such reasons would be: Smith is not such a bad chap; his death would leave his wife and seven children destitute; we need Smith to play catcher in the company softball game next week; etc. Giving up analytic truth (iii) leads to a paranoic concept of the past, since an agent legitimately can challenge knowledge claims based on ostensible traces merely because he begins to consider good reasons for these claims to be false. There could hardly be a more radical change in our ordinary concept of the past.

There are many moves that a defender of backward causation might make at this point. First, he might stipulate, as he has a perfect right to, that on every occasion on which Jones deliberates about making E to have happened in spite of there being numerous ostensible traces of not-E it is subsequently discovered that all of these traces are unveridical; new traces are unearthed that show that all the eyewitnesses were having delusions and that the motion pictures of not-E are phonies, etc. This, however, is irrelevant, since it still remains the case that Jones is required, in violation of (iii), to give up a knowledge claim based on ostensible traces because of reasons rather than evidence for its being false. It is also unavailing to stipulate that it does not in fact ever happen that Jones begins to deliberate about making E happen when he and others have ostensible traces of not-E. The kind of absurdity that has been shown to follow from the assumption of backward causation is a *conceptual* rather than an *empirical* one. Questions concerning what a defender of backward causation would be required to say if certain logically possible things were to happen are relevant to determining what he means by "cause," "deliberate," "trace," etc. The above refutation of the Case of the Retro-Warning is based on a description of a logically possible state of affairs, and in eliciting the queer way in which Jones would have to speak in such a state of affairs it reveals that his concept of trace and therefore of the past is *radically* different from the ordinary one.

A defender of backward causation might question the supposition that it is logically possible for Jones to begin to deliberate about making E to have happened when he and others have ostensible traces of not-E. If such a supposition is not logically possible, then Jones is spared the absurdity of having to give up his nonintentional knowledge claim based on these ostensible traces when he begins to deliberate about doing L so as to make these ostensible traces unveridical. The reply is that if we want, as would a defender of backward causation, backward deliberation and intention, to be a true analogue to ordinary future deliberation and intention, then it should be logically possible for an agent to give up a nonintentional knowledge claim because he begins to deliberate. An agent can claim to have nonintentional knowledge that M will not occur and then withdraw this claim, as he would be logically required to, when he begins to deliberate about doing L so as to bring about M. By doing L he does not change the future—what will be will be—but he makes it different than it would be if he were not to do L. Analogously, it should be possible for Jones to make a nonintentional knowledge claim that E did not occur and then withdraw this knowledge claim when he begins to deliberate about doing L so as to make E to have happened. What has been has been, but by doing L Jones makes the past different than it would have been if he were not to do L.

It might be claimed that it is only a contingent fact that there is no future analogue to trace. If, as is logically possible, we were to have a faculty that is a future analogue to memory, such as precognition, then we could have noninferential knowledge of the future as well as the past.[15] In such a case an analogous logical clash would arise between ordinary forward deliberation and precognition as that which was shown to arise between backward deliberation and trace: there could be a situation in which an agent calls into question the veridicality of one of his ostensible precognitions of the future merely because he begins to deliberate and not because he has come upon any fresh evidence to indicate that the future is different than are the ostensible precognitions of it.

The obvious retort is that since the existence of precognition would result in a logical absurdity it is not a *contingent* fact that we do not possess such a faculty. Relative to our present conceptual system it is logically impossible that there be such a future analogue to memory. If we are to allow for the possibility of precognition, it is necessary to jettison a family of concepts having to do with agency, such as deliberation and intention. It is not logically possible for an agent to precognize without interruption the decisions he will make as a result of future deliberations, whereas it is logically possible for an agent to remember without interruption the decisions he made as a result of past deliberations.[16] If an agent were to precognize without interruption the decision he will make as a result of a future deliberation, he would know what decision he will make when he deliberates in the future, and this violates analytic truth (iv) that it is not logically possible that an agent deliberate about whether to do X and at the same time either know that X will occur or know that X will not occur. This brings out a crucial disanalogy between memory and precognition. It also shows that determinism, interpreted as the doctrine that an *agent* in principle could retrodict and predict every event on the basis of instantial premises and scientific laws, is false.

In addition to radically transforming our concept of the past, the Case of the Retro-Warning also requires a drastic change to be made in our concept of experimentation. According to this case, event L is the sufficient cause of a past event E. A causal claim should be amenable to experimental verification, although it may not be practically feasible to do so. The causal claim that an event C in a situation S causes event E is experimentally verified by making C happen in S and then observing what results. An agent's claim to be able to bring about M by doing L is experimentally verified by having him do L under controlled conditions and then waiting to see—to directly verify—whether M happens. Jones's causal claim to be able to bring about a *past* event E by doing L cannot be verified in this manner, for while we can wait for him to do L we cannot wait to directly observe whether E happens. In this case what we must "wait for" after he does L is not the occurrence of E but indirect evidence of E's having occurred in the past. This indirect evidence consists of traces. Traces, by definition, are enduring states of an object: the footprints in the sand, the marks on the photographic plate, as well as a person's memories, are enduring states of an object. Were traces not enduring states, there would be no basis for an agreement in judgment between inquirers existing at different times subsequent to the event about which judgment is made. This means that all of the traces of E (not-E) that are in principle available to us after Jones does L are also in principle available to us before Jones does L. Thus we need not wait for the experiment to be performed in order to verify its outcome: before Jones does L we are in just as good a position to verify whether E occurred as we are after he does L. Jones is performing only a mock experiment.

Jones might say that the ostensible traces of E (not-E) cannot be trusted until after he does L. But if we cannot trust ostensible traces before he does L why should they be any more trustworthy after he does L? He might say that once he forms an intention to do L he has intentional knowledge of E and therefore has a basis on which to determine the veridicality of these ostensible traces. This is viciously circular since, according to analytic truth (i'), Jones has intentional knowledge of an event E that is not one of his actions if, and only if, he has intentional knowledge of one of his own actions L and *knows that* L *is sufficient to bring about* E. L is a sufficient cause of E, Jones would need evidence that is independent of his intentions. If Jones should use his intention to do L as the decisive factor in determining whether E occurred, he would sever himself from the rest of the scientific community. He would have a private science. He could go on cherishing the belief that he brings about E by doing L, only he probably would do so in a padded cell.

Backward causation also creates havoc for our concepts of responsibility and punishment. Let us suppose that E is a highly undesirable event and there is a law against bringing it about, anyone who does so intentionally being culpable and subject to punishment. On some occasion E happens, and, in accordance with the above Case of the Retro-Warning, it has no proximate cause other than Jones's subsequent action of doing L. Therefore, since an illegal event has occurred that is a result of Jones's intentional action L, we can hold him responsible—culpable—for this and punish him accordingly. Thus we are punishing him for some action that he has not yet performed. But part of the justification of punishment is to reform the character of the criminal so that he will not perform illegal acts in the future. However, this justification cannot apply to our punishment of Jones, for if the punishment does succeed in reforming Jones so that he will not do L in the future, then we will have punished him for a crime that he does not commit.

NOTES

1. The following authors deal with this question: M. Dummett and A. Flew, "Can an Effect Precede its Cause?" (symposium), *Aristotelian Society Supp.* 28 (1954): M. Black, "Why Cannot an Effect Precede its Cause?" *Analysis* 16 (1956); A. Flew, "Effects Before Their Causes? Addenda and Corrigenda," *Analysis* 16 (1956); M. Scriven, "Randomness and the Causal Order," *Analysis* 17 (1956); A. J. Ayer, *The Problem of Knowledge* (London: Macmillan, 1956), pp. 170–175; D. F. Pears, "The Priority of Causes," *Analysis* 17 (1957); A. Flew, "Causal Disorder Again," *Analysis* 17 (1957); R. M. Chisholm and R. Taylor. "Making Things to Have Happened," *Analysis*, 20 (1960); M. Dummett, "Bringing about the Past," *Philosophical Review* 23 (1964), reprinted in *The Philosophy of Time*, edited by Gale; S. Gorovitz, "Leaving the Past Alone," *Philosophical Review* 23 (1964); and R. M. Gale, "Why a Cause Cannot Be Later Than Its Effect," *The Review of Metaphysics* 19 (1965). Also to be consulted in this connection are the articles by C. D. Broad, C. J. Ducasse and A. Flew in *The Philosophy of C. D. Broad*, ed. P. Schilpp (New York: Tudor, 1959).

2. The way in which we have posed the question of whether or not we could give up this analytic truth involves acceptance of some form of the conventionalist's theory of necessity; however, the same sort of question could be raised if we operated with a platonic theory of necessity. Since the platonist denies that necessity is dependent in any way on linguistic rules, he would not allow us to speak of denying, or giving up, an analytic truth by changing linguistic rules. In regard to cases where supposed analytic truths were denied, e.g., development of non-Euclidean geometries, he would say that this shows only that they really were not analytic truths but only believed to be such. But, then, we could raise the question of whether the claim that a present event cannot cause a past event really is an analytic truth or is only believed to be one.

3. This example appears in H. L. A. Hart and A. M. Honore, *Causation in the Law* (Oxford: Clarendon, 1959), p. 190. I am deeply indebted to this excellent book throughout this chapter.

4. Russell, "On the Notion of Cause," in *Mysticism and Logic* (London: Allen and Unwin, 1950); and R. Taylor's two articles, "Causation," *Monist* 47 (1963), and "Can a Cause Precede Its Effect?" *Monist* 48 (1964).

5. It might be thought that there are counterexamples to the claim that we cannot remember the future, such as "I remember that there is a picnic tomorrow." The latter is obviously elliptical for "I remember that there is a picnic scheduled (planned) for tomorrow," in which case I am remembering my past state of knowledge and not a future event. The reason is that it could be true that I remember (in the success sense of "remember") that there is a picnic tomorrow without there being a picnic tomorrow: the picnic that was scheduled or planned for tomorrow could be rescheduled. Similar considerations would hold for our memory of events occurring prior to our birth. For a discussion of these cases see Norman Malcolm's three lectures on memory in *Knowledge and Certainty* (Englewood Cliffs: Prentice-Hall, 1963).

6. For a more detailed discussion of this point see my article, "Professor Ducasse on Determinism," *Philosophy and Phenomenological Research* 22 (1961).

7. It might be argued that the introduction of experimental control of L violates condition (4), which requires that E not be a proximate or remote cause of L. This is not so, for if we were successful in making L happen when it is not preceded by E, it would show only that not-E is on that occasion a remote cause of L (since it is our knowledge of not-E that causes us to bring about L), not that E is a cause of L.

8. One might argue that since K_2 is a sufficient proximate cause of K_1, and K_1 a sufficient proximate cause of K, and K a sufficient proximate cause of L, therefore K_2 is a sufficient cause of L. And if this is so there could not be an

instance in which an event of type K_2 occurs without being followed by an event of type L. And since L is a sufficient proximate cause of E, it entails that E must occur every time K_2 occurs, in violation of the stipulation. This argument fails because it requires us to speak of a remote cause of L, namely, K_2, as a sufficient cause of L. As pointed out in Section I, we cannot speak of a remote cause as sufficient because the concept of a situation in which it is sufficient has no application to a remote cause. K_2 is sufficient for K_1 in a situation C. And K_1 is sufficient for K in a situation D. But then it is possible for K_2 to occur in C and sufficiently cause K_1 but the situation in which K_1 occurs is not situation D, and therefore it is not sufficient for K.

9. Dummett and Flew, "Can an Effect Precede Its Cause?" p. 32.

10. This holds true even if a proximate cause$_3$ is not linked with its effect by some process or sequence of events: in Section I such causality at a temporal distance was not countenanced.

11. This formula is neutral as to whether backward causations$_3$ operates at a temporal distance. In most counterstipulation-examples it does operate at a temporal distance.

12. We are counting nonoccurences and negative states of affairs as events.

13. It is logically possible for an agent to deliberate about whether to do X and at the same time know of the occurrence of some event of which X is a sufficient cause since there could be a sufficient cause of this event other than X. Also, someone beside himself might be able to do X so as to bring about this event. For example, Jones may be part of a conspiracy, each party to which has vowed to blow up the airplane on which they all are passengers. It is possible for Jones to deliberate about whether he should detonate his bomb so as to blow up the airplane even though he knows that the plane will blow up: what he is deliberating about is whether he should be the person to blow it up.

14. Evidence to the effect that he can do L and that L is sufficient to bring about E can figure in the agent's deliberation, but this evidence by itself does not enable him to infer the occurrence of either L or E.

15. I am using "knowledge" here in such a way that that X know that p entails that p. Intentional knowledge, as pointed out above, does not qualify as knowledge in this sense.

16. An agent remembers without interruption an event X if between X and his present memory there is no lapse in his state of remembering X, as there would be if he were to suffer from amnesia during this time. Analogously, an agent precognizes without interruption an event X if between X and his present precognition there is no lapse in his state of precognizing X, as

there would be if he were to suffer from some future analogue to amnesia—call it "aforeknowlia"—during this time. The reason for requiring uninterrupted precognition is that otherwise an agent could now precognize the future occurrence of M but subsequently suffer from aforeknowlia and then honestly begin to deliberate about whether to do M.

11

AN IDENTITY THEORY OF THE *A*- AND *B*-SERIES

Coauthored with Michelle C. M. Beer

The temporal perspectives of past, present, and future have been the most problematic aspects of time. For once we are confronted with the present or now we feel compelled to find some honest work for it to do. And what else could this be but for it to "advance" into the future at the plodding rate of one minute per minute as it successively bestows its exalted gift of existence upon eagerly awaiting events? To avoid having to countenance this paradoxical sort of sui generis change, often called *temporal becoming*, a long line of philosophers have attempted to show that the *A*-Series of events running from the past to the present and to the future is reducible to, and thus is nothing more than, the *B*-Series of events running from earlier to later. This has usually taken the form of a linguistic reduction in which a proposition describing an event as past, present, or future is claimed to be either identical with, or entailed by one describing an event as earlier than, simultaneous with or later than another event or moment of time. The former is an *A*-proposition and is expressible through the use of a temporal indexical or tensed sentence that is not freely repeatable in that its use on successive occasions with the same meaning can express propositions differing in truth-value; the latter is a *B*-proposition and is expressible through the use of a freely repeatable or tenseless sentence that describes a temporal relation between two events and/or moments. Some philosophers, doubting the viability of a linguistic reduction, have attempted to ontologically downgrade the present and temporal becoming to a second-class, mind-dependent status, as if this made the notion of temporal becoming any less troublesome.

In *The Language of Time*[1] it was argued that *A*-propositions cannot be reduced to *B*-propositions, but that discussion is now quite obsolete, for there subsequently has been a rash of new accounts of indexical discourse, which can be used to mount new types of linguistic reductions, as well as other types of reductions in which Fregean *de dicto A*-propositions are shown to be replaceable by *de re* propositions that are an ontological mixed bag of the real-life referent of the indexical term and the sense of the predicative expression. This essay will develop a new version of a reduction of the *A*- to the *B*-Series, called the "coreporting thesis," that eschews any attempt to dispense with *A*-propositions in favor of *B*-propositions but instead claims that for every *A*-proposition there is a *B*-proposition that reports one and the same event. This coreporting thesis will be found to have all the therapeutic value of the older linguistic reductions. It also shows the absurdity of the psychological reduction, since the identity of an event's occurring now with its occurring at some time cannot be mind-dependent any more than any individual's being self-identical can. Before presenting and defending the coreporting type of reduction, we shall discuss the different sorts of reductions that can be based upon recent theories of indexicals.

I. THE POSSIBLE WORLDS REDUCTION

Saul Kripke's path-breaking work on rigid designators and indexicals can be deployed to mount both an identity and entailment type of linguistic reduction.[2] A rigid designator's referent in a counterfactual proposition is identical with its referent when employed in a categorical proposition. Its referent, in other words, remains constant across worlds in which its actual world's referent exists. Thus, if "*d*" is a rigid designator, the proposition expressed by "*d* might not have been *d*" is necessarily false. Indexical terms are rigid designators by this test; for it is necessarily false that here might not have been here or that now might not been now. That a student impatiently sitting through a three-hour lecture says, "If only it were 2 p.m. now rather than 9 a.m., I would be sailing on the bay," hardly is a counterexample. She is not envisioning a situation in which now is a different time than it is any more than you envision being a different person when you say to someone, "If I were you, I would pay attention." You are merely saying that anyone in that person's situation prudentially ought to be paying attention, and all our impatient student is saying is that it is now 9 a.m. and she is not sailing but at a later and better time, 2 p.m., she does.

Proper names, including coordinates and dates, also are rigid. As a consequence, a proposition expressed by an identity sentence employing only proper names and/or indexicals in any combination is necessarily true if true at all. A consequence of this is that for every *A*-proposition there is a *B*-proposition that has the same truth-value in every possible world as does the *A*-proposition. Let our example of an *A*-proposition be the proposition expressed by using at 3 p.m. March 15, 2003 EST, for short t_7, the sentence:

(1) Event *E* occurs now.

The use of "now" in (1) denotes the moment of time t_7. Therefore, the proposition expressed by using at t_7 the sentence,

(2) Now is t_7.

is necessarily true, since there is no possible world or counterfactual situation in which now—this moment of time, t_7—is not identical with t_7. From this it follows that the *B*-proposition expressed by the use at any time of

(3) Event E occurs (tenselessly) at t_7.

has the same truth-value in every possible world as does the A-proposition expressed at t_7 by the use of (1).

When this result is combined with the definitions of propositional identity or entailment in terms of the semantics of possible worlds, we get either an identity or entailment reduction. If we say that proposition p is identical with proposition q just in case they have the same truth-value in every possible world, it follows that the propositions expressed by the appropriate uses of (1) and (3) are identical. This definition, however, has the unwanted result that there is only one necessarily true (false) proposition. Moreover, it does not do justice to the role propositions play as intentional accusatives. It is not unreasonable to suppose that, given any proposition p and any proposition q, a necessary condition for p being identical with q is that the sentences expressing them be interchangeable in all contexts *salva veritate*. And yet it seems clearly possible for someone who understands the proposition expressed by (1) at t_7 and the proposition expressed by (3) to believe that E occurs now but not believe that E occurs (tenselessly) at t_7.

And if we say that p entails q just in case there is no possible world in which p is true and q false, then by this definition we have the result that the proposition expressed by (3) entails the proposition expressed by (1) at t_7. But this definition is too weak for those philosophers who demand of entailment deducibility using only premises that are both necessary and a priori. For, in order to deduce the proposition expressed by (1) at t_7 from that expressed by (3), we must make use of the proposition expressed by (2) at t_7, which, although necessary, is not knowable a priori.

II. THE ELIMINATIVE REDUCTION

John Perry's important and lucid articles on indexicals can serve as the basis for a very radical sort of reduction in which A-propositions are eliminated entirely, shown to be nonexistent, in favor of B-propositions.[3] Perry argues that the traditional Fregean theory of propositions does not fit sentences employing indexical terms, unless we are willing to countenance propositions that can be expressed or apprehended at only one time or place or by only one person. The source of the difficulty is that the sense of a sentence, which Frege identifies with the thought expressed, must be "complete in every respect." The sense of the nonindexical sentence, "E occurs (tenselessly) at t_7," is complete in that it is the result of combining the incomplete sense of "E is (tenselessly) occurring" with the sense-completer, "at t_7." But since the referent of an indexical term is relative to its context of use, an indexical term cannot be said to serve as a sense-completer unless we attribute to it a sense that varies with the context and is apprehendable only in that context. Every time "now" is tokened it has a different sense that can be grasped only at that time. As a result, the proposition or complete, unified sense expressed by a tokening of "E occurs now" at t_7 can be apprehended or thought only at t_7; and only Jones can grasp or apprehend the proposition she expresses by tokening "I am Jones."

Perry cannot accept the notion of propositions of limited accessibility and suggests that the proposition expressed by an indexical sentence in some context be replaced in its role as object of belief with what he calls a *de re* proposition, this being an ontological mixed bag composed of the value or referent the indexical term has in that context—the time, place, or person it denotes—and the incomplete sense of the sentence. By identifying the information conveyed by the tokening of an indexical sentence in a certain context with a *de re* proposition, Perry's theory has the consequence that the information conveyed by the use at t_7 of "E occurs now" is equivalent to that conveyed by the use at any time of "E occurs (tenselessly) at t_7," and that, as a result, there is no loss of information when an *A*-proposition is replaced by a *B*-proposition.

Perry's elimination theory of indexical propositions may ultimately prove right, but it cannot be accepted without major refinements so as to meet some difficulties. On Perry's theory, for example, the object of Hume's first-person belief that he himself is the author of the *Treatise* is the pair composed of a person—Hume—and an abstract entity—being-the-author-of-the-*Treatise*. But this suffers from the same problem as does Russell's multiple relation theory of belief in not being able to account for the unity in the proposition believed.[4] In believing that he himself is the author of the *Treatise*, Hume believes a single thing that has a peculiar complex unity; but a *de re* proposition has no unity, even if it is taken to be an ordered couple, being a mere laundry list or a roster with a comma between each name. Furthermore, we say that indexical propositions not only are objects of belief but also bearers of truth-values. Yet it is difficult to see what, on Perry's theory, could be the bearer of a truth-value. It cannot be a *de re* proposition since the latter lacks an internal articulation and unity. Nor can it be the sense of the sentence, which Perry identifies with its role, namely, a rule or function that takes us from a context of use to a truth-value.

III. THE EPISTEMIC REDUCTION

Hector-Neri Castañeda, in his outstanding work on indexicals, accepts Fregean propositions of limited accessibility and rejects any version of an identity or entailment reduction of them to nonindexical propositions.[5] Castañeda's account of *quasi-indicators*, however, can serve as the basis of a weak reductive theory according to which a person who has no location in time, and thereby cannot use any temporal indexical sentences, can know A-propositions. A quasi-indicator makes an anaphoric reference within an *oratio obliqua* construction attributing a propositional attitude to someone and indicates what sort of indexical reference this person made. In the sentence, "At t_7 Jones knows that it is then t_7," the occurrence of "then" within the *oratio obliqua* clause functions as a quasi-indicator in that it both makes an anaphoric reference to t_7 and indicates that Jones made a present-tense indexical reference to that time. As a result, Castañeda claims, a person who is not in time, such as a timelessly eternal God, can know the very same proposition as is expressed by someone through the use of an indexical sentence, in virtue of the principle of the transitivity of knowledge that holds that if A knows that B knows that p, then A knows that p. Thus, a timeless God can know that Jones knows at t_7 that it is then t_7. From this, in conjunction with the principle of the transitivity of knowledge, Castañeda concludes that God knows the very same A-

proposition as does Jones—the proposition Jones would express at t_7 by tokening "It is now t_7."

There are problems in this line of reasoning. First, the principle of the transitivity of knowledge does not hold in general. Just as A can know that the proposition expressed by B is true but not know it because she lacks a suitable justification for this proposition, A can know that B knows this proposition and lack this needed justification. We can know, for example, that Einstein knows that $E=mc^2$ but not know that $E=mc^2$ because we do not understand the relevant theoretical concepts; what we know is only that it is true that $E=mc^2$. Furthermore, the principle seems to have exceptions when A is not able to specify or express the proposition known by B, and this is exactly the predicament God is in. We can know on the basis of what Jones's friends tell us that her favorite proposition, is true but not know this proposition; for although we are able to identify the proposition, we do not know which proposition it is in the sense of not being able to specify or express it. Likewise, God can identify the A-proposition known by Jones and know that it is true but does not know which A-proposition Jones knows because God cannot specify or express it in *oratio recta*. In the sentence, "God knows that Jones knows at t_7 that it is then t_7," the final "that"-clause—"that it is then t_7"—does not specify a complete proposition since the quasi-indicator "then" occurs as a free variable, no longer being bound by the occurrence of "at t_7" outside of the "that"-clause. While "that it is then " does identify an A-proposition, it does not do so in a specifying manner, as does the tokening now of "that it is now t_7." It might be argued that this problem of failing to specify a complete proposition in the final "that"-clause can be easily solved by moving the "at t_7" from outside to inside the final "that"-clause, resulting in "God knows that Jones knows that at t_7 it is then t_7." But if so, then neither God nor Jones knows any A-proposition at all; for the proposition that at t_7 it is then t_7 is identical with the tautology that t_7 is t_7, which is a B-proposition since it is expressed by a freely repeatable sentence. Assuming that there are Fregean A-propositions, the proposition that it is now t_7, by Leibniz's Law, is not identical with the proposition that t_7 is t_7 (or that at t_7 it is then t_7), the reason being that only the latter has the property of being knowable a priori.

IV. THE COREPORTING THESIS

This reduction accepts Fregean A-propositions of limited accessibility and grants that no B-proposition is identical with, entails, or has the same informational content as any A-proposition. The claim is that for every A-proposition there is a B-proposition that reports one and the same event. And, as a result, McTaggart's B-series of events running from the past, to the present, and to the future is identical with his A-Series of events running from earlier to later. This reduction is based on the Fregean sense-reference distinction and attempts to show that for every A-proposition there is a B-proposition that reports one and the same event, in spite of its having a different sense. It finds its inspiration in theories of scientific reductions that attempt to show that sentences, such as "There is a flash of lightning" and "There is a flow of ionized particles," could report one and the same event although they express different propositions. Let us say that the event reported by a proposition is the event referred to by the participial nominalization of the sentence expressing the proposition. Thus, the event reported on a given occasion by the use of the temporal indexical sentence "Jones is running now" is the event referred to on that occasion by "Jones's running now," while the event reported at any time by the use of the non-indexical sentence "Jones is (tenselessly) running at t_7," is the event referred to by "Jones's running at t_7." Given Frege's sense-reference distinction, it is clear that two sentences can differ in sense and yet be coreporting. This can be seen if we appeal to the following criterion that provides a sufficient, though not necessary, condition for coreferentiality: If two n-adic participial nominalizations refer to the same relata and have the same predicates, then they are coreferring. Applying this criterion to dyadic participial nominalizations, it follows that if the participial nominalizations "a's having R to b" and "c's having S to d" are such that $a = c$ and $b = d$ and "R" is synonymous with "S," then they are co-referring. Thus, "The wife of President Bill Clinton is (tenselessly) speaking at t_7," differs in sense from "The junior senator from New York is (tenselessly) speaking at t_7," and yet it reports the same event, since the participial nominalizations of these sentences are coreferring.

The coreporting thesis requires only one more tenet—that temporal indexical terms, as they are used on a particular occasion, are referring terms that denote times. The temporal indexical "now," like "this time," refers to a time, just as the spatial indexical "here" refers to a place. This is shown by the fact that "now" can be used to answer such questions as "At what time is Jones running?" and "When does the race begin?" The sentences "Now is t_7," and "Now is the time at which the race begins," therefore, are used to assert an identity between times, just as "Here is 42nd Street and Broadway" is used to assert an identity between places. That "now," like "this time" and "the present," is used to refer to a time shows the absurdity of the common account of temporal becoming, used by both friends and foes of becoming, according to which it involves the shift or advance of the present or now to ever-later times or events. For how can this very time—the present or now—cease to be identical with itself or become a different time at ever-later times?

From the tenet given above, in conjunction with the criterion for coreferentiality, it follows that for every *A*-proposition there is a *B*-proposition that reports the same event. For example, if it is now t_7, the *A*-proposition expressed by now tokening

(4) Jones is running now.

reports the same event as does the *B*-proposition expressed by tokening at any time

(5) Jones is (tenselessly) running at t_7.

The reason for this is that the participial nominalizations, "Jones's running now" and "Jones's running at t_7," which are respectively synonymous with "Jones's running being simultaneous with now" and "Jones's running being simultaneous with t_7," are coreferring since they refer to the same relata and have the same predicate.

The coreporting thesis, although simple and obvious, has important consequences. First, it establishes the identity of the *A*-Series and the *B*-series, since it shows that an event's having an *A*-determination—its being past, present, or future—is identical with that event's bearing a temporal relation to some moment of time. The coreporting thesis thereby helps to demystify the concept of time because it checks our inclination to think that the referent of "now" must be something queer—a transcendent spotlight of presentness that mysteriously advances to ever-later times. Philosophers who are friends of becoming might nevertheless claim that, while the use of "now" refers to a moment of time, it also expresses the irreducible property of presentness that advances to later and later times.[6] This response, however, overlooks the fact that, on the coreporting thesis, every time "now" is tokened it has a different sense and thus expresses a different property—the property of being now—so that it is impossible that there be another time that has that very property. Consequently, whatever is expressed by "now" is not a mysterious property that shifts to ever-later times, but an individual essence or haecceity that individuates a moment of time.

Secondly, the coreporting thesis not only undercuts some of the bad philosophizing by the friends of becoming, but also performs this service for some of the misbegotten efforts by its foes. Consider in this connection the claim that temporal becoming is mind dependent because events are present or occur now only in relation to a perceiver. Adolf Grünbaum, who, along with Russell, is a leading spokesperson for this view, claims that although the occurrence of a physical event at a clock time is independent of any relation to a mind, the occurrence of a physical event now or at the present time is not. What qualifies a physical event at time t as being present or now, Grünbaum states, "is that at the time t at least one human or other *mind-possessing* organism M is conceptually aware of experiencing the event at that time."[7] If the coreporting thesis is correct, this mind dependence theory is absurd. For, according to the mind dependence theory, an event's being present or occurring now is mind dependent but that same event's occurring at a moment of time is not. But, given that an event's occurring now is identical with its occurring at a moment of time, it follows from Leibniz's law that an event's occurring now both is and is not mind dependent, which is clearly contradictory. The coreporting thesis, moreover, undercuts Grünbaum's argument for the mind dependence of an event's being present or occurring now, which is based upon the alleged fact that physics takes no cognizance of now or the present.[8] Since physics takes cognizance of times, it also takes cognizance of now. Scientific realism need not cower before the *A*-Series!

It might be asked why, if the coreporting thesis is so simple and obvious, it has eluded philosophers for so long? We offer two brief conjectures. First, some philosophers have failed to properly distinguish between the sense and reference of referring terms. A clear-cut example is supplied by Grünbaum's argument against taking "now" in the judgment, "It is 3 p.m. EST now," to denote a time, as the coreporting thesis contends. Grünbaum argues that unless "now" designates a particular content of conceptualized awareness,

> then there would seem to be nothing left for it to designate other than either the events already identified as occurring at 3 p.m. EST or those identified as occurring at some other time. In the former case, the initially informative temporal judgment "It is 3 p.m. EST now" turns into the utter triviality that the events of 3 p.m. EST occur at 3 p.m. EST! And in the latter case, the initially informative judgment, if false in point of fact, becomes self-contradictory.[9]

The argument seems to be that if "now" denotes 3 p.m. EST, then when we say "Now is 3 p.m. EST," we really are saying "3 p.m. EST is 3 p.m. EST," which is like arguing that if Tully is Cicero, then to say "Tully is Cicero" is to assert the triviality "Cicero is Cicero." This plainly involves a sense-reference confusion.

The second reason for the failure to take cognizance of the coreporting thesis is a more profound one that involves a confusion between the *how* and *what* of an indexical reference. Wittgenstein, in the second half of the *Blue Book*, argues that the referent of an indexical use of "I" is something queer—a nonempirical ego for which we lack criteria of identity—because the substitution of any description or proper name for "I" changes the proposition expressed.[10] While there might be something odd about an indexical reference to oneself, it does not follow that there is anything odd about what gets denoted. Wittgenstein seems to have forgotten that he could truly say "I am Wittgenstein"; and, thus, "I" refers to what "Wittgenstein" does—a person. And since he has criteria of identity for Wittgenstein he also has them for what he denotes by his use of "I."

The coreporting thesis, of course, does not settle the issue of what constitutes the nature of time. While it commits us to the existence of moments of time, it does not commit us to any particular view about what a moment of time is, and thus we are left with the problem of analyzing the nature of a moment of time.[11] But we can make far greater progress in clarifying the nature of a moment than we can in analyzing the nature of some mysterious, transcendent entity or property that shifts relentlessly to later and later times.

NOTES

1. Richard M. Gale, *The Language of Time* (New York: Routledge & Kegan Paul, 1968).

2. "Identity and Necessity," in *Identity and Individuation*, ed. M. K. Munitz (New York: New York University Press, 1971).

3. "Frege on Demonstratives," *The Philosophical Review* 86 (1977): 474–97; and "The Problem of the Essential Indexical," *Nous* 13 (1979): 3–21.

4. For a fuller account of this problem see R. M. Gale, "Propositions, Judgments, Sentences, and Statements," in the *Encyclopedia of Philosophy*, ed. P. Edwards (New York: Macmillan, 1967).

5. See his "'He': A Study in the Logic of Self-Consciousness," *Ratio* 8 (1966): 130–57; "Indicators and Quasi-Indicators, *American Philosophical Quarterly* 4 (1967): 85–100; and "Omniscience and Indexical Reference," *The Journal of Philosophy* 64 (1967).

6. This objection has been raised by Quentin Smith in his response to an earlier draft of this paper. See his "The Co-reporting Theory of Tensed and Tenseless Sentences," *The Philosophical Quarterly* 40 (1990): 213–22.

7. "The Status of Temporal Becoming," in *The Philosophy of Time*, ed. R. M. Gale (New York: Anchor Doubleday, 1967), p. 333.

8. Ibid., p. 337.

9. Ibid. Grünbaum is assuming that a moment of time can be defined in terms of a class of simultaneous events.

10. The same sort of reasoning imbues Castañeda's "On the Phenomeno-Logic of the I," in *Proceedings of the XIVth International Congress for Philosophy*, vol. 3, pp. 160–66.

11. For a rather wild, metaphysical account of moments of time as parts of an absolute space-time receptacle see R. M. Gale's *Negation and Non-Being, The American Philosophical Quarterly* Monograph No. 10 (1976).

12

DISANALOGIES BETWEEN SPACE AND TIME

While space and time obviously are different, for space is space and time is time, it still might be the case that they are analogous in all philosophically important respects. It is not difficult to find some disanalogies between them. While "Kiss me now" sounds a bit desperate, it has none of the lewd overtones of "Kiss me here." "Wish you were here" sounds more intimate than "Wish you were now." And "There is no time like the present" doesn't sound quite as chauvinistic as "There is no place like here." Such disanalogies, however, are of more interest to a lover, vacationer, or travel agent than a philosopher.

For the philosopher bent on clarifying our concepts of space and time, only a modally based disanalogy will count as important.[1] A modal disanalogy requires that the spatial or temporal analogue to a given sentence or proposition has a different modal status, in which a spatial or temporal analogue to a given sentence is formed by substituting for every temporal term in it a corresponding spatial one and vice-versa. In forming analogues the temporal indexical term "now" and "this time" are to be replaced respectively by "here" and "this place" and a date expression by a proper name of a place. For the time being we will agree to substitute "in front of" for "later than." It will be seen that it does not matter if "to the rear (right, left) of" is substituted instead.[2]

It might be thought that the most obvious and important modal disanalogy concerns the fact that there is no spatial analogue to temporal becoming: while it is necessary for the reality of time that there be a now or present that inexorably shifts to ever-later times, it is not necessary for the reality of space that there be a here that shifts in some spatial direction. The following pair of analogues attempts to make this modal disanalogy explicit:

T1. Every event later than now will happen.
S1. Every event in front of here will happen.

Unlike T1, S1 is not a necessary truth, since some of the events that occur in front of here might have already happened.

This, unfortunately, is a bogus modal disanalogy, since there is a temporal component of T1, the future-tensed "will happen," that fails to get replaced in S1 by a corresponding spatial expression. The proper analogy is:

T2. Every event later than now happens later than now.
S2. Every event in front of here happens in front of here.

But both are necessary truths, and therefore there is no modal disanalogy. There appears to be a totally trivial sense in which here and now "shift" in analogous manners, viz. it is necessary that tokenings of "now" at different times denote different times just as it is necessary that tokenings of "here" at different places denote different places. It will be see that appearances deceive here. To avoid against bogus disanalogies, such as T1-S1, we must be scrupulous in making fully explicit all of the temporal and spatial elements in our analogues, something that I failed to do in my *The Language of Time*. I caution the reader to watch me carefully, since I am not to be trusted.

There is no way to articulate the becoming-based modal disanalogy because this concept of becoming is absurd. A contradiction can be deduced from the claim that the present or now shift to ever-later times. The first step in this deduction is to point out that "now," like "this time" and "the present," is a singular referring expression that is used to denote a moment of time, whatever a moment of time might turn out to be upon analysis. This is borne out by the fact that sentences such as "Now is the time for all good men to come to the aid of their country" and "This time is noon of June 29, 1996" are used to assert an identity between times. These temporal demonstratives behave in the typical way that indexical words do in that they are rigid designators in Kripke's sense, meaning that the sentence "Now might not be now" expresses a necessarily false proposition whenever tokened. Ask yourself under what conceivable counterfactual circumstances this very time—now—would not be this time. There are none. Therefore, it is impossible for now (the present, this time) to shift to a later time; for then this time would cease to be identical with this time, i.e., would cease to be identical with itself, certainly a manifest repugnancy.

That an impatient bridegroom says to his bride in the course of the wedding ceremony, "If only it were now 11 p.m. rather than 1 p.m., we would be making love," hardly constitutes a counterexample. He is no more envisioning a situation in which now is a different time than it is than I am envisioning being a different person when I say to you, "If I were you, I would sell my IBM stock." I am merely saying that anyone in your situation prudentially ought to sell IBM, and all our overeager bridegroom is saying is that it is now 1 p.m. and they are not making love and at a later and better time, 11 p.m., they will be making love.

Although the conception of temporal becoming dear to the hearts of *A*-Theorists is absurd, there still might be significant modal disanalogies between our temporal and spatial indexical perspectives. I will follow a three-stage format in my pursuit of these disanalogies. I begin with our untutored common-sense beliefs, often expressed in metaphorical and pictorial terms, as to how time and space differ. Next, I refine these beliefs by translating them into more precise literal statements, being careful to make explicit all of their temporal and spatial commitments. Finally, I attempt to explain and justify these beliefs by unearthing the underlying modal disanalogies that serve as their cash backing. Sometimes these disanalogies will be formulated in the formal mode in which explicit mention is made of words and their rules of use. It will attempt to unearth them within our concepts of *agency* and *objectivity*.

I. AGENCY-BASED DISANALOGIES

Whether an agent fills space and time in modally disanalogous ways will depend crucially on how we define an "agent." I will be making a somewhat technical or jargonistic use of "agent," the justification for which will come at the end of this section when I discuss the connection of my use of "agent" with certain forensic uses of "person." According to my use, it is required that an agent, in addition to being rational and self-conscious, has as its overriding goal to achieve self-realization. An agent will rationally deliberate about the best way to achieve this goal and will then intentionally carry out her decisions in a free, morally responsible manner. Since an agent's summum bonum is to be an active and free cause of her own self-realization, an agent accepts a causal theory of value in which the goodness of an outcome, result, upshot, denouement, or culmination depends in part upon its being brought about in the right way, the right way involving the agent as an active and free cause. Means and ends interpenetrate, each deriving its meaning and value from its functional relation to the other. As is the case with other causal theories, such as those for perception, memory, and reference, we are able to recognize in many cases when a given sequence is or is not of the right sort, but notoriously are not able to specify in general what is the right sort of causal sequence.

To summarize, an agent is a rational, self-conscious being who deliberates about the best way to achieve self-realization and then intentionally carries out her decisions in a free, morally responsible manner. For the time being we will accept this as a merely stipulative definition for the sake of the ensuing discussion. It now is to be shown that this concept of agency entails striking modal disanalogies between the manner in which an agent exists in space and time consisting in there necessarily being a direction to time but not space, regardless of its dimensionality.

Some important and startling modal disanalogies concerning an agent's axiological commitments follow logically from my concept of an agent when it is conjoined with the following modal disanalogies concerning causation and the dependent notions of deliberation and choice:

> T3. An action performed now can bring about something later but not earlier than now.[3]
>
> S3. An action performed here can bring about something in front of but not to the rear of here.

in which the "can" is the weakest one of mere logical or conceptual possibility. No difference is made if "to the rear (right, left) of here" is substituted for "in front of here" in S3, as will be the case with all of the modal disanalogies to follow.

The T3-S3 modal disanalogy entails this modal disanalogy:

> T4. An agent can now deliberate about and make choices and have intentions in respect to her conduct later but not earlier than now.
>
> S4. An agent can here deliberate about and make choices and have intentions in respect to her conduct in front of but not to the rear of here.

There might be circumstances in which I have the capacity and opportunity to bring about things only to the front but not to the rear of here—I would literally have my back to the wall—but it is still *logically* possible that I bring about something to the rear of here and thus *logically* possible that I deliberate about doing so. And thus T4 and S4 differ modally, T4 alone being necessarily true. Similar considerations hold for T3 and S3, provided their use of "can" is interpreted as expressing logical possibility.

Given that an agent's summum bonum or primary project is to be the right sort of cause of her own self-realization and that causation cannot go temporally backwards though it logically can go in any spatial direction, it follows that an agent, in virtue of being rational, will have axiological commitments that are modally disanalogous between space and time. These disanalogies hold only for my "agents," not for human beings in general; for it is well known that human beings in different cultures and socioeconomic groups value the past, present, and future differently, some being more future oriented, while others give greater importance to the past or present. For this reason, the following would not express a modal disanalogy:

> T5. *Human beings* care more about what befalls them later rather than earlier than now.
> S5. *Human beings* care more about what befalls them in front of rather than to the rear of here.

Let us begin with the old saws, "All's well that ends well" and "Consider no man fortunate until after he is dead." That it sounds funny to say, "All's well that spatially terminates well in front of here" or "You should count no man fortunate except from a place in front of where he dies," is some indication that we have modal disanalogies in these cases, but it is not easy to give an explicit formulation of them.

Plainly, the following pair of analogues will not do, since they both seem to be *contingent* generalizations and false ones to boot:

> T6. A temporal succession of events is good if it temporally terminates later than now in a good state of affairs.
> S6. A spatial order of events is good if it spatially terminates in front of here in a good state of affairs.

Lynne McFall has presented me with numerous counterexamples to T6, consisting in cases in which a death-bed conversion or final moment of beatific bliss does not render good or valuable a life that prior to that was one of long and unremitting immorality or suffering. The moral of these examples is that the length and intensity of evil that leads up to the favorable upshot or culmination must be taken into account.

The McFall-type counterexamples might be met by requiring that the earlier succession of events is both the right sort of an agent-cause of the terminating state and is morally outweighed by it, resulting in:

> T7. A temporal succession of events is good if it temporally terminates later than now in a state of affairs that morally outweighs it and for which it is the right sort of agent-cause.
> S7. A spatial order of events is good if it spatially terminates in front of here in a state of affairs that morally outweighs it and for which it is the right sort of agent-cause.[4]

Whereas T7 seems a plausible candidate for being a necessary truth, S7 does not, since an agent does not necessarily give greater axiological value to any one particular spatial direction over the others.

There are other ways of reformulating T6 that might work as well as or even better than the T7 way, as for example:

> T8. An agent holds that if it is better to be in state Y than state X, then it is better to be in state X now and state Y later rather than earlier than now, provided that she brings Y about out of X in the right sort of agency manner.
> S8. An agent holds that if it is better to be in state Y than state X, then it is better to be in state X here and state Y in front of rather than to the rear of here, provided that she brings Y about out of X in the right sort of agency manner.

T8, for example, requires that an agent who believes that it is better to be a philosophy professor than a pickpocket believe that it is better to be a pickpocket now and a philosophy professor later than now rather than vice-versa, provided that she agency-causes the professorial state to evolve from the pickpocket one in the right way, as, for example, by using her ill-gotten gains to pay her way through graduate school. But without any additional information, our agent will be indifferent between being a pickpocket here and a philosophy professor in front of here rather than vice-versa. Given additional information, the agent might prefer the former, since here could be New York City, a good place for a pickpocket, and Pittsburgh could be in front of here, a good place for a philosophy professor but a bad place for a pickpocket due to its being economically depressed. But this hardly shows that S8 is a *necessary* truth, for this preference is based on extra nonspatial information of a contingent sort, whereas the preference in T8 is not based on any extra nontemporal information of a contingent sort, thereby showing that T8, unlike S8, is logically necessary.

It is interesting to note that the T8-S8 modal disanalogy underlies the prevalent soul-building theodicy, which holds that God is justified in permitting past evils if they serve as a necessary condition for an agent to grow freely in morally desirable ways. In determining the goodness of a world we do not just mechanically add up the goods and evils in it, but also consider the temporal plot into which they enter. Their spatial plot or concatenation is irrelevant. The greater value that T8 accords to the future does not mean that progress is inevitable or that future persons are to be given a privileged status when formulating social policies, a point that was forcefully made in discussion by George Kline.

Phil Quinn has presented me with a counterexample to T8's necessity that indicates the need to further qualify it. He imagines an agent of age sixty who has been poor health all his life reasoning as follows:

> It is better for me to be rich than to be poor, for wealth is bound to be helpful in the project of self-realization if wisely used. But clearly it is not better for me to be poor now and rich later, provided I earn my wealth, than for me to be poor now and rich earlier. Even if I can still earn a fortune at my age, by the time I have done so I will be too old and feeble to make much use of it in advancing my project of self-realization. But if I had a fortune when I was a mere youth, I would have spent it all on my project of self-realization and would have made a lot more progress in this project than I actually did, which in turn would have given me internal resources I do not now have to enable me to make the best of my present poverty.

One way to meet this ingenious counterexample is to require that we consider only the intrinsic value of the successive states X and Y in T8, thereby precluding consideration of their instrumental value in promoting other goods, such as that of self-realization, which is what

Quinn's sixty-year-old man does. A technical device for assuring that only the intrinsic values of X and Y be considered is to require that they be described in "temporally pure" ways. A descriptive predicate "F" is temporally pure just in case the proposition expressed by "A is F at time t_7," in which "A" is a nondescriptive denotator of an individual, is such that it (i) does not entail that there are any times other than t_7 and (ii) is compatible with there being any number of instances of F at times other than t_7. Condition (i) rules out "drinking the fatal glass of beer" since it entails that the drinker dies at some future date as a result of the drinking and (ii) does so for "drinking the first (last) glass of beer" since this entails that the drinker does not drink a glass of beer at any earlier (later) time.

Another agency-based axiological asymmetry between past and future that has no modally equivalent spatial analogue concerns this difference between an agent's attitudes toward her past and future finitude:

> T9. An agent regrets that her existence does not extend beyond some time later than now but does not regret in the same way that her existence does not extend beyond some time earlier than now.
> S9. An agent regrets that her existence does not extend beyond some place in front of here but does not regret in the same way that her existence does not extend beyond some place to the rear of here.

The reason for the "in the same way" qualification will emerge from the ensuing discussion. S9 is not a necessary truth; for, an agent's regret that she does not exist at some place in front of here is based on contingent considerations that are not necessary for her being agent; e.g., Las Vegas could be in front of here and she loves to gamble in different casinos and thus would regret her never existing in Vegas. But is T9 necessary?

To establish the necessity of T9 it must be shown to be a logical consequence of my definition of an agent. Since an agent has as its summum bonum her own self-realization and there is no upper limit on the possibility for the development of one's character, knowledge, ability, talents, etc., an agent ought to regret its future demise.[5] To be sure, it might take only a finite future time for an agent to realize all of her present first-order intentions, but because there is no upper bound to an agent's potential for self-realization, it is of the very essence of an agent always to be on the make, always to be incomplete. Thus, at every time an agent has a second-order intention always to have a new intention, always to have its projected horizon recede as it succeeds in satisfying former intentions; and, thus, death always represents a cutting off of its possibility for a fuller self-realization of its inherent potentialities.

Annette Baier has pointed out that there could be extratemporal contingent considerations that could lead an agent not to regret her death, such as her now suffering from an incurable illness that prevents her from progressing now or in the future in her self-realization project. This problem could be met by stipulating that her agency is not impaired later than now.

> T10. An agent regrets that her existence does not extend beyond some time later than now but does not regret in the same way that her existence does not extend beyond some time earlier than now, *provided nothing prevents her from functioning as an agent later than now.*

But, in contradistinction from T10, a necessary truth does not emerge when the analogous restriction is made in S9:

> S10. An agent regrets that her existence does not extend beyond some place in front of here but does not regret in the same way that her existence does not extend beyond some place to the rear of here, *provided nothing prevents her from functioning as an agent in front of here.*

An agent might grow weary of being an agent for nonmedical reasons and thus no longer want an unlimited future. This, however, is just a case of an agent no longer being an agent, and thus not a counterexample to T10.

An agent might regret that her past existence is finite—she is an historian of ancient Greece and thus regrets having been born too late to have been an eyewitness to the going-ons in that era. But while her past finitude limits her knowledge, it does not limit in any way her opportunity to realize herself and, in particular, as an historian, her excellence as an historian not being diminished by her not having certain data that it is not possible for her to obtain. Since the agent's regret at having a finite future is not topic specific, unlike the historian who regrets that her past is finite, T10's temporal asymmetry between past and future is unscathed by this example. This is the reason for the "does not regret in the same way" qualification in T10.

T10 ceases to be a necessary truth when applied to human beings in general. Mystical individuals seem to have no asymmetry in their attitudes to birth and death, since they take time to be unreal. Derek Parfit has argued that we would be happier if we lacked the T10-type of temporal bias. He imagines a passive, contemplative sort of chap named "Timeless" who is not concerned with being an agent but only with finding a psychologically satisfying way of viewing the world around him. Timeless is someone

> who takes life's pleasures as they come. And, to the extent that we are like this ... we would be happier if we lacked the bias towards the future. We would be much less depressed by ageing and the approach of death. If we were like Timeless, being at the end of our lives would be more like being at the beginning. At any point within our lives we could enjoy looking either backward or forward to our whole lives.... I have claimed that, if we lacked the bias towards the future, this would be better for us.... On any plausible moral view, it would be better if we were all happier.[6]

Timeless poses no threat to T10's necessity, since he is not an agent. Whether it is better to be an agent, and thereby have a T10-type bias, is an entirely different matter. No doubt Timeless has more peace of mind, is in a more mellow mood, than an agent. He is happier in the feeling-happy sense. But whether it is better to have the sort of psychological happiness of a Timeless than be in the mentally perturbed state of a striving, incomplete agent is irrelevant to the truth of T10. I happen not to share Parfit's "ethical" intuitions. I believe that those who have a capacity to become agents have an obligation to do so, even at the expense of their ataraxia.

It is an empirical fact that most human beings prefer that their painful experiences be in the past and their pleasurable ones in the future but do not have the analogous spatial preference, it mattering not at all whether their pains and pleasures occur in any particular direction from here. It does not seem to be necessary that *human beings* have these preferences, but is it necessary that *agents* do? Is the following a modal disanalogy?

> T11. An agent prefers that her painful experiences occur earlier than now and her pleasurable experiences later than now.
> S11. An agent prefers that her painful experiences occur to the rear of here and her pleasurable experiences in front of here.

While it is obvious that S11 is not necessary, that T11 is must be argued.

Before attempting this, the descriptions of the painful and pleasurable experiences in T11 must be restricted to temporally pure ones, so that no demands are made on what obtains or fails to obtain at times earlier or later than that at which the pleasure or pain occurs. Without such a restriction the following sort of counterexample can be produced. It is reasonable for an agent to prefer that a painful amputation of her leg occur in the future instead of the past, since this gives her more time in which she has use of the leg and thereby a leg up on her self-realization project. But the description of a pain as "the pain of having one's leg amputated" is temporally impure because it entails that one has this leg before the painful experience and lacks it afterwards.

It is very difficult to show why T11 is necessary, assuming that it is. Plainly, we can't do so by saying that a past pain, since it already has become present, is of no moment whereas a future one, since it has yet to do so, is. For this is just to say that the past pain has already happened while the future one has not yet happened, leaving unexplained why this difference should be significant. And, for reasons already given, we cannot explain why T11 is necessary by invoking the notion of temporal becoming that involves a shift of the present moment to ever-later times.

Given that it is better to be in a pleasurable than a painful state, it could be claimed that T11 is a special instance of

> T8. An agent holds that if it is better to be in state Y than state X, then it is better to be in state X now and state Y later rather than earlier than now, provided that she brings Y about out of X in the right sort of agency manner.

The problem with this derivation is that an agent's T11 preference does not seem to require that she be a causal agent in respect to the painful and pleasurable experiences in question. Thus, there is a possible range of cases to which T11 applies but T8 does not, and therefore the necessity of T11 is yet to be explained.

Another possible way of grounding T11 in the concept of an agent is supplied by the following phenomenological insight of William James:

> The fact is that our consciousness at a given moment is never free from the ingredient of expectancy. Every one knows how when a painful thing has to be undergone in the near future, the vague feeling that it is impending penetrates all our thought with uneasiness and subtly vitiates our mood even when it does not control our attention; it keeps us from being at rest in the given present.[7]

It could be objected that James's phenomenological generalization is at best a contingent truth about human beings, and thus cannot establish the necessity of T11. But agents, unlike human beings, are not as a contingent matter of fact expectors and anticipators but are essentially so. And anticipation of an impending harm is not only upsetting but, more important, distracting, thereby undermining their efficiency as agents. Furthermore, a future pain is harmful to their self-realization in a way in which a past pain is not. Thus, it is fitting and proper for an agent to have T11-type preferences. This defense requires that T11 be restricted to anticipated and remembered pleasures and pains.

It is not hard to tell a story in which a future pain is not deleterious to an agent's self-realization but even necessary for it. In such a case an agent does not prefer that the pain is in the past. Therefore, it seems necessary to add yet another restriction to T11, requiring that the pleasures and pains are respectively beneficial and deleterious for self-realization.[8] My defense of T11's necessity is starting to take on too many epicycles to be very convincing, but, unfortunately, it is the best that I am able to do right now.

In concluding this section, I will consider Richard Bernstein's very trenchant objection to my general procedure for deriving agency-based modal disanalogies: My stipulatively defining "agent" in such a way that it entails the desired axiological modal disanalogies is nothing but a trivial exercise in gerrymandering. The plums that I gleefully pull out of my pie have been put there by me. My response is in two stages. Even if I am gerrymandering, my task hardly is trivial, since, as the preceding discussion attests, it is no easy matter to show that my concept of an agent entails these disanalogies. One of the major tasks for philosophy, going back to Plato's science of "dialectics," is to articulate the logical interconnections between different concepts. Furthermore, my concept of an agent isn't all that gerrymandered. It is similar to a prevalent definition of what a person is in the normative or forensic sense, the sense that qualifies an individual to be a bearer of rights, such as to be treated always as an end and never as a mere means. Thus, my concept is not made up out of the blue solely for the purpose of establishing modal disanalogies but is modeled on an important tradition for understanding the normative concept of personhood. That my agency-based analysis of personhood is controversial is readily granted, but that is not grounds for the charge of gerrymandering.

II. OBJECTIVITY-BASED DISANALOGIES

The doctrine of temporal becoming as involving a shifting now was supposed to offer a theoretical explanation for our gut feeling that our past-present-future perspective is objective in a way in which our here-there one is not. Because this doctrine is contradictory and thus explains nothing, it does not follow that we must give up our gut beliefs that there is a sense in which we are prisoners of time but not space, are spatially but not temporally free and rangy, and the like. You can choose to leave Pittsburgh for a wild weekend in Ambridge or McKeesport but can't choose to leave the twentieth century for a high old time in the seventeenth century. It is just such beliefs in the coercive power of time that caused some of our forefathers to prostrate themselves before a god of time but not one of space. Our fear of heights—or in the case of the comedian Steven Wright, widths—is an entirely different matter. I will now attempt to legitimize these beliefs by unearthing the objectivity-based modal disanalogies that underlie them.

Our concept of objectivity comprises two components: being nonselective or imposed independently of our will, and being common to or shared by different observers. It will be shown that for each component there are modal disanalogies between space and time.

A. Nonselectivity Disanalogies

There are three different sort of nonselectivity disanalogies: (i) perceptual, (ii) referential, and (iii) locomotive.

(i) For the sake of simplicity the discussion will be confined to visual perception, but it admits of generalization to the other senses. Space is an order of coexistent objects and time an order of successive events. Visual experience presents us with coexistent objects but not successive events.[9] At any given time we can see only those events and objects that happen or exist at that time. This gives rise to the following modal disanalogy:

T12. I can now see only what is happening now.
S12. I can here see only what is happening here.

in which "can" again is that of mere logical possibility, thus rendering it irrelevant whether I have a stiff neck that prevents me from turning my head.

While it is clear that S12 is not necessary, there is cause to doubt that T12 is necessary, due to the fact that light signals have a finite velocity, resulting in what is seen being earlier than the seeing of it. One way to meet this difficulty is to revise T12-S12 as:

T13. I can now see only what happens now or earlier than now.
S13. I can here see only what happens here or to the rear of here.

Because perception is a causal process, this modal disanalogy rests on the T3-S3 one concerning the impossibility of backward causation.

Another way to circumvent the problem is to adopt the convention that "now" in T12 refers to the class of events that are directly perceivable by me, the observer, i.e., all those events are are causally connectible with my here-now by a rectilinear light ray. This convention for saving the necessity of T12 squares with the Special Theory of Relativity and is less cumbersome, and therefore will be adopted in what follows. Thus a tokening of "now" or "this time" refers to the simultaneity class of events that stand in this light-ray relation, the cone of the past, to the time and place of the tokening.

The T12-S12 modal disanalogy, in turn, gives rise to this modal disanalogy:

T14. I can here and now choose whether to see events that occur now or then (or later than now).
S14. I can now and here choose whether to see objects that exist here or there (or in front of here).

in which "choose" distributes over the disjunction: "I can choose p or q" is short for "I can choose p and I can choose q." Again, stiff necks are irrelevant.

(ii) Because visual perception is selective among places but not times, there will be a selectivity in the use of spatial indexical terms that is lacking for temporal indexical terms. We will confine ourselves to the "primary use" of an indexical term, i.e., one in which it does not pick up its reference by falling within the scope of some other referring term. A primary use of "this place" is spatially selective whereas a primary use of "this time" is not:

T15. I can choose whether my primary use here and now of "this time" denotes now or then (or a time later than now).
S15. I can choose whether my primary use now and here of "this place" denotes here or there (or a place in front of here).

This modal disanalogy, cast in the formal mode, results from a difference in the rules of use for these indexical terms. The rule of use for "this place" specify that the the denotatum of a tokening of it is the place ostended by the speaker. (Remember that I can point to the place I occupy.) No such act of ostending enters into determining the denotatum of a tokening of "this time." To be sure, I can choose when to token "this time," but given that I token it at the time I do, I have no choice but to refer to that time. Herein I am requiring that the time at which a temporal indexical term is used be kept constant when we ask counterfactual questions about its referent. This could be called be the principle of "contextual constancy."

It might come as a surprise, but exactly the same sort of disanalogy holds between the rules for the primary use of "here" and "now." *Pace* what was tentatively granted above, a token of "here" need not denote the place at which it is tokened, thereby giving rise to this modal disanalogy:

T16. A primary use of "now" must denote the time at which it is tokened.[10]

S16. A primary use of "here" must denote the place at which it is tokened.

A counterexample to S16 is my saying, "Place the piano here," as I point to some place in front of me.

It might be countered that S16 becomes necessary when restricted to a "naked" use of "here," i.e., a use in which there is no accompanying ostensive act of pointing, gesturing, or staring. This must be granted; however, this restriction to a naked use gives rise to a different modal disanalogy:

T17. I can choose whether or not to use "now" nakedly.

S17. I can choose whether or not to use "here" nakedly.

Whereas, admittedly, S17 is necessary, T17 is not, since, as T15 has shown, a use of "now" or "this time" cannot involve an act of ostending.[11] Therefore, every primary use of "here," including the naked one, involves selection of some sort, unlike the primary use of "now."

(iii) Not only is our past-present-future perspective, unlike our here-there one, nonselective in regard to perception and reference, it also is so in regard to our power of locomotion. We can move about in space at will but not time, thus the reason for it making sense to say, "Come here" but not "Come now," assuming it is only the locomotive sense that is relevant. We can return to the same place but not the same time, which yields this modal disanalogy:

> S18. I can exist here both now and at some time, t_2, later than now, and there at some time, t_1, temporally between now and t_2.
> T18. I can exist now both here and at some place, P_2, in front of here, and then at some place, P_1, spatially between here and P_2.

This modal disanalogy is a consequence of the conceptual truth that a material object can occupy the same place at different times but not the same time at different places:

> S19. I can exist here both now and then.
> T19. I can exist now both here and there.

A philosopher of the likes of Richard Taylor would not accept these as genuine modal disanalogies. He would claim that a physical object is composed of both spatial and temporal parts. Thus, he would claim that both S18 and T18 are necessary truths; just as I can exist both here and there by having different spatial parts of myself occupy these two places I can exist here both now and then by having different temporal parts of myself happen at these two times.

He is wrong, however, in his claim that physical objects, as contrasted with events, have temporal as well as spatial parts. When a man has his legs amputated, as did Ronald Reagan in an old movie, he can ask, "Where's the rest of me?" for he is referring to some of his former spatial parts. But he cannot claim to be incomplete now because some of his "temporal parts," i.e., events in his history, are not happening now. If my view of someone is obstructed so that I see only his back, I say that I see only a part of him, but I do not say this if I do not see some events in his past and future history. I would say that I see only part of his *history* rather than part of the *man*.

It might be replied that while we do not at present speak of a physical object's temporal parts, this might not be due to it being conceptually absurd to do so but simply because we have not yet had the proper contingent occasion to do so. It might be that the reason why we do not now speak of temporal parts is that an object's parts are connected with its sortal nature, and so far it has proven advantageous for the purpose of devising intellectually satisfying scientific systems of classification and successfully interacting with our environment to define the sortal or essential nature of objects solely in terms of how their spatial parts are concatenated. Think of the periodic table of elements in this connection. There are, however, conceivable circumstances in which it would no longer prove advantageous to define an object's essence exclusively in spatial terms; how it fills time, its history, would then be at least partially determinative of its nature. In fact, this is already the case in some areas of subatomic physics. It is part of the definition of certain kinds of mesons that they have a half-life of a certain duration. In such cases in which the definition of an object's essence makes demands upon its history, it might be appropriate to talk of an object's temporal as well as its spatial parts. Since our present spatially biased system of definitions of essences or sortal natures is revisable in this manner, it is doubtful that S18-T18 and S19-T19 are genuine modal disanalogies.

The reply to this is that this essay is a study in descriptive rather than revisionary metaphysics. The concern is with how we actually do conceive and talk about the world. No doubt, if we were radically to revise our empirical beliefs, this would occasion a conceptual revolution, such as is envisioned in the preceding response. *How* we play the language-games we do is a different question than *why* we do. A proper answer to the latter is not given by a description of linguistic rules but by an account of why the world rewards those who play them.

Fortunately, there are locomotive-based modal disanalogies that do not rest on an object's having only spatial parts. Because I can choose to move in any spatial direction but cannot backwardly cause something to happen, there is this modal disanalogy:

S20. I can choose here and now whether my use of "here" later than now denotes a place in front of or to the rear of here.
T20. I can choose now and here whether my use of "now" in front of here denotes a time later or earlier than now.

Other modal disanalogies that have the same conceptual underpinnings are:

S21. I can choose here and now whether to occupy here later than now.
T21. I can choose now and here whether to occupy now in front of here.

and

S22. I can choose here and now to occupy here at all times between now and five minutes later than now.
T22. I can choose now and here to occupy now at all places between here and five feet in front of here.

The reason for these two modal disanalogies is that I can now choose to bring something about neither in the past nor the present. Whether I now occupy both here and certain places in front of here, by having different spatial parts of me occupy them, can be caused only by past events, such as an earlier decision of mine to overeat to that I would occupy these places now.

B. *Shared-perspectives Disanalogies*

To complete my account of the objectivity-based modal disanalogies between our spatial and temporal indexical perspectives, it remains to consider the other component of our concept of objectivity—that of being common to or shared by different observers. There is a sense in which both spatial and temporal indexical facts are objective. It is open to public verification both that some place is here and that some time is now, as well as that some event occurs here and that some event occurs now. The disanalogy I seek is implicated in the nature of the agreement in judgment or the unanimity test for verifying such facts. Because it is a necessary truth that

> S23. Two observers who exist now at different places can both see what happens here now.

but false, and necessarily false at that, given my above convention for the use of "now." that

> T23. Two observers who exist here at different times can both see what happens now here.

it follows that our here-there perspective is perceptually transcendable in a way in which our past-present-future one is not. Whereas only observers who exist now can directly verify or see what occurs now, observers who do not exist here can directly verify or see what occurs here. This is a variation on the T12-S12 modal disananlogy. Thus, while it is necessarily true that

> T24. Observers who can directly verify (see) what occurs now share the same temporal indexical perspective, i.e., they both exist now.

it is not necessarily true that

> S24. Observers who can directly verify (see) what occurs here share the same spatial indexical perspective, i.e. they both exist here.

Often observers who do not occupy here can have a better view of what is here than do those who are here.

Thus, our agreement in judgment or unanimity test for objectivity, which, I might add, is only one of the relevant tests for objectivity, shows a modal disanalogy between now and here in regard to their being shared by or common to the *relevant* observers. The relevant observers for directly verifying or seeing what occurs now must share the same temporal indexical perspective but not the same spatial indexical perspective; they must all exist now but needn't all exist here. This is why it seemed less chauvinistic to say that there is no time like the present rather than there is no place like here. Even if, *per impossible*, we could converse with Plato via some mysterious telephone connection, his testimony as to what he then perceives would be irrelevant for the purpose of determining what is happening now. Our unanimity test, therefore, presupposes a shared or common now among the relevant observers but not a common here. And given that one mark of the objective is to be shared or common, it follows that our past-present-future perspective is objective in a way in which our here-there one is not. And when this modal disanalogy is conjoined with the nonselectivity modal disanalogy between these two kinds of indexical perspectives, there results a powerful conceptual case for now but not here being objective. These modal disanalogies are the cash that underlies our common-sense beliefs and feelings about being prisoners of time but not space, being spatially but not temporally free and rangy, and the like. There is no need, thank God, to appeal to the doctrine of temporal becoming to explain and justify them.

CONCLUSION

What connection, if any, is there between the agency-based axiological modal disanalogies and the various objectivity-based modal disanalogies? One would hope that there is a deep connection, and, fortunately, this hope is not disappointed. That our temporal but not our spatial indexical perspectives are objective gives an ontological grounding to an agent having axiological biases in favor of the future but not any spatial direction from here. If the past-present-future perspective were to be nonobjective, an agent's axiological biases in favor of the future would be merely subjective. There would be a serious and depressing bifurcation between agents and nature. The value-preferences of agents would be based on a mistaken view of reality in which how things are taken to be by agents is not how they really or objectively are. If I am right, this is not the case. The irreducibly tensed perspective of an agent as someone whose major concern is "What should I now?" is grounded in nature's own perspective.

NOTES

1. I am fully aware that in making use of modal notions I am imposing on the good will of many readers. For those who are willing to countenance such notions, I give them license to fill in their own favorite account of modality in terms of linguistic rules, platonic forms, possible worlds, metaphysical necessities, and the like; while for those who view the modal distinction between necessity and contingency as an untenable dualism, I leave them free to reinterpret my talk about necessity in a Quineian way concerning how deeply embedded or central in our web of belief a given proposition is. For the latter my project is to show that there are truths about time whose spatial analogues are not as deeply embedded or central in our web of belief.

2. Strictly speaking, "event" should be replaced by "object," since objects are composed of spatial parts and events of temporal parts. And since objects exist but do not happen, "happens" should be replaced by "exists." No harm is done here by not making such replacements, but we must be on our guard to see that no harm results in subsequent cases. Furthermore, none of the disanalogies that figure in this paper are based on a difference in the dimensionality of space and time. They hold even if space were to be only one dimensional.

3. For a defense of this see chapter 5 of my *The Language of Time* (London: Routledge & Kegan Paul, 1968).

4. The agent-causation in S7 must be of the simultaneous sort, such as figures in the laws of classical physics, for otherwise some temporal component of T7 would fail to be translated in S7.

5. I am assuming that an agent cannot perform a so-called supertask, consisting in the performance of an infinite number of distinct acts in a finite time by performing each task in half of the time of its immediate predecessor.

6. *Reasons and Persons* (Oxford: Oxford University Press, 1984), pp. 176–77.

7. *The Will to Believe and Other Popular Essays in Philosophy* (Cambridge, MA: Harvard University Press, 1979), p. 67.

8. It is worth pointing out that what an agent prefers from a tensed perspective might differ from what she prefers from a tenseless one. If an agent existing now has a choice between suffering one unit of pain tomorrow or eight units of pain yesterday, she will prefer to have already suffered eight units of pain yesterday rather than one unit of pain tomorrow; but if this same

agent adopts a tenseless Myth of Ur perspective on her life and is given the choice between suffering one unit of pain at t_9 or eight units of pain at t_7, she will prefer to suffer one unit of pain at t_9 rather than eight units of pain at t_7. Assume, as is possible, that tomorrow is t_9 and yesterday is t_7. In this case her tensed preferences conflict with her tenseless ones. This result should not surprise us, for we know that coreferring expressions that differ in sense are not intersubstitutible *salva veritate* within the scope of the verb "prefer," since it creates a nonextensional context. Thus, even though t_7=yesterday and t_9=tomorrow, these coreferring expressions, given that they differ in sense, are not intersubstitutible *salva veritate* within the scope of "prefer."

9. This might be challenged by appeal to the doctrine of the specious present according to which each pulse of perceptual experience has a sensory content comprised of successive events, thereby enabling us to perceive a succession of events in a single pulse of experience. This has the consequence that when I see an arm rise I really am seeing a Hindu-type god, and thus am seeing not a temporal succession but a concatenation of coexistent arms, and that when I hear the final note of a melody I am hearing a chord. (If Mozart had an auditory specious present of thirty minutes, being able to hear an entire symphony all at once, he must have had some horrible headaches.) For a fuller account see my essay, "From the Specious to the Suspicious Present: The Jack Horner Phenomenology of William James," *Journal of Speculative Philosophy* 11 (1997).

10. Sean Gallagher has shown that there are some surface counterexamples to this, e.g., "Now he has won" and "Now he will do it." But these are stylistic variants respectively for "He has just won" and "He will do it shortly."

11. It is interesting to note that there are some analogous ways in which we can choose the context for our use of spatial and temporal indexical terms. For example, for both type of indexes, one can adopt the rule of having their referent determined either *quoad* the place or time of the tokening, as is usual, or *quoad* the place or time of the perception of the tokening.

NONBEING

13

NEGATIVE STATEMENTS

Among the perennial disputes in philosophy is that between the friends and foes of negative facts or events. The latter argue that negative facts are either reducible to or dependent upon positive facts, while the former, believing in the ontological equality of these two kinds of facts, are ready to rebut these arguments. It is assumed by the disputants that we are able to distinguish between positive and negative facts. This distinction requires that we be able to discriminate between positive and negative statements, since a positive (negative) fact is what is stated by a true positive (negative) statement. If there is no reasonably clear-cut criterion for distinguishing between these two kinds of statements, the dispute between friends and foes of negative facts is like a game played with unmarked dice: in neither case can one determine the winner. The aim of this paper is to examine how such a criterion is to be constructed.

While there is a rich literature on whether negative facts are reducible to or less "real" than positive ones, almost nothing has been done toward devising a criterion for distinguishing between negative and positive statements. This oversight might be explained by the confidence we place in our preanalytic intuitions as to which statements are negative. This confidence may be overconfidence, for, as Frege pointed out, there are many cases in which our intuitions are indecisive, e.g., "This shirt is striped," "Jones is dead," etc.[1] To overcome this indecision we must replace our preanalytic intuitions with a precise criterion for distinguishing between negative and positive statements. Of course, any adequate criterion must yield results that agree with our preanalytic intuitions in those cases in which they are strong and decisive. Without such strong intuitions there would be data neither for launching our task of devising a criterion nor checking its adequacy once it is formulated. Keeping one eye on these intuitions, we shall get on with the task of devising a criterion by first criticizing criteria that have been proposed.

An adequate criterion for distinguishing between positive and negative statements must enable us to determine when a statement is positive and when negative. A criterion for determining when one statement is the negation of another will not enable us to do this. Thus we can bracket as irrelevant any proposed analysis or definition of the connective "~" in terms of its role in inference or the contradictory of a statement. It may be that for the purposes of formulating logical principles and laws there is no need to specify when a statement is negative, as opposed to being negated, but this does not show that there is something illegitimate in our quest for a criterion for a negative (positive) statement. Logic is not the whole of philosophy.

The criterion that most readily comes to mind is a grammatical one. A negative statement is one that is made through the use of a sentence that is grammatically negative, i.e., contains some negative word such as "not" or some negative prefix such as "un." Any such criterion, as Ayer has shown, leads to an absurd consequence, that two different sentences can be used to make statements either that are the same yet differ in quality or that are equivalent but yet different.[2] Consider the sentences, "Hayes is the fastest man" and "There is no other man who is as fast as Hayes." By any grammatical criterion the former is positive and the latter negative. Yet it seems plain that the statements made by the use of these sentences are the same. But then a given statement is both positive and negative, which is absurd. And it would be equally absurd to claim that these sentences are used to make equivalent but nonidentical statements, thus allowing one of the statements to be positive and the other negative in relation to these two different sentences. Since grammatically dissimilar sentences can be used to make the same statement, it is clear that our quarry is not to be found hiding in a grammar book. This is analogous to the impossibility of giving a grammatical criterion for a statement that describes an event as being past (present, future). In English these temporal determinations are made through the use of tensed verbs and copula, but in some other languages these same determinations are made through very different grammatical means.[3]

If grammar cannot supply a criterion for distinguishing between positive and negative statements, maybe psychology can. Many philosophers have claimed that negation signifies a person's mental act of denying, rejecting, or rebutting a statement that is actually made or envisioned as being made by someone.[4] Accordingly, a negative statement is one that expresses a subject's act of denying some statement, a positive statement not being made in rebuttal of some statement. By making negative facts and events dependent upon a subject's mental act of denial, this theory is attractive to those philosophers who cannot get themselves to believe that such facts and events are "objective." Without subjects—persons—there are no acts of denial, and without acts of denial there are no negative facts. If negation really is denial, then the opposite of a negative statement is an affirmative rather than a positive statement, the act of denial being opposed to the act of affirmation. That I choose to contrast negative with positive statements indicates that I do not accept the view that negation is denial.

This psychological criterion for distinguishing between negative and positive statements in terms of the mental acts of denial and affirmation just won't do. First, a statement that is negated need not be one that is ever made by anyone or even envisioned as being made. The minor premise in a *modus tollens* argument negates the consequent of the hypothetical statement in the major premise, but this consequent statement has not been asserted nor need it be imagined as being asserted.

Secondly, a statement that is denied may be either positive or negative, and the same goes for the statement denying it. I might say that it is not the case that it is not raining, herein it being the denied statement that is negative and the denial that is positive, double negation just being a polite or diplomatic way of making a positive statement.

It would seem that the psychological criterion, at best, enables us to determine when one statement is the denial of another, but it does not indicate which one is negative. This failure also marks Dewey's revision of the psychological criterion, according to which a negative statement is one that rejects a certain fact as not being relevant to the furtherance of an inquiry into some problem, as not being a fact of the case:

> Negative propositions ... represent subject-matters to be eliminated because of their irrelevancy to the evidential function of material in the solution of a given problem.[5]

The question that this theory of negation leaves unanswered is how we determine when some rejected subject-matter or statement is negative rather than positive. I might be engrossed in solving some mathematical problem, and thus the fact that my lamp is blue would rightly be rejected as not being a relevant fact of the case. Still it is a positive fact, regardless of how useless it is in furthering this inquiry.

There are further difficulties with the view that negation is denial that arise from there being conceptual truths pertaining to the negation of a statement that do not hold for the denial of a statement. It is necessarily true that for every statement s, either it is not the case that s or it is not the case that it is not the case that s. If negation is denial then "it is not the case" means the same as "I deny." If so, it should be necessarily true, but is not, that for every statement s, either I deny that s or I deny that not-s (or I deny that I deny that s). Moreover, that s is false is entailed by that it is not the case that s but not by that I deny that s. It would seem that negation is part of the factual or informative content of a statement or Thought (in Frege's sense); its function is not a pragmatic one of expressing the propositional attitude of the speaker.[6]

In behalf of the exorcism of negative events and states it is often said that they are not perceived but inferred or judged on the basis of what is actually presented to our senses; e.g., we see that the table is blue, but must infer that it is not green on the basis of what we do actually see.[7] This can be made to serve as a criterion for distinguishing between positive and negative statements that predicate a sensible property of a spatiotemporal individual. A statement of this kind is positive if the event or state it reports is perceivable, otherwise negative. The major difficulty with this perceptual criterion is that certain events and states that should be classified as negative according to our preanalytic intuitions can correctly be said to be perceived, either with or without a "that" preceding the grammatical accusative of the perceptual verb; e.g., "I see (that) the chair is not blue."[8] It is no help to say that the negative state of affairs of the chair's not being green, unlike the positive one of its being blue, is not actually imprinted on our retina or on a photographic plate, since this just pushes the problem one stage further back, it being we who must *look* at the retina or photographic plate and determine what it is that we *see*. An appeal to what can be pictured would be equally of no avail.

At this point, having begun to despair at our repeated failures to find a criterion, we might attempt a simple-minded solution. A singular statement is positive if it entails that its subject has the property signified by its predicate, otherwise it is negative. But this gets us nowhere. A singular referential statement could entail that its subject has the property signified by its predicate and still not be positive, since the property in question might be a negative one, such as nonblue. This criterion can work only if we first have a criterion for distinguishing between positive and negative properties or predicates. We feel that blue is a genuine or real property, while nonblue is a mere pretender, getting whatever determinateness it has from its positive complement, blue. But the problem is how to go beyond mere intuition and formulate an explicit criterion for a "real" property, i.e., a positive property.

A. Quinton has attempted to distinguish between natural and nonnatural or arbitrary classes, it being a positive or genuine property alone that determines the former; and he has used this distinction as a basis for determining which of two complementary properties is the positive one.[9] For Quinton a natural class is determined by a property that is ostensively teachable, since the things it applies to share some common perceivable property.[10] As a result, a natural class will be open ended and have members that are representative of the whole.[11] Blue determines a natural class, because it can be ostensively taught. After having a few instances of blue pointed out, and perceiving the property common to these instances, we are able to go on successfully identifying blue things. The class of nonblue things is nonnatural, since nonblue cannot be learned in this ostensive manner.

Several things are doubtful about Quinton's criterion. First, we feel that an adequate criterion for distinguishing between positive and negative properties should be logical, having to do with a basic difference between the logic of predicates for these two kinds of properties. Instead we are given a criterion based on the alleged ostensive teachability of positive properties. However, the ostensive teachability of a property depends on all sorts of extralogical features of a psychological and sociological sort. Ayer asks us to imagine a tribe whose language contains only two color words, "blue" and "eulb," which means a color that is not blue.[12] They attach a mana to blue things and are forbidden to use "blue" except at certain sacred rites. It is reasonable to suppose that the youth of this tribe are first ostensively taught eulb and then have "blue" defined for them as the complement of eulb. Here it is the negative complement that is ostensively taught and the positive one that is defined in terms of it.

An even more telling objection is that this criterion really is nothing but a variation on the discredited perceptual criterion, and is subject to all of its difficulties. A positive property alone is ostensively teachable. Why? Because the things it applies to share some common *perceptible* property, unlike the members forming the extension of a predicate signifying a negative property. But, as seen above, it is correct to say that we perceive a negative property. This should not surprise us, since what is perceived is so dependent upon linguistic, psychological, and sociological facts involving the perceiver, as well as features of the immediate context of perception.

Ayer has claimed that in respect to a pair of complementary properties there is no criterion by which it can be shown that one of them alone is a "real" or "genuine" property. His denial is based on acceptance of the principle of significant contrast as the criterion for a meaningful predicate. If one member of a pair of complementary predicates satisfies this principle, so does the other:

> The fact is that every significant predicate has a limited range of application. Its correct use is determined both by the fact that there is a set of occasions to which it applies and by the fact that there is a set of occasions to which it does not apply. This being so, it must always be possible to find, or introduce, a predicate that is complementary to the predicate in question, either in the wide sense, as applying to all and only those occasions to which it does not apply, or, in a narrow sense, as applying to all and only the occasions of this sort that fall within a certain general range.[13]

"Blue" applies to blue things and to nothing else, while "eulb," interpreted as the narrow complement of "blue," applies to things that are a color that is not blue and to nothing else. What is common to all things to which the former applies is that they are blue and in respect to the latter that they are a color that is not blue. Neither signifies a more genuine or real property or universal than the other.

Ayer makes quick work of Cook Wilson's attempt to show that a negative term does not signify a "true" universal. According to Wilson:

> If Aness, Bness and Cness are all different in the sense that every A is not B, every B not A, &c., it would follow as before that Cness was a species of not-Aness and at the same time a species of not-Bness. But, if a universal is a differentiation of two different universals, either these two are related themselves as true genus and species or they mutually involve one another so that each necessitates the other. Thus though not-Aness and not-Bness exclude one another, either one is a species of the other, or each involves the other, but both these alternatives are self-contradictory.[14]

Let A, B, and C be respectively blueness, greenness, and redness. These universals are species of color and are different from each other in the required sense, since every blue thing is not green, etc. The complements of blueness and greenness are respectively nonblueness and nongreenness. Redness is a species of each of these, since that something is red entails that it is nonblue and that it is nongreen. According to Wilson's criterion for a true universal, since redness differentiates both nonblueness and nongreenness there must be some relation of necessitation between them; that something is nonblue entails and/or is entailed by that it is nongreen. Plainly these relationships fail to hold, since if an object is green (blue) it is nonblue (nongreen), but cannot without contradiction be nongreen (nonblue). In regard to true universals—positive ones—this relation of necessitation holds; e.g., navy blueness differentiates blueness and coloredness, but blueness necessitates coloredness.

To this Ayer replies:

> Now, if we were obliged to hold that either of the complementary predicates to "blue" and "green" entailed the other, let alone that each entailed the other, we should certainly be involved in contradiction; for it can easily be shown that if this were so the same thing might be, in the one case, both blue and not blue and, in the other, both green and not green. But why should we have to make any such assumption? No reason has been given for supposing that just because the complementary predicates to "blue" and "green" have a number of other predicates, such as "brown" and "red" and "yellow," subsumed under them both, they must therefore stand in any relation of logical necessity to one another. And if it be alleged that this is true of all universals that have any common specification, the answer may be that it is just such cases as these that provide a counter-example.[15]

This way of dismissing Cook Wilson's criterion completely misses the point. In the paper from which the preceding quotation is taken, Ayer is trying to formulate a criterion for a negative statement. He very likely is right in challenging Wilson's criterion as a criterion for a "true" universal. Wilson may be guilty of linguistic imperialism here, of arbitrarily stipulating a definition of "universal," not a very serious offense since this is a term of philosophical jargon. This is irrelevant, however, to whether this is an adequate criterion of a negative universal or property, which is what Ayer is supposed to be seeking. What shall be shown is that Ayer's own criterion, which is based on the level of specificity between complementary predicates, fails and that something like Wilson's criterion can work.

It must be borne in mind that Ayer is seeking a criterion for a negative *statement*. This comes out in his rejection of any grammatical criterion based on determination of when a *sentence* is negative:

> When philosophers contrast affirmative with negative statements, the distinction with which they are concerned applies not to the grammatical form of different sentences but to the different ways in which they are used.[16]

After showing that a psychological as well as an ostensive teachability criterion will not work, he goes on to reject any attempt, such as that of Cook Wilson above, to distinguish between negative and positive predicates by showing that only the latter signify a real universal or property. In respect to a pair of complementary predicates, if either satisfies the principle of significant contrast—Ayer's criterion for a meaningful predicate—so does the other.

Although both of a pair of complementary predicates can be meaningful, and thus express a real property, Ayer claims that in certain cases one of the pair is negative, and, what is more, can be shown to be such by a criterion that yields results generally in agreement with our intuitions. On the basis of this criterion it can be determined when a statement is positive and when negative. The following is Ayer's specificity criterion:

> Let us say of any two singular referential statements S and S', that is, statements which refer to a particular individual and ascribe some property to it, that S is a specifier of S' if and only if S' is not a component of S, S entails S', and S' does not entail S. And let us say that a singular referential statement S' is absolutely specific, with respect to a given language L, if there is no statement expressible in L which is a specifier of S. Further let us say that a statement has the first degree of specificity, with respect to a language L, if it is not absolutely specific but has no specifiers expressible in L which are not themselves absolutely specific, that it has the second degree of specificity if it is not absolutely specific, or specific to the first

> degree, but has no specifiers which are not themselves absolutely specific or specific to the first degree, and so on. Then among complementary pairs of singular referential statements it may happen that one member of the pair has a higher, that is, a less, degree of specificity than the other. In that case the more specific statement may be said to be affirmative and the less specific to be negative.[17]

Notice that Ayer is not saying that a statement is affirmative ("positive" in my terminology) in relation to some statement of which it is a specifier and negative in relation to some other statement that specifies it. This would yield the strange consequences that the statement that a is blue is positive in relation to the statement that a is colored but negative in relation to the statement that a is azure. Rather, according to this criterion, it is the case that, in English, that a is blue is positive, since it is more specific than is the statement predicating of a the complement of blue-nonblue.

Once we have determined the class of positive singular referential statements by this criterion, the quality of quantified statements can be determined as follows:

> An existential statement may be said to be affirmative if and only if it is entailed by an affirmative singular referential statement. A universal, or particular, statement may be said to be affirmative if and only if the singular referential statements which are obtained from it by giving values to its variables are affirmative. The class of negative statements, with respect to a given language, may then be held to consist of all and only those statements that have affirmative statements for their complementaries.[18]

By the use of the principle of quantifier negation certain quantified statements can be made through the use of either a grammatically affirmative or negative sentence. This will not result in ambiguous classifications, since there is no way of instantiating a negatively quantified statement nor any way of deriving such a statement by means of generalization from a singular statement.

Does Ayer's criterion work? In answer to this it will be argued that: (1) his criterion should not be relativized to a language; (2) it is not possible to compare the level or degree of specificity of singular referential statements predicating complementary properties of the same individual without reference to a hierarchical system of classification containing these properties; (3) his vertical criterion based on the level of specificity, even when applied to complementary properties within a hierarchical system, yields counterintuitive results, which can be avoided by a horizontal criterion concerned with connections between properties on the same level of specificity within a system. Various limitations in this horizontal criterion will then be indicated; and, finally, it will be shown that there are versions of Cook Wilson's criterion, interpreted as a criterion for a positive rather than a "true" universal or property, which succeed in distinguishing between negative and positive properties and are not subject to these limitations.

(1) According to Ayer's criterion a statement is positive (negative) only in relation to some specific language. He writes:

> Thus, while for the members of our imaginary tribe the statement that an object was blue would not be more specific than the statement that it was eulb, to say in English that an object is blue is to make a more specific statement than to say that it is not blue; for whereas the statement that an object is not blue is specified by such statements as that it is red, or that it is green, or that it is colourless, the statement that it is blue is not specified by any statement at this level. Accordingly the statement that the object is blue counts, with respect to the English language, as affirmative by this criterion, and the statement that it is not blue as negative.[19]

By so relativizing his criterion to a specific language, Ayer is inconsistent with his own objection to a grammatical criterion. According to this objection, a grammatical criterion can yield ambiguous results, a given statement being both positive and negative, depending upon whether it is made through a positive sentence or a synonymous negative sentence. Ayer assumes that a statement cannot have more than one quality; if it is negative, it is not positive (or neither the one nor the other). But, Ayer tells us, a statement could be negative if made by the use of a sentence in one language, e.g., "*a* is not blue" in English, but neither positive nor negative if made by the use of a sentence in a different language, e.g., "*a* is eulb" in the language of his tribe—Tribese. If the seeming contradiction of a statement's having incompatible qualities can be explained away by relativizing a statement's quality to a language, then relativizing its quality to a sentence should be an equally good, or bad, way out.

More important than the charge of inconsistency, which is only ad hominem, is the fact that Ayer's attempt to relativize a statement's quality to a language involves a distorted conception of a statement. Judging from what Ayer says on page 38 of his article, a statement has to do with the way in which a sentence is used. This seems to fit the definition of a statement as the what-is-said (-believed, -judged, etc.), which is indicated through an *oratio obliqua* construction. It will be left an open issue whether such intentional accusatives can be reduced to acts of stating (etc.) or properties of such acts. It will be assumed that if two sentences are used to make the same statement, the statements they make have the same entailment relations, i.e., they entail and are entailed by the same statements. Granting this as a necessary condition for statement identity, it can be shown, *pace* Ayer, that one and the same statement cannot differ in its quality relative to different languages. For this to happen a given statement must differ in its level or degree of specificity relative to its complementary statement in different languages. To ensure that this cannot happen all we need show is that a statement cannot differ in its level of specificity in different languages. It will be seen that our assumption concerning statement identity ensures that this cannot happen.

Ayer's example of a statement that differs in its specificity level in different languages is the statement that is made both through the use of the English sentence "*a* is not blue" and the Tribese sentence "*a* is eulb." It is claimed that these sentences are used to make statements that differ in their level of specificity, since the speakers of Tribese, because of its paucity of color words, cannot, as can speakers of English, express statements—e.g., that *a* is red (green, etc.)—that are specifiers of that *a* is not blue. Forgetting, but only for the moment, about infimae species of blue, red, etc., it follows that the statement that *a* is not blue is absolutely specific in Tribese but of the first degree of specificity in English.

Ayer faces a dilemma here. Either the speakers of Tribese and English make the same statement or they do not. If they do not, it is not one and the same statement that has different levels of specificity in different languages; and, if they do, then, according to our assumption for statement identity, these statements have the same entailment relations and therefore the same degree or level of specificity.[20] On either horn it turns out that Ayer fails to produce an example of a *single* statement having different levels of specificity in different languages. And if such an example cannot be produced, a statement cannot differ in quality relative to different languages. Of course, we cannot identify or refer to a statement except by using a sentence in some language, but in using this sentence we are not referring to it. In saying, "the statement that *s*," I refer to the statement that *s*, not to the *sentence* '*s*.'

(2) Even when Ayer's specificity criterion is not relativized to a language there are problems. One concerns how we are to compare the respective levels of specificity of *wide* complements. Consider in this connection the pair of wide complementary properties, number, and nonnumber. That *a* is a number is of at least the sixth degree or level of specificity, since it has specifiers belonging to six different levels of specificity; in inverse order of specificity some of them are that *a* is a real number, a rational number, an integer, a positive integer, a positive odd integer, the number seven. Nonnumber, being the wide complement of number, applies to everything that is not a number, e.g., an organism. Organism is a property of at least the third degree of specificity, since it is specified by statements on three different levels; some of them are that *a* is an animal, a man, a Caucasian. This makes it appear as if nonnumber is of the fourth degree of specificity, and therefore positive, since it is more specific than its complement, number. If this counterintuitive result should bother us, we no doubt could find some specifier of nonnumber, such as *thought of a number*, which would make nonnumber appear to be of a higher degree of specificity than number, and therefore the negative member of the pair. Obviously, something has gone wrong, for a given property cannot be both positive and negative.

The way out of this difficulty is to restrict Ayer's specificity or vertical criterion to *narrow* complements. This narrowing of the universe of discourse requires that the complementary properties in question be species of some common genus. Blue and color that is not blue are narrow complements, since they both specify color. We can now state Ayer's vertical criterion as follows:

> (V) A property is positive if and only if it is more specific than its narrow complement, i.e., is specified by properties on fewer horizontal levels.

A property is negative if less specific than its narrow complement, and neither positive nor negative if on the same level of specificity as its narrow complement. This criterion presupposes a classificatory system containing the narrow complements to be tested. Such a system is made up of both a vertical and horizontal dimension. The vertical dimension is determined by relations of being a specifier of, which hold between the infimae species and the species on the next higher level, and so on up to the summum genus of the system. The degree or level of specificity of a property is determined by its position in this vertical dimension. A horizontal level of the system is determined by a group of incompatible species having the same degree of specificity. It will be seen that this reliance on a classificatory system is a weakness in criterion (V).

(3) There are problems with criterion (V). First, if a genus logically could have only two species, then each of these is the narrow complement of the other. But then there is a pair of narrow complements neither of which is positive, since neither is more specific. Dry and damp, odd and even, are examples of such complements. Therefore, to say that a is even (odd) or that a is damp (dry) is not to make a positive statement (nor a negative one), which runs counter to our intuitions that they are positive statements.[21] This difficulty can be met by placing an ad hoc restriction on (V), so that it applies only to properties that belong to a classificatory system that admits the logical possibility of there being more than two species on anyone of its horizontal levels.

Another kind of counterintuitive result, which cannot be met by any ad hoc restriction, is the following. Suppose there is a genus G

which has C, D, and E for its species, but C alone has species, and these species have infimae species. Therefore, that a is C is specified by statements on more horizontal levels—two—than its narrow complement that a is a G that is not C, it being specified by statements on only one level. An example of this would be where G is color and C, D, and E are blue, green, and red, respectively, and blue alone has species, such as azure, which themselves have infimae species, such as kazure (a determinate shade of azure). The statement we make by using the sentence, "a is red (green)," is not exactly the same, although a close cousin of, the one which we ordinarily make, since these differ in their entailment relations. That a is blue is negative, since its narrow complement is specified by statements on fewer horizontal levels. It is not logically impossible that colors should be organized in this way, it being a contingent fact that there are the species of color there are and that these species have the species they have, and so on. Even if colors were to have the strange stratification envisioned above, we would not want to say that blue is a negative property.

This counterintuitive result can be avoided by replacing the vertical criterion (V) with the following horizontal one:

(H) A property is positive if it is not specified by any property on the same horizontal level as its narrow complement, otherwise it is negative.[22]

This horizontal criterion meets both of the preceding objections. First, both damp and dry (odd and even) will now check out as positive, since none of these properties is specified by a property on the same horizontal level as its narrow complement. Secondly, regardless of whether there are determinate shades of the different species of color and determinate shades of these determinate shades, and so on, that a is a color that is not blue is specified by statements containing predicates on the same horizontal level as its narrow complement, e.g., that a is red.

The horizontal criterion (H), like the vertical criterion (V), presupposes a genus-species or determinable-determinate classificatory system, because it assumes that we already know when two properties are on the same level of specificity within a system. By presupposing a classificatory system, these criteria face certain difficulties. One is due to the fact that not all singular referential statements have predicates signifying properties that fit a genus-species or determinable-determinate type of classification; e.g., "Smith is (is not) a member of the Elks," "The carburetor is (is not) the defective part of the automobile."[23] Being a member of the Elks (being the defective part of the automobile) is not a property contained within a genus-species classification. That it is not is seen by the unanswerable nature of the question, "What property on the same level of specificity as being a member of the Elks is incompatible with it?" Our intuitions tell us that statements that refer to some set or whole and say that some member or part of this set or whole does not have a certain property are negative, but neither criterion (V) nor (H) can be utilized to show that they are.

Another difficulty with both (V) and (H), which will be discussed in section (4), is that by presupposing a classificatory system they presuppose the very distinction they are trying to explicate. Just why will become clearer after we have formulated some versions of Cook Wilson's criterion that do not presuppose a classificatory system—a task to which we now turn.

(4) What is distinctive about the Cook Wilson criterion is that it is based solely on a difference in the kind of logical relations into which positive and negative properties enter, without presupposing any classificatory system. It will be shown that (i) there are several viable versions of a Cook Wilson type criterion and (ii) they are superior to both the vertical criterion (V) and the horizontal criterion (H).

(i) According to Cook Wilson, "if a universal is a differentiation of two different universals, either these two are related themselves as true genus and species or they mutually involve one another so that each necessitates the other."[24] This can serve as the basis for the following criterion for a negative property:

(W) A property P is negative if and only if there is a property P_1 such that:

(a) P and P_1 are both specified by a property P_2; and
(b) neither P entails P_1 nor P_1 entails P.

A property that fails to satisfy (W) is positive. To say that a property F entails a property F_1 means that that something is F entails that it is F_1. To say that a property F specifies a property F_1 means the following: (a) F entails F_1; (b) F_1 does not entail F. A property may specify another without being either a determinate or species of it. This is due to conditions (a) and (b) being necessary but not sufficient for a determinable-determinate or genus-species relation.[25]

Unfortunately, (W) does not work, since it is satisfied by properties that obviously are positive. E.g., let P be blue, P_1 be nonazure, and P_2 be navy blue. P_2 specifies both P and P_1, and P does not entail P_1 nor does P_1 entail P. P_1 is itself negative, and it might be thought that (W) could be protected against this kind of counterexample by restricting P_1 to positive properties; however, this would make (W) viciously circular. This circularity can be avoided by restricting P_1 to a property *of the same quality as P*. Being of the same quality as, no doubt, is epistemically or psychologically less primitive than being positive (negative); but there is no reason why we cannot take it as being logically primitive and devise a criterion for distinguishing between negative and positive properties in terms of it. In other words, it is being assumed that we have the concept of being of the same quality as, and, as a result, can segregate properties into two groups, each member of one group being of the same quality as every other member of that group and no member of one group being of the same quality as any member of the other group. A criterion will now be formulated for determining which group contains the positive properties and which the negative. It is as follows:

(W)$_1$ A property P is negative if and only if there is a property P_1 such that:
  (a) P_1 is of the same quality as P;
  (b) P and P_1 are both specified by a property P_2; and
  (c) neither P entails P_1 nor P_1 entails P.

This criterion is an improvement. Blue no longer turns out to be negative, for while it is true that blue and nonazure are both specified by navy blue and there is no entailment relation between blue and nonazure, the latter is not of the same quality as blue. There still remains a counterexample to $(W)_1$. Imagine that there is a property *aoi* that denotes a part of the spectrum that overlaps the part denoted by blue. Let us call the part of the spectrum that is both blue and aoi *flue*. Flue specifies both blue and aoi, even though blue and aoi are of the same quality and stand in no entailment relation, thereby satisfying $(W)_1$. This counterexample can be met by requiring P_2 to be of a different quality from *P*:

> $(W)_2$ A property *P* is negative if and only if there is a property P_1 such that:
> (*a*) P_1 is of the same quality as *P*;
> (*b*) *P* and P_1 are both specified by a property P_2 that is not of the same quality
> as *P*; and
> (*c*) neither *P* entails P_1 nor P_1 entails *P*.

Any property that fails to satisfy some condition of $(W)_2$ is positive.

There still remain counterexamples to $(W)_2$ that can be met by restricting the sort of properties that can be substituted for the property variables *P*, P_1, and P_2. Here is one example. Let the property to be tested *P* be blue. There is a property P_1—square—such that: (a) P_1 is of the same quality as P_i (b) *P* and P_1 are both specified by a property P_2 blue-and-square-and-nonred—which is not of the same quality as *P*; and (c) neither *P* entails P_1 nor P_1 entails *P*. The reason why P_2 differs in quality from the positive property *P* is that a conjunctive property, at least according to my intuitions, is negative if anyone of its conjuncts is; a disjunctive property is positive if any one of its disjuncts is. This is analogous to a conjunction being contingent if any one of its conjuncts is and a disjunction being necessary if anyone of its disjuncts is.

Admittedly, blue-and-square-and-nonred is a strange sort of a property, if it is one at all. How can we restrict the properties over which the property variables of $(W)_2$ range so as to eliminate this kind of a counterexample? One way is to restrict the range of properties to "atomic" properties, i.e., a property that contains a constituent property that entails every one of its constituent properties. Red, for example, is atomic; for while it is a conjunction of red and colored, its former constituent entails every one of its constituent properties. This restriction eliminates the above counterexample, since blue-and-square-and-nonred obviously is not atomic. This, however, is not a good way of restricting $(W)_2$, since, while it would work for determinate properties, e.g., red, it would be inapplicable to properties that are a species of some genus, e.g., square is a conjunction of quadrilateral-and-equiangular-and-equilateral, no one of whose constituents entails everyone of its constituents. This unwanted result can be avoided if we restrict $(W)_2$ instead to "qualitatively homogeneous properties," i.e., properties all of whose constituents are of the same quality. Again, we have had to make use of our logically primitive notion of "being the same quality as." It is apparent that blue-and-square-and-nonred is not qualitatively homogeneous. I do not think it would be accurate to call such a property "qualitatively indefinite," since, as indicated above, a conjunction one of whose conjuncts is negative is itself negative. Restricted in this way, I believe that $(W)_2$ works.

There are simpler alternatives to $(W)_2$ that also are based on a difference in the kind of logical relations sustained by negative and positive properties, without a classificatory system being presupposed. Condition (b) of $(W)_2$ can alone serve as a criterion for a negative property, since a negative property specifies only another negative property whereas positive properties specify both positive and negative properties. By once again making use of the primitive notion of having the same quality as, this can be expressed as follows:

$(W)_3$ A property P is negative if and only if it specifies no property that is not of the same quality.

A property that does not satisfy some condition of $(W)_3$ is positive. There are specification relations going up a genus-species classification, e.g., from man to animal, but there also are specification relations going down this classification when we insert for each property its wide complement, e.g., from nonanimal to nonman. But positive properties, in addition to specifying other positive properties, also specify negative properties, i.e., properties of different quality. E.g., blue specifies, in addition to color, nonred, but nonred, as the wide complement to red, specifies no positive property, i.e., property differing in quality from it.[26] Again, it is necessary to restrict $(W)_3$ to qualitatively homogeneous properties; otherwise, nonred color would have to count as positive, since it specifies color, which differs from it in quality.

Another difference between positive and negative properties in respect to their logical relations, which also can serve as a criterion, is the following:

$(W)_4$ A property P is negative if and only if there is no property of the same quality as it with which it is incompatible.

To say that two properties are incompatible means that it is logically impossible for them to be coinstantiated. Red is incompatible with blue, which is of the same quality as it, but there is no property of the same quality as nonred with which it is incompatible. $(W)_4$ also must be restricted to qualitatively homogeneous properties; for nonred color, an obviously negative property, is incompatible with some other property of the same quality—noncolored.

It might be wondered how criteria $(W)_2$–$(W)_4$ would work for a property such as striped or speckled. To say of a surface that it is speckled means that parts of its surface are of one color and its other parts are not of this color. Thus, this property is qualitatively heterogeneous, and as a result these criteria do not apply to it. What we can do is to apply our criteria to each of its atomic constituents. It turns out to be a conjunctive property, and since one of its constituents is negative it is negative. My intuition concerning the quality of conjunctive (disjunctive) properties one of whose conjuncts (disjuncts) is negative (positive) are not too strong, and there may be exceptions to the rule that a conjunctive (disjunctive) property with a negative (positive) conjunct (disjunct) is negative (positive). We might eschew trying to classify qualitatively heterogeneous properties, and instead confine ourselves to the classification of their atomic constituents.

(ii) Some viable versions of a Cook Wilson type criterion, viz. $(W)_2$–$(W)_4$, have been presented, and it will now be shown that they are superior to the vertical criterion (V) and the horizontal criterion (H). First let us consider how adequately these criteria handle properties, e.g., damp and dry, which specify a genus that logically could have only two species. It has been shown that (H) is superior to (V) in this regard, since (H) alone can apply to these kinds of properties. Criteria $(W)_2$–$(W)_4$ are at least the equal of (H), since they too require us to classify these properties as positive. E.g., damp is incompatible with a property of the same quality—dry—thereby failing to satisfy some condition of $(W)_4$; and, moreover, it fails to satisfy some condition of $(W)_3$ since it specifies a property of a different quality, e.g., nonnumber.

While criteria (H) and $(W)_2$–$(W)_4$ are right in general to classify such properties as positive, there are "teleological" counterexamples in which one of the two logically possible species of a given genus is considered to be natural, fit, or proper to the kind of things that instantiates it. When a thing of this kind does not have this "natural" property it suffers a "privation" in the sense of Aristotle and Aquinas. In such teleological cases a statement predicating the narrow complement of this natural property is to be classified as negative. E.g., under the genus of organism having eyes there are only two possibilities—having the ability to see and being blind. Yet to say that a man is blind is to make a negative statement according to my intuitions, the reason being that we think it fit or natural for a man to be able to see. Similarly, to say that a man is dead is to make a negative statement according to my intuitions, since life seems to be a more natural and desirable state than death.

The superiority of $(W)_2$–$(W)_4$ over (V) and (H) rests on the fact that the former alone do not presuppose a genus-species type classificatory system that contains the property to be tested. Two difficulties arise for (V) and (H) over the presupposition. First, as already indicated, their generality is limited, because they cannot be applied to properties that do not fit a genus-species or determinable-determinate classification, e.g., being a member of the Elks. But criteria $(W)_2$–$(W)_4$ can successfully handle such cases; e.g., being a member of the Elks is positive since it fails to satisfy $(W)_4$, being a member of the Elks being incompatible with being a number. It also fails to satisfy $(W)_3$, since it specifies being a non-number, which differs from it in quality.

The major difficulty with presupposing a genus-species type classification is that it seems to presuppose the very distinction it is supposed to explicate. A genus-species type classification itself presupposes a distinction between positive and negative properties. The reason is that such a classification cannot be determined by negative properties, only by positive ones. The species of a given genus must be mutually incompatible, otherwise there would be cross-classifications. A negative genus, according to $(W)_3$, can have as a species, be specified by, only another negative property. But, according to $(W)_4$, a negative property is not incompatible with any other negative property, i.e., property of the same quality as itself. Thus, from $(W)_3$ and $(W)_4$ it can be deduced that no two species of a negative genus are incompatible. And for this reason negative properties cannot determine a genus-species classification. Of course a negative genus can have species that are positive properties, since a positive property can specify a property of a different quality. But these positive species need not be incompatible. E.g., nonred has among its positive species justice and action, but they are not incompatible since something could be a just action.

Not only do $(W)_2$–$(W)_4$ not presuppose a genus-species classification, but they explicate the distinction between positive and negative properties in terms of those features of positive properties that make them alone fit for determining such a classification. A philosophically illuminating criterion for distinguishing between positive and negative properties must not just yield results in agreement with our preanalytic intuitions; if this were all that is required, a perfectly adequate criterion would be that a property P is positive if and only if it is of the same quality as red. In addition, this criterion must indicate those features of positive and negative properties that explain why the former play a role in the development of systems of knowledge that the latter cannot, why negative properties are epistemically of no significance. One of the jobs we want properties to do is to help us in constructing classificatory systems of the genus-species sort, but this is just what negative properties cannot do. The great value of $(W)_2$–$(W)_4$ is that they explain why negative properties are unfit for this purpose. One can sympathize with a Cook Wilson who denies that negative properties are "real" or "genuine" universals. Plato's science of dialectics, I suspect, consists in constructing hierarchical classifications of the Forms, his relation of "mingling" or "blending" being that of being specified by. There could be no such a science if we allow negative Forms into the realm of Being.[27]

NOTES

1. "Negation" in *Translations from the Philosophical Writings of Gottlob Frege*, ed. Max Black and P. T. Geach (Oxford: Blackwell, 1952), pp. 125–26.

2. A. J. Ayer, "Negation," *The Journal of Philosophy* 49 (1952): 797–815, reprinted in his *Philosophical Essays* (London: Macmillan, 1954). All references to this article are from the pagination in the latter book. See pp. 36–37.

3. For a fuller account see ch. 3 of my book, *The Language of Time* (London: Routledge & Kegan Paul, 1968).

4. For a defense of this see: Immanuel Kant, *Critique of Pure Reason*, (London: Macmillan, 1963), A709, B737; C. Sigwart, *Logic*, vol. 1, sec. ed. (London: Swan Sonnenschein, 1895), p. 119; F. H. Bradley, *The Principles of Logic*, vol. 1, sec. ed. (London: Oxford University Press, 1922), pp. 114–15; Bernard Bosanquet, *Knowledge and Reality* (London: Swan Sonnenschein, 1892), p. 216; and *Logic*, vol. 1, sec. ed. (Oxford: Clarendon, 1911), p. 278; Henri Louis Bergson, *Creative Evolution* (New York: Modern Library, 1944), p. 312; Sidney Hook, *The Quest for Being* (New York: St. Martin's Press, 1961), p. 147; and Hans Regnell, "On Negation and Negative Facts," *Theoria* 17 (1951), pp. 210–21.

5. *Logic: The Theory of Inquiry* (New York: Holt, 1938), p. 183.

6. Another significant difference between negation and denial is that "I deny" is a performative verb while "It is not the case" is not. To say in appropriate circumstances, "I deny that s," is thereby to deny that s; however, to say, even in appropriate circumstances (e.g., one in which I have evidence for not-s), "It is not the case that s," is not for it thereby not to be the case that s.

7. For a discussion of this question see G. Buchdahl, "The Problem of Negation," *Philosophy and Phenomenological Research* 22 (1961), pp. 163–78.

8. This point is made by Richard Taylor in "Negative Things," *The Journal of Philosophy* 49 (1952), p. 33, and Morris Lazerowtiz, "Negative Terms," reprinted in *The Structure of Metaphysics* (New York: Humanities Press, 1955), pp. 197–98.

9. "Properties and Classes," *Proceedings of the Aristotelian Society* 63 (1957–1958), especially p. 48 ff.

10. Ibid., pp. 47 and 58.

11. Ibid., pp. 36 and 37.

12. Ayer, "Negation," p. 49 ff.

13. Ibid., p. 48. I assume that Ayer's principle of significant contrast requires only that for a predicate to be meaningful it must be *logically* possible for both it and its complement to apply to something, not that both actually do have an application. The problem with assuming the latter is explored in my

article, "Hook's Views on Metaphysics" in *Sidney Hook and the Contemporary World,* ed. P. Kurtz (New York: John Day, 1968).

14. John Cook Wilson, *Statement and Inference* (Oxford: Clarendon, 1926), vol. 1, p. 254.

15. Ayer, "Negation," pp. 52–53.

16. Ibid., p. 38. We shall see that Ayer's criterion, because it is relativized to a language, betrays his own declared objective.

17. Ibid., p. 62. Ayer uses "affirmative" instead of "positive." My reasons for preferring the latter term have been given in my argument against negation being the same as denial.

18. Ibid., p. 63.

19. Ibid., p. 62. By placing colorless on the same "level" as red, green, and blue, Ayer is taking it to mean something like transparent or white, both of which are specifiers of color. Colorless as the complement of colored means not subject to color determinations. But if Ayer is using colorless in this way he is inconsistent when he later says (on p. 63) that one of the paradoxical consequences of his specificity criterion is that "the statement that an object is coloured will have to count as negative: for it is less specific than the statement that the object is colorless." For his criterion applies only to complementary predicates. If colorless is a specifier of color, it cannot also be its complement.

20. Which horn we pick is based on what criteria we adopt for determining when two persons have made the same statement or said the same thing. A tough criterion would require that each person can verbally formulate all of the statements that the other claims are entailed by or entail this statement. According to this criterion the speakers of Tribese and English do not make the same statement.

21. Ayer concurs. See ibid., p. 63.

22. Ayer, without indicating it, shifts from his vertical criterion to a horizontal one when he says on p. 62: "Whereas the statement that an object is not blue is specified by such statements as that it is red, or that it is green ... the statement that it is blue is not specified by any statements *at this level*." My italics.

23. H. H. Price's contribution to the symposium on "Negation" in the *Proceedings of the Aristotelian Society,* Supplementary Volume 9 (1929), pp. 97–111, is very helpful on this point.

24. Cook Wilson, *Statement and Inference,* p. 254.

25. For an indication of what additional conditions are required for a definition of these two relations see John Woods, "On Species and Determinates," *Nous* 1 (1967): 243–54.

26. It might be contended that there are properties not of the same quality as nonred that it specifies, viz., being an entity, being something, being self-identical with itself, etc. These "properties" will not be counted as properties, since they logically must have a universal extension. We shall also not countenance as properties any property that logically must have a null extension.

27. Much of the work on this paper was done during the spring term of 1968 while I held a Charles E. Merrill Fellowship at the University of Pittsburgh. I profited immensely from discussions with the following: Alan Ross Anderson; Nuel D. Belnap, Jr.; Joseph Camp; Jose Alberto Coffa; Charles Hamblin; Philip Quin; Nicholas Rescher; Michael Rohr; Robert Schultz; Thomas Schwartz; and Martin Tweedale.

14

ON WHAT THERE ISN'T

The status of negative events and facts is a perennial source of embarrassment, for they seem to be just as inescapable as they are unpalatable. These are some reasons for their being considered logical undesirables. Reality becomes overcrowded, since every positive event or state carries on its back an infinite or indefinite number of negative fleas: my being in Pittsburgh now requires my not being in Cleveland now, my not being in Chicago now, etc., etc.! Second, for those who hold that there is no entity without identity, negative events are found wanting, since there seem to be no criteria for individuating and counting them, or even for determining how many of them there are: we can individuate and count occurrent forest fires but not nonoccurrent ones. Third, for those who believe that reality must be determinate, negative events fail to make the grade, since they are not properly determinate: something could not be just the nonoccurrence of a forest fire or a non- (forest fire) since this would be compatible with its having only negative properties and thus being nothing at all. Finally, harking back to the hallowed principle of Parmenides that Being Is, Not-Being is not, it would be contradictory to say that there *are* things that are not or do not occur.

On the other side of the ledger there seem to be equally powerful reasons for countenancing negative events and states. The first and foremost reason is that since every true proposition about the world supposedly corresponds with some event, there must be a negative event corresponding to every true negative proposition about the world. Second, there can be no determinate reality without negative facts, since something can be a definite individual only if it has finite boundaries, which require that it is *not* the same as everything else. Third, change requires temporal passage consisting in the shift of the present to ever-later times; however, this requires that there be a past and future, which are the *no*-longer and the *not*-yet. Fourth, we seem to perceive negative things such as lacks and absences, but whatever we perceive must exist. Fifth, for those who believe in real essences or substantial natures, there are objective teleological negations consisting in a certain kind of object not realizing all of its natural functions. And, finally, it seems to be inconsistent to say that there are no negative facts, for supposedly there will be at least one negative fact consisting in there not being any negative facts.

Herein we have the ingredients of an all-too-common embarrassment in philosophy. An entity of type x appears queer or bogus, yet also appears inescapable. The typical response by the friends of x's is to argue that they are not so queer as charged, while that of the foes of x's is ontologically to downgrade x's so that they need not be countenanced as ultimate constituents or features of reality. Both moves have been made in the negative fact dispute. The foes of negative things, in their efforts to show that there aren't such entities or that they have a second-class existence that is dependent upon positive reality, have defended one or more of the following theses:

(1) Negative statements are reducible to positive ones;
(2) The world is fully describable in positive statements;
(3) There are no negative events; and
(4) Negative events are subjective in the sense of being

dependent upon the unfulfilled desires or expectations of a conscious being.

My efforts will be directed toward attacking (1) and defending (2) and (3). Space will not permit treatment of (4), but for the record I believe that it is false.

(1) NEGATIVE STATEMENTS AS REDUCIBLE TO POSITIVE ONES

This is the most extreme form that the ontological downgrading of negative events and facts takes. Its aim is well expressed by a popular song from the 1940s: "Accentuate the positive, eliminate the negative." The song also cautions us against messing with Mr. Inbetween, which, I take it, is a warning against having anything to do with certain Polish logicians. If a negative statement is reducible to a positive one, it would undermine the major reason for introducing negative events; for the correspondent of a true negative statement about the world is the positive event that serves as the correspondent of the positive statement to which it is reduced.

At the basis of all such reductive analyses are the concepts of *otherness* (or *difference*) and *incompatibility*. These concepts are quite different, although they are often confounded with each other. To say that x is other than y means that x is not identical with y, whereas to say that x is incompatible with y is to make the stronger claim that they are logically not coinstantiable. Redness is other than, but not incompatible with, crimsonness. With this distinction in mind, we can now consider various kinds of otherness and incompatibility analyses of two prominent negative statements—the singular denial and the negative existential—such as:

(S) My pen is not red.

and

(E) There are no unicorns.

According to one version of the otherness account, they are rendered as:

(S1) Every property of my pen is other than redness.

and

(E1) Every property of every existent thing is other than unicornness.

In some otherness analyses it is propositions rather than properties that are quantified over, as in the following:

(S2) Every true proposition is other than that my pen is red.

and

(E2) Every true proposition is other than that there are unicorns.

Many see these analyses as trivial, the charge being that they fail to clarify the structure of negative events or facts. More specifically, (S1) and (S2) do not bring out the way in which (S) is verified or confirmed. It is not verified by inspecting every property of my pen or cataloguing every true proposition and finding that each of them is other than redness or the proposition that my pen is red but by discovering some positive property of my pen that logically excludes its being red, this being its color. This sort of objection would apply to the following nominalistic versions of the otherness analysis:

(S3) Every red thing is other than my pen.

and

(E3) Every existent thing is other than any thing that is a unicorn.

They are nominalistic because they quantify over concrete individuals alone. While (S3) is logically equivalent to (S), it no more constitutes an analysis of (S) than does "All nonblack things are nonravens" constitute an analysis of "All ravens are black." Just as we wouldn't count an instance of a nonblack thing that was not a raven as a confirming instance of "All ravens are black," we wouldn't count an instance of a red thing that is not the same as my pen as a confirming instance of "My pen is not red." It is highly implausible to say that this supposedly singular statement really is about every object in the world.

It would be more revealing to analyze (S) and (E) in terms of incompatibility, as do the following:

(S4) There is a positive property of my pen that is incompatible with redness.

and

(E4) Every existent thing has some positive property that is incompatible with unicornness.

According to a more refined version of the incompatibility analysis, the function of a singular denial is to eliminate one possible qualification of the subject within some disjunctive set of mutually incompatible properties. In a proposition like (S) the property denied of the subject is a determinate or species of some determinable or genus and its function is to affirm of the subject some determinate or species of this determinable or genus that is incompatible with the one denied. Accordingly, (S) turns into:

(S5) The color of my pen is incompatible with redness.

It would be reasonable to render (E) as:

(E5) Every existent animal has some species-type property that is incompatible with unicornness.

In some cases the denied predicate indicates a part of some whole, as in, "The defective part (of the car) is not the carburetor," and would be rendered as, "The defective part (of the car) is some part of the car one of whose positive properties is incompatible with carburetorness."

In an even more fine-grained analysis the disjunctive set in question, whether made up of determinates, species, or parts, is spelled out in the *analysans*, minus the rejected member, so that (S) and (E) become:

(S6) My pen is either blue or green or yellow, etc.

and

(E6) Every existent animal is either a horse or a man or a dog, etc.

These analyses are the only versions of the incompatibility analysis that are nominalistic.

These more fine-grained versions of the incompatibility analysis face certain problems that are peculiar to them. First, there are counterexamples, e.g., that the soul is not a fire shovel, in which we do not want to predicate of the subject the generic property of which the denied property is a species. Such counterexamples have been charged with vacuousness because they are tautological. At any rate, it would be reasonable for a defender of an (S5)-type analysis to restrict it to contingent negative denials. Against an (S6)-type analysis it could be claimed that it is a contingent fact that there are certain determinate shades of color, and thus (S) could be true and (S6) false. Moreover, there is the medical problem of completing the disjunction in (S6), since there may be an infinite number of determinate shades of color; if there should be a superdenumerable infinity of such determinates, the difficulty is logical rather than medical. Waiving this problem of completing the analysis, there is the further difficulty of how we could ever know that the disjunction was complete. Another problem with (S6) is that it presents us with a disjunctive state or fact, but such states are just as puzzling for many philosophers as are negative ones. Because of these problems with (S6)—and (E6)—type analyses, we shall consider only the less fine-grained versions of the incompatibility account; and, if it should turn out that there are some difficulties peculiar to an (S5)-type analysis, possibly due to its attempt to specify the genus, etc. within which the elimination takes place, we shall go with the least fine-grained version, (S4).

There is another kind of analysis of a negative statement, based on the axiomatic method in constructing logical systems, that might be held to succeed in reducing negative to positive statements. In constructing such a system, we can select entailment and universal quantification as primitive notions and can define negation in terms of them as follows: "not-p" means that if p is true then every proposition is true. Since the consequent of this conditional is necessarily false, for if every proposition were true then the proposition that some proposition is false is also true, it follows that p is false and thus not-p is true. Thus we could analyse (S) and (E) as:

(S7) If my pen is red, then every proposition is true.

and

(E7) If there is a unicorn, then every proposition is true.

Any necessarily false proposition, e.g., that $1 + 1 = 3$, could serve as the consequent in these analyses.

In some axiomatic systems, the stroke operation is taken as the sole primitive connective. In such a system (S) and (E) could be rendered as:

(S8) That my pen is red/that my pen is red.

and

(E8) That there are unicorns/that there are unicorns.

in which the stroke operator "/" means *not both true*.

None of these axiomatic accounts have been seriously considered as reductive analyses of negative to positive statements. The reasons are not hard to find. First, primitiveness in an axiomatic system is one thing and conceptual primitiveness another. There seems to be nothing conceptually primitive about the stroke operator, since it can be explained only in terms of negation. The above analyses just supply us with novel ways of saying that a given proposition is false. This objection would hold if we took material implication as a primitive notion and read the "if . . . then" in (S7) and (E7) as material implication. Second, these analyses do nothing to clarify the nature or structure of negative facts or states, and in this respect suffer from the same sort of triviality as do the otherness analyses. Finally, against (S7) and (E7) it could be claimed that a contingently false statement—that my pen is red—does not entail a necessarily false statement. For these reasons we will not give further consideration to the above axiomatic analyses of negation.

The moment of truth has now arrived in which it must be determined whether any of the preceding analyses succeed in reducing a negative to a positive statement. The standard objection to them is that both otherness and incompatibility are negative relations, the former meaning "is *not* the same as" and the latter "is *not* coinstantiable with," and therefore these analyses are viciously circular. A further charge of circularity is raised against the universally quantified versions of these analyses. To say that every property of my pen is other than redness means, according to the principle of quantifier negation, that there is *no* property of my pen that is the same as redness. These oft-made charges of circularity have not moved the proponents of these analyses. This sort of an impass is all too common in reductive metaphysics. An attempt is made to reduce x-type entities to y-type ones—by translating statements that are about or report x's into ones that are about or report y's alone. For this reductive analysis to succeed it is necessary that the statement about y's in the *analysans* entail the statement about x's in the *analysandum*; but then it can be charged that this makes the analysis viciously circular. The reply is that this charge of circularity is nothing but a variation on the paradox of analysis objection to any analysis. The way out of this impass is to devise adequate criteria for statements that are about x's and those that are about y's.

Only then can it be determined whether the statement in the *analysans* is an *x*-type statement and as a result the analysis is viciously circular. Unfortunately, the dispute between the friends and foes of negative facts has not been informed by any such criteria for negative and positive statements; and thus their dispute has taken on the strange quality of a crap game played with unmarked dice.

It was toward finding a way out of this impass that I attempted, in a previous article, to devise adequate criteria for positive and negative statements.[1] The best that can be done here is to give a brief summary of my results, which can then be put to work in mediating the circularity controversy. First, criteria will be devised for nonquantified singular statements, in which only one of the predicate's arguments, if it has more than one, is taken as the subject, the other arguments being considered part of the predicate; e.g., a statement of the form "*aRb*" can be parsed so that its predicate is either "_*Rb*" or "*a*R_." The problem reduces to that of determining when a predicate in such a uniquely parsed statement expresses a positive rather than a negative property.

My criteria will employ as a logically primitive notion that of *being of the same quality as*, i.e., being both positive or both negative. Being of the same quality as, no doubt, is epistemically or psychologically less primitive than being positive (negative) in quality; but there is no reason why we cannot take it as being logically primitive and devise criteria for distinguishing between negative and positive properties or predicates in terms of it. In other words, it is being assumed that we have the concept of *being of the same quality as*, and, as a result, can segregate properties or predicates into two groups, each member of one group being of the same quality as every other member of that group and no member of one group being of the same quality as any member of the other group. Criteria will now be devised for determining which group contains the positive properties and which the negative. These criteria are:

(C) A property is positive if there could be a property of the same quality that is incompatible with it.

and

(C1) A property is positive if there could be a property of different quality that is entailed by it.

To say that a property P entails a property Q means that a statement that *a* is P entails that *a* is Q. Any property that fails to satisfy either of these criteria is negative. These criteria allow for there being complementary properties, each of which is positive, e.g., odd and even.

Adequate criteria for distinguishing between positive and negative properties must yield results in agreement with our preanalytic intuitions and also be philosophically illuminating. That these criteria satisfy the former requirement can be seen by considering clearcut cases of positive and negative properties, e.g., redness and nonredness. Redness satisfies both (C) and (C1), since it is incompatible with greenness, which is of the same quality, and it entails nonblueness, which is not of the same quality. Nonredness turns out to be negative since it satisfies neither of these criteria.

A philosophically illuminating criterion must not just yield results in agreement with our preanalytic intuitions; if this were all that is required, a perfectly adequate criterion would be that a property is positive if and only if it is of the same quality as redness. In addition, this criterion must indicate those logical features of positive and negative properties that explain why the former play a role in the development of systems of knowledge that the latter cannot, why negative properties are epistemically of no significance. One of the jobs we want properties to do is to enable us to construct classificatory systems of the genus-species and determinable-determinate sort. The inability of negative properties to determine such classificatory systems is explained by my criteria. The species of a given genus must be mutually incompatible, otherwise there would be cross-classifications. A negative species, according to (C1), can have as a genus only another negative property, the reason being that a species must entail its genus but negative properties entail only negative properties. But according to (C) a negative property is not incompatible with any other negative property, i.e., property of the same quality as itself. Thus, from (C1) and (C) it can be deduced that no two species of a negative genus are incompatible. And for this reason a classificatory system cannot be determined by negative properties.

To ward off counterexamples to my criteria, some restrictions must be placed on what is to count as a property. It might be contended that there are properties not of the same quality as nonred that it entails, viz., being an entity, being something, being identical with itself, etc. Thus, nonred satisfies (C1) and must be classified as positive. These "properties" will not be counted as properties, since they logically must have a universal extension. We shall also not countenance as properties any property that logically must have a null extension. Another difficulty for my criteria is that a property like being a nonred color, which intuitively we take to be negative, entails being colored, which differs in quality from it, thereby satisfying (C1). One of the peculiarities of such a property is that it is "qualitatively heterogeneous," i.e., is equivalent to a conjunction of properties that differ in quality and no conjunct of which is redundant in that it is entailed by the other conjuncts. Therefore, my criteria will be restricted to "qualitatively homogeneous" properties, i.e., properties that are either atomic, as is a determinate property, or equivalent to a conjunction of properties that are of the same quality and no conjunct of which is redundant. There still remains the question of how to determine the quality of qualitatively heterogeneous properties. According to my intuitions, a conjunctive property is negative if anyone of its nonredundant conjuncts is; thus, a qualitatively heterogenous property is negative. Concerning disjunctive properties, my intuitions are that such a property is positive if any one of its disjuncts is. One thing is for sure (and this is all that will be required for the purposes of this essay), a conjunction or disjunction every conjunct or disjunct of which is positive (negative) is positive (negative).

So far our concern has been to determine the quality of predicates in non-quantified singular statements. How should we classify quantified statements? It is reasonable to hold that a quantiified statement is positive if and only if an existential instantiation of it has a predicate that satisfied either (C) or (C1). This, I believe, would yield results in accord with our preanalystic instuitions.

My criteria can now be utilized in determining whether otherness and incompatibility statements are negative. In the first place, the fact that some of these statements are universally quantified does not thereby establish that they are negative, for there are universal statements, such as that everything is tangible, that we would want to count as positive because their existential instantiation—that this is tangible—has a predicate that satisfies either (C) or (C1). The more powerful form of the circularity charge is the claim that the predicates "is other than redness" and "is incompatible with redness" are negative. These predicates mean respectively "is not the same as redness" and "is logically not coinstantiable with redness." Their complements are "is the same as redness" and "is logically coinstantiable with redness." The former obviously satisfies both (C) and (C1), since "it is incompatible with" is a determinate of blueness, which is of the same quality, and entails "is not a determinate of blueness," which differs in quality. "Is not the same as redness" satisfies neither (C) nor (C1), and thus counts as negative. By similar considerations it can be shown that "is incompatible with redness" also is negative. It is concluded that otherness and incompatibility analyses, in all of their versions, fail to reduce negative to positive statements because they are viciously circular.

(2) THE WORLD AS FULLY DESCRIBABLE IN POSITIVE STATEMENTS

Although these analyses fail as *reductive* analyses, one or more of them might succeed in supporting one of the other theses that attempt to ontologically downgrade negative events. One of these theses holds that the world is fully describable in positive terms alone. The idea is that reality is wholly determinate and positive, whatever lacks, absences, or privations there are being a logical consequence of this positive reality. This might be termed the redundancy theory of negation. Is it true that every negative fact about the world is entailed by some positive fact about the world? Let us first deal with the more limited question of whether every singular denial that refers to a concrete individual or spatiotemporal region is entailed by some positive singular statement.

An affirmative answer is not supported by an otherness type

analysis of a singular denial, such as (S), for my pen could lack redness without this being a logical consequence of some positive property of my pen. An affirmative reply, however, does find support in the incompatibility analyses, even in the least fine-grained version, such as (S4). According to these analyses whenever an object lacks a positive property o it is due to its possession of some other positive property o' that is incompatible with o. This means that a singular statement predicating o' of this object entails that it lacks o. While it is clear that the incompatibility analyses of singular denials establish the affirmative reply, there are serious objections to the incompatibility analyses. One kind of objection is based on alleged counterexamples to these analyses. Another holds that a positive statement entails a negative one only if some additional negative premise is assumed. Still another objection holds that the incompatibility analyses lead us straight into the ontological argument.

Concerning the counterexample-type objections, a common claim is that a substance, like water, could be colorless, odorless, and tasteless without these lacks being a logical consequence of any of its positive properties. Such examples are not sufficiently clear, for in saying that an object is colorless we could mean, among other things, that it is white, drab, transparent, or lacking in a stable color. The latter is what we mean when we say that water is colorless; for while water reflects colors and thus appears colored, its color quality is ephemeral, varying with the things it reflects. The sense in which the number seven is colorless is different again; but its failure to appear colored obviously is entailed by some positive property it possesses. Since seven is a number, it follows that it is not extended, which in turn entails that it cannot appear to have a color. But might not an extended object lack any color because of the contingent negative fact that it is invisible? The Shadow and the Invisible Man are not examples, since both of them are white men. What is needed is a permanent invisible man—call him Son of Invisible Man. But even this is not a clear-cut counterexample because it is plausible to hold that it is a conceptual truth that an ordinary extended material object is visible. And until this conceptual issue is settled, Hollywood better not sink millions in making *Son of Invisible Man*.

But, it might be urged, a particular individual could lack extension without this being a logical consequence of its positive properties or nature. The following line of reasoning, based on the requirement that singular identifying expressions have definiteness of reference, could be advanced against this possibility. Such an expression can be used successfully to identify some individual only if this expression has a sense or meaning that includes a sortal type concept that makes it possible for us to pick out, individuate, and reidentify individuals of that sort. An adequate sortal concept must completely determine its referent's position in "logical space," i.e., for any property F it must either entail that the referent has F or some property incompatible with F or entail that it lacks F. Just as seven is nonextended and non-visible, etc. because of the logical requirements of the positive sortal concept under which we identify numbers, so too Lamont Cranston is extended and visible, at least some of the time, because of what is entailed by the positive sortal concept under which we identify men.

This essentialist-type defense of the incompatibility analysis of singular denials is not completely satisfying, for it relies too much on the obscure notion of a sortal or substantial concept. One might agree that there couldn't be a man who was permanently invisible but still urge that there could exist something—call it what you will—that is exactly like a man except that it is invisible; and, what is more, this lack is not entailed by its sortal nature, whatever it is. The essentialist response is that this odd individual must have a sortal nature that entails this lack; e.g., we could invent the sortal or substantial concept *Shman* for it and require that shmen are not visible. While this individual's invisibility is now entailed by its sortal nature, it could be argued that *Shman* is a conjunctive property one of whose conjuncts is negative; it is short for being exactly like a man except for not being visible. That we represent the sortal concept by a single, affirmative-looking word hides from us the fact that it is in part a negative property. I am not sure what to say in response to this.

The second objection, fortunately, is more easily met. According to it, the positive statement that my pen is blue entails that it is not now red only if we assume as an additional premise that blueness is incompatible with redness, which is a negative statement; thus, it is false that a singular denial is entailed by a positive statement alone. To me this makes as much sense as saying that the statement that Elsie is a cow entails that she is an animal only if we assume as an additional premise that every cow is an animal, or saying that a set of premises p entail a statement q only if we assume as an extra premise that p entails q. In other words, this objection is based on a completely confused notion of what an enthymemic argument is. There is nothing incomplete about any of the above arguments or entailments.

A very different sort of objection to the incompatibility analysis claims that it establishes a sound ontological argument for the necessary existence of a Greatest Conceivable Being or the universe as a whole. This objection, obviously, would not impress philosophers who accept ontological arguments, but we shall consider it anyway. How does the incompatibility analysis support such ontological arguments? According to this analysis whenever something does not exist it is because of some positive existent reality that logically excludes it. But, by definition, no existent reality could logically exclude the existence of a Greatest Conceivable Being; therefore, it is necessarily true that such a Being exists. The same argument can be given for the necessary existence of the universe. According to the incompatibility analysis if the universe were not to exist, there would have to exist something else that logically excluded it. But, by definition, whatever exists is part of the universe; therefore, it is necessarily true that the universe exists. Because the incompatibility analysis establishes such ontological arguments, it is reduced to absurdity, assuming that these arguments are absurd.

A defender of the incompatibility analysis who does not want to be committed to the above ontological arguments has a reasonable way out of this difficulty. He can argue along Kantian lines, though no doubt with a British accent, that it is meaningless to apply ordinary concepts, such as negation, to the universe as a whole or to some transcendent being. Our concepts are tethered to an intraworld use, and any application of them to the world as a whole or what transcends the world results in categorical absurdities. While it is meaningful to say that some object is nonexistent (or absent from the world) or that some existent object might not have existed, it makes no sense to say these things of the universe. The defenders of the incompatibility analysis need not go so far as to deny the meaningfulness of applying the concept to negation to the universe as whole or a transcendent being. He can simply restrict the incompatibility analysis to the intraworld uses of negation and then respectfully ask of those who apply negation to the world as a whole or something transcendent what they mean. He had better not hold his breath waiting for an answer.

So far it has been argued, although not too convincingly, that every singular denial is entailed by some positive statement, but this does not establish that every negative fact about the world is entailed by some positive one, or, in other words, that the world can be completely described in wholly positive terms. Negative existentials are tricky to handle. While a statement denying that there are o's is not entailed by any conjunction of positive singular statements, it is entailed by a positive quantified statement that refers to every existent thing and predicates of each of them some property that is incompatible with $o$ness and says that every existent individual is identical with one of these aforementioned individuals. The negative existential (E) is entailed by this statement: "a is a dog and b is a man and c is a ball and every existent individual is identical with a or b or c." To show that this conjunctive statement is positive it only need be shown that every one of its conjuncts is, since a conjunctive property or statement is positive if every one of its conjuncts is. There can be no doubt about the positiveness of its singular conjuncts, but some might be suspicious of its final conjunct. Being a universal statement its quality is determined by reference to its existential instantiation, e.g., "This is identical with a or b or c." This singular statement counts as positive, since it contains a disjunctive predicate, every disjunct of which is positive. Negative universal statements can easily be treated along similar lines.

The above way of handling negative existentials provides a way of answering a familiar objection to the possibility of giving a complete description of the world, viz., that for such a description to be complete it must not only list all the facts there are about the world about also the metafact that there are no facts about the world other than these, which, supposedly, is negative fact. We can easily comply with the demand that our complete description of the world in wholly positive terms include this meta-fact by formulating our description as follows: "It is a fact that $F1$ and $F2$ and $F3$ and every fact is identical with $F1$ or $F2$ or $F3$," in which $F1$, $F2$, and $F3$ are all the positive nonmetafacts there are.

(3) THE UNREALITY OF NEGATIVE EVENTS

There still remains the question whether there are negative events. Because negative statements are not reducible to positive ones does not establish that there are, for not every statement reports or describes an event, e.g., that $2 + 2 = 4$. In other words, the irreducibility of negative to positive statements hows that there are ineliminable negative facts, but not all facts are about an event. The problem of negative events, it will be recalled, arose from the following dialectic: supposedly we need negative events to serve as the correspondents in the world of certain true negative statements but such events are alleged to be queer because there are no criteria of identity for them in virtue of which they can be picked out, individuated, reidentified, and counted. I shall attempt to extricate us from the coils of this dialectical puzzle by establishing the following: there are familiar senses of a *negative event* as an unfulfillment, failure, omission, or privation in which there are negative events, but such events are logically unobjectionable since there are criteria of identity for them; second, the correspondence theory of truth does not require the introduction of any logically objectionable kind of negative events, such as occurrences of negative event-types or nonoccurrences of positive event-types; and, finally there *really* aren't any negative events, since the familiar, unobjectionable kind of negative events are reducible to the occurrence of a positive event-type.

First, a few words about what counts as an event and how it is determined what event a statement reports. My usage of the term *event* will be somewhat technical in that it is unusually generic, species of "events" being *changes, happenings, occurrences, processes, states,* and the like. What all of these terms have in common is that they meaningfully can replace the "it" in one or more of the following questions: "When does *it* occur (begin, end)?" and "How long does *it* take?" Any expression that meaningfully can replace the "it" in such questions will count as an event-expression. A statement reports an event if the participial nominalization of the sentence used to make this statement counts as an event-expression, the (or an) event it reports being the one referred to by this nominalized expression. The statement that S is ϕing reports an occurrence of S's if ϕing. That two and two equals four does not report any event, since it is absurd to ask "How long does two and two's equalling four take?" or "When does two and two's equalling four begin (or end)?"

There is no established usage of the term *negative event* in either ordinary or philosophical discourse, but in philosophy it sometimes is used to mean an unfulfillment or nonrealization of some possibility, an act of omission or refraining, or a privation. Idealist logicians called these kind of negative events "significant" negations. The logical features of some of these significant negations will be sketched so as to determine whether they are logically objectionable.

First we shall consider the unfulfillment or nonrealization of some possible event. What is a possible event? Does it suffer the ignominious fate of the possible fat man in the doorway? I hope to give an account of possible events that will show they have adequate criteria of identity, which, moreover, are purely extensional. Very roughly, a possible event E is a concrete object or state of affairs S that could easily develop into an E at a certain place and time if certain fairly common things were to happen. Possible events aptly could be called "conditional possibilities." Questions about the identity of possible events or conditional possibilities are purely extensional, for the concrete individuals S and R are the same possible event E if S is identical with R. S is identical with R if and only if they are coincident in space and time and have the same sortal nature. Identity questions about propositions asserting conditional possibilities also are extensional; for that it is conditionally possible that S will become an E at place P and time T is the same as that it is conditionally possible that R will become an E at place P and time T if the event of S's becoming an E at place P at time T is identical with R's becoming an E at place P at time T, which will be true if S is identical with R.

Just as there is no problem of determining the number of conditionally possible E's there are because questions about their identity are purely extensional, there is no problem in determining how many such possibilities go unfulfilled or unrealized. When a possible E in respect to a certain region of space and time is prevented or warded off by the efforts of either man or nature, there is a possible E that goes unrealized at that spatiotemporal region. Whereas more than one event of a given type cannot occur in the same spatiotemporal region, more than one possible E can go unrealized in a given spatiotemporal region. This would be the case if numerically distinct concrete objects or states of affairs S and R are each possible E's in respect to the same spatiotemporal region and both fail to become E's.

Some examples would help to clarify this brief sketch of conditional possibilities and their criteria of identity. That sinister character, Smokey the Bear, says that only you can prevent forest fires. He may not realize it, but he is immersed in an ontology of unrealized possible events right up to the peak of his hat—the one he took off the boy scout he killed. There are concrete situations, such as untended campfires and dropping of lighted matches in a forest, that in the normal course of things could easily develop into a forest fire at some place and time. Herein we have our possible events, in this case possible forest fires. When one of these possible forest fires is prevented from becoming a forest fire, be it through the efforts of man or nature, there is a possible forest fire that fails to occur at some spatiotemporal region.

Because we can in principle determine the number of possible forest fires there are in respect to a given spatiotemporal region, we can determine how many possible forest fires go unrealized at this region. More than one could go unrealized at a given region if the following were to occur. Two unattended campfires are burning at the same time in close proximity to each other. Each is a possible forest fire. Even though only one forest fire would occur were each of these campfires to develop into a forest fire, and this holds even though the event of one campfire's becoming a forest fire is numerically distinct from the other's becoming a forest fire, the campfires are numerically distinct possible forest fires. If you should stamp out one of them and I the other, we would have prevented different possible forest fires. In such a case two different possible forest fires would fail to occur in the same spatiotemporal region. By countenancing unrealized possible events we do not run the risk of making the universe into an overcrowded slum; there will not be an infinite or indefinite number of possible events that go unrealized at a given spatiotemporal region but at best only a few, if there are any at all. Furthermore, the nonrealization of a possible event does take up any room, thus the inappropriateness of talk about crowded slums.

It must be reiterated that the account of a possible event E in terms of a concrete object or situation S that could easily develop into an E at a certain place and time if certain fairly common things were to happen is very rough and sketchy. The phrases "could easily" and "fairly common" tell us nothing until we plug in for "E" a description of a specific kinds of event and for "S" a description of an object or situation. The more detailed our descriptions are, the more precise these phrases become; e.g., if the untended campfire is burning in a dry forest in a very high wind, the fairly common things that would enable it to develop into a forest fire might be merely the absence of outside intervention, such as a person stamping out the fire or a sudden downpour. But this contextual filling in does not precisely fix the meaning of these phrases. For the concept of possible event is inherently vague, as is attested to by the fact that it is meaningful to say of a possible event that it is barely or very possible. Because the concept of a possible event is vague does not show that there are no criteria of identity for possible events, only that these criteria are to some extent vague. Our concept of a bald man is also vague, but no one would want to deny that there are criteria, vague though they are, for picking out and individuating bald men.

There is a kind of possible event or conditional possibility for which we do not have criteria of identity in virtue of which it can be picked out and individuated. It is a "higher order" possible event—an event that becomes an identifiable possible event only when some other possible event(s) is realized. A higher order possible event is not possible in respect to a specific place and time; and, thus, our reference to it is ineliminably general. My favorite example of such a higher order conditional possibility is the following. The wolfman looks out of the window and sees that the moon is about to become full. Realizing that it is getting to be his time of the month, he takes precautions against his leaving the room by locking the door, knowing that when he has his claw-like hands he won't be able to work the lock. He thereby prevents one escape of the wolfman from his room, but how many maidens in the village does he prevent from getting eaten up? Knowing the wolfman as well as we do, we might hazard a rough inductive guess that there are three; but we cannot identify which three possible assaults he has prevented. While he has prevented *some* possible assault(s), there is no way in which they can be identified and counted; our reference to them is ineliminably general. Only if he were to get out of his room (he conveniently forgot to shut the window) and have an opportunity to assault someone could we make a singular identifying reference to a possible assault, for herein there will be a possible assault in respect to a specific region of space and time.

Higher order conditional possibilities sometimes are designated by phrases in which "possible" contracts a noun that refers to an object rather than an event, as in *"a* is a possible assassin." In such cases the object-noun is paralleled by a verb that indicates what an object must do or what we must do to it for it to qualify as an object of that kind—in our example "to assassinate." When a psychologist says that *a* is a possible assassin he means, very roughly, that if a number of different things were to happen, such as *a*'s being in a good position to assassinate an important person, etc., he very likely would assassinate him. If we were to reform *a* so that he no longer has the proclivities of an assassin, we would prevent a possible assassination, but our reference to this possible event (s) must remain ineliminably general. Not all uses of "*a* is a possible assassin" indicate a higher order possible event. There are at least two other uses of it, epistemic and decisional, meaning "There is some evidence that *a* assassinated someone" (said by a police officer) and "*a* is suitable to be picked to assassinate someone" (said by a mafioso), respectively. With enough imagination we could find some honest work for the possible fat man in the doorway; for there could be a decisional use of "*a* is a possible fat man in the doorway," supposing we had to select someone of bulk to stand in the doorway and prevent others from getting through.

There is another kind of unrealized possible event that rests on the passage of time. Whatever actually occurs or obtains at present has the real possibility of continuing or lasting on into the future. When this possibility of its continuance is negated by the passage of time, there is a possibility that goes unrealized. It is not the passage of time itself that destroys or negates this possibility but the events that become present, and this they do, if the incompatibility analysis be correct, by logically excluding the continuance of this past event. When S has been ϕing but has just ceased to do so, it is "significant" to say that S is not now ϕing or is no longer ϕing. These temporal possibilities differ from conditional possibilities in that whereas the latter involve a concrete situation S that could easily develop into a different event E if certain things were to happen, the former involve a concrete event E that, because actual, has the possibility of continuing as one and the same event. But in regard to both kinds of possible events we have extensional criteria of identity. We count unrealized possibilities by counting concrete situations or events. The number of temporally possible events that go unrealized now is determined by counting the past events that have just ceased to occur or obtain.

So far we have treated one kind of significant negation—the unfulfillment or nonrealization of a possible event—and have attempted to show that the sort of "negative events" they report are logically unobjectionable since we have criteria or identity for them, which, moreover, are extensional. There are other kinds of "significant" negative events consisting in acts of omission or failure to live up to one's obligations, duties, or expectations. There are constitutive rules for various practices that dictate what a person must do in certain situations, as well as rules of strategy that dictate what a person ought to do in certain situations if he is to engage in the practice skillfully. Since we have purely extensional criteria of identity for persons being in such situations, we can count the number of times they fail to follow either a constitutive rule or a rule of strategy, e.g., the number of times a person fails to signal for a turn or to keep his promise. Such acts of failure or omission, since they involve a person's not following a rule when in a relevant situation, are logically unobjectionable. Yet another kind of logically unobjectionable negative event is a state of privation, which consists in a substance of a certain kind lacking some property that is considered to be natural or proper to that kind of substance. A man can suffer a privation because he is blind, lame, or deaf, but not because he cannot fly or dematerialize. Thus, we can count the number of privations a given substance suffers.

The above sort of "significant" negative events do not disturb us, because we have adequate criteria of identity for them. Before asking whether these significant negative events are reducible to positive events, it will be asked whether such significant negative events can serve as the correspondents in the world for every true negative statement about a concrete individual or spatiotemporal region, which we shall call a negative statement about the world. Unfortunately, the answer seems to be negative, for it is true that a forest fire is not occurring now in the Sahara Desert, although no possible forest fire goes unrealized there now, and also true that Jones, who is now in bed making love to his wife, is not now signalling for a turn, although he does not fail to do so.

Idealist logicians, of course, would have heaped scorn on such negations and have called them "insignificant." Insignificant or not they still are perfectly meaningful and, moreover, true. A statement can be true even though there might be some pragmatic absurdity in asserting it, e.g., that I do not exist or that I cannot utter any English words. Since there does not appear to be a significant negative event to serve as the correspondent of every true negative statement about the world, there remains the problem of what sort of an event can serve as the correspondent in such cases. Herein there is a temptation to introduce as the correspondent a logically objectionable kind of negative event consisting in either the occurrence of a negative event-type or the nonoccurrence of a positive event-type. It will be argued that these kinds of negative events can serve as the correspondents of insignificant negations.

One way of conceiving of insignificant negative events is as the occurrence of a negative event-type. The statement that a forest fire did not occur in the Sahara Desert yesterday corresponds with the occurrence of a non-(forest fire) in the Sahara Desert yesterday. The concept of a non-(forest fire), however, is logically objectionable, since it supplies us with no criteria of identity for non-(forest fires). An adequate concept of a certain type of concrete individual must supply us with criteria for picking out and individuating such individuals. A negative event-type is not a demarcating or delineating concept in that it does not enable us to mark off what goes on or obtains in one spatiotemporal region from its spatiotemporal surroundings. The concept of a forest fire has such a demarcating function, for it makes it possible to unify the goings-on in some spatiotemporal region as a *single* event that has a beginning and end with all of the goings-on in the subregions of this spatiotemporal region being parts of this single event. That a negative event-type does not have such a demarcating and unifying function is seen by the in principle unanswerable nature of questions like, "Is the non-(forest fire) that occurred here during the last ten minutes distinct from or part of the same non- (forest fire) as occurred here during the ten-minute interval prior to this time?" and "Is the non-(forest fire) that is now occurring here distinct from or part of the one occurring in the next room now?" Furthermore, like the concept of a nonman, the concept of a non-(forest fire) does not supply us with any criteria for determining how many of them there are. There is no nonarbitrary answer to the question "How many non-(forest fires) or nonmen are there?." We might try to answer it by determining the number of positive events or objects there are, but this would require that we make use of some system of positive event or object sortals; but then it would not be the concept of a non-(forest fire) or nonman, nor the entire battery of negative event-types, that made it possible for us to answer this question.

The other kind of negative correspondent for an insignificant negation was a nonoccurrence of a positive event-type, e.g., the nonoccurrence of a forest fire. The above objections apply with equal force to this kind of negative event. While we can in principle determine the number of possible forest fires that did not occur, we cannot determine the number of forest fires simpliciter that did not occur or how many nonoccurrences of a forest fire there were. We might try to determine the number of nonoccurrences of forest fires there are by determining how many spatiotemporal regions there are that are of the proper size to accommodate a forest fire but that do not contain any forest fire. If space and time are continuous, there will be a superdenumerable number of such nonoccurrences. But again it is our battery of positive rather than negative event-types that makes it possible for us to individuate the individuals in question. Our criteria of identity for places and times is dependent upon the criteria of identity supplied by positive object- and event-types.

For the reasons just given, it is concluded that the concept of a negative event as the occurrence of a negative event-type or the nonoccurrence of a positive event-type is bogus. It might be objected that if these event concepts are bogus, then so are negative concepts for objects and properties, such a nonman and nonred; for we no more have criteria of identity for the latter than we do for insignificant negative events. But, if this is so, I am guilty of a serious inconsistency, for my criteria for distinguishing between positive and negative properties had to make use of such logically objectionable negative concepts. Restricting criteria (C) and (C1) to qualitatively homogeneous properties required us to employ purely negative concepts, such as nonred, etc. How can this seeming inconsistency be explained away?

My criteria are for negative and positive *predicates* (or properties, if we choose to speak in the material mode). A predicate expression of the form "_is o" is meaningful if and only if it satisfies the principle of significant contrast, i.e., it must be possible for the predicate to be true of some individual and possible for it to be false of some individual. Purely negative predicates or qualitatively homogeneous negative predicates, such as "_ is a nonman," satisfy the significant contrast principle and thus are meaningful. But not every meaningful predicate is convertible into a genuine referring expression by the use of this transformation: "_ is o" into "_ is identical with some o." Put roughly, only substantial predicates or those that restrict such predicates admit of such transformation, e.g., "_ is a man" into "_ is identical with some man." The predicate "_ is red," although perfectly meaningful, is not transformable into "_ is identical with some red," since "a red" is a bogus referring expression, due to its failure to supply us with any criteria of identity. This should not shock us, for when such a predicate is joined with a suitable expression to form a complete assertion, it is the subject expression that takes care of the referring by supplying criteria of identity for the kind of things it refers to. The way out of my difficulty should now be apparent. "_ is a non-(forest fire)" and "_ is identical with some nonman" because "non-(forest fire)" and "nonman" supply us with no criteria of identity for their referents.

If the above kind of insignificant negative events cannot serve as the correspondents of true but insignificant negative statements about the world, what, if anything, could perform this function? Either of two strategies might be adopted to answer this question. First, it could be argued that an insignificant negation does not report an *event*, while according to the second strategy, which is the one that will be argued for, it reports an event but it is a positive event. Let us explore the first way out.

Let us recall Jones, who is still in bed making love to his wife. It is true though insignificant to say that:

(N) Jones is not now signalling for a turn.

To show that (N) does not report an event, an (S2) type of analysis can be given of it, viz.;

(N1) Every true proposition is other than that Jones is now signalling for a turn.

A variant of (N1), which amounts to the same thing, is:

(N2) The statement that Jones is now signalling for a turn does not correspond with the facts.

Although both (N1) and (N2) are negative, due to their use respectively of "is other than" and "does not correspond with," neither reports an event; for it makes no sense to ask of either every true proposition's being other than that Jones is now signalling for a turn or the statement that Jones is now signalling for a turn not corresponding with the facts when it begins or ends or how long it takes. Such questions are senseless because a relation between propositions or between propositions and facts is not a relation between temporal entities and thus not subject to temporal distinctions. The insignificant negation (N), therefore, does not correspond with any event but with some fact about a relation of otherness between propositions or noncorrespondence between a proposition and the facts.

This way out of the problem of finding a correspondent for an insignificant negation is not completely convincing. Its plausibility depends on whether either (N1) or (N2) constitutes a proper analysis of (N). It is not enough that they be an equivalent paraphrase of (N), since for any event-reporting statement we can find some equivalent paraphrase that does not report an event: e.g., that Jones is now running finds an equivalent paraphrase in that the statement that Jones is now running is identical with some true proposition, but this hardly shows that the former statement does not report an event, for we would not consider the latter to be a proper analysis of it. Does either (N1) or (N2) constitute a proper analysis of (N)? For reasons given previously, there are grounds for doubting that any otherness analysis, of which (N1) and (N2) are variants, constitutes a proper analysis. Both (N1) and (N2) fail to bring out the way in which (N) is verified, for they turn (N) into a universal statement that must be verified or confirmed by an exhaustive enumeration of every true proposition or fact. Since it is doubtful that they constitute a proper anlaysis of (N), it is doubtful that they establish that (N) does not report an event.

The other strategy, I believe, is the more promising one. It employs some version of the incompatibility analysis to show that (N) reports a positive event and thus has a positive event as its correspondent. Obviously, this way out will be no more successful than is the incompatibility analysis. While we have seen some difficulties with the analysis, especially in its more fine-grained versions, it still must be considered a highly plausible analysis, unlike the otherness analysis. It will be assumed as an article of faith that these difficulties, especially the one concerning the nature of substantial or sortal concepts, can be met. Using the least fine-grained version of the incompatibility analysis—(S4)—we could analyze (N) into:

(N3) Jones now has some positive property that is incompatible with signalling-for-a-turn-hood.

There is no question that (N3) reports an event, for it is meaningful to ask of Jones's having some positive property that is incompatible with signalling-for-a-turn-hood when it begins or ends, or how long it lasts or obtains. The question is whether it reports a positive event. Jones's having some positive property (or instantiating some positive event-type) is a positive event without doubt. The incompatibility of this positive property or event-type with signalling-for-a-turn-hood is a negative relation, which accounts for why (N3) is a negative statement. This relation, however, is not an event, since it is absurd to ask when some positive property's being incompatible with signalling-for-a-turn-hood begins or end, or how long it goes on or takes. Such a relation of incompatibility holds between abstracta and therefore is a timeless relation not subject to temporal distinctions. Thus, it turns out that the negative element in (N3) does not have to do with the kind of event it reports but with a negative relation between the positive property instantiated in the event it reports and some other positive property. The only kind of negative facts required to account for the truth of insignificant negations like (N) are facts about negative relations between positive properties. Maybe this is why Plato was content to confine his treatment of negation in the *Sophist* to relations between the forms.

Some might question whether there are criteria of identity for the event-type or -sortal consisting in Jones's having some property that is incompatible with signalling-for-a-turn-hood. It seems that we can individuate and count instances of this event-sortal. In principle it can be determined how many positive things Jones is now doing or undergoing that are incompatible with his signalling for a turn, e.g., swimming in a pool, making love to his wife in bed (I was careful to specify that it occurs in bed for some well-coordinated persons can accomplish this feat while driving a car and signalling for a turn with their free hand), etc.

It should be pointed out for those who still adhere to the otherness analysis that there is a version of it according to which (N) reports a positive event. (N) can be analyzed in an (S1)-type manner into:

(N4) Every (positive) property of Jones is now other than signalling-for-a-turn-hood.

This statement reports an event and moreover a positive one; for the properties that Jones now has that are incompatible with signalling-for-a-turn-hood are positive ones.

So far it has been shown how we can give an incompatibility analysis of an insignificant singular negative statement, such as (N), according to which it reports a positive event. There are other kind of insignificant negations, e.g., the negative existential statement that a forest fire is not now occurring in the stratosphere. Herein there is no possible forest fire that goes unrealized now in the stratosphere. For the reasons given by Russell in his theory of descriptions, a less misleading way of formulating this statement is as "There is no forest fire that is occurring now in the stratosphere." This statement can be given an (E4)-type of analysis in that every object in the stratosphere now has some property (or collectively has such a property) that is incompatible with forest-fire-hood. If the stratosphere should now be devoid of objects, this universal statement will be true—vacuously true, to use a pun, but still true. Again, the important point is that the event it reports—every object in the stratosphere's having a positive property that is incompatible with forest—fire-hood—is a positive event.

There is only one thing more to be shown: that significant negative statements about the world also have a positive event(s) as their correspondent when true. This will be accomplished by showing that the negative component of a significant negation is identical with an insignificant negation, which we know reports a positive event, while the other components describe positive events, such as the occurrence of a possible event, etc. More precisely, a significant negative statement entails both an insignificant negative statement and a statement that reports some positive event consisting in the occurrence or existence of a possible event or a person being in a situation governed by some constitutive rule or rule of strategy, etc. From this it follows that significant negations, when true, correspond to positive events alone. Some examples will help clarify this sketch.

Jones is now making a turn at an intersection but does not signal. Herein there occurs a significant negative event consisting in his failure to signal for a turn, which is reported by:

(N') Jones is now failing to signal for a turn.

This statement entails, first:

> (N) Jones is not now signalling for a turn.

This is an insignificant negative statement and it has been shown to correspond with a positive event consisting in some positive thing that Jones is now doing or undergoing that logically excludes his signalling for a turn. (N'), in addition, entails:

> (R) Jones is now in a situation that is governed by a rule that requires him to signal.

This statement also reports a positive event, his being in a situation governed by a rule being a positive event. Therefore, (N') reports only positive events.

Another example consists in a lighted cigarette being dropped in a dry forest. This concrete occurrence or situation is a possible forest fire in respect to a certain place S and time T. For some reason this situation does not develop into a forest fire at S and T. It is true to say:

> (C) A possible forest fire is not realized at S and T.

This statement entails that

> (C1) A forest fire does not occur at S and T.

and

> (C2) There is some situation that is a possible forest fire in respect to S and T.

The insignificant negation (C1) corresponds with some positive event that logically excludes the occurrence of a forest fire at S and T, such as the trees in S growing greenly during T, while (C2) corresponds with another positive event—the dropping of a lighted cigarette in a dry forest.

The conclusion of this paper, therefore, is that what exists or occurs in the world is wholly positive, what negative facts there are being facts about relations between abstracta, such as properties and propositions.

NOTE

1. "Negative Statements", *The American Philosophical Quarterly* 7 (July 1970), reprinted in this volume.

15

NONBEING AND THE RECEPTACLE

Chapter 1* was in effect a long footnote to Plato's theory of nonbeing in the *Sophist*. This chapter will be a long footnote to his account in the *Timaeus* of another kind of nonbeing—the Receptacle or empty space. Nonbeing in the form of a void or Receptacle played a crucial role in Greek philosophy. It was the major point at issue between the Eleatics and Atomists, if we are to trust Aristotle's account of the history of philosophy:

> For some of the ancients had thought that what *is* must necessarily be one and motionless, since what is void is nonexistent, and there could be no motion without a separately existing void, and again there could be no plurality of existents without something to sepa-

---

*"Chapter 1," "this chapter," etc. refer to this as published in Richard Gale, "Negation and Nonbeing," *American Philosophical Quarterly* Monograph Series 10 (1976).

rate them.... But Leucippus thought he had arguments which would assert what is consistent with sense perception and not do away with coming-into-being and perishing and motion and the plurality of existents. He agrees with sensible appearances to this extent, but he concedes to those who maintain the One that there would be no motion without void, and says that what is void is not-being, and that no part of what *is* is not-being—for what *is* in the strict sense is wholly and fully being. But such being, he says, is not one; there is an infinite number of them, and they are invisible because of the smallness of their mass. They move in the void (for there *is* void), and when they come together they cause coming-to-be, and when they separate they cause perishing.[1]

Plato's reason for postulating a Receptacle was different from that which prompted the Atomists to accept a void, this being the need for a formless realm in which the Forms could be instantiated. I believe that Plato was right in his Receptacle Theory and shall advance further considerations for its acceptance. The first concerns the need to postulate a Receptacle if we are to offer an adequate explanation of the ultimate grounds of individuation of spatiotemporal (concrete) individuals. The second argues that a Receptacle is needed if an adequate account is to be given of the objectivity of concrete individuals. Yet another useful function can be found for the Receptacle, this being to serve as the ground of the genuine possibility that there be Nothing rather than something. The Receptacle, like all metaphysical constructs, is mysterious and elusive; our only access to it is by reference to those metaphysical problems to which it gives an intellectually satisfying resolution. The more such problems we can find for it to solve, the more determinate its nature becomes for us.

I. THE RECEPTACLE AND THE GROUNDS OF INDIVIDUATION

Our concern in this section is with the problem of the ultimate grounds of individuation of concrete individuals. This is a paradigm problem of "hard-core" metaphysics, not just in the obvious sense that it is totally lacking in any redeeming social value (bless its heart) but also in that it may prove to be as intractable as are the problems of the hard-core unemployed and hard-core criminals. But before we despair of there being any answer to our problem and thus its being a genuine problem, we should make a valiant effort to find an answer. If every answer we can think of is either false or unintelligible, this will constitute good inductive grounds for doubting that there is any explanation to be given of what grounds the identity and individuation of concrete things.

There are some preliminary problems concerning the formulation of the question of individuation. Often it is posed in a self-defeating manner; e.g., "When are *two* individuals identical?" to which the correct reply is "Never!" This should not make us despair and seek refuge in a metalinguistic reformulation of our question, for there are perfectly good object-language formulations. E.g., "Under what conditions are there two objects rather than one?" or "What are the necessary and sufficient conditions for a and b to be identical (diverse)?" In the latter formulation the use of the proper names "a" and "b" leaves it undetermined whether these names are coreferential.

In a small college town in Ohio, just off Interstate 80 behind Kinky's Hamburger House, is the Philosophical Hall of Fame. In its basement is the wax museum Hall of Philosophical Horrors that houses specimens of the "queer" entities by which past philosophers attempted to explain the grounds of individuation. In the first glass case there is a part of the Receptacle, in the next case some prime matter, next a case with a substratum in it, then one containing a thing-in-itself, and last a case that has just been flown in from Iowa City in which there is a bare particular. The funny thing about these glass cases is that you see the same thing in each one of them—nothing. That is why it is called the *Hall of Philosophical Horrors* and the specimens it houses *queer,* for they are inaccessible entities of the I-do-not-know-what type. Leibniz's principle of the Identity of Indiscernibles, less misleadingly called the principle of Dissimilarity of the Diverse by McTaggart, has been the only attempt to give a "nonqueer" solution to the problem of individuation, for what explains the diversity between concrete individuals is some difference in the properties they instantiate. Since this principle promises to free us of these philosophical horrors, it deserves to be considered first. Unfortunately, it will turn out that this principle works only if it is willing to countenance "properties" that introduce one of the above "queer" entities. Once it is established that this philosophical vice squad is not without vice, it will be argued that the Receptacle is indeed needed and although it is somewhat queer it is not *that* queer.

The usual formulation of the Identity of Indiscernibles is:

(L) For every x and y, if x and y have all their properties in common, then $x = y$.

in which x and y range over concrete individuals and no restrictions are placed on what is to count as a property. (L) is supposed to serve as an explanation of the ultimate grounds of individuation and thus hold for every *conceivable* concrete individual. It can do this only if it is a necessary truth.

It is well known that, depending upon what restriction is placed upon a property, (L) can be true but trivial or exciting and false. If we permit the relations of identity and diversity to count as properties, (L) is necessarily true since, given any two diverse individuals a and b, a alone will have the "property" of being identical with a (diverse from b). Should (L) be allowed to employ such "properties"? The only way of answering this question is to see what (L) is advertised as doing. Herein (L) is advertised as providing an analysis or account of the ultimate grounds of the identity and individuation of concrete individuals. Unless it is restricted to properties that do not involve identity and diversity, it will make use of the very concept it is advertised as analyzing and thereby will suffer from vicious circularity.[2]

It may be necessary to place even further restrictions on properties in (L). Given any two sortally similar concrete individuals a and b, a alone will be spatiotemporally coincident with a. (The reason for the proviso that a and b be sortally similar is that I think it possible for diverse objects that are sortally dissimilar to be spatiotemporally coincident, e.g., a statue and the lump of stuff it is made of.) As a consequence, necessarily, given any two concrete individuals, they will differ either in their sortal properties or in their spatiotemporal coincidence properties. Two questions arise at this point. Should (L) be permitted to count being spatiotemporally coincident with *a*, as a property? And, even if it should, does the use of such a property introduce some "queer" entity from the Hall of Philosophical Horrors?

It would seem that (L) is no more justified in using the "property" of being spatiotemporally coincident with *a* than it was in using that of being identical with *a*, and for the same reason. (L) is advertised as providing an explanation of *a*'s identity and individuation, but it does so by using a proper name for *a*. This looks like a vicious circularity in the order of *explanation*, because we explain *a*'s individuation in terms of *a* itself. What is more, since (L) is supposed to explain the grounds of individuation of concrete individuals *in general*, it should not be permitted to use any property that is expressed by the use of a proper name for a concrete individual.

Another problem with (L)'s use of being spatiotemporally coincident with *a* is that it is very difficult to analyze this without quantifying over space and/or time or parts of this Receptacle, thereby invoking some "queer" entity from the Hall of Philosophical Horrors. E.g. "*a* is spatiotemporally coincident with *b*" means "*a* and *b* exist at the same times and at every time in their history *a*'s boundaries coincide with *b*'s." Also, the concept of being spatiotemporally coincident with *a* involves criteria of genidentity for *a*, but again it is doubtful that they can be formulated without quantifying over places and times. In order to determine *a*'s path in space-time—the spatiotemporal region it occupies—criteria of identity over time or persistence for *a* are needed. This in turn requires criteria for the spatiotemporal continuity of an object. It is doubtful that such criteria can be specified without quantification over places and/or times.[3]

For the above reasons let us accept the restriction of (L) to properties that can be expressed without the use of a proper name for a concrete individual.[4] Because it is impossible for sortally similar concrete individuals to be spatiotemporally coincident, it seems to follow that necessarily, for any two sortally similar concrete individuals *a* and *b*, there will be some ordered quadruple composed of one temporal and three spatial coordinates that is true of *a* alone, e.g., being, at x_1, y_2, z_3, at t_4. This sort of "property," to be sure, is expressed through the use of proper names, but they are not names of *concrete* individuals. One might quibble that since their denotata are in space and time they qualify as concrete individuals. There are far more questionable aspects of this way of establishing the necessity of (L).

The first problem concerns how we manage to name places and times in the spatiotemporal coordinate system that is appealed to. It might be said that such a name is equivalent to some definite description that contains no proper name, e.g., "the individual that has ϕ_1 ... ϕ_n." But then we would beg the question in favor of (L) if we were to say that no more than one individual could have ϕ_1 ... ϕ_n. Another problem concerns the denotata of these names, assuming that they cannot be replaced by definite descriptions of empirical individuals for the reason just given. Their denotata are places and times, which seem to be "queer" entities for which we lack criteria of identity.[5]

Let us make another attempt to discern between a and b, which we can assume to be coexistent discs of the same color, shape, size, etc. Ultimately, we are prepared to distinguish between them by the use of spatial indexical signs—spatial demonstratives. E.g., it is true of a alone that it is here (or bears some determinate spatial relation to here).[6] If it be objected that there is a possible world W_1 consisting of a and b alone and thus no language-users, the reply is that there is another possible world W_2 in which there is a language-user who indexically discerns between them and we can keep the referent of his use of "here" constant in all possible worlds, even W_1. This might be more perspicuously expressed by the following counterfactual truth: "a is here and would be here even if it were not so designated," as tokened in W_2.

Although indexical signs are not proper names in the ordinary sense, and thus escape the restriction placed upon (L) above, the need to employ them should give us pause.[7] (L) is supposed to provide a "nonqueer" explanation of the grounds of individuation by showing that diverse individuals can always be distinguished between by purely *descriptive* means. Indexical signs, since they can be used and understood only by beings in space and time, do not seem to be purely descriptive devices. Even if such signs are always used in conjunction with some description, they still seem to be singular designators that cannot be replaced by descriptions alone, at least descriptions that could be understood by God. And, since indexical signs seem to have some irreducible designatory function, there is the fear that their denotata might be "queer" entities.

We have found that ultimately we are prepared to distinguish between concrete individuals by the use of spatial and temporal demonstratives, and the question now arises as to what we are ontologically committed to by our use of "*a* is at this place (time)." At a first glance we seem to be committed to the existence of places (times) in a Receptacle,[8] but many philosophers would argue that appearances deceive in this case. Among such philosophers are the defenders of the relational theory of space and time who hold that:

(*a*) the ultimate bearers of spatial and temporal characteristics are empirical objects and events; and,
(*b*) all spatial and temporal designations are analyzable into spatial and temporal relations.

It will be argued that spatial and temporal indexical signs constitute a counterexample to both these tenets.

According to (*b*), the indexical proposition that *a* is at this place (time) is to be analyzed into a nonindexical proposition that describes a spatial (temporal) relation between *a* and some other individual, e.g., the proposition that *a* has spatial (temporal) relation R to b (or the ϕ). Such analyses must fail because their *analysans* is not logically equivalent to their *analysandum*.[9]

In defense of tenet (*a*) one of two things might be said. First, it might be denied that indexical signs are referring expressions. It could be claimed that "here" and "now" are adverbs of manner that can be perspicuously paraphrased as "herely" and "nowly" (or "presently"). This is implausible. While it is true that "here" and "now" are adverbs—indicating where and when some event occurs—it is dubious that they are adverbs of manner. It is not just that "herely" and "nowly" look contrived but that they do not indicate the manner in which an action is done; to waltz here is not a manner of waltzing as is to waltz gracefully. Moreover, "here" and "now" can be used to answer the question as to where and when—at what place and time—a certain event occurs.

A more plausible way of defending (*a*) is to accept indexical signs as referring expressions but claim that they are always used to designate some empirical object or a part of such an object. The use of a spatial demonstrative, e.g., is accompanied by an act of pointing or staring and at the end of the index finger or in its line of sight is some empirical object that serves as its denotatum. Thus, when we say that *a* is here we might mean that *a* occupies this part of the floor or some piece of cloth, etc.

This way of defending (*b*) fails for two reasons. First, it accounts for our ability to distinguish indexically between discs *a* and *b* by bringing in other empirical objects or parts thereof—parts of the floor or cloth—but this just pushes our problem of the ultimate grounds of individuation one stage further back, for we still owe an explanation of the grounds of the diversity between the different parts of the floor or cloth. Were we to say that they in turn occupy different empirical parts of some further object, e.g., another floor or cloth, we would be launched on an infinite regress that is vicious not because we might run out of plywood or gabardine but because it makes it impossible for us to answer our initial question concerning the grounds of the diversity between *a* and *b*. This is analogous to trying to account for their diversity in terms of a diversity between the atoms that compose them, for we still owe an explanation of the grounds of the diversity between these atoms. It was to check this vicious regress that Aristotle introduced his prime matter as constituting the *ultimate* grounds of individuation.

In the second place, not every conceivable use of an indexical sign has an empirical referent. When the speaker in possible world W_1 says "*a* is in this place," he cannot be referring to an empirical place, i.e., part of an empirical object, since *ex hypothesi* the only empirical objects in W_2 are *a*, *b*, and the speaker.

A summary is now in order. Our discussion began by considering principle (*L*), since it is the only traditional account of individuation that promises to give a "nonqueer" solution. But it was found that the only way to protect (*L*) from counterexamples, e.g., discs *a* and *b* in W_1, was to allow being here (now) to count as a "property." It turned out that such indexical properties seemed to involve a reference to places (times) in a Receptacle, and thus (*L*) seems to be on all fours with other "queer" accounts of individuation. It is true that we ultimately are prepared to discern between concrete individuals by "this"-ing and "that"-ing or "now"-ing and "then"-ing them, and it is now time that we face up to the problems raised by the ontological commitment of these indexical terms to "queer" entities—the Receptacle and the individual places and times in it.[10] We shall do this by giving a sketch of the Receptacle Theory of individuation and considering various objections to it. By responding to these objections, hopefully in a successful manner, this theory will get filled out and distinguished from objectionable kinds of "queer" accounts of individuation.

It is necessary to account for the grounds of the possibility of there being a counterexample to (L), when it is restricted to *purely descriptive* properties, i.e., those that are expressible without the use of any singular designator (e.g., proper noun, indexical sign, definite description). A basic principle of Aristotelian philosophy is that every possibility must be grounded in some actuality. It is hard to know what to make of this principle. Is it a necessary truth or only a regulative idea of reason? One thing seems certain. We are unhappy when we must countenance some ungrounded possibility, and one ought to accept the Aristotelian principle to the extent that he always does his best to find a ground in actuality for a possibility.

The possibility of there being more than one instantiation of any purely descriptive property, e.g., discs a and b in W_1, is grounded in an actual being—the spatiotemporal Receptacle—which is ontologically prior to whatever exists or occurs in it. This Receptacle is a realm of formless, unstructured extension and duration in which we can house duplicate objects and events. The ultimate grounds of diversity between sortally similar objects and events is that they occupy different spatiotemporal regions in this Receptacle. This is the ontological explanation for the epistemic possibility of our distinguishing between duplicate individuals by the use of indexical signs. It is in virtue of its occupying a region in the Receptacle that an object is "this"-able. The Receptacle is the ground of an object's being a *Dasein*—a being *there*.

That the Receptacle is a spatiotemporal one represents a significant departure from Plato's conception of the Receptacle as being only spatial. While he attributed to the space of his Receptacle a reality that is independent of concrete individuals, time is accorded a second-class status, being said to be dependent upon empirical events in the manner described by tenet (*a*) above of the relational theory of time. This disparity in his treatment of time indicates that he did not introduce his Receptacle to explain the ontological grounds of the possibility of duplication, since he was well aware of the possibility of duplication in time as well as in space. He even held to a cyclical theory of history that involved the large-scale duplication of sequences of events. He introduced his merely spatial Receptacle in order to explain how concrete objects are "images" or "reflections" of the forms, since there must be some medium in which the imaging or reflecting takes place. Even so, he should have realized that there is a parallel problem of explaining how forms of events get "imaged" or "reflected" in a temporal medium.

The metaphors of the Receptacle "imaging" and "reflecting" forms is a troublesome one that should be clarified. A sortal form is instantiated or exemplified by a concrete individual. To use a Brecht title: A MAN'S A MAN. Let us say that a man instantiates$_1$ the form of manness. A man cannot exist without occupying a region of the Receptacle. This region, however, is not a man in the sense of being identical with some man but rather that in which a man exists. Let us say that this region of the Receptacle instantiates$_2$ the form of manness. In Whitehead's terminology, there is an "ingression" of this form at that Receptacle region.

This Receptacle Theory account of instantiation and individuation contrasts favorably with the rival "bare particular" account.[11] According to the latter a concrete individual contains a bare particular, i.e., an individual that is natureless in the sense of having no essential properties, which is the ultimate bearer of all its properties, including its sortal form. The diversity between two concrete individuals is grounded in a diversity between the bare particulars contained in them. Although Receptacle places and times play the same role as do bare particulars in grounding the diversity between concrete individuals, there are radical differences between them. Whereas bare particulars are said to be *in* concrete individuals, according to the Receptacle Theory it is the latter that are *in* regions of the Receptacle. Furthermore, for the Receptacle Theory it is concrete objects that instantiate$_1$ sortal forms, whereas for the Bare Particular Theory it is bare particulars that do. The latter theory, taking the referent of "this" to be a bare particular, analyzes "This is a man" into "This bare particular instantiates$_1$ the form of manness," whereas the Receptacle Theory, taking the referent of "this" to be a region of the Receptacle, analyzes it as "A man is in this region of the Receptacle" or "This region of the Receptacle instantiates$_2$ the form of manness." These differences are all in favor of the Receptacle Theory.

Certain versions of the Receptacle Theory impute a determinate metric and topology to the Receptacle, thereby limiting to only one the number of systems of spatiotemporal geometry that could correctly characterize physical space-time. E.g., according to the Newtonian theory of absolute space and time, the geometry of spacetime must be flat. The objection to this version of the Receptacle Theory is that there is more than one spatiotemporal geometry that could correctly characterize physical space-time, and it is up to science to determine which in fact does give the best description of physical space-time. The system of spatiotemporal geometry that best describes the physical world is neither necessary nor determinable a priori.

However powerful this objection may be against certain versions of the Receptacle Theory, it leaves my version untouched; for my Receptacle has as its essential properties only those that are common to every possible empirical space-time system. The Receptacle is the minimum space-time system, every possible empirical space-time being embeddable in it. Its only essential features, therefore, are extension and duration. These features determine no determinate metric and topology of space-time nor any way of partitioning it into space- and time-like intervals. Since every possible space-time system must be embeddable in the Receptacle, the Receptacle must have infinitely many dimensions, assuming that it is possible for empirical space to have any number of dimensions. Another essential property of the Receptacle is that it has the potentiality of becoming any one of numerous determinate space-time systems. With the instantiation$_2$ of forms of the Receptacle, it acquires some determinate metric and topology, which could vary from one region of the Receptacle to another. Although the Receptacle can acquire a determinate metric and topology, its possession of this spatiotemporal structure is an accidental property, for it can change over both space and time in respect to its determinate structure.

According to the Receptacle Theory of individuation, there is only *one* Receptacle, the grounds of diversity between any two sortally similar concrete individuals is their occupying different regions in *the* Receptacle. In recent years many attempts have been made to produce counterexamples to the Kantian thesis that necessarily all places (times) are parts of a single spatial (temporal) system.[12] One such attempt holds that it is possible for there to exist two or more coterminous spatial realms or worlds that are not spatially related, neither being any distance or direction from the other, and, as a consequence, it is possible that there exist an object in one realm that is sortally similar to an object in the other realm even though they do not occupy different places in a single Receptacle. The story by which the possibility of there being two spatially unrelated realms is made intelligible is that of the consistent "dream."

A person—or better, persons—in order to give the required agreement in judgment for supporting an objectivity claim, find that when they go to sleep or lose consciousness in the spatial realm they are in, they immediately begin to "dream" that they wake up in another spatial realm, and when they go to sleep in this realm they immediately begin to "dream" that they wake up in the former realm, and so on. Each of these realms qualifies as being an objective or real world since each is internally consistent and persons can deliberate in advance about how to act in it. That they are spatially unrelated is supported by the inability of persons to come upon any object in one of these realms when they occupy the other realm. This requires that no physical object or process carries over from one realm to the other; only the memories of persons do. To produce a counterexample to the Receptacle Theory of individuation, we merely need to add to the story of the consistent "dream" that in each of the spatial realms there exists a penny, being sure to add that these pennies differ in some of their properties so that there can be no doubt that they are diverse from each other.

One reason that this story does not constitute a decisive counterexample to the Receptacle Theory is that it requires us to accept a highly debatable Cartesian view of persons. Since no physical object can carry over from one realm to the other, a person who successively occupies these realms must have or, better, be a mind that is successively related in a Cartesian manner to different bodies. Even if we are willing to grant the Cartesian assumptions of the story, there is a good rebuttal open to the Receptacle Theory. The Receptacle, it will be recalled, has infinitely many dimensions, every possible empirical space-time system being embeddable in it. What happens when a person passes from one spatial realm to the other is that he passes into higher-order dimensions of space than the three dimensions of his initial spatial realm. This allows these spatial realms to be parts of a single spatial system, and thereby the pennies in question do occupy different places in a single Receptacle. The recipe for escaping from the three-dimensional space of our everyday world is: Go to sleep, perchance to "dream."

There is a far more powerful objection to the Receptacle Theory of individuation that applies to any theory of individuation that introduces "queer" entities. Such theories account for the ground of individuation of ordinary concrete individuals by reference to some ultimate kind of individuals—places and times in the Receptacle, bare particulars, substrata, etc. But what are the grounds of individuation of these ultimate individuals?

There are three equally disastrous responses to this question. The first response is to say "Don't ask," to which the appropriate response is "Why didn't you say that in the first place when you were asked about the grounds of individuation of ordinary concrete individuals?" Entities should not be multiplied beyond necessity, especially when they turn out to be mysterious I-do-not-know-what type of entities. A second response attempts to give the same account of their grounds of individuation as was given for ordinary concrete individuals; e.g., the diversity between two bare particulars is grounded in a diversity between the bare particulars contained in them, or the diversity between two regions of the Receptacle is due to their occupying different regions in some second-order Receptacle. This response obviously generates a vicious infinite regress. The third response attempts to give an account of the identity and individuation of the "queer" individuals in terms of ordinary concrete individuals, which seems to result in a vicious circle. The Bare Particular Theory seems to fall prey to this, for the rule it apparently follows in counting and distinguishing between bare particulars is "One bare particular per ordinary concrete object."

First it will be shown that this objection is telling against the version of the Receptacle Theory that takes *both* the Receptacle and its individual places and times to be ontologically prior to concrete individuals. Then it will be argued that there is a viable version of the Receptacle Theory that escapes this objection, viz., the one according to which *only* the Receptacle as a whole has ontological priority, there being a mutual dependency on the ontological although not epistemological order between Receptacle places and times and concrete or empirical individuals.

Against the first version it often is objected that we do not perceive Receptacle places and times as such but only regions or stretches of space and time that either separate empirical individuals or constitute their boundaries and locations. As a result we cannot make identifying references to Receptacle places and times without making identifying references to empirical individuals. But this only shows that in the epistemic order—the order of experience—receptacle places and times are not prior, not that they are not prior in the order of nature or being. It is possible for a certain kind of entity, e.g., a theoretical entity in a physical theory, to be prior in the latter but not the former sense. Even if this Aristotelian distinction be granted, the first version still is in trouble. If Receptacle places and times are prior in the ontological order, there should be criteria of *identity* for them, although not necessarily criteria for making *identifying* references to them, which are completely independent of those for empirical individuals. This patently is not the case, as attested to by the unanswerable nature of the following identity-questions: "How many Receptacle places or times are there?"; "Are these places and times punctual?"; "What are the criteria of identity over time for a Receptacle place?"; "What are the criteria for its being the same time at spatially separated places in the Receptacle?" The latter question is especially troublesome because the Receptacle is supposed to have as its essential properties only those that are common to every possible space-time system and thus cannot determine a specific way of dividing space-time into space- and time-like intervals. That we might be able to pick out indexically a spatial region of the Receptacle as such, by cupping our hands, does nothing toward supplying answers to identity-questions about such a region.

It will now be argued that a viable version of the Receptacle Theory of individuation need take only the Receptacle as a whole as having ontological priority, it having the potentiality of becoming subdivided into actual places and times with its instantiation$_2$ of sortal forms of objects and events. This version is in accord with Plato's own account:

> Only in speaking of that *in* which all of them (earth, air, fire, and water) are always coming to be, making their appearance and again vanishing out of it, may we use the words "this" or "that"....[13]

I take it that Plato's point is that only the Receptacle as a whole is an actual individual, "that in which" referring to this individual. It is because the Receptacle is an actual individual that it is "this"-able.

While the imputation of ontological priority to Receptacle places and times was dubious because they lacked independent criteria of identity, there is no problem in assigning such an exalted status to the Receptacle as a whole. We have criteria of identity for it with a vengeance. It is a conceptual truth that there can be only one Receptacle, since there can be only one system of spatiotemporal relations, our nocturnal "travelers" notwithstanding. We even can indexically pick out this unique Receptacle by delimiting some region with an ostensive gesture as we say "the spatiotemporal system of which this region is a part." It would be wrong to object that this ostensive gesture, e.g., cupping of the hands or circling with the index finger, does not point to a region of the Receptacle but rather the hands or index finger of the speaker. This would be to confound *what* is picked out with the *way* in which it is picked out. An index finger used in an act of ostension no more points to itself than a hammer hammers itself.

This logically preexistent Receptacle, in virtue of its having extension and duration, has the potentiality of becoming subdivided into actual places and times with its instantiation$_2$ of sortal forms of objects and events. In a like manner it has the potentiality of acquiring a determinate metric and topology. An analogy with the way in which a mass object can get subdivided into distinct parts might be helpful. Imagine an unlimited expanse of snow. It does not yet contain any parts that have a distinct identity of their own. But in virtue of its being an expanse of snow, it has the possibility of becoming subdivided into distinct parts, as it would if a cup were impressed upon it. The cup-shaped regions of the expanse of snow are actual regions in this expanse. Similarly, the regions of the Receptacle that are formed from its instantiation$_2$ of forms are actual regions, though they were not that before.

Against our claims that the Receptacle becomes divided up into actual regions with the existence of empirical individuals, it might be objected that since such regions are nothing apart from such individuals, they are nothing. This is no more cogent than saying that because a substance is nothing apart from its qualities, it is not anything in conjunction with its qualities.[14] Similarly, because places and times are nothing apart from empirical individuals, it does not follow that they are nothing in conjunction with them.

Nevertheless, it might be objected against the reality of such regions that their criteria of identity are in terms of those for empirical individuals. Unfortunately, as we have seen, the criteria of identity for the latter seem to make reference to Receptacle places and times, since there seems to be no way to analyze the concept of spatiotemporal continuity without quantifying over places and times. There seems to be a vicious circularity afoot here, for the criteria of identity over time for a place depend upon some selected empirical individual(s) remaining numerically one and the same over this interval, but equally the criteria of identity over time for an empirical object make reference to places being numerically one and the same at different times. Some have tried to escape this vicious circularity by arguing that the case of a continuously observed empirical individual is epistemically privileged, and all other reidentifications, whether of other empirical individuals or of places, can be based upon these privileged reidentifications.[15] This way out confounds the epistemological order with the ontological order. Very likely, in the order of *identifying* references, empirical individuals are prior to places and times, but this does nothing to show that the criteria of *identity* for the former are independent of the latter. Criteria of identity for a certain type of individual involve the conditions for *being* an individual of that type, and not the conditions under which an individual of that type can be *known* or identifyingly referred to.

The most promising way out of the seeming vicious circularity is to deny that there is anything vicious about it. What's wrong with a teepee? Why must everything be a layer cake? While a circularity in the epistemological order is indeed vicious (for how can we ever get to know anything or succeed in making an identifying reference or reidentification?), there is nothing vicious about a mutual dependency in the ontological order. Many of the most satisfying ontological explanations make use of principles or entities that mutually involve and support each other like the legs of a teepee. Even the Receptacle does not occupy its Olympian heights in isolation from other individuals with which it is interdependent.

The role of the Receptacle, its raison d'être, is to be that in which forms can be instantiated$_2$, even in ways which counterexample a suitably restricted principle (L). The nature of the Receptacle, therefore, is dependent upon the forms, which, in turn, are dependent upon the Receptacle, since they are what can be instantiated$_2$, thus bringing in the Receptacle. While an ontological theory can have a hierarchical structure, as does mine, which gives ontological priority to the Receptacle and the forms over both empirical individuals and places and times, it still can have horizontal levels comprised of entities that are mutually dependent upon each other.[16]

II. THE RECEPTACLE AND THE OBJECTIVITY OF EXPERIENCE

It now will be argued that the same Receptacle that was seen to serve as the grounds of individuation also serves as the grounds of objectivity of experience. What this amounts to is the claim that it is necessary that *objective particulars*, i.e., perceptible objects that exist independently of experience, be located in the spatiotemporal Receptacle. While no one would question the need for a temporal dimension, some would deny that objective particulars *must* be located in space as well. A persuasive case for this not being necessary has been made out by P. F. Strawson in his highly original and imaginative chapter on "Sounds" in *Individuals*. Through a detailed criticism of his effort, we hope to show that the concept of an objective particular requires that objective particulars be located in space as well as in time.

The question whether objective particulars must be in space is given an epistemic twist by Strawson in terms of his general principle that we cannot have a concept of a certain type of individual unless we have experientially grounded criteria of identity for individuals of that type. Accordingly, it turns into the question of whether criteria of identity for objective particulars could be formulated in terms of sense experiences that are not representative of things as being in space.[17] He puts aside visual experiences, since they seem to be representative of space, at least a two-dimensional space. Kinaesthetic and tactual experiences also seem to be representative of space, and there can be no doubt that in combination they are. Olfactory and gustatory experiences, neither alone nor in conjunction, are representative of space, but Strawson chooses not to work with them since he thinks there is little hope of establishing the possibility of a world of objective smells or tastes.

It is auditory experience that he thinks holds out the best chance for success. He argues, convincingly in my opinion, that auditory experiences *alone* are not representative of space. Our ability to locate a sound in space on the basis of an auditory experience is dependent (in some way that is left unspecified) upon correlations between auditory experiences and other kinds of experiences of a visual, kinaesthetic, or tactual sort. This ability often depends upon having knowledge of a sound's cause, but such knowledge is not based upon auditory experiences alone.

It is Strawson's aim to show that criteria of identity for objective sound particulars can be formulated exclusively in terms of auditory experiences, thus establishing the logical possibility of there being a no-space world composed of objective sounds. These sounds would resemble commonsensical sounds in that both can occur when not actually heard. (A tree that falls in a forest devoid of sentient beings does make a loud noise, unless it falls into a snow bank or pile of leaves.) They differ from commonsensical sounds only in not being in space.

According to Strawson our purely auditory criteria of identity for objective sound particulars must enable us, first, to distinguish numerically between sounds, even in cases in which sounds are qualitatively the same, and, second, to reidentify sounds, even in cases in which there has been a lapse in our perception of them. The latter is crucial to our ascription of a mind-independent status to the sounds of the no-space world. No mere regularity in uninterrupted auditory experiences would suffice.

If we were continually to hear a repetition of an *A-B-C-D* sequence of sounds, we would be able to distinguish numerically between an occurrence of one *A*-type sound and earlier or later occurrences of this same type of sound, but we would have no grounds for holding that these sequences of sounds could occur even when not actually heard.

To make sense of a sound occurring when unperceived, the no-space world of sounds must be given some dimension analogous to space so that we can say where a sound is when it fails to be heard:

> We must have a dimension other than the temporal in which to house the at present unheard sensory particulars, if we are to give a satisfactory sense to the idea of their existing now unperceived, and hence to the idea of reidentification of particulars in a purely auditory world.[18]

This would make the no-space world of sounds analogous to our ordinary spatial world, for which

> the crucial idea is that of a spatial system of objects, through which oneself, another object, moves, but which extends beyond the limits of one's observation at any moment.... This idea obviously supplies the necessary non-temporal dimension for, so to speak, the housing of the objects which are held to exist continuously, though unobserved.[19]

The necessity for a nontemporal dimension in which unperceived sounds are housed can be established in a way that Strawson does not explicitly consider, although he says things that suggest it. This consists in showing a fatal flaw in the most likely way of making out a case for the logical possibility of there being objective sound particulars that occur only in the dimension of time, this consisting in the application of a well-founded inductive generalization to a case in which there is a gap in perception. It works in the following way.

Let us suppose that on n number of occasions an A-B-C-D sequence of sounds is heard and no sound of any one of these types is ever heard except in such a sequence. This observed regularity justifies the inductive generalization that every A-B sequence of sounds is followed by a C-D sequence.[20] On occasion $n + 1$ an A-B-E-D sequence is heard rather than an A-B-C-D sequence. The question is whether C occurred on this occasion even though not actually heard. It is claimed that our above inductive generalization justifies an affirmative answer, and thereby a case has been made out for the possibility of sounds existing unperceived even though not housed in any nontemporal dimension analogous to space.

The obvious rebuttal to this argument is that the $n + 1$ occasion, the one on which sequence A-B-E-D was heard, constitutes a counterinstance to the inductive generalization that every A-B sequence is followed by a C-D sequence. How might this seeming counterinstance be neutralized? There are two ways in which seeming counterinstances to empirical generalizations are met. It will be seen that neither is of any avail in the above case.

The first way is to show that a perceptual error occurred: on occasion $n + 1$, C was misheard as E, or the observer only thought he heard E, while it was C that he really heard. We can determine that a perceptual error occurred only if we have criteria for determining what objectively is the case. But it is just such criteria that are lacking in the above case: we cannot appeal to the empirical generalization that every occurrence of A-B is followed by C-D to establish that a perceptual error occurred on occasion $n + 1$, since this would render the "empirical" generalization unfalsifiable by experience. It is this generalization that is supposed to give us a criterion for determining what objectively is the case, but it seems to face a counterinstance.

The second way of meeting a seeming counterexample is to show that the observer was not in a *position* to observe what was there to be perceived; e.g., he or the object had moved away, he was looking in the wrong direction, his view was blocked, etc. The fact that on some occasion I saw a burning log and later saw ashes in place of this log does not refute the generalization that a log burns down continuously into ashes, provided that I had moved away in the interim or had my view of the log blocked, etc. It is apparent that all of these explanations invoke a spatial dimension in which are housed coexistent objects, one of which is an observer capable of moving in relation to these other objects. Since the above no-space world contains no nontemporal dimension that houses coexistent sounds, this sort of explanation cannot be offered. Without such a dimension, there is no way our inductive generalization can be saved from the seeming counterinstance.

If the above line of reasoning is correct, it bears out Strawson's claim that a no-space world of objective sounds must contain some nontemporal dimension in which coexistent sounds are housed. But for exactly what features of space must analogues be found in this nontemporal dimension? According to Strawson it is not simply that of distance, so that one sound can be said to move nearer to another or be further away from one sound than it is from another, but that of an observer, who is one sound among others, and can move in relation to these other sounds. This would make the analogy with the way in which material objects fill space rather precise in that the observer is a material object or at least has a body that is one object among others and that can move in relation to these objects. This would enable us to dispose of the seeming counterinstance on occasion $n + 1$ by saying that the observer—the hearer—had moved away from the place in the nontemporal dimension at which sound C occurred and therefore wasn't properly positioned to hear C, which is a species of the second sort of way of meeting a seeming counterinstance to an empirical generalization.

The problem is how we can derive from the properties of sound alone a nontemporal dimension having the above analogous features to space. There are three properties of sound: pitch, volume, and timbre. Only pitch and volume determine a serial ordering, and either of them could be selected to determine this dimension. Strawson elects to work with pitch, no doubt because there are rich spatial metaphors concerning pitch; e.g., we speak of the pitch of one note as being closer to that or another than it is to that of some third note, of one note becoming closer in pitch to another, of higher and lower pitches. Such analogies between pitch and space will be familiar to students of the Schillinger System in which melodies are represented on graphs.

Strawson concocts the following description of a possible sound world in which pitch alone determines the nontemporal dimension in which objective sound particulars are housed. Auditory experience contains a sound, called the "master-sound," which is unique in its timbre and continuity. The sound varies in pitch and when it is at certain pitches other sounds are heard, some of which have the kind of unity possessed by a musical composition. E.g., at pitch level L of the master-sound a unitary musical composition M is heard, while at level L' a different composition M' is heard. When the master-sound remains at L composition M can be heard in its entirety, as well as repetitions of it. As the master-sound gradually moves up or down in pitch from L there is a gradual decrease in the volume of M, and as its pitch approaches close to L there is an increase in the volume of M.

The master-sound serves as the surrogate in the sound world for the body of the observer in the spatial world, its pitch being the position from which the observer hears other sounds, and changes in its pitch representing his change of position in the pitch-dimension. This can serve as an explanation of why certain sound-sequences cannot be heard at certain pitches of the master-sound, i.e., at certain positions in the pitch-dimension. In saying that the pitch of the master-sound gives the position of the observer, we do not mean to impute self-consciousness to him.[21] It is we, the story-tellers, who talk about his position and change of position, not the observer who does.

The sounds or sound-sequences that are heard at the different pitch-levels of the master-sound qualify as objective particulars because there are criteria for reidentifying them when they are not continuously heard, as well as for distinguishing between qualitative and numerical identity within the pitch-dimension itself and not just within the time-dimension. Imagine a case in which the mastersound is at pitch-level L and M is being heard:

Then suppose the master-sound changes fairly rapidly in pitch to level L' and back again to L; and then M is heard once more, a few bars having been missed. Then the sound-particular now being heard is reidentified as the same particular instance of M. If, during the same time, the master-sound had changed not from L to L' and back again to L, but from L to L', then even though M may be heard once more, a few bars having been missed, it is not the same particular instance of M that is now heard, but a different instance.[22]

In the final sentence Strawson commits himself to the possibility of the principle of the Identity of Indiscernibles being counterexampled within the pitch-dimension, which is to say that we can draw the distinction between qualitative and numerical identity within this dimension. Just as the same purely descriptive property can be instanced at two or more places in space, the same sound universal or pattern of universals can be instanced at two or more places (pitches) in the pitch-dimension.

There is a minor flaw in Strawson's account. It is clear that there is a need for some kind of clock. This comes out in his claim that the same particular instance of M is heard only if the master-sound changes "fairly rapidly" from L to L' and back again. He has not provided the observer with any way of determining when such a change occurs rapidly enough. This difficulty can be gotten around by imagining a Jimmy Durante–type of observer who has his own inner clock or standard of temporal congruence that is marked by his continual hearing of "boop-boop-bee-doop."

Has Strawson's ingenious account of his Wonderful World of Sounds shown that there could be objective particulars that are not in space? Two different kinds of arguments will be advanced to show that he has not. The first type challenges Strawson's unstated assumption that there are exclusively auditory criteria of identity for sounds, in virtue of which it can be determined both when a sound persists and when it is distinct from some coexistent sound. The second type is based upon there being crucial conceptual disanalogies between the way in which physical individuals occupy space and the way in which sounds occupy the pitch-dimension, which renders the latter dimension logically incapable of housing objective particulars.

Strawson's account assumes that we have purely auditory criteria for the persistence of a sound as well as for distinguishing between coexistent sounds. This is quite dubious. What criteria we have are not only imprecise but also seem to require a reference to the causal source of a sound, and thus invoke knowledge that is not gained from auditory experience alone. If we have a continuous and phenomenologically invariant auditory experience, do we hear numerically one and the same sound particular throughout this time? The only way of answering this question is by reference to the causal source of our auditory experience. At the old Savoy Ballroom there was a large bandstand on which two bands could be seated. The music went on continuously; when one band stopped playing the other immediately began to play. I remember once hearing Count Basie's band playing the "Two O'Clock Jump" and when they played a sustained chord they stopped playing and without any perceptible break Cootie Williams's band began to play this chord. On this occasion I heard two phenomenologically similar sounds, the first of which was produced by Basie and the second by Williams. My criteria of identity are based on the causal source of my auditory experience, but obviously my knowledge of such causes is not based on auditory experience alone.

A similar problem arises for sustained auditory experience in which there is phenomenological alteration. Strawson assumes that the master-sound persists even though it changes in its pitch. But this is gratuitous since we have no criteria for a sound's persisting that are independent of its causal source. The glissando sound we hear remains one and the same sound-particular throughout if it is produced by someone sliding his finger up a violin or guitar string. But the glissando would be composed of numerically distinct successive sounds if it were instead produced by a very rapid playing of an eight-tone scale on an eight-tone piano (there isn't one yet), even though we cannot phenomenologically distinguish between one sound and its immediate successor.

It also is dubious that there are purely auditory criteria for distinguishing between simultaneously heard sounds. It would seem that our ability to distinguish between the notes of a heard chord depends ultimately upon our knowledge of some nonauditory feature of the situation in which it is produced. If this be so, Strawson has no right to assume that the master-sound is numerically distinct from the sounds that are alleged to accompany it at its different pitches.

I suspect that the reason Strawson failed to see the dependency of our criteria of identity for sounds upon their causal source is that he leaned too heavily upon the radio analogy by which he first introduced the master-sound. The master-sound is said to be analogous to "the persistent whistle, of varying pitch, which, in a wireless set in need of repair, sometimes accompanies the programmes we listen to."[23] The way in which we hear different sound-sequences at different pitch-levels of the master-sound is compared to gradually "tuning-out one station and tuning-in another. ... Only ... instead of a tuning-knob being gradually turned, we have the gradual alteration in the pitch of the master-sound."[24] Our ability to distinguish between the persistent whistle and the programs that accompany it, as well as to distinguish between different programs, is based on knowledge of how these sounds are produced.

The preceding arguments against Strawson's Wonderful World of Sounds are not decisive because our criteria of identity for sounds are so imprecise. Some arguments based upon *crucial* conceptual disanalogies between space and the pitch-dimension will now be advanced. And they are decisive. What will make these disanalogies *crucial* is that they concern the very grounds of individuation for objective particulars.

The first crucial disanalogy to be argued for is that whereas it is possible for (L), the Identity of Indiscernibles, when restricted to purely descriptive properties, to be counterexampled within the spatial-dimension(s), it is not possible for it to be counterexampled within the pitch-dimension. In other words, the distinction between qualitative and numerical identity has a possible application within the spatial-dimension(s) but not within the pitch-dimension. Strawson would deny that there is this disanalogy. In the lengthy quotation above, he claims that if M is heard at pitch-level L of the master-sound, which then changes to pitch-level L'' at which M is heard, "it is not the same particular instance of M that is now heard, but a different instance." Although these two tokenings of the sound-type M are qualitatively identical, they are numerically distinct because they occur at different places (i.e., pitches) in the pitch-dimension. It will be illuminating to see why there could not be any such use of the distinction between qualitative and numerical identity within the pitch-dimension.

The tokening of M at L is supposed to be diverse from that at $L"$ because they occur at different positions in the pitch-dimension, which would make the grounds of individuation for sounds quite analogous to that for coexistent spatial individuals. But whereas Strawson tells us how to determine the position in this dimension of the master-sound, he says nothing about how we are to determine the position of a non–master-sound.[25] If the position of the master-sound at any given time is to be determined by its pitch, we should expect the same to hold true for all sounds. Since, *ex hypothesi*, the tokenings of M at L and $L"$ have *all* their purely descriptive properties in common, they have the same pitch (or are in the same key), and thereby are at the same position. If we should persist in holding that nevertheless there are two tokenings of M, we would be working with a principle of individuation for sounds that is radically disanalogous to that for spatial individuals, for which it is necessarily true that sortally similar diverse individuals are not spatiotemporally coincident.

Even if we were to hold that only the master-sound's position is determined by its own pitch, the position of every other sound being determined by the pitch-level of the master-sound from which it is heard, principle (L) still could not be counterexampled within the pitch-dimension. The tokenings of M are supposed to constitute a counterexample to (L). Although they have all their purely descriptive properties in common, they nevertheless are diverse because they occupy different positions, this being due to their being heard at different pitch-levels of the master-sound. They do not, however, have all their purely descriptive properties in common, since they have different relational properties; one has the property of being heard at pitch-level L of the master-sound while the other has instead the property of being heard at pitch-level $L."$ It is not only the master-sound type that can be tokened only once within the pitch-dimension but every sound type that can be so tokened.

The disanalogy between space and the pitch-dimension consisting of (L)'s being capable of counterexample within the former alone is a consequence of an even more fundamental conceptual disanalogy between the two. The pitch-dimension, unlike a spatial-dimension, is an empirically determined dimension in that its parts or positions are generated or determined by differences in the empirical properties, viz., pitches, they instantiate. In other words, (L) is necessarily true of positions in the pitch-dimension but not of places in space. Whereas diverse positions in the pitch-dimension cannot have all their purely descriptive properties in common, diverse places in space could—e.g., the places occupied by the qualitatively indiscernible discs a and b in W_1. This, of course, is not to say that diverse places never differ in their properties, for one place might instantiate$_2$ a form that another place does not. Since (L) is necessarily true of the positions in the pitch-dimension, it is necessarily true of the sounds contained in this dimension, And since (L) is not necessarily true of the parts of space, places, it is not necessarily true of the objective particulars in space.

This more fundamental disanalogy between space and the pitch-dimension explains why only the former can account for the ultimate grounds of individuation of coexistent objective particulars. To account for the ultimate grounds of the diversity between such particulars, we must invoke some realm or dimension(s) within which they can simultaneously occupy different positions. If this realm is an empirically determined one, the positions in it are themselves objective particulars; e.g., the positions in the pitch-dimension are not universals—pitch-types—but objective particulars that instantiate$_1$ these types. But then we will have failed to account for the grounds of individuation of these objective particulars. Obviously we are launched on a vicious infinite regress if we try to account for their individuation in terms of their occupying different positions in some other empirically determined dimension(s). Since the space of the Receptacle is not an empirically determined realm, being nothing but pure extension, it can serve as the grounds of individuation of objective particulars. This is in substantial agreement with Plato's somewhat poetical account of the Receptacle:

> Hence that which is to receive in itself all kinds must be free from all characters ... that which is duly to receive over its whole extent and many times over all the likenesses of the intelligible and eternal

things ought in its own nature to be free of all the characters. For this reason, then, the mother and Receptacle of what has come to be visible and otherwise sensible must not be called earth or air or fire or water, nor any of their compounds or components.[26]

NOTES

1. Aristotle, *De Generatione et Corruptione*, 1.8.324b32–325a32.

2. A more precise way of stating this restriction is as follows: for every property φ, a proposition predicating or denying φ of any given substance x is not entailed by a proposition that x is diverse from some given substance.

3. "Absolute and Relational Theories of Space and Space-Time," in *Foundations of Space-Time Theories*, ed. John S. Earman, Clark N. Glymour, and John J. Stachel, Minnesota Studies in the Philosophy of Science, vol. 8 (Minneapolis: University of Minnesota Press, 1977), pp. 303–373.

4. A proper name can always be converted into a contrived verb, e.g., "Jones" into "jonesaizes." It could be claimed that, for any two individuals a and b, only a will have the property of $a$izing. This seems to be no help in supporting (L), for either "$a$izing" means "being identical with a," in which case we have not avoided the use of a proper name, or it is equivalent to some description, e.g., "being $\varphi_1 \ldots \varphi_n$," in which case we can't be sure it won't be satisfied by both a and b.

5. For a fuller account see my paper, "O'Connor on the Identity of Indiscernibles," *Philosophical Studies* 24 (1973): 412–15.

6. Similar considerations apply to our ability ultimately to discern indexically between qualitatively similar events in a cyclical history, e.g., only one of the events is now (or bears some determinate temporal relation to now). Although my treatment of spatial and temporal indexical signs is parallel in this essay, I believe that there are important differences between them. For an account of this see my paper "'Here' and 'Now'," *Monist* 53 (1969): 396–409.

7. For a fuller treatment see my article, "Indexical Signs, Egocentric Particulars, Token-Reflexive Words" in the *Encyclopedia of Philosophy*, ed. P. Edwards (New York: Macmillan, 1967).

8. The ontological commitments of indexical signs is strikingly portrayed in Wittgenstein's remark: "'Put it *here*'–indicating the place with one's finger—that is giving an *absolute* spatial position." *Zettel* (Oxford: Blackwell, 1967), #713.

9. For a very elaborate defense of this see chapter 3 of my book *The Language of Time* (London: Routledge & Kegan Paul, 1968).

10. As argued above, another way in which (L) becomes committed to a spatiotemporal Receptacle is by permitting being spatiotemporally coincident with to count as a property.

11. For a forceful presentation of this account see Edwin Allaire, "Bare Particulars," *Philosophical Studies* 14 (1963): 1–8, and "Another Look at Bare Particulars," *Philosophical Studies* 16 (1965): 16–21. Both articles are reprinted in *Universals and Particulars*, ed. M. Loux (New York: Anchor Books, 1970).

12. For a critical discussion of these various attempts see my review of Richard Swinburne's *Space and Time* in *The Journal of Philosophy* 67 (1970): 300–16.

13. Plato, *Timeaus*, 49E. Quoted from p. 180 of F. M. Cornford's *Plato's Cosmology* (New York: Liberal Arts Press, 1952).

14. This example is borrowed from J. M. E. McTaggart's *The Nature of Existence* (Cambridge: Cambridge University Press, 1927), 1: 69.

15. For a skillful working out of this approach see David Wiggins, "The Individuation of Things and Places," *Proceedings of the Aristotelian Society*, Supplementary Volume 37 (1963), pp. 177–202 reprinted in Loux, *Universals and Parliculars*.

16. Concerning the Demiurge, who is conspicuously absent in my account, all I have to say is "Don't ask!"

17. The sense of *objective particular* that we are working with is weaker than the one employed by Strawson. For him an objective particular must not only be capable of existing when not actually perceived but also be distinguishable by a subject of experience from his own states of consciousness, which is to require self-consciousness on the part of this subject. Whether the possibility of self-consciousness depends on the representation of objects as being in space will not be considered. Strawson's answer to this question is indecisive, since he thinks that our concept of the self is not sufficiently precise.

18. *Individuals* (New York: Anchor Books, 1963), p. 67.

19. Ibid., p. 66.

20. The mere fact that the premises of this inductive argument do not report spatial phenomena is not of itself grounds for challenging it.

21. The reader is referred back to the distinctions made in footnote 17 above.

22. *Individuals*, p. 70.

23. Ibid, p. 68.

24. Ibid., p. 69.

25. This oversight infects Jonathan Bennett's reconstruction of Strawson's sound world in his *Kant's Analytic* (Cambridge: Cambridge Univer-

sity Press, 1966), p. 37. For an insightful discussion of Strawson's sound world see M. R. Ayers, "Perception and Action," in *Knowledge and Necessity*, ed. G. N. A. Vesey, Royal Institute of Philosophy Lectures, vol. 3 (1968–69) (London: Macmillan, 1970).

26. *Timaeus*, 50E–51.

16

COULD LOGICAL SPACE BE EMPTY?

It is an honor to have this opportunity to salute G. H. von Wright on his sixtieth birthday. There is no living philosopher of whom I have a higher regard either as a philosopher or as a man. Although this von Wright Festschrift is to deal with the philosophy of Wittgenstein, it would seem appropriate, under other circumstances, to have a Wittgenstein Festschrift that dealt with the philosophy of von Wright.

This essay will consider a gut metaphysical issue: Could there exist objects that do not participate in any positive events or states of affairs? An adequate answer must be based upon a fairly extensive and systematic analysis of a family of interrelated concepts concerning substances, modality, and fact (event). Probably the most powerful and intriguing attempt to answer it is found in Wittgenstein's *Tractatus*. Herein an affirmative reply, which takes the form of the thesis in 2.013 that "logical space" could be empty, is entailed by an integrated set of metaphysical assumptions. Through a critical analysis of the text it will be shown that logical space could not be empty. First, it will be shown that 2.013 is inconsistent with the account given in 2.0131 and 2.0251 of the "form of an object," and then it will be shown that alternative ways of interpreting, and even reconstructing, these passages either contradict 2.013 or are philosophically indefensible. Since an adequate analysis of the form of an object entails that logical space could not be empty, it is 2.013 that must be given up, but to do so we must modify the severe logical atomism of the *Tractatus*, viz. the thesis that no two atomic propositions are incompatible with each other.

1. LOGICAL SPACE

Logical space, in brief, is the totality of possible atomic facts.[1] A complete description of these facts can be given by listing every atomic proposition, the reason being that the sense of an atomic proposition—what it represents—is a possible atomic fact and there is no possible atomic fact that is not represented by some atomic proposition.

For Wittgenstein, as for Aristotle, possible facts are ontologically dependent upon substance, called *objects* in the *Tractatus*.[2] Each object has a *form*, also called its *nature* and *essence*, which is comprised of its different possibilities for entering into determinate relations with other objects. Since an atomic fact is a configuration of objects, the form of an object can be said to be the possible atomic facts in which it is a relatum or constituent. An object's possibility of being configured in some determinate way with other objects is called a *formal* or *internal* property and is said to be an essential property in that "it is unthinkable that its object should not possess it." (4.123) If an object *a* has the formal property of having the possibility of having relation *R* to *b*, *a* could not fail to have this property: *a*'s possession of this modalized property is in no way endangered by the failure of this possibility to be realized. The sum total of the formal properties of objects determines the totality of possible atomic facts, and thereby determines logical space.

The world is identified with the totality of existing atomic facts, i.e., the possible atomic facts that are realized or actualized. (2.04) The set of true atomic propositions completely describes the world, and it is a subset, although as we shall soon see, not necessarily a proper subset of the set of atomic propositions that completely describes logical space. This is the point made in 1.13: "The facts in logical space are the world." If we substract the world from logical space, we are left with the unrealized or nonexistent possible atomic facts. Since the nonexistence of a possible fact is a negative fact (2.06), a complete description of negative facts can be obtained by subtracting the set of atomic propositions that describes the world from the set that describes logical space and negating every remaining proposition. Reality is identified with the totality of both positive and negative facts—the existence and nonexistence of possible atomic facts.

Our concern is with whether logical space could be empty in the sense that every possible atomic fact goes unrealized, in which case every atomic proposition is false; there would be no existent atomic facts, only negative facts, a complete description of which could be given by negating every atomic proposition. Wittgenstein seems to commit himself in 2.013 to the possibility of there being this kind of bizarre no-world reality:

> Each thing is, as it were, in a space of possible atomic facts. This space I can imagine empty, but I cannot imagine the thing without the space.[3]

When it is said in 2.024, "Substance is what subsists independently of what is the case," we could add, in accordance with 2.013, "and independently of anything at all being the case."

Our reading of 2.013 is perfectly consistent with 2.0122:

> Things are independent in so far as they can occur in all possible situations, but this form of independence is a form of connection with atomic facts.[4]

There is no incompatibility with the above account of 2.013, since 2.0122 does not require that any of the *possible* situations in question be actualized or realized; accordingly, the *atomic facts* referred to at the end of the passage must be construed as *possible atomic facts*. Objects are dependent not upon actual atomic facts but upon other objects, since their formal properties involve their possibilities of being configured with other objects. More will be said about this ontological interdependency between objects.

Because of the metaphorical nature of 2.013, one might not be convinced that we have rendered it correctly. But even without appeal to 2.013 it can be shown that the *Tractatus* entails the possibility of every atomic proposition being false. That this is possible is a logical consequence of two of the most fundamental theses of the *Tractatus*, viz.:

(A) Every proposition is a truth-function of atomic propositions.
(B) Atomic propositions are logically independent of each other in that no atomic proposition entails any other one or its negation. (1.21, 2.061, 2.062, and 4.211)

These theses entail that if there are n atomic propositions there are 2^n possible combinations of truth-values for them, which is exactly what is said in 4.28. Alternatively, if logical space is comprised of n possible atomic facts there are 2^n possibilities of existence and nonexistence for them, which is what is said in 4.27. One of these 2^n possibilities is represented by the bottom row of a standard truth table (as in 4.31)—the case in which every atomic proposition is false. But this is exactly the case in which logical space is empty. The top row of the truth table represents the case in which logical space is full—the case in which there are positive facts alone since the set of atomic propositions that describes the world is a subset but not a proper subset of the set of atomic propositions that describes logical space. When we subtract the world from logical space, there is no remainder.

Although I am confident that we have given the correct interpretation of 2.013, and thereby what it means for logical space to be empty, it is not crucial for the purpose of this essay that one accepts this interpretation. What is crucial is that Wittgenstein is committed in the *Tractatus* to the possibility of every atomic proposition being false and thus every possible atomic fact going unrealized. And this he plainly is committed to in virtue of theses (A) and (B) above.

2. FORMAL PROPERTIES

We now turn to the question of whether the claim that logical space could be empty (i.e., every atomic proposition could be false) is consistent with the account of the form of an object that is given in the following passages:

> Space, time, and colour (being coloured) are forms of objects. (2.0251)
> A spatial object must be situated in infinite space. (A spatial point is an argument place.) A speck in the visual field, though it need not be red, must have some colour: it is, so to speak, surrounded by colour-space. Notes must have *some* pitch, objects of the sense of touch *some* degree of hardness, and so on. (2.0131)

It will be argued that these passages entail the impossibility of logical space being empty. First, it will be argued for color and pitch and then for space and time.

Color and Pitch. In 2.0131 we are told that a colored object, such as a speck in the visual field, "must have *some* colour" and that a note "must have some pitch." By "*some* color (pitch)" it is natural to assume that Wittenstein means some determinate color (pitch). Since being colored is a formal property according to 2.0251, it would seem to follow that that an object has a determinate color is an atomic fact. But since an object that has the formal property of being colored must have some determinate color, it follows that there must be at least one existent atomic fact. And, thus, logical space is not empty. Similiar considerations hold for pitch.

Let us consider various strategies for eliminating this alleged inconsistency in the *Tractatus* and see how far each one gets us. First, one might say that Wittgenstein was not serious about color being a formal property, since in 2.032 he claimed, "In a manner of speaking, objects are colourless." To understand this somewhat metaphorical passage we must relate it to the immediately preceding passage, 2.0231:

> The substance of the world can only determine a form, and not any material properties. For it is only by means of propositions that

material properties are represented—only by the configuration of objects that they are produced.

What is being claimed here is that a determinate property of an object, such as its determinate color or pitch, is one of its "material" properties, and thus is not entailed by its formal properties. Its formal properties entail only the possibility of its having this determinate property. Objects are colorless, then, in the sense that whatever color they have is not one of their essential or formal properties.

Another strategy for avoiding the inconsistency is to deny that Wittgenstein accepted the thesis that an object cannot be colored or have a pitch without having some determinate color or pitch. Not only does this fly in the face of what is said in 2.0131 but it also seems inconsistent with his insistence that reality, as well as the sense of a proposition, be completely determinate. Moreover, it seems to me absurd to claim that an object can be colored in the straightforward categorical sense without having some determinate color.

Yet another strategy is to bring in 6.3751 wherein it is claimed that a proposition predicating a determinate color of an object cannot be atomic since it is incompatible with another proposition predicating some other determinate color of the same object. If we are to take Wittgenstein at his word when he says that being colored is a formal property and that an object cannot be colored without having some (determinate) color, it requires that the property of being colored be analyzed or construed in such a manner that the possible facts in which a colored object must be a constituent will indeed be atomic. This requires that we analyze a proposition that predicates some determinate color of an object into an atomic proposition.

It is hard to imagine what such an analysis would be like. That a is red could not be analyzed into that a (or some other object) stands in some determinate spatial relation R to other objects, for the latter obviously is not atomic since incompatible with the proposition that a stands in some other determinate spatial relation R' to these other objects. Nor would it do to analyze it into that a is darker than (or stands in some determinate color relation to) some other object(s), since the latter again fails to be atomic since incompatible with that a

is lighter than this other object. Later, conclusive reasons will be given for the impossibility of analyzing any empirical proposition into an atomic proposition, the concept of the latter being an impossible one.

Even if, *per impossible*, such an analysis could be given, it would still be of no avail in avoiding the inconsistency mentioned above. Let us assume that we have succeeded in analyzing being colored in such a way that for every fact about an object having a determinate color we can produce some counterpart atomic fact. Since it is a conceptual truth that an object cannot be colored without having some determinate color, it also should be a conceptual truth that an object cannot be colored in this new sense without being a constituent in one of these counterpart atomic facts. If this conceptual truth were not to hold for the latter, we would have good reasons for rejecting the preferred analysis.

There is a different, and more promising, strategy for avoiding the alleged inconsistency. So far we have interpreted a formal property of an object as if it were a *monadic* property that belongs *categorically* to an object. But this does not square with what Wittengenstein explicitly says about formal properties, for he says that a formal property is the possibility of being configured with other objects. A formal property is a modalized relation. For our purposes what is important is that formal properties are to be construed in an iffy manner, not that they are relations; for the text of the *Tractatus* is not decisive in respect to whether properties are objects, and, as a result, the relational counterpart to being colored is the "relation" of exemplifying coloredness. The significance of construing formal properties as mere possibilities is that it would enable us to make sense of the idea of logical space being empty, this being the case in which the various possibilities that objects are subject to in virtue of their form go unrealized.

Before we can evaluate the success of this strategy, we must determine the nature of these iffy properties. We might construe being colored or having a pitch as the possibility of bearing some determinate color or pitch relation to other objects, e.g., the possibility of being darker than or a minor third lower than. But an object can be darker than or a minor third lower than only if it has a determinate color or pitch of its own. This has the consequence that an object cannot have the iffy formal property of having the possibility of bearing some determinate color or pitch relation to other objects unless it categorically has some determinate color or pitch. Thus, it is not conceivable that an object have one of these iffy formal properties and logical space be empty.

One might give a different sort of iffy analysis, which we shall call the "radical iffy" analysis, according to which being colored or having a pitch is to be construed as the possibility of being colored or having a pitch. Although this analysis has no textual support, it is worth considering on its own. Again the question is whether an object could have these sort of radically iffy formal properties without being a constituent in at least one atomic fact. In support of an affirmative answer to this question it might be claimed that it is not absurd to conceive of a material object that is always invisible although it has the possibility of being visible. If so, there could be an object that has the possibility of being colored although it never has any determinate color.

But this permanently invisible object has the possibility of being colored only because it categorically has certain properties, among which are being in space and time, being physical, etc. As a result logical space is not empty. Furthermore, that an object can have the possibility of being colored without actually being colored seems to constitute a good reason for denying that being colored is a formal property; for a formal property is an *essential* property, one that "it is unthinkable its object should not possess." (4.123) There are further difficulties with the radical iffy analysis of formal properties that will be considered after we have discussed space and time as formal properties.

Space and Time. So far our argument against the possibility of logical space being empty has been based on a consideration of only two of Wittgenstein's examples of formal properties. But being colored and having a pitch, as witnessed by the case of the permanently invisible object, hardly are paradigmatic essential properties. One might dismiss the foregoing argument as only showing that Wittgenstein chose poor examples. However, if any properties should count as essential in the sense of 4.123, it should be space and time. If it can be shown that objects could not have these formal properties and logical space still be empty, our case for there being an inconsistency in the *Tractatus* will be greatly strengthened. First, considerations will be advanced to show that logical space could not be empty if objects have the form of space or time, and, then, some strategies for escaping from the inconsistency will be considered and shot down.

In 2.0251 space and time are said to be forms of objects, and in 2.0131 it is claimed that "a spatial object must be situated in infinite space." From these two passages it can be concluded that any object that has the form of space actually is in space; similar considerations hold for time. The question arises as to whether an object can actually be in space or time without there being some actual atomic fact in which it is a constituent. A negative reply is warranted. An object cannot be in space without having some determinate shape and size. An object cannot be in time without either itself having some determinate duration or, if it be a terminal event consisting in the beginning or end of some process or state, there being some process or state that has a determinate duration. Again, it can be objected that these determinate facts are not atomic, since that an object has a certain determinate shape is incompatible with its having some other determinate shape. And, again, the reply must be that whatever might be the counterpart atomic facts to these determinate facts (and it will be argued that there couldn't be any such atomic fact) it should still be the case that an object can be in space only if it is a consistuent in some actual counterpart atomic fact.

Spatial and temporal objects must also be subject to determinate indexical facts. A spatial object must either be here (at this place) or bear some determinate spatial relation to here. A temporal object must either occur (exist) now (at this time) or bear some determinate relation of precedence or subsequence to now. That there must be such indexical facts if anything is to be in space or time, as I discovered from the reactions to my book, *The Language of Time*, in which this is argued for, is highly mooted.

That there must be determinate facts if an object is in space and time holds on both an absolute and relational theory of space and time. According to the absolute theory, if an object is in space and time there will be determinate facts about its spatial and temporal relations to absolute places and times. It is interesting to note that there are passages in the *Tractatus* that seem to accept an absolute theory of space:

A spatial object must be situated in infinite space. (A spatial point is an argument place. (2.0131. See also 3.411)

The explanation of the analogy that is drawn between a spatial point and an argument place is that just as an argument can be filled by a constant, a spatial point can be occupied by an object, though it need not be.

According to the relational theory, space and time are networks of spatial and temporal relations between empirical objects. Thus, if an object is in space and time there will be determinate facts about its spatial and temporal relations to other objects. An interesting argument can be screwed out of the *Tractatus* for the impossibility of an object being in time without there being atomic facts, if the relational theory of time is accepted.

A consequence of the relational theory of time is that there cannot be time without change. Since the objects of the *Tractatus* are unalterable, the only sort of change recognized by the *Tractatus* is change in the way objects are configured. (2.0271) Objects serve as the substrata that underlie change. This shows that not all objects are timeless or eternal, since objects cannot change in their relations to each other unless they endure in time, or at least one of them endures if it be assumed that the relations in question are between a particular and universals.[5] If any object has the form of time, it actually is in time, if we may paraphrase 2.0131. If an object is in time, there is time. If there is time, there is change. And if there is change, there are differences between the way objects are configured at different times. But a configuration of objects is an atomic fact. Therefore, if an object is in time, there are atomic facts.

As was the case with color and pitch, one might try to show the possibility of logical space being empty by offering some sort of iffy analysis of the forms of space and time. One might offer a radical iffy analysis of them as being mere possibility of being in space and time, it being possible that an object would possess such possibilities although they go unactualized. Not only is this analysis inconsistent with what is explicitly said in 2.0131, it also is philosophically unviable. If an object has the form of space and time but is not actually in space and time, existing nowhere and nowhen, it follows that it does not exist, e.g., Santa Claus. The objects of the *Tractatus* are existent, although according to its unusually narrow theory of meaningfulness, we cannot say that an object(s) exists, this being "ladder" talk.

Nor is it of any avail to offer the other version of the iffy analysis according to which having the forms of space and time is construed as having only the possibility of entering into spatial and temporal relations with other objects. An object cannot have such possibilities without actually being in space and time; and this mobilizes all of the preceding objections to logical space being empty in this case. Furthermore, there are considerations internal to the *Tractatus* that have the consequence that logical space is not empty if an object has the possibility of entering into spatial or temporal relations with other objects. It works in the following way.

It will be recalled that the only sort of ontological dependence objects have is upon each other, since their formal or essential properties involve the possibility of their entering into configurations with each other. This means that when we specify a formal property of an object, we must introduce another object, i.e., we must use a proper name that refers to another object or existentially quantify over other objects. This is a consequence of these passages:

> An atomic fact is a configuration of objects (things). (2.01)

> It is essential to things that they should be possible constituents of atomic facts. (2.011)

> In logic nothing is accidental: if a thing occur in an atomic fact, the possibility of the atomic fact must be written into the thing itself. (2.012)

Thus, if there is an object, it must be a possible constituent in some atomic fact, say that $a R b$. But the use of the proper name "b", according to the *Tractatus*, ontologically commits us to the existence of b, since there cannot be a proper name that fails to denote an existent object.

According to the above version of the iffy analysis, if a has the form of space (time), it has the possibility of entering into a spatial (temporal) relation with some other object(s), say b. (Whether we actually specify the other object(s), or merely quantify over objects, is not important for the sake of this argument, since, in either case, we are ontologically committed to the existence of some other object(s).) Now a cannot have the possibility of having spatial relation R to b unless b exists and moreover itself has the form of space. b cannot have the form of space without existing in space. (2.0131) Since both a and b exist in space and there is a single spatial system (2.0131), it follows that a and b stand in some determinate spatial relation to each other. Thus, if a has the possibility of standing in a spatial relation to some other object, b, it follows that it does in fact stand in some determinate spatial relation to b.

One might object to the foregoing arguments against the possibility of logical space being empty that they take Wittgenstein's examples of formal properties too literally. Since it is not the task of the *Tractatus* to give any examples of atomic facts, neither can it have been its task to give any examples of formal properties, since such a property is nothing but the possibility of being a constituent in an atomic fact. Wittgenstein's examples of color, pitch, space, and time, accordingly, are not be taken literally but only as examples whose function is to illustrate the logical role played by formal properties, in particular their logical interconnections with possible atomic facts.

This escape into the fog is unsatisfying for several reasons. First, as seen above, since it is a conceptual truth that an object cannot be colored, have a pitch, be spatial, or be temporal without having some determinate or specific form of these properties, we should expect the same conceptual truth to hold for those properties, whatever they might be, which are the formal property counterparts to these properties.

Second, the claim that logical space could be empty entails that the world could be wholly iffy, that objects could possess only dispositional properties, none of which get actualized. The author of the *Tractatus* was convinced that existence could not be completely conditional, and with this I am in agreement. The closest thing we have to a completely iffy or dispositional analysis of objects is phenomenalism. In addition to the numerous and, in my opinion, formidable objections to phenomenalism, it still does not turn out that everything has a purely iffy existence, for it is necessary to speak about the empirical places and times at which various sense data could be had. In cases in which no actual sense data of an object are had we must say something like, "If someone had been in room 709 of Schenley Hall on September 4, 1975, at 3 p.m., he would have had desk-like sense data." But the criteria of identity for the empirical place and time in question are logically dependent upon those for material objects and events, thus rendering the analysis viciously circular.

Third, if we allow for the possibility of there being objects that have only dispositional properties, none of which get actualized, what is to distinguish between the case in which nothing exists, not even objects, and the one in which they exist but none of their possibilities for being a constituent in atomic facts gets realized? There is no answer, and this shows the absurdity of countenancing the possibility of logical space being empty. This does not mean that it is absurd to countenance the possibility of there being no objects, in which case there would be no logical space. For certainly there is a sense in which it is possible for there to be nothing—no things or objects.[6]

Fourth, if logical space were empty, we would not be assured of there being any ground of individuation for objects. If logical space were empty, we could not distinguish between objects in terms of their material or contingent properties, since they would have none. Neither is there any assurance that we could do so by appeal to their formal properties, since, as Wittgenstein rightly indicates in 2.0233, it is possible for two objects to agree in all their formal properties. But, then, there would be no grounds of individuation for these objects. And this shows the absurdity of the supposition that logical space could be empty. It can be shown, although I do not now have the space to do it, that what serves as the ultimate grounds of individuation for empirical objects is their being noncoincident in space and/or time: it is a conceptual truth that sortally similiar objects do not coincide in space and time.[7] But this requires that objects be in space and time; and it has already been shown that objects cannot be in space and time without being subject to certain kinds of determinate facts.

Fifth, if logical space were empty, there would be absences, lacks, wants, and privations that have no positive ground in that there is no positive fact about the world that entails that there is such a lack, want, etc. While there might be some lacks, etc. that are contingent relative to what positively is the case, e.g., a man who simply lacked an odor without this being entailed by any of his positive properties, it seems inconceivable that all lacks, etc. would be contingent in this sense.[8]

3. THE WAY OUT OF THE INCONSISTENCY

Since it is logically impossible, for all of the foregoing reasons, that logical space be empty, the way out of the inconsistency is to modify the severe logical atomism of the *Tractatus*. It will be recalled that the possibility of logical space being empty is a logical consequence of two fundamental *Tractatus* theses:

> (A) Every proposition is a truth-function of atomic propositions; and,
> (B) Atomic propositions are logically independent of each other in that no atomic proposition entails any other one or its negation.

One or both of these theses must be the culprits. That language is truth-functional, although quite dubious, is nevertheless not an absurd thesis.

Thesis (B), on the other hand, is absurd; and thus is the one that ought to be given up or altered. Thesis (B) represents Wittgenstein's severe version of logical atomism. It goes beyond Humean atomism, which required only that no atomic proposition entails any other one, by adding the further proviso that no two atomic propositions are mutually incompatible. It is this additional proviso that renders his version of logical atomism absurd. Let us see why.

Atomic propositions are said to describe the world, say something, convey information, and the like. Tautologies and contradictions are both found to be vacuous in this respect, and as a result are said to be senseless, although not nonsensical. True atomic propositions, moreover, comprise the natural sciences. It is for this reason, no doubt, that

Wittgenstein did not speculate in the *Tractatus* (although he did in the *Notebooks*) about the form such propositions would take; for it is up to the scientist, not the philosopher, to discover this, and this may have to await the coming of the scientific millennium.

The informative role that atomic propositions are assigned, however, could not possibly be played by propositions that are mutually compatible. An informative proposition must be logically incompatible with at least one contingent proposition—the more such propositions it is incompatible with, the more informative it is. Alternatively, a predicate in an informative proposition must be logically incompatible with at least one contingent predicate, i.e., a predicate that both could be true of something and could be false of something. Since an atomic proposition is both positive and compatible with every other atomic proposition, an atomic proposition cannot be incompatible with any positive proposition. Unfortunately, the only sort of positive propositions that meet this condition are *necessary* truths. But that is an entity (self-identical, etc.) that is noninformative, its predicate not being incompatible with any contingent predicate.[9]

A valiant and ingenious attempt has been made by Stenius to show how an atomic proposition, subject to the restrictions of Wittgenstein's severe version of logical atomism, could be informative. It will be instructive to consider his attempt and note where and how it fails. Stenius makes clear that he accepts the above necessary condition for a proposition being informative, for he says that "a proposition cannot have a factual content unless, in stating something as being the case, it excludes something else from being the case."[10] He begins by considering a model world consisting of five rectangular parallelepipeds. A complete description of this world must specify the length, height, and width of each of these objects. Following the use of the term in physics, Stenius says that "a world has as many dimensions as it has mutually independent components of description." Our model world has fifteen such dimensions. Each of these dimensions comprises an infinite number of possible facts or values in that there is an infinite number of values that the length (height, width) of an object can take. The possible facts of any given dimension are mutually incompatible and thereby do not count as atomic facts.

What is needed if we are to show how an atomic proposition could be informative is a world with multivalued dimensions only of whose possible values or facts counts as atomic; an affirmation of this value or fact would be informative since it would entail the negation of at least one other possible and contingent value. One-valued dimensions would not work, because an affirmation of a dimension's one possible value would not logically exclude any other contingent value or fact either of this or any other dimension. Toward this end Stenius modifies his model world as follows. Whereas we presently think of each of its fifteen dimensions as having an infinite number of possible values, "we might simply restrict the number of *values* that are regarded as possible in each dimension" to two possible values:

> Assume that the possible values of the length, width and height of P_1 (one of the parallelepipeds) are, say, 4.6 yds and 2.3 yds, 3.0 yds. and 1.5 yds, and 0.8 yds and 0.4 yds, only two values (the one of which is double the other) being considered logically possible in each dimension, and that a corresponding restriction holds true for the remaining parallelepipeds.

The model world now consists of fifteen two-valued dimensions such that the affirmation of any one of the two possible values in one of these dimensions entails the negation of the other possible value.

All that remains is to show how only one of the possible (and contingent) values or facts in each dimension is to count as atomic. Since an atomic fact or proposition must be positive, Stenius accomplishes this by making one of the possible values in each dimension positive and the other negative:

> We could agree upon regarding the assertion of one of these values only—say the greater one—as a *positive* statement, whereas the assertion of the other value is regarded as a mere *negative* of this. If now the positive statement is considered to describe an atomic state of affairs, then according to this interpretation the *negative* statement does not describe an atomic state of affairs—because the negation of an atomic state of affairs is not atomic but logically compounded. So according to this interpretation every dimension contains only *one*

atomic state of affairs properly so called, and therefore *all atomic states of affairs* properly so called are *independent of one another.*

An assertion of the *positive* value in one of these two-valued dimensions counts as atomic; however, it is informative because it logically excludes the other possible (and contingent) value, which, because it is negative, does not count as atomic.

It will be argued that the above attempt by Stenius to rescue Wittgenstein's concept of an atomic proposition from the charge of being a contradiction in terms both fails as an exegesis of the *Tractatus* and, more seriously, is philosophically unacceptable.

The first problem concerns Steinus's claim that a dimension in the description of the world could have different possible values in different possible worlds. That what is possible could vary from one possible world to another is totally at odds with the *Tractatus*. What is common to every possible world is a certain form:

> It is obvious that an imagined world, however different it may be from the real one, must have *something*—a form—in common with it. (2.022)

This form is logical space. It is the totality of possible atomic facts and is determined by the formal properties of objects.

"Objects are just what constitute this unalterable form." (2.023) The same objects must exist in every possible world, for these possible worlds are ontologically grounded in the forms of these objects. As a consequence of these theses, if an object, any parallelepiped P_1 in Stenius's model world, has the possibility of having any one of an infinite number of different lengths, it has this possibility in every possible world; otherwise its form would vary from one world to another, and as a result different possible worlds would not have a form in common. But this is just what is denied in Stenius's account. The form of P_1 varies from one possible world to another because the possible values of its length vary from one of these worlds to the other; these possible worlds are not in the same logical space.

More serious than a mere exegetical failure is an incoherence in

Stenius's account of the possible values of a dimension. What does Stenius mean by "possible" when he speaks of the values of a dimension in some world? At the outset he seems to mean values that are possible relative to the physical theories and laws that most accurately characterize the world in question, for he says in defense of his assumption that each of the fifteen dimensions of his model world could have a finite number of possible values that "the assumption of such 'discrete' dimensions cannot be regarded as too artificial in the age of quantum theory." However, soon after he introduces this *physical* sense of possible values of a dimension, Stenius says that in his imagined world of two-valued dimensions only two values are "considered *logically* possible in each dimension." And further on he says that "the assertion of one of the values of a dimension is in that case *logically equivalent* to the negation of the other." Herein he has shifted from the physical to the logical sense of "possible."

How are we to resolve this equivocation? Plainly, it must be done in favor of the *logical* sense of "possible," for it is essential to his account that the affirmation of any one of the two possible values of a given dimension *logically* (and not just physically) entail the negation of the other possible value. Stenius, therefore, is committed to relativizing logical possibilities and logical entailments to possible worlds. Not only does he fail to offer any justification for this radical thesis but does not even tell us what it could mean. Obviously, to say that in a given possible world a dimension has only two possible values cannot mean the same as, nor be justified by appeal to, what is physically possible in that world; for this would amount to the abolishment of the logical sense of "possible." Someone who relativizes logical possibility to possible worlds would be apt to analyze "p is logically possible relative to world W" as "p is the case in some world to which W has access." Unfortunately, it is difficult to understand why this relation of accessibility is not universal among possible worlds, thus rendering it extremely unlikely that p could be logically possible relative to W but not be logically possible relative to some other possible world.

Even if there were some way of getting around the problem of relativizing logical possibilities to possible worlds, Stenius's account still would face an insuperable objection. It is essential to his account that one and only one of the two possible and incompatible values of a given dimension count as positive; if both were to count as positive, the assertion of either of them would fail to express an atomic proposition since it would be logically incompatible with some positive proposition. It will be shown that Stenius's selection of one of these values as being positive and the other as negative not only is arbitrary, which he readily grants, but also is at variance with our preanalytic intuitions regarding what propositions (facts, values, properties) are positive. First, it must be shown why our preanalytic instuitions are central in this matter.

The distinction between positive and negative facts (propositions) runs deep in the *Tractatus*: an atomic proposition must be positive; the world is composed of positive facts alone, reality of both positive and negative facts. The closest that Wittgenstein comes to giving an account of the distinction between positive and negative facts is in 2.06: "We also call the existence of atomic facts a positive fact, and their non-existence a negative fact." This distinction falls back upon our ordinary intuitions regarding what is positive and negative, for the existence of a fact will not count as positive (or negative) unless the fact is itself positive (or negative); e.g., the existence of the fact that a is nonred is a negative fact, its nonexistence a positive fact. Atomic facts or propositions, whatever form they may ultimately take, must count as positive according to our ordinary, preanalytic intuitions. It is essential, therefore, that Stenius succeed in showing that the assertion of only one of the two possible values of a given dimension count as positive according to these intuitions; and it is just this that he has completely failed to do.

In this connection consider his claim that in the world in which the only two possible values of the length of P_1 are 2.3 and 4.6 yds, we can regard the assertion of the 4.6 value as positive and therefore the assertion of the correlative value, 2.6, as negative. First, this is based on the dubious assumption that for every pair of correlative values or terms one of them must be positive and the other negative, to which there are numerous counterexamples, e.g., odd-even, wet-dry, etc. Second, *pace* Stenius, it is intuitively apparent that the proposition that P_1 is 4.6 yds is of the same quality as the proposition that P_1 is 2.3 yds;

they are both positive or both negative. Third, according to our preanalytic intuitions, they are both positive. Furthermore, these intuitions can be borne out by appeal to adequate criteria for distinguishing between positive and negative values (properties, predicates). It is claimed that the following criteria, which employ as a logically primitive notion that of *being of the same quality as*, yield results that are in agreement with our preanalytic intuitions:

(C) A property (predicate or value) is positive if and only if there could be a property of the same quality that is logically incompatible with it.

and

(C_1) A property is positive if and only if there could be a property of different quality that is logically entailed by it.

To say that a property P entails a property Q means that a statement that a is P entails that a is Q. Any property that fails to satisfy either of these criteria is negative.

It is clear that according to these criteria both being 2.3 yds and being 4.6 yds count as positive, as they should. There be a property, e.g., being 2.4 yds, which is logically incompatible with and of the same quality as being 2.3 yds; and similarly for being 4.6 yds. Notice that even if we followed Stenius in relativizing logical possibilities to possible worlds, so that there could be a world in which the only possible length of P_1 is 2.3 yds, it still would be true that there *could* (in some other possible world) be a value of the same quality as 2.3 yds that is logically incompatible with it.

For the above reasons we conclude that Stenius has failed to show how an atomic proposition could be informative. Every dimension must be one-valued! Because the concept of an atomic proposition is an impossible one, we can understand our failure to find any examples of a formal property. A formal property is a possibility of being a constituent in an atomic fact. Because of the requirement that atomic propositions be logically compatible, possession of a formal property cannot give its possessor the possibility for being a constituent in two or more mutually incompatible atomic facts; this is why being colored, spatial, etc. could not count as formal properties, for that a is colored entails that it is possible that a is red and that it is possible that a is blue, etc. The absurdity in this is that a formal property must have informative properties as its specifiers; but, according to the *Tractatus*, the specifiers of a formal property cannot be informative since they must be compatible with every positive property.

It should be clear by now that the only hope for being able to give an adequate account of an atomic proposition, as well as of a formal property, is to drop the requirement that atomic propositions be mutually compatible. In giving up this requirement we leave most of the fundamental doctrines of the *Tractatus* in tact. The only one that must be surrendered is Wittgenstein's cherished hope that every contradiction could be shown to be such by truth-tabular methods. It would be nice if this could be done. But what right do we have to assume a priori that God will be this good to us? And, as is well known, the surrender of this faith (in the 1929 "Some Remarks on Logical Form") leads to Wittgenstein's later philosophy, in which the scope of logic is vastly expanded so as to encompass logical grammar as well as truth-functional logic.

NOTES

1. Some interpreters might claim that logical space contains molecular facts as well. But since molecular facts are truth-functions of atomic facts, and thus are uniquely determined by atomic facts, they should not carp at my definition of "logical space."

2. Since possibility is ontologically dependent upon the existence of objects, it will be nonsensical to ask whether it is possible for obects (or some particular object a) not to exist. While it is true that an object can neither begin nor cease to exist, it by no means follows that it is necessary that it exist. Modal distinctions, in other words, do not apply to the existence of objects. Objects are the brute given of the *Tractatus* ontology, and, to paraphrase 6.44 so that it applies to objects rather than the world, *that* objects exist is the mystical.

3. Throughout I follow the Pears and McGuinness translation, with two

exceptions: I render "Sachverhalt" as "atomic fact" and "Elementarsatz" as "atomic proposition." The only commentator who realizes that something shocking is being said in 2.013 is Wilfrid Sellars in "Naming and Saying" (reprinted in *Essays on Wittgenstein's* Tractatus, ed. Copi and Beard [London: Routledge & Kegan Paul, 1963], p. 263) who says that in this passage Wittgenstein "suggests the intriguing possibility that we can make sense of the idea that the language we use might have no application." This is not an accurate account, for our language does apply to the case in which there are only negative facts. To describe it we only need negate every atomic proposition. Only if there were no objects would our language, according to the *Tractatus*, have no application.

4. When it is said that things "can occur in all *possible* situations," he must mean "all possible situations relative to their nature"; for otherwise it would turn out that all objects have the same nature, since they can occur in exactly the same possible facts or situations, viz., all of them.

5. That objects change in their configurations to each other shows that objects are not eternal in the sense of being timeless. David Keyt, in a specious argument in "Wittgenstein's Notion of an Object," reprinted in Copi and Beard, *Essays on Wittgenstein's* Tractatus, p. 294, holds that objects are timeless because no temporal distinctions apply to them. He supports this by appeal to the *Tractatus* prohibition against saying that an object(s) exists; since we cannot say that an object exists, neither can we say that it did (does now, or will) exist. But this overlooks other kinds of temporal distinctions that might apply to objects; e.g., we can say of objects a and b that they once stood in relation R to each other but no longer do.

6. The nature and viability of this possibility is explored in section 2 of chapter 3 of my book *Negation and Non-Being, American Philosophical Quarterly* Monograph Series, vol. 10 (Oxford: Blackwell, 1976).

7. For an elaborate defense of this, see section 1 of chapter 2 of ibid.

8. For an exploration of this problem see chapter 1 of ibid. According to the *Tractatus*, no negative fact—the nonexistence of an atomic fact—is entailed by any existent atomic fact, since no two atomic facts are incompatible. This makes it difficult to understand the sense of 2.21 ("A picture agrees with reality or fails to agree; it is correct or incorrect, true or false") and 2.223 ("In order to tell whether a picture is true or false we must compare it with reality") in the case in which there are only negative facts. Herein there is no world with which we can compare an atomic proposition so as to discover that it is false. It won't do to say that we determine this by consulting a list that gives a complete description of reality to see whether it has a "true" or "false" next

to it; for this merely pushes the difficulty back to how this list was drawn up. The point about the difficulty of determining the falsity of an atomic proposition in the case in which logical space is empty is consigned to a footnote because it is an epistemological point; and epistemological considerations cannot be appealed to either in defense or criticism of a *Tractatus* thesis.

9. Even Wittgenstein's examples of formal properties or predicates satisfy this necessary condition, for that *a* is colored (spatial, temporal) entails that it is not a prime number. Noninformative predicates or properties are those that logically must have either a universal or null extension.

10. Erik Stenius, *Wittgenstein's Tractatus: A Critical Exposition of Its Main Lines of Thought* (Ithaca, NY: Cornell University Press, 1960), p. 43. One assumes that the "something else" that is excluded is a contingent something else.